AutoCAD LT® 2005 FOR DUMMIES®

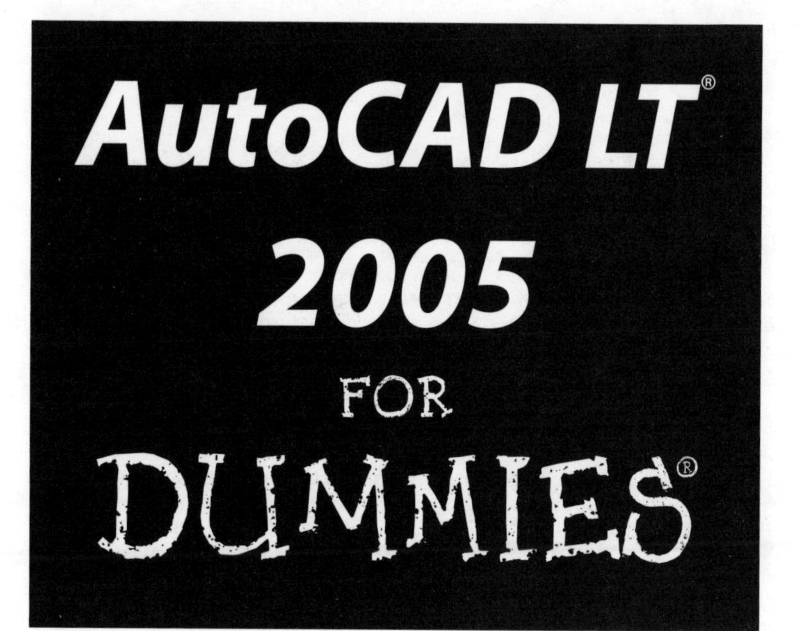

by Mark Middlebrook

Wiley Publishing, Inc.

AutoCAD LT® 2005 For Dummies®

Published by
Wiley Publishing, Inc.
111 River Street
Hoboken, NJ 07030-5774

Published by Wiley Publishing, Inc., Indianapolis, Indiana

Published simultaneously in Canada

Library of Congress Control Number: 2004104564

ISBN: 0-7645-7280-6

Manufactured in the United States of America

10 9 8 7 6 5 4 3 2 1

1O/QZ/QX/QU/IN

About the Author

Mark Middlebrook used to be an engineer but gave it up when he discovered that he couldn't handle a real job. He is now principal of Daedalus Consulting, an independent CAD and computer consulting company in Oakland, California. (In case you wondered, Daedalus was the guy in ancient Greek legend who built the labyrinth on Crete. Mark named his company after Daedalus before he realized that few of his clients would be able to pronounce it and even fewer spell it.) Mark is also a contributing editor for *CADALYST* magazine and Webmaster of `markcad.com`. When he's not busy being a cad, Mark sells and writes about wine for Paul Marcus Wines in Oakland. He also teaches literature and philosophy classes at St. Mary's College of California — hence "Daedalus." *AutoCAD LT 2005 For Dummies* is his second book on AutoCAD LT and his seventh on the AutoCAD family of programs.

Dedication

To the engineers at Middlebrook + Louie, and especially to Hardip Pannu, who first prodded me into writing about AutoCAD LT. They helped me realize that AutoCAD LT is every bit as interesting — and peculiar — as AutoCAD. Also to the Structural Engineers Association of Northern California, who invited me to teach AutoCAD LT classes for their members on several occasions. It was during those courses that I developed some of the ideas for the material in this book.

Author's Acknowledgments

Thanks to Acquisitions Editor Terri Varveris, who first suggested resurrecting *AutoCAD LT For Dummies* after an interval of five years and four LT versions and whose enthusiasm got the project off on the right foot. This was my first opportunity to work with Project Editor Nicole Sholly, and I only hope it's not the last. She brought to bear just the right balance of pressure and patience and demonstrated at all times that the book was in dexterous yet gentle hands. Dave Byrnes carried out his duties as tech editor with skill, verve, and unerring insight into the particularities of AutoCAD LT. As always, his thoughtful suggestions inspired me to think about how to describe some things more carefully and thereby helped make the book perceptibly better.

Publisher's Acknowledgments

We're proud of this book; please send us your comments through our online registration form located at www.dummies.com/register/.

Some of the people who helped bring this book to market include the following:

Acquisitions, Editorial, and Media Development

Associate Project Editor: Nicole Sholly

Acquisitions Editor: Terri Varveris

Copy Editor: Rebecca Senninger

Technical Editor: David Byrnes

Editorial Manager: Kevin Kirschner

Media Development Manager: Laura VanWinkle

Media Development Supervisor: Richard Graves

Editorial Assistant: Amanda Foxworth

Cartoons: Rich Tennant (www.the5thwave.com)

Production

Project Coordinator: Courtney MacIntyre

Layout and Graphics: Andrea Dahl, Denny Hager, Joyce Haughey, Stephanie D. Jumper, Lynsey Osborn, Heather Ryan

Proofreaders: Laura Albert, Andy Hollandbeck, Dwight Ramsey, TECHBOOKS Production Services

Indexer: TECHBOOKS Production Services

Publishing and Editorial for Technology Dummies

Richard Swadley, Vice President and Executive Group Publisher

Andy Cummings, Vice President and Publisher

Mary Bednarek, Executive Editorial Director

Mary C. Corder, Editorial Director

Publishing for Consumer Dummies

Diane Graves Steele, Vice President and Publisher

Joyce Pepple, Acquisitions Director

Composition Services

Gerry Fahey, Vice President of Production Services

Debbie Stailey, Director of Composition Services

Contents at a Glance

Table of Contents

Part III: Annotation for Communication 201

Introduction

AutoCAD came into being over two decades ago, at a time when most people thought that personal computers weren't capable of industrial-strength tasks like CAD. (The acronym stands for Computer-Aided Drafting, Computer-Aided Design, or both, depending on whom you talk to.) AutoCAD LT was born over a decade ago, as a much lower-cost alternative for those who needed most, but not all, of AutoCAD's impressive CAD muscle.

It's remarkable that, after all this time, AutoCAD and AutoCAD LT remain the king and prince of the microcomputer CAD hill by a tall margin. Many competing CAD programs have come to challenge AutoCAD and LT, many have fallen, and a few are still around. One hears rumblings that the long-term future of CAD may belong to special-purpose, 3D-based software such as the Autodesk Inventor and Revit programs. Whether or not those rumblings amplify into a roar remains to be seen, but for the present and the near future anyway, AutoCAD is where the CAD action is, and LT puts you in the center of it.

The only problem with LT, as those in the know often call it, is that sometimes it's a little *too* much like full AutoCAD. In its evolution, AutoCAD LT, like AutoCAD, has grown more complex, in part to keep up with the increasing complexity of the design and drafting processes that AutoCAD is intended to serve. Just drawing nice-looking lines is not enough anymore. If you want to play CAD with the big boys and girls, you need to appropriately organize the objects you draw, their properties, and the files in which they reside. You need to coordinate your CAD work with other people in your office who are working on or making use of the same drawings. You need to be savvy about shipping drawings around via the Internet.

AutoCAD LT 2005 provides the tools for doing all these things, but figuring out which hammer to pick up or which nail to bang on first isn't always easy. With this book, you have an excellent chance of creating a presentable, usable, printable, and sharable drawing on your first or second try without putting a T square through your computer screen in frustration.

What's Not in This Book

Unlike many other *For Dummies* books, this one does tell you to consult the official software documentation sometimes. AutoCAD LT is just too big and complicated for a single book to attempt to describe it completely.

This book focuses on AutoCAD LT 2005. I do occasionally mention differences with previous versions, going back to the highly popular AutoCAD Release 14 and AutoCAD LT 97, so that everyone has some context and upgraders can more readily understand the differences. (Chapter 1 includes a rundown of the version history of AutoCAD and LT.) I also mention the important differences between full AutoCAD LT and AutoCAD, so that you know what you're missing.

Who Are — and Aren't — You?

Together, AutoCAD and AutoCAD LT have a large, loyal, and dedicated group of longtime users. (Autodesk claims to have sold more copies of AutoCAD LT than of AutoCAD, as of a few years ago.) This book is not for the sort of people who have been using AutoCAD LT for a decade, who plan their vacation time around Autodesk University, or who consider 1,000-page-plus technical tomes about AutoCAD as pleasure reading. This book *is* for people who want to get going quickly with AutoCAD LT, but who also know the importance of developing proper CAD techniques from the beginning.

However, you do need to have some idea of how to use your computer system before tackling AutoCAD LT — and this book. You need to have a computer system with LT (preferably the 2005 version). A printer or plotter and a connection to the Internet are big helps, too.

You also need to know how to use Windows to copy and delete files, create a folder, and find a file. You need to know how to use a mouse to select (highlight) or to choose (activate) commands, how to close a window, and how to minimize and maximize windows. Make sure that you're familiar with the basics of your operating system before you start with AutoCAD LT.

How This Book Is Organized

If you saw the impressive and apparently random piles of stuff cluttering my desk while I was writing this book, you'd wonder how I could organize a chapter, never mind an entire book. Nevertheless, I hope you find that the book reflects some concerted thought about how to present AutoCAD LT in a way that's both easy-to-dip-into and smoothly-flowing-from-beginning-to-end.

The organization of this book into *parts* — collections of related chapters — is one of the most important, uh, parts of this book. You really can get to know AutoCAD LT one piece at a time, and each part represents a group of closely related topics. The order of parts also says something about priority; yes, you have my permission to ignore the stuff in later parts until you master most of the stuff in the early ones. This kind of building-block approach can be especially valuable in a program as powerful as AutoCAD LT.

The following sections describe the parts that the book breaks down into.

Part I: Lighting Up LT

Need to know your way around the AutoCAD LT screen? Why does LT even exist, anyway? What's the difference between AutoCAD and AutoCAD LT, and is LT right for you? What's that funny command line thing with all the text at the bottom of the LT screen thing? How do I get started drawing stuff in AutoCAD LT?

Part I answers all these questions — and more. In particular, Chapters 2 and 3 provide some crucial information about how AutoCAD LT is different from other programs and how you, the budding CADet, need to deal with those differences. If you want to make drawings that look good, plot good, and are good, read this stuff!

Part II: Geometry Rules

The second part starts with a detailed tour of the essential task of drawing setup. In CAD, setting up a new drawing is a nontrivial but vital job. With the information in Chapter 5, you can get the job done correctly and fairly quickly before moving on to the more fun activities of actually drawing stuff.

After the drawing setup preamble, the bulk of this part covers the trio of activities that you probably spend most of your time in AutoCAD LT doing: drawing objects, editing them, and zooming and panning to see them better on-screen. These are the things that you do in order to create the *geometry* — that is, the CAD representations of the objects in the real world that you're designing. By the end of Part II, you will be pretty good at geometry, even if your ninth grade math teacher told you otherwise.

Part III: Annotation for Communication

CAD drawings do not live on lines alone — most of them require quite a bit of text, dimensioning, and hatching in order to make the design intent clear to the poor chump who has to build your amazing creation. (Whoever said "a picture is worth a thousand words" must not have counted up the number of words on the average architectural or mechanical drawing!) This part shows you how to add these essential features to your drawings.

After you gussy up your drawing with text, dimensions, and hatching, you probably want to create a snapshot of it to show off to your client, contractor, or grandma. Normal people call this process *printing*, but CAD people call it *plotting*. Whatever you decide to call it, I show you how to do it.

Part IV: Collaboration Makes the Drawings Go 'Round

A good CAD user, like a good kindergartner, plays well with others. AutoCAD LT encourages this behavior with a host of drawing- and data-sharing features. Blocks and external reference files encourage the re-use of parts of drawings, entire drawings, and bitmap image files. CAD standards serve as the table manners of the CAD production process — they define and regulate how people create drawings so that sharing can be more productive and predictable. AutoCAD LT's Internet features enable sharing of drawings well beyond your hard disk and local network.

The drawing- and data-sharing features in AutoCAD LT take you way beyond old-style, pencil-and-paper design and drafting. After you know how to apply the techniques in this part, you are well on your way to full CAD-nerd-hood (you may want to warn your family beforehand . . .).

Part V: The Part of Tens

This part contains guidelines that minimize your chances of really messing up drawings (your own or others'), and techniques for swapping drawings with other people and accessing them from other computer programs. I've packed a lot of meat into these three chapters — juicy tidbits from years of drafting, experimentation, and fist-shaking at things that don't work right, not to mention years of compulsive list-making. I hope that you find these lists help you get on the right track quickly and help you stay there.

Icons Used in This Book

This icon tells you that herein lies a pointed insight that can save you time and trouble as you use AutoCAD LT. In many cases, tip paragraphs act as a funnel on AutoCAD's impressive but sometimes overwhelming flexibility: After telling you all the ways that you *can* do something, I tell you the way that you *should* do it in most cases.

The Technical Stuff icon points out places where I'm delving a little more deeply into AutoCAD LT's inner workings or pointing out something that most people don't need to know about most of the time. These paragraphs definitely are not required reading the first time through, so if you come to one of them at a time when you've reached your techie detail threshold, feel free to skip over it.

This icon tells you how to stay out of trouble when living a little close to the edge. Failure to heed its message may have unpleasant consequences for you and your drawing — or maybe for both of you.

You have a lot to remember when you're using AutoCAD LT, so I've remembered to remind you about some those things that you should be remembering. These paragraphs usually refer to a crucial point earlier in the chapter or in a previous chapter. So if you're reading sequentially, a remember paragraph serves as a friendly reminder. If you're not reading sequentially, this kind of paragraph may help you realize that you need to review a central concept or technique before proceeding.

This icon points to new stuff in AutoCAD LT 2005. It's mostly designed for those of you who are somewhat familiar with a previous version of AutoCAD or LT and want to be alerted to what's new in this version. New LT users starting out their CAD working lives with AutoCAD LT 2005 will find this stuff interesting, too — especially when they can show off their new book-learnin' to the grizzled AutoCAD veterans in the office who don't yet know about all the cool, new features.

A Few Conventions — Just in Case

You probably can figure out for yourself all the information in this section, but here are the details just in case.

Text you type into the program at the command line, in a dialog box, in a text box, and so on appears in **boldface type**. Examples of AutoCAD LT prompts appear in a `special typeface`, as does any other text in the book that echoes a message, a word, or one or more lines of text that actually appear on-screen. Sequences of prompts that appear in the LT command line area have a shaded background, like so:

```
Specify lower left corner or [ON/OFF] <0.0000,0.0000>:
```

(Many of the figures — especially in Chapters 6 and 7 — also show AutoCAD LT command line sequences that demonstrate LT's prompts and example responses.)

Often in this book you see phrases such as "choose File⇨Save As from the menu bar." The funny little arrow (⇨) separates the main menu name from the specific command on that menu. In this example, you open the File menu and choose the Save As command. If you know another way to start the same command (for example, in this example, type **SAVEAS** and press Enter), you're welcome to do it that way instead.

Many AutoCAD LT commands have shortcut (fewer letter) versions for the benefit of those who like to type commands at the LT command prompt. In this book, I format command names with the shortcut letters in uppercase and the other letters in lowercase so that you can become familiar with the shortcuts and use them if you want to. So when you see an instruction like "run the **DimLInear** command to draw a linear dimension," it means "for a linear dimension, type **DIMLINEAR**, or **DLI** for short, at the command line, and then press the Enter key."

Where to Go from Here

I suggest that you start by at least skimming Chapter 1 and then reading Chapters 2, 3, and 5 fairly carefully. Chapter 4 gives you a gentle, hands-on introduction to all the main parts of the CAD drawing production process — feel free to work through the example or simply skim it during your next bus ride or unoccupied moment on the couch. With the information in these chapters under your belt, you're ready to dip into any other place in the book.

If you plan to use AutoCAD LT to create full drawings from scratch, you probably want to continue straight on to Chapters 6 through 8 and then 9 through 13. These chapters cover all the essential activities for creating and editing drawings. Then dip into the remaining chapters depending on your additional CAD needs or curiosity.

If you plan to plug into an existing CAD process — for example, viewing, plotting, or making minor changes to drawings created by AutoCAD users, you can jump directly from the first five chapters of the book to any other chapter. For example, go directly to Chapter 8 to figure out how to zoom and pan in order to get a better look at the details of a large, complex drawing, or skip to Chapter 12 when your task is to plot an AutoCAD drawing.

Part I
Lighting Up LT

"Oh, big surprise – another announcement of cost overruns and a delayed completion date."

In this part . . .

AutoCAD LT is more than just another application program, it's a complete environment for drafting. So if you're new to LT, you need to know several things to get off to a good start — especially how to use the command line area, draw precisely, and control object properties. These key techniques are described in this part of the book. The final chapter in this part takes you on a quick trip through the drawing, editing, and plotting CAD process, so that you have an idea what the scenery will look like in the remaining parts of the book.

If you've used earlier versions of AutoCAD, you'll be most interested in the high points of the new release, including some newer interface components. The lowdown on what's new is here, too.

Chapter 1

Why Be LT?

In This Chapter

- Detecting the LT difference
- Finding where CAD fits
- Reaping the benefits of DWG

AutoCAD LT is one of the best deals around — a shining example of the old 80/20 rule: roughly 80 percent of the capabilities of AutoCAD for roughly 20 percent of the money. Like AutoCAD, AutoCAD LT runs on mainstream Windows computers and doesn't require any additional hardware devices. With AutoCAD LT, you can be a "player" in the world of AutoCAD, the world's leading CAD program, for a comparatively low starting cost.

AutoCAD LT is a close cousin to AutoCAD. Autodesk, the company that makes the two programs, created AutoCAD LT by starting with the AutoCAD program, taking out a few features to make the program a little simpler to use (and to justify a lower price), adding a couple of features to enhance ease of use compared to full AutoCAD, and then testing the result.

The LT Difference

AutoCAD LT 2005, shown in Figure 1-1, is almost identical to AutoCAD 2005 in the way it looks and works. The opening screen and menus of the two programs are nearly indistinguishable, with LT missing a small number of the commands found in the AutoCAD 2005 menus.

In fact, the major difference between the programs has nothing to do with the programs themselves. The major difference is that AutoCAD LT lacks support for several programming languages that software developers and even some advanced users employ to create utilities and industry-specific applications for AutoCAD. AutoCAD supports add-ons written in Microsoft's Visual Basic for Applications (VBA), in a specialized AutoCAD programming language called AutoLISP, and in a specialized version of the C programming language called the AutoCAD Runtime Extension (ARX).

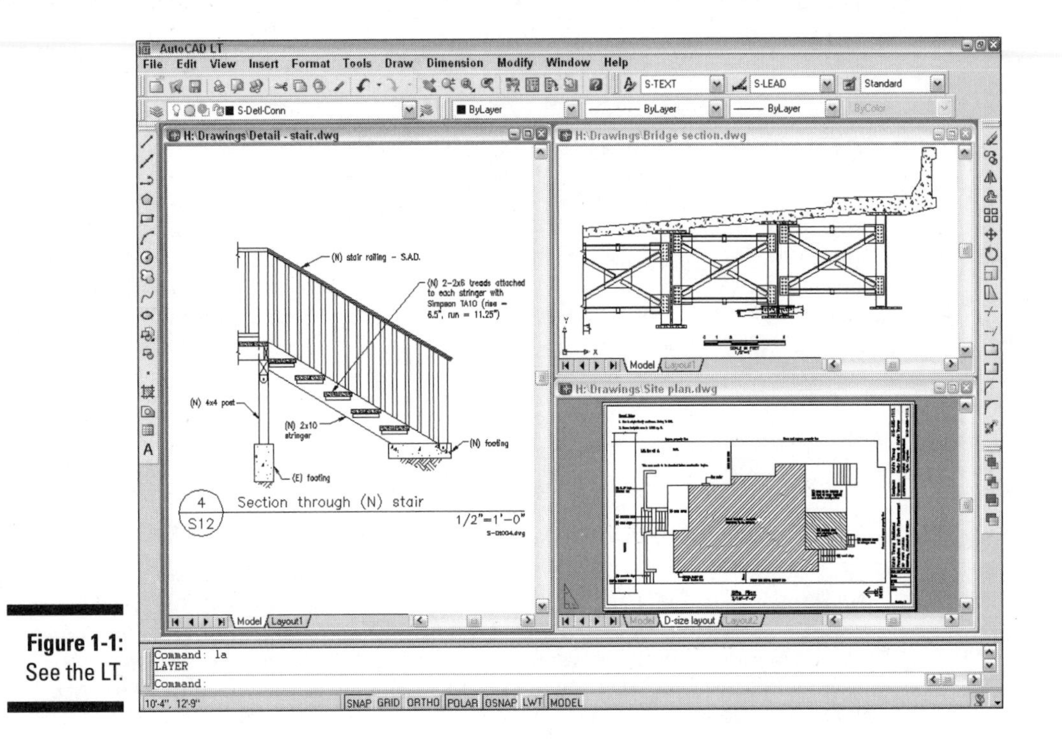

Figure 1-1: See the LT.

Software developers, including Autodesk's own programmers, use AutoCAD's support for these programming languages to develop add-on programs that work with AutoCAD. For example, AutoCAD includes a set of handy utility commands called the Express Tools, and Autodesk used AutoLISP and other AutoCAD programming languages to create them. Other software developers create specialized applications for architectural drafting or other industry-specific needs.

AutoCAD LT doesn't support any of these programming languages, so most of the utilities and applications developed for AutoCAD don't work with LT. AutoCAD LT does include the same menu and script customization features that AutoCAD has. As a result, a few very simple AutoCAD add-ons do work with LT. For example, you can purchase or download *block libraries* — collections of drafting symbols — that work with LT.

AutoCAD LT also has only limited 3D support. You can view and edit 3D objects in AutoCAD LT, so you can work with drawings created in AutoCAD that contain 3D objects. You also can extrude a 2D object, which gives you a limited ability to create 3D models. (CAD people call this ability "2½ D" because it's limited to giving 2D objects depth in one direction.) However, you cannot create 3D surfaces or solids.

The lack of 3D object creation in LT is not as big of a limitation for many people as you may think. Most companies use CAD to create 2D drawings most of the time. Although 3D modeling can be effective for some kinds of work, it requires a lot more skill and sophistication on the part of the user. It also begs for more computing power. A reasonably current, no-frills computer that runs AutoCAD LT quite respectably is brought to its knees if you try to do real 3D modeling and rendering with AutoCAD on it.

Although you may hear claims that AutoCAD LT is easier to master and use than AutoCAD, the truth is that they're about equally difficult (or easy, depending on your nerd IQ). The LT learning curve doesn't differ significantly from that of AutoCAD. AutoCAD was originally designed for maximum power and then modified somewhat to improve ease of use. AutoCAD LT shares this same heritage.

The most notable example of this penchant for power over ease of use is the command line (that text area lurking at the bottom of the AutoCAD LT screen — see Chapter 2 for details). But fear not; this book guides you around the bumps and minimizes the bruises.

Letting the CAD Out of the Bag

Depending on whom you ask, CAD stands for Computer-Aided Drafting or Computer-Aided Design. A few people cover both bases by calling it CADD: Computer-Aided Drafting and Design. (AutoCAD presumably is short for "Automatic CAD" — it's certainly not limited to drawing cars.) Most people use CAD programs for drafting — creating and modifying drawings that guide the construction of something. A design task, by contrast, involves making decisions such as "how many veeblefetzers can I cram into this crawl space?" or "how big does this beam need to be to ensure that the 500-member synchronized polka dancing team doesn't bring down the building?" Documenting these decisions is part of your CAD work, too, so computer-aided design is not a bad name. Just remember that you'll probably use AutoCAD LT primarily for drafting.

AutoCAD LT is, first and foremost, a program to create *technical drawings;* drawings in which measurements and precision are important because these kinds of drawings often get used to build something. The drawings you create with LT must adhere to standards established long ago for hand-drafted drawings. The upfront investment to use AutoCAD LT certainly is more expensive than the investment needed to use pencil and paper, and the learning curve is much steeper, too. Why bother? The key reasons for using AutoCAD LT rather than pencil and paper are:

- **Precision:** Creating lines, circles, and other shapes of the exactly correct dimensions is easier with AutoCAD LT than with pencils.
- **Modifiability:** Drawings are much easier to modify on the computer screen than on paper. CAD modifications are a lot cleaner, too.

- **Efficiency:** Creating many kinds of drawings is faster with a CAD program — especially drawings that involve repetition, such as floor plans in a multistory building. But that efficiency takes skill and practice. If you're an accomplished pencil-and-paper drafter, don't expect CAD to be faster at first!

CAD programs have some similarities to other kinds of programs that are used for drawing. Here's a quick rundown on some major types of drawing programs that you may recognize, and how they relate to CAD programs:

- **Paint programs:** You use these programs to create *bitmapped images*. The computer stores a bitmapped image as a bunch of *pixels* (short for "picture elements," the little dots on your screen). The standard format for bitmapped images in Windows is a *BMP* (BitMaP) file. Most people prefer to use other formats, such as TIF, GIF, or PCX, that offer file compression. The Paint program that comes free with Windows is, as you may expect, a prototypical example of a simple paint program. Adobe Photoshop, for all its sophistication, is a grown-up paint program.

  The biggest difference between a paint program and CAD is that you can't easily modify geometrical objects in a paint program; after you draw a line, for example, you can't select it again as a line — just as a bunch of pixels. If the line crosses other lines or images, selecting it again just as a line is nearly impossible. So, creation is easy in a paint program, but editing things such as lines and arcs is hard, and precision is next to impossible.

  In the CAD world, paint-type images are referred to as *raster images*.

- **Illustration programs:** You use an illustration program to create *vector-based images*. The computer stores vector-based images as a set of geometrical objects (such as lines and arcs), using any of a variety of formats. Adobe Illustrator and CorelDraw are draw programs; Visio is an example of a specialized form of draw program called a *diagramming program*.

  The biggest difference between a CAD program and a draw or diagramming program is the degree of support for precision. In a draw program, you can create an image easily, but creating a precise one is difficult. In a CAD program, creating an image can be somewhat difficult, but making it precise doesn't require much additional work. CAD programs also offer robust support for CAD-specific features, such as dimensioning and hatching.

If your previous computer drawing experience is limited to a paint program, AutoCAD LT presents a fairly steep learning curve for you — you have to "think different," to quote the ads of a large computer company known more for its design cachet than its adherence to grammatical norms. In CAD, you create geometrical *objects* rather than just images, and that difference introduces a whole new set of things that you need to think about as you draw and edit.

If you've used a draw program or a diagramming program, and especially if you've used one to do complicated, precise work, you don't face such a steep learning curve. After you understand how to select objects, enter commands, and print, you can get rolling.

In either case, you need to pay close attention to controlling object properties and precision — Chapter 3 shows how. Paint and draw programs and the types of images that you create with them usually permit a fairly loose approach to properties and precision. AutoCAD LT *permits* the loose approach, but drawings created that way won't work well for you or for the intended audience.

Wherever you start from, figuring out how to use AutoCAD LT offers many rewards. AutoCAD is the best-selling CAD program in the world, and billions of dollars worth of drawings have been created with it. By using AutoCAD LT, you inherit much of the AutoCAD infrastructure. You also gain the ability to create precise, well-documented drawings that can be used, edited, and reused by millions of other designers and drafters.

The Importance of Being DWG

One of AutoCAD LT's key advantages is its use of the same DWG ("drawing") file format as full AutoCAD. AutoCAD LT reads and writes DWG files, using almost exactly the same computer code as in AutoCAD because the same company creates both programs and uses much of the same programming work for both. Thanks to this common parentage, an AutoCAD user and an AutoCAD LT user can almost always share files smoothly, although users of any other pair of CAD programs usually can't share files without bumping into compatibility problems.

To understand the importance of smooth DWG exchange, think of a similar problem involving word processing. If you create a document in Microsoft Word and send it to someone who uses WordPerfect, the recipient can open it, but the formatting frequently changes — page breaks may move, tables may look a little different, special characters may mysteriously transmogrify, and so on. Fixing the problems can cost lots of time and money.

File exchange is much more common and frequent among CAD users than it is among users of other kinds of programs. Many CAD projects involve dozens of designers and drafters working at several different companies. CAD file exchange also is much more fraught with potential compatibility problems. Properties, precision, and plotting vary from one CAD program to the next. These differences frequently show up on the screen, printed output, or both. And remember that companies use CAD files to build airplanes, buildings, and medical instruments such as pacemakers; errors literally can be life threatening.

To quickly sum up years of technical work by Autodesk and its competitors, as well as discussions, articles, online debates, and even lawsuits, DWG compatibility is notoriously hard to achieve. The only program that offers nearly flawless file compatibility with AutoCAD is AutoCAD LT.

As you probably expect, the DWG format isn't static — Autodesk changes it every few years in order to accommodate new features. In some cases, an older version of AutoCAD or LT can't open a DWG file that's been saved by a newer version of AutoCAD.

- A newer version of AutoCAD *always* can open files saved by an older version.
- *Some* previous versions of AutoCAD can open files saved by the subsequent one or two versions. For example, AutoCAD LT 2004 can open DWG files saved by AutoCAD 2005 or LT 2005. That's because Autodesk didn't change the DWG file format between AutoCAD 2004 and AutoCAD 2005.
- You can use the Save As option in newer versions to save the file to some older DWG formats. For example, AutoCAD LT 2005 can save to the previous format, namely the AutoCAD 2000 DWG format.

Table 1-1 shows which versions use which DWG file formats.

Table 1-1 AutoCAD Versions and DWG File Formats

AutoCAD Version	*AutoCAD LT Version*	*Release Year*	*DWG File Format*
AutoCAD 2005 (A2k5)	AutoCAD LT 2005	2004	Acad 2004
AutoCAD 2004 (A2k4)	AutoCAD LT 2004	2003	Acad 2004
AutoCAD 2002 (A2k2)	AutoCAD LT 2002	2001	Acad 2000
AutoCAD 2000i (A2ki)	AutoCAD LT 2000i	2000	Acad 2000
AutoCAD 2000 (A2k)	AutoCAD LT 2000	1999	Acad 2000
AutoCAD Release 14 (R14)	AutoCAD LT 98 & 97	1997	Acad R14
AutoCAD Release 13 (R13)	AutoCAD LT 95	1994	Acad R13
AutoCAD Release 12 (R12)	AutoCAD LT Release 2	1992	Acad R12

Life is easier when your co-workers and colleagues in other companies all use the same version of AutoCAD or AutoCAD LT. That way, your DWG files, add-on tools, and even the details of your CAD knowledge can mix and match among your workgroup and partners. In the real world, you probably work with people — at least in other companies — who use AutoCAD versions as old as Release 14.

AutoCAD LT 2005 does not include an option for saving files to the R14 DWG file format. This omission creates problems if you want to send DWG files to clients or consultants who are still using AutoCAD Release 14. (And a surprising number of these folks are out there — R14 was popular, and AutoCAD 2000 through 2004 didn't tempt everyone to upgrade.) To get around this limitation, you can save to the R12 DXF format, which AutoCAD Release 14 can open — see Chapter 17 for instructions.

Why Workalike Works

In addition to DWG compatibility, another, subtler reason exists for viewing AutoCAD LT as your best choice for a lower-priced CAD program. And, like DWG compatibility, this reason relates to AutoCAD's position as the industry standard for CAD. Choosing AutoCAD LT makes sense because of all the industry experience and products that exist for AutoCAD and therefore, to a large extent, for AutoCAD LT.

This book is a great example of how LT and its users benefit from full AutoCAD. My book *AutoCAD 2005 For Dummies* provides the source material for much of this book. *AutoCAD LT 2005 For Dummies* is easier to justify economically — not to mention easier for me to write! — because of AutoCAD.

Similar reasoning applies to many books, articles, courses, and products related to AutoCAD and AutoCAD LT. The AutoCAD connection provides the base for AutoCAD LT-related products, and AutoCAD itself provides an upgrade path in case LT can't meet all your needs.

As I mention earlier in this chapter, not all AutoCAD-compatible products work with AutoCAD LT. You can't use the add-on programs and utilities developed with one of the AutoCAD customization programming languages, such as AutoLISP or the AutoCAD Runtime Extension (ARX). Before you buy any product that was developed to work with AutoCAD, ask whether it supports AutoCAD LT, too.

Working with AutoCAD veterans

Watching an experienced AutoCAD user work can be a bewildering experience. In all likelihood, the old pro moves quickly and unpredictably between the program's menus, toolbars, and command line. You may see that person start a command or process in one part of the screen, continue it in another, and complete it in a third.

Also, you may see AutoCAD veterans using a program that looks a lot different from your version of AutoCAD LT. They may have an old version of AutoCAD, they may be running one or more add-on programs (mostly not compatible with LT), or they may have customized and rearranged the AutoCAD screen beyond recognition.

AutoCAD veterans use a confusing mixture of very fast, efficient approaches and old hang-overs from previous versions that are no longer the best way to work. A novice AutoCAD or LT user can't easily distinguish which is which when getting help from an experienced user.

Unless you have an unusually thoughtful, patient, and otherwise unoccupied AutoCAD veteran nearby, you probably shouldn't get most of your beginning AutoCAD instruction from a veteran. Turn to this book as a resource for the basics of using AutoCAD LT and save your questions for when you need to know how your company does things, or for when no other source (neither this book, the AutoCAD LT Help files [which I describe in Chapter 2], nor your own trials and tribulations) provides a quick, satisfactory answer. You get brownie points for going it alone as much as you can — and then are more likely to get a quick, helpful answer just when you need it.

The final, but perhaps most important, AutoCAD-related advantage of AutoCAD LT is all the AutoCAD knowledge that's likely to be in the heads of your co-workers. If you have colleagues with AutoCAD experience, you have an experienced technical support staff on call nearby. Although you don't want to wear out your welcome (using this book can help you answer the easy questions yourself), this informal support network, plus any formal AutoCAD support in your organization, is an invaluable resource. And as your LT knowledge grows, you can help other LT and AutoCAD users with their problems in return.

Chapter 2

AutoCAD LT 2005 Screen Test

In This Chapter

- Touring the AutoCAD LT 2005 screen
- Going bar-hopping: title bars, the menu bar, toolbars, and the status bar
- Commanding the command line
- Discovering the drawing area
- Making the most of Model and Layout tabs
- Dabbling with palettes
- Setting system variables and using dialog boxes
- Using online help

AutoCAD LT 2005 is a full-fledged citizen of the Windows world, with toolbars, dialog boxes, right-click menus, a multiple-document interface, and all the other trappings of a real Windows program. But lurking beneath that pretty face — and literally beneath the drawing area, right at the bottom of the LT program window — is a weird but essential holdover from the DOS days: the command line area. The command line is one of the few un-Windows-like things in AutoCAD LT that you have to come to terms with, and this chapter shows you how.

Like the rest of the book, this chapter is written for someone who has used other Windows programs but has little or no experience with AutoCAD. If you've had any experience with recent Windows versions of AutoCAD or LT, much of this chapter is old hat for you. Do make sure, though, that you're familiar with the interface features that were added to AutoCAD 2005 and AutoCAD LT 2005: palettes and the additional buttons on the right end of the status bar.

AutoCAD LT Does Windows — Sort Of

Although AutoCAD LT looks pretty much like other Windows programs, aspects of the program's appearance — and some of the ways in which you work with it — are quite different from other programs. You can, in many

Screens in black and white

The screen shots and descriptions in this chapter reflect the *default* configuration of AutoCAD LT — that is, the way the screen looks if you haven't messed with the display settings. You can change the appearance of the screen with settings on the Display tab of the Options dialog box (choose Tools⇨Options⇨Display) and by dragging toolbars and other screen components.

One display modification you may want to make is to change your drawing area background to black because the normal range of colors that appears in most drawings is easier to see against a black background. (On the Display tab I mention in the previous paragraph, click the Colors button, choose Model Tab Background in the Window Element list, and then choose Black in the Color list.) I left the drawing area background white when I created the figures for this book because they show up better that way on the printed page.

cases, tell the program what to do in at least four ways — click a toolbar icon, pick from the pull-down menus, type at the command line, or select from the right-click menus — none of which is necessarily the best method to use for every task. The experience is much like that of having to act as several different characters in a play; you're likely to forget your lines (whichever "you" you are at the time!) every now and then.

As with other Windows programs, the menus at the top of the AutoCAD LT screen enable you to access most of the program's functions and are the easiest-to-remember method of issuing commands. When you want to get real work done, you need to combine the pull-down menus with other methods — especially typing options at the command line or choosing them from the right-click menu. I show you how throughout this book.

Passing the LT Screen Test

When you launch AutoCAD LT after first installing it, the opening screen, shown in Figure 2-1, displays an arrangement of menus, toolbars, palettes, and a new, blank drawing. You can close the Tool palettes and Info palette for now — I describe how to open and use them later in this chapter.

Standard Windows fare

As shown in Figure 2-1, much of the AutoCAD LT screen is standard Windows fare — title bars, a menu bar, toolbars, and a status bar.

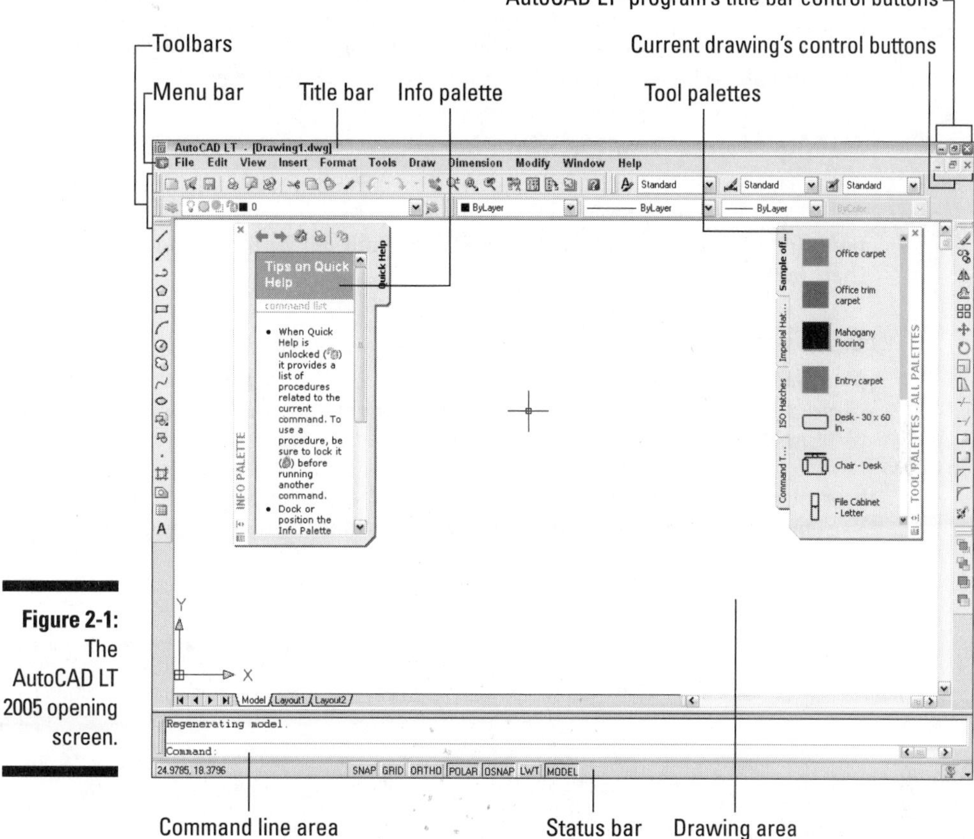

Figure 2-1: The AutoCAD LT 2005 opening screen.

A hierarchy of title bars

Like most Windows programs, AutoCAD LT has a *title bar* at the top of its program window that reminds you which program you're in (not that you'd ever mistake the LT window for, say, Microsoft Word!).

- At the right side of the title bar is the standard set of three Windows control buttons: Minimize, Maximize/Restore, and Close.
- Each drawing window within the AutoCAD LT program window has its own title bar. You use the control buttons on a drawing window's title bar to minimize, maximize/restore down, or close that drawing, not the entire LT program.

As in other Windows programs, if you maximize a drawing's window, it expands to fill the entire drawing area. (AutoCAD LT 2005 starts with the drawing maximized in this way.) As shown in Figure 2-1, the drawing's control buttons move onto the menu bar, below the control buttons for the LT program window; the drawing's name appears in the LT title bar. To un-maximize the drawing so that you can see any other drawings that you have open, click the lower un-maximize button. The result is as shown in Figure 2-2: a separate title bar for each drawing with the name and controls for that drawing.

Making choices from the menu bar

The *menu bar* contains the names of all the primary menus in your version of AutoCAD LT. As with any program that's new to you, spending a few minutes perusing the menus in order to familiarize yourself with the commands and their arrangement is worth your time.

Cruising the toolbars

As in other Windows programs, the toolbars in AutoCAD LT 2005 provide rapid access to the program's most commonly used commands. LT ships with toolbars in this default arrangement (as shown in Figure 2-3):

- **Standard toolbar:** Located on top, just below the menu bar; file management and other common Windows functions, plus some specialized AutoCAD LT stuff, such as zooming and panning.

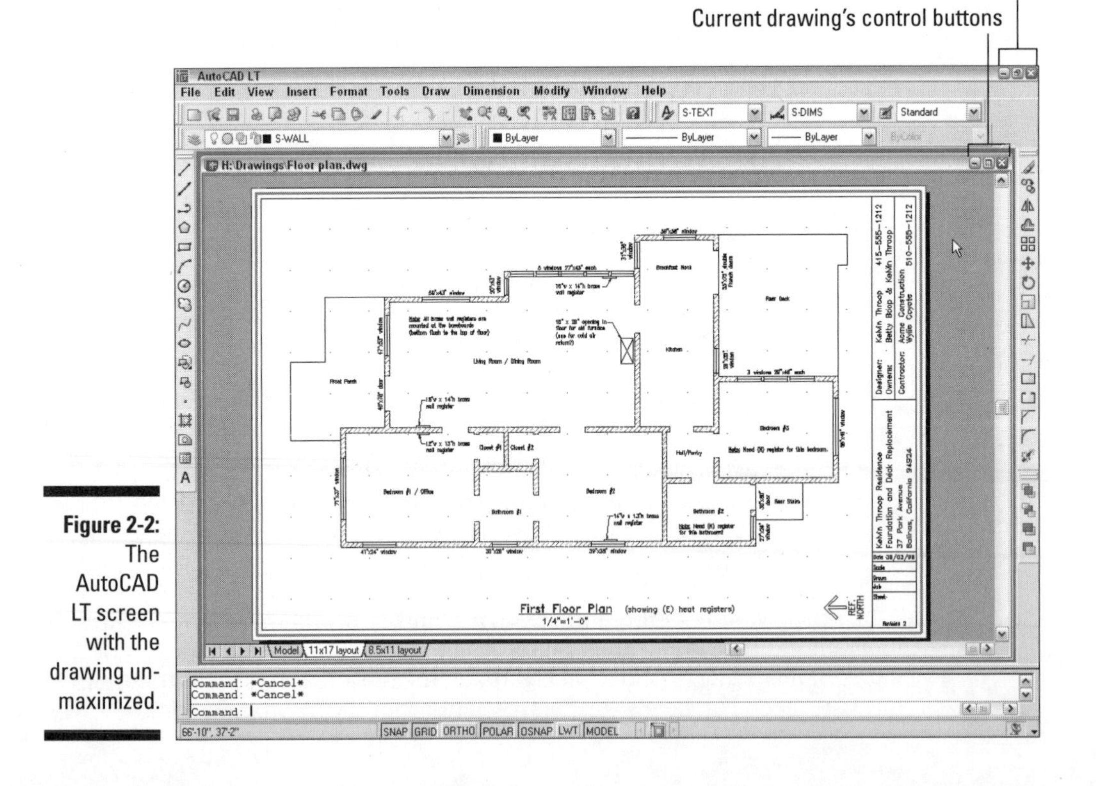

Figure 2-2: The AutoCAD LT screen with the drawing un-maximized.

- **Styles toolbar:** To the right of the Standard toolbar; analogous to the left part of the Formatting toolbar in Microsoft programs, but formatting of LT's text, dimension, and table styles. (Table styles are new in AutoCAD LT 2005.) Chapters 9 and 10 cover these features.
- **Layers toolbar:** Beneath the Standard toolbar; commands and a drop-down list for manipulating layers, which are LT's fundamental tools for organizing and formatting objects. Chapter 3 contains the layer lowdown.
- **Properties toolbar:** To the right of the Layers toolbar; analogous to the right part of the Formatting toolbar in Microsoft programs, but formatting of AutoCAD LT's properties, such as colors, linetypes, and lineweights. See Chapter 3 when you're ready to play with LT's object properties.
- **Draw toolbar:** Vertically down the far-left edge of the screen; the most commonly used commands from the Draw menu. Chapter 6 covers most of the items on this toolbar.
- **Modify toolbar:** Vertically down the far-right edge of the screen; the most commonly used commands from the Modify menu. Chapter 7 shows you how to use almost everything on this toolbar.

- **Draw toolbar:** Beneath the Modify toolbar; commands for controlling which objects appear on top of which other objects. (This toolbar existed in previous versions, but in AutoCAD LT 2005 the toolbar is turned on by default.) Chapter 13 mentions these features.

You can rearrange, open, and close toolbars as in other Windows programs:

- To move a toolbar, point to its border (the double-line control handle at the leading edge of the toolbar is the easiest part to grab), click, and drag.
- To open or close toolbars, right-click any toolbar button and choose from the list of available toolbars, as shown in Figure 2-3.

Hot-wiring the menu bar

Some standard tips and tricks for Windows are especially useful in AutoCAD LT. Control-key shortcuts for the most popular functions — Ctrl+S to save, Ctrl+O to open a file, and Ctrl+P to print — work the same way in LT as in most other Windows programs. Use them!

Also worth remembering are the Alt-key shortcuts, which are available for all menu choices, not just the most popular ones. To fly around the menus, just press and hold the Alt key and then press the letters on your keyboard that correspond to the underlined letters on the menu bar and in the menu choices. To bring up the SAVEAS command, for example, just press and hold the Alt key, press F for File, and then press A for Save As.

Figure 2-3: A toolbar tasting.

The AutoCAD LT screen shown in Figure 2-3 shows the default toolbar arrangement, which works fine for most people. Feel free to close the Draw Order toolbar; you aren't likely to use its features frequently. You may want to turn on a couple of additional toolbars, such as Object Snap and Dimension, as you discover and make use of additional features. Throughout this book, I point out when a particular toolbar may be useful.

If you're not satisfied with just rearranging the stock AutoCAD LT toolbars, you can customize their contents or even create new ones. The procedures are beyond the scope of this book; they involve bouncing among the Commands, Toolbars, and Properties tabs on the Customize dialog box in not entirely intuitive ways. Resist slicing and dicing the stock LT toolbars until you're at least somewhat familiar with them. If you want to get creative thereafter, go to the Contents tab of the AutoCAD LT 2005 online help and choose Customization Guide⇨Basic Customization⇨Create Custom Toolbars.

LT toolbar buttons provide *ToolTips,* those short text descriptions that appear in little yellow boxes when you pause the cursor over a toolbar button. A longer description of the icon's function appears in the status bar at the bottom of the screen.

Looking for Mr. Status Bar

The *status bar* appears at the bottom of the AutoCAD LT screen, as shown in Figure 2-4. The status bar displays and allows you to change several important settings that affect how you draw and edit in the current drawing. Some of these settings don't make complete sense until you use the LT commands that they influence, but here's a brief description, with pointers to detailed descriptions of how to use each setting elsewhere in this book:

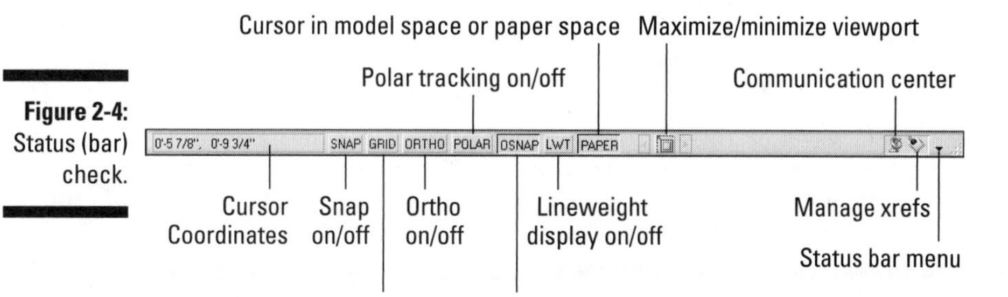

Figure 2-4: Status (bar) check.

- **Coordinates of the cursor:** The *cursor coordinates* readout displays the current X,Y,Z location of the cursor in the drawing area, with respect to the origin point (whose coordinates are 0,0,0). It's a bit like having a GPS (Global Positioning System) device in your drawing. Chapter 3 describes AutoCAD LT's coordinate conventions and how to use this area of the status bar.

  If the coordinates in the lower-left corner of the screen are grayed out, coordinate tracking is turned off. Click the coordinates so that they appear in dark lettering that changes when you move the cursor in the drawing area.

- **SNAP, GRID, and ORTHO mode buttons:** These three buttons control three of AutoCAD LT's tools for ensuring precision drawing and editing:
  - **Snap** constrains the cursor to regularly spaced hot spots, enabling you to draw objects a fixed distance apart more easily.
  - **Grid** displays a series of regularly spaced dots, which serve as a distance reference.
  - **Ortho** constrains the cursor to horizontal and vertical relative movement, which makes drawing orthogonal (straight horizontal and vertical) lines easy.

  See Chapter 5 for instructions on how to configure these modes and Chapter 3 for information about why, when, and how to use them in actual drawing operations.

- **POLAR tracking mode button:** Polar tracking causes the cursor to prefer certain angles when you draw and edit objects. By default, the preferred angles are multiples of 90 degrees, but you can specify other angle increments, such as 45 or 30 degrees. See Chapter 3 for instructions on how to specify the polar tracking angles that you prefer. Clicking the POLAR button toggles polar tracking on or off. Ortho and polar tracking are mutually exclusive — turning on one mode disables the other.
- **Running Object Snap (OSNAP) button:** *Object snap* is another AutoCAD LT tool for ensuring precision drawing and editing. You use object snaps to grab points on existing objects — for example, the endpoint of a line or the center of a circle. When you turn on *running object snap,* LT continues to hunt for object snap points. Chapter 3 contains detailed instructions on how to use this feature.
- **Lineweight (LWT) display mode button:** One of the properties that you can assign to objects in AutoCAD LT is *lineweight* — the thickness that lines appear when you plot the drawing. This button controls whether you see the lineweights on-screen. (This button doesn't control whether lineweights appear on plots; that's a separate setting in the Plot dialog box.) Chapter 3 gives you the skinny (and the wide) on lineweights.
- **MODEL/PAPER space button:** As I describe in the section "Main course: The drawing area" later in this chapter, the drawing area is composed of overlapping tabbed areas labeled Model, Layout1, and Layout2 by default. The Model tab displays a part of the drawing called *model space,* where you create most of your drawing. Each of the remaining tabs displays a *paper space layout,* where you can compose a plot-able view with a title block. A completed layout includes one or more *viewports*, which reveal some or all the objects in model space at a particular scale.

  The MODEL/PAPER status bar button (not to be confused with the Model *tab*) comes into play after you click one of the paper space layout tabs. The MODEL/PAPER button provides a means for moving the cursor between model and paper space while remaining in the particular layout.

  - When the MODEL/PAPER button says MODEL, drawing and editing operations take place in model space, inside a viewport.
  - When the button says PAPER, drawing and editing operations take place in paper space on the current layout.

  Don't worry if you find model space and paper space a little disorienting at first. The paper space layout setup information in Chapter 5 and plotting instructions in Chapter 12 can help you get your bearings and navigate with confidence.
- **Maximize/Minimize Viewport button** (paper space layouts only): When you're looking at one of the Layout tabs instead of the Model tab, the status bar displays an additional Maximize Viewport button. Click this button to expand the current paper space viewport so that it fills the entire drawing area. Click the button — now called Minimize Viewport — again to restore the viewport to its normal size. (Chapter 5 describes viewports.)

- **Communication Center:** This button opens a dialog box containing recent AutoCAD-related headlines that Autodesk thinks you may find useful. The headlines are grouped into categories called *channels*: Live Update Maintenance Patches, Articles and Tips, Product Support Information, and so on. Each headline is a link to a Web page with more information, such as how to download a software update or fix a problem. Click the Settings button to select channels you see in the Communication Center window.
- **Manage Xrefs:** You won't see this combination button and notification symbol until you open a drawing that contains xrefs (external DWG files that are incorporated into the current drawing). Chapter 13 tells you how to use xrefs and what the Manage Xrefs button does.
- **Status Bar menu:** When you click the easy-to-miss downward-pointing arrow near the right edge of the status bar, you open a menu with options for toggling off or on each status bar button. Now you can decorate your status bar to your taste.

You can open dialog boxes for configuring many of the status bar button functions by right-clicking the status bar button and choosing Settings. Chapters 3 and 5 give you specific guidance about when and how to change these settings.

A button's appearance shows whether the setting is turned on or off. Depressed, or down, means on; raised, or up, means off. If you're unclear whether a setting is on or off, click its button; its mode changes and the command line reflects its new setting — <Osnap off>, for example. Click again to restore the previous setting.

Take an order: The command line area

If the title bars, menu bar, and status bar are the Windows equivalent of comfort food — familiar, nourishing, and unthreatening — then the command line area, shown in Figure 2-5, must be the steak tartare or blood sausage of the LT screen feast. It looks weird, turns the stomachs of newcomers, and delights AutoCAD aficionados. The hard truth is that you have to like — or at least tolerate — the command line if you want to become at all comfortable using AutoCAD LT.

```
Command: foo
Unknown command "FOO".  Press F1 for help.
Command:
```

Figure 2-5: Learn to obey the command line.

You need to get up close and personal with the command line for four reasons:

- **The command line area is LT's primary communications conduit with you.** This reason to pay attention to the command line is the most important. AutoCAD LT frequently displays prompts, warnings, and error messages in the command line area. If you don't keep an eye on this area, you miss a lot of vital information. You'll continually be frustrated because you won't "hear" what LT is trying to tell you.
- **The command line is an efficient way to run some commands and the only way to run a few others.** Instead of clicking a toolbar button or a menu choice, you can start a command by typing its command name and then pressing the Enter key. Even better, you can type the keyboard shortcut for a command name and press Enter. Most of the keyboard shortcuts for command names are just one or two letters — for example, L for the LINE command and CP for the COPY command. Most people who use the shortcuts for the commands that they run most frequently find that their AutoCAD LT productivity improves noticeably. Even if you're not worried about increasing your productivity with this technique, some commands aren't on the toolbars or pull-down menus. If you want to run those commands, you have to type them!
- **After you start a command — whether from a toolbar, from a menu, or by typing — the command line is where LT prompts you with options for that command.**

  You activate one of these options by typing the uppercase letter(s) in the option and pressing Enter.

  In many cases, you can activate a command's options by right-clicking in the drawing area and choosing the desired option from the right-click menu, instead of by typing the letter(s) for the option and pressing Enter. But if you don't watch the command line, you probably won't realize that there *are* any options!
- **You sometimes need to type coordinates at the command line to specify precise points or distances.** Chapter 3 describes this technique in detail.

You don't have to click in the command line area to type command names, keyboard shortcuts, or command options there. AutoCAD LT knows that your typing is supposed to go to the command line. The only exception is when you're within a text command (you're adding a text note to the drawing itself); in that case, the text appears in the drawing, not in the command line area.

The following steps demonstrate how you use the command line area to run commands, view and select options, and pay attention to messages from LT:

1. **Type L and press Enter.**

   AutoCAD LT starts the LINE command and displays the following prompt in the command line area:

   ```
   LINE Specify first point:
   ```

2. **Click a point anywhere in the drawing area.**

   The command line prompt changes to:

   ```
   Specify next point or [Undo]:
   ```

   LT always displays command options in square brackets. In this case, the Undo option appears in brackets. To activate the option, type the letter(s) shown in uppercase and press Enter. (You can type the option letter(s) in lowercase or uppercase.)

3. **Click another point anywhere in the drawing area.**

   AutoCAD LT draws the first line segment.

   If you find that you're able to draw only horizontal and vertical lines and you want a little more angular freedom, click the toolbar's ORTHO button on the toolbar in order to turn off ortho mode. Similarly, you may want to turn off the SNAP and OSNAP buttons during this "get acquainted with the command line" set of steps in order to remove some of LT's precision constraints. Chapter 3 describes how to use these buttons to ensure precision when you do real drafting.

4. **Click a third point anywhere in the drawing area.**

   LT draws the second line segment. The command line prompt changes to:

   ```
   Specify next point or [Close/Undo]:
   ```

   LT now displays two options, Close and Undo, separated by a slash.

5. **Type U and press Enter.**

   LT undoes the second line segment.

6. **Type** 3,2 **(without any spaces) and press Enter.**

   LT draws a new line segment to the point whose the X coordinate is 3 and the Y coordinate is 2.

7. **Click several more points anywhere in the drawing area.**

   LT draws additional line segments.

8. **Type X and press Enter.**

   LT displays an error message (because X isn't a valid option of the LINE command) and reprompts for another point:

   ```
   Point or option keyword required.
   Specify next point or [Close/Undo]:
   ```

   Option keyword is programmer jargon for the letter(s) shown in uppercase that you type to activate a command option. This error message is AutoCAD LT's way of saying "I don't understand what you mean by typing 'X.' Either specify a point or type a letter that I do understand."

9. **Type** C **and press Enter.**

   LT draws a final line segment, which creates a closed figure, and ends the LINE command. The *naked command prompt* returns (that is, `Command:` at the bottom of the command line area, with nothing after it):

   ```
   Command:
   ```

   The naked command prompt indicates that the program is ready for the next command.

10. **Press the F2 key.**

    LT displays the AutoCAD LT Text window, which is simply an enlarged, scrollable version of the command line area, as shown in Figure 2-6.

    The normal three-line command line area usually shows you what you need to see, but occasionally you want to review a larger chunk of command line history ("What was LT trying to tell me a minute ago?!").

11. **Press the F2 key again.**

    The AutoCAD LT Text window closes.

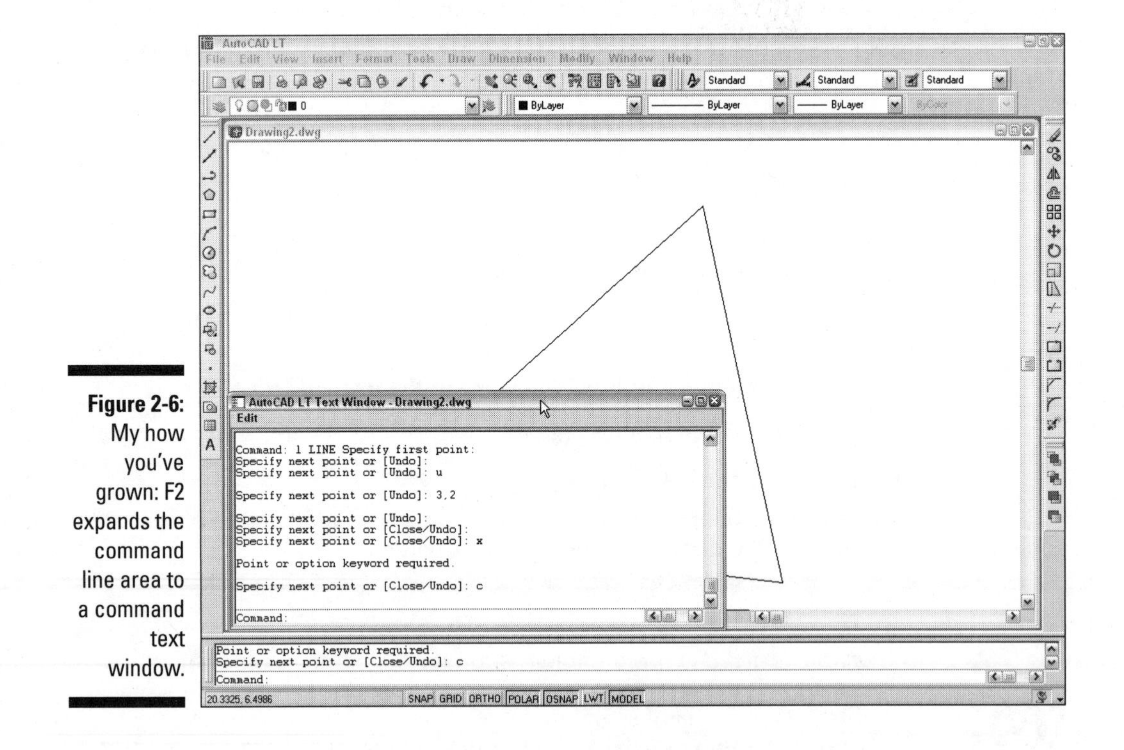

Figure 2-6: My how you've grown: F2 expands the command line area to a command text window.

AutoCAD LT is no *vin ordinaire*

The back-and-forth needed to get AutoCAD LT to draw and complete a line is a great example of the program's power — and its power to confuse new users. It's kind of like a wine that tastes a bit harsh initially, but that ages better than something more immediately drinkable.

In other programs, if you want to draw a line, you just draw it. In AutoCAD LT, you have to press Enter one extra time when you're done just to tell the program you really are finished drawing. But the fact that the Line command remains active after you draw the first line segment makes it much faster to draw complicated, multisegment lines, which is a common activity in a complex drawing.

This example is just one of how AutoCAD LT favors ease of use for power users doing complex drawings over ease of learning for beginners, who frequently forget to hit Enter that extra time to close out a command.

Here are a few other tips and tricks for using the command line effectively:

- **Use the Esc key to bail out of the current operation.** You get confused sometimes about what you're doing in AutoCAD LT and/or what you're seeing in the command line area. If you need to bail out of the current operation, just press the Esc key one or more times until you see the naked command prompt. As in most other Windows programs, Esc is the cancel key. Unlike many other Windows programs, AutoCAD LT keeps you well informed of whether an operation is in progress. The naked command prompt indicates that LT is in a quiescent state, waiting for your next command.
- **Press Enter to accept the default action.** Some command prompts include a default action in angled brackets. For example, the first prompt of the POLygon command is

  ```
  Enter number of sides <4>:
  ```

  The default here is four sides, and you can accept it simply by pressing the Enter key. (That is, you don't have to type **4** first.)

  AutoCAD LT uses two kinds of brackets in command line prompts.

  - Command options appear in square brackets: [Close/Undo].

    To activate a command option, type the letter(s) that appear in uppercase and then press Enter.

  - A default value or option appears in angle brackets: <>.

    To choose the default value or option, simply press Enter.

- **Observe the command line.** You discover a lot about how to use the command line simply by watching it after each action that you take. When you click a toolbar button or menu choice, AutoCAD LT types the name of the command automatically, so if you're watching the command line, you absorb the command names more-or-less naturally.

  When LT types commands automatically in response to your toolbar and menu clicks, it usually adds one or two extra characters to the front of the command name.

  - AutoCAD LT usually puts an underscore in front of the command name (for example, _LINE instead of LINE). The underscore is an Autodesk programmers' trick that enables non-English versions of LT to understand the English command names embedded in the menus.
  - AutoCAD LT sometimes puts an apostrophe in front of the command name and any underscore (for example, '_ZOOM instead of ZOOM). The apostrophe indicates a *transparent* command; you can run the command in the middle of another command without canceling the first command. For example, you can start the LINE command, run the ZOOM command transparently, and then pick up where you left off with the LINE command.

- **Leave the command line in the default configuration initially.** The command line area, like most other parts of the AutoCAD LT screen, is resizable and relocateable. The default location (docked at the bottom of the LT screen) and size (three lines deep) work well for most people. Resist the temptation to mess with the command line area's appearance — at least until you're comfortable with how to use the command line.
- **Right-click in the command line area for options.** If you right-click in the command line area, you see a menu with some useful choices, including Recent Commands — the last six commands that you ran.
- **Press the up- and down-arrow keys to cycle through the stack of commands that you typed recently.** This way is handy to recall and rerun a command, although it doesn't work for commands that you chose from the toolbars or menus. Press the left- and right-arrow keys to edit the command line text that you typed or recalled.

Main course: The drawing area

After all these screen hors d'oeuvres, you're probably getting hungry for the main course — the AutoCAD LT drawing area. The drawing area is where you do your drawing, of course. In the course of creating drawings, you click points to specify locations and distances, click objects to select them for editing, and zoom and pan to get a better view of what you're working on.

Most of this book shows you how to interact with the drawing area, but you need to know a few things up front.

The Model and Layout tabs (Model and paper space)

One of the initially disorienting things about AutoCAD LT is that finished drawings can be composed of objects drawn in different *spaces,* which LT indicates with the tabs along the bottom of the drawing area (Model, Layout1, and Layout2 by default).

- *Model space* is where you create and modify the objects that represent things in the real world — walls, widgets, waterways, or whatever.
- *Paper space* is where you create particular views of these objects for plotting, usually with a title block around them. Paper space comprises one or more *layouts,* each of which can contain a different arrangement of model space views and different title block information. (In most cases, you use only one layout per drawing file — the layout whose tab is labeled Layout1 by default.)

When you click the Model tab in the drawing area, you see pure, unadulterated model space, as shown in Figure 2-7. When you click one of the paper space layout tabs (Layout1 or Layout2, unless someone has renamed or added to them), you see a paper space layout, as shown in Figure 2-8. A completed layout usually includes one or more *viewports,* which are windows that display all or part of model space at a particular scale. A layout also usually includes a title block or other objects that exist only in the layout and don't appear when you click the Model tab. (Think of the viewport as a window looking into model space and the title block as a frame around the window.) Thus, a layout displays model space and paper space objects together, and AutoCAD LT lets you draw and edit objects in either space. See Chapter 5 for information about creating paper space layouts and Chapter 12 for the lowdown on plotting them.

As I describe in the "Looking for Mr. Status Bar" section in this chapter, after you click one of the layout tabs, the status bar's MODEL/PAPER button moves the cursor between model and paper space while remaining in the particular layout. (As shown in Figures 2-7 and 2-8, the orientation icon at the lower-left corner of the AutoCAD LT drawing area changes between an X-Y axis for model space and a drafting triangle for paper space as an additional reminder of which space the cursor currently resides in.) Chapter 5 describes the consequences of changing the MODEL/PAPER setting and advises you on how to use it.

This back-and-forth with the MODEL/PAPER button is necessary only when you're drawing things while viewing one of the paper space layouts. In practice, you probably won't encounter that situation very often. Instead, you do most of your drawing on the Model tab and, after you set up a paper space layout, click its layout tab only when you want to plot.

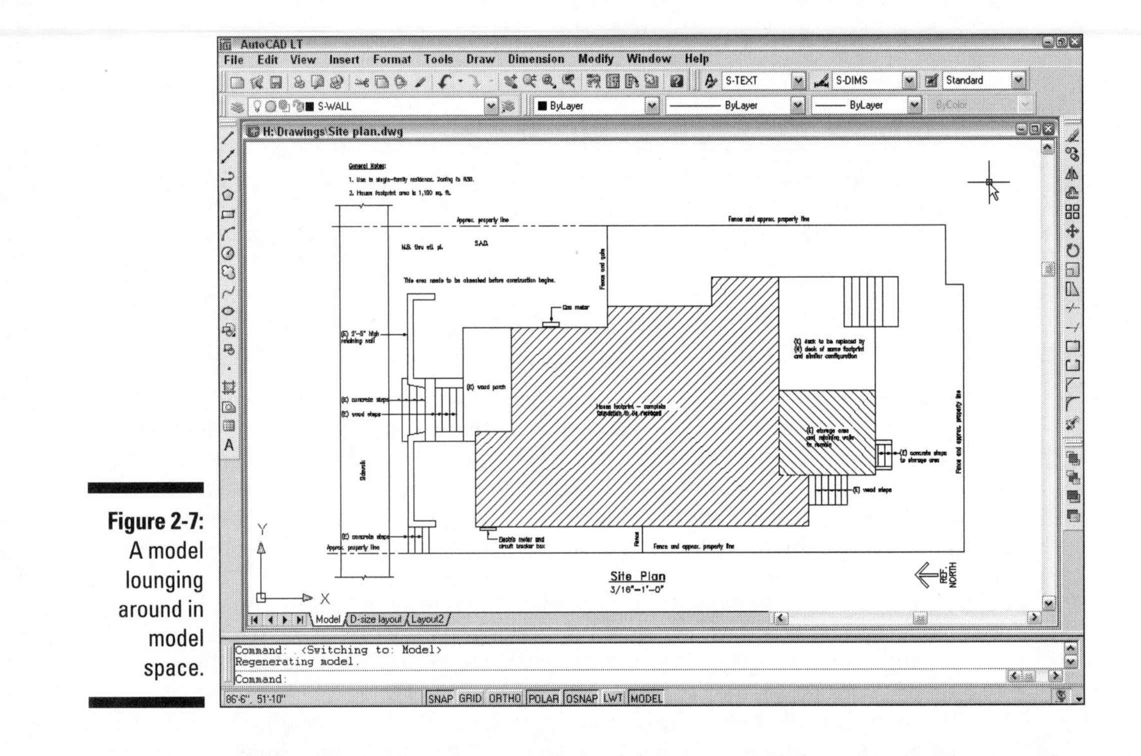

Figure 2-7: A model lounging around in model space.

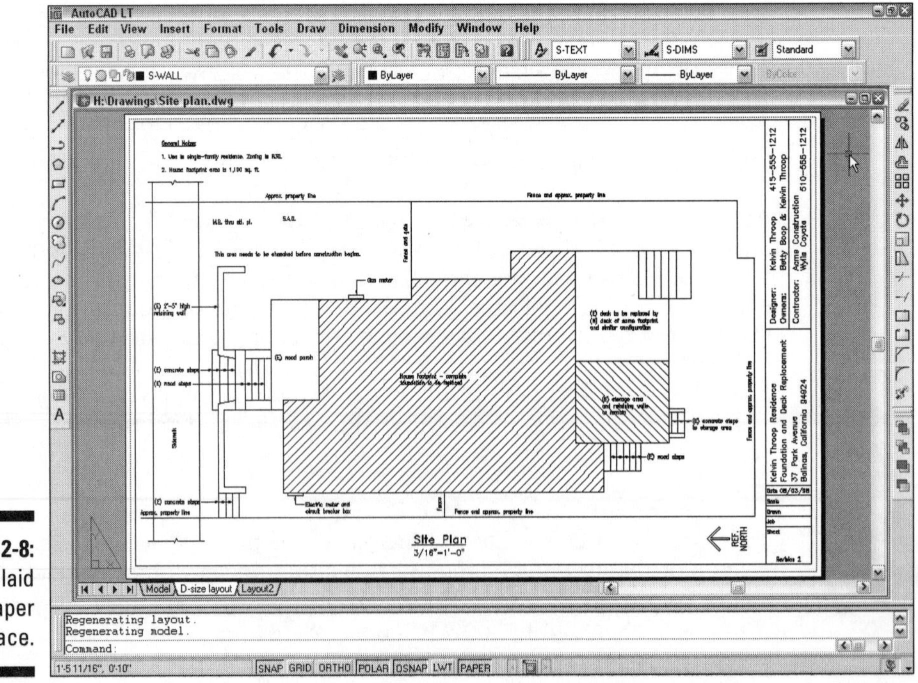

Figure 2-8: Freshly laid out in paper space.

Drawing on the drawing area

Here are a few other things to know about the AutoCAD LT drawing area:

- Efficient, confident use of LT requires that you continually glance from the drawing area to the command line area (to see those all-important prompts!) and then back up to the drawing area. This sequence is not a natural reflex for most people. Get in the habit of looking at the command line after each action that you take, whether picking something on a toolbar, on a menu, or in the drawing area.
- Clicking at random in the drawing area is not quite as harmless in AutoCAD LT as it is in many Windows programs. When you click in the LT drawing area, you're almost always performing some action — usually specifying a point or selecting objects for editing. Feel free to experiment, but look at the command line after each click. If you get confused, press the Esc key a couple of times to clear the current operation and return to the naked command prompt.
- In most cases, you can right-click in the drawing area to display a menu with some options for the current situation.

A Palette Cleanser

In AutoCAD LT 2005, two features called Properties and DesignCenter, plus a toolbar-like interface called Tool Palettes appear in spiffy modeless dialog boxes, or *palettes*.

- **Properties and DesignCenter:** Controls object properties and named objects (layers, blocks, and so on), respectively. Chapter 3 shows you how.
- **Tool Palettes:** Resembles a stack of painter's palettes, except that each palette holds *content* (drawing symbols and hatch patterns) and/or *commands* (toolbar-like macros — a new feature in AutoCAD LT 2005) instead of paints. Chapters 11 and 13 help you unlock your inner Tool Palette artistry.

You toggle these palettes on and off by clicking three buttons near the end of the Standard toolbar or by pressing Ctrl+1 (Properties), Ctrl+2 (DesignCenter), or Ctrl+3 (Tool Palettes). Figure 2-9 shows all three toggled on.

Modeless is just a fancy way of saying that these dialog boxes don't take over AutoCAD LT in the way that *modal* dialog boxes do. Modal dialog boxes demand your undivided attention. You enter values, click buttons, or whatever, and then click the OK or Cancel button to close the dialog box. While the modal dialog box is open, you can't do anything else in LT. A modeless dialog box, on the other hand, can remain open while you execute other commands that have nothing to do with the dialog box. You return to the modeless dialog box when or if you need its features.

Be careful not to muddle modal and model. *Modal* and *modeless* refer to the two general classes of dialog boxes. *Model* refers to the activity of drawing a representation of something in a CAD program, to the drawing thusly created, and to the AutoCAD LT space in which one creates it.

Manipulating AutoCAD LT modeless dialog boxes — or *palettes* — is similar to manipulating a regular Windows dialog box, except that the title bar is along the side instead of at the top. In other words, you click and drag the title strip along the side to move the palette. If you experiment with the control buttons at the bottom of this strip (or right-click anywhere on the strip), you quickly get the hang of what you can do with these palettes. In particular, turning on the auto-hide feature causes the dialog box to "roll up" into the strip so that it's not taking up much screen space. When you point the cursor at the strip, the palette unfurls again.

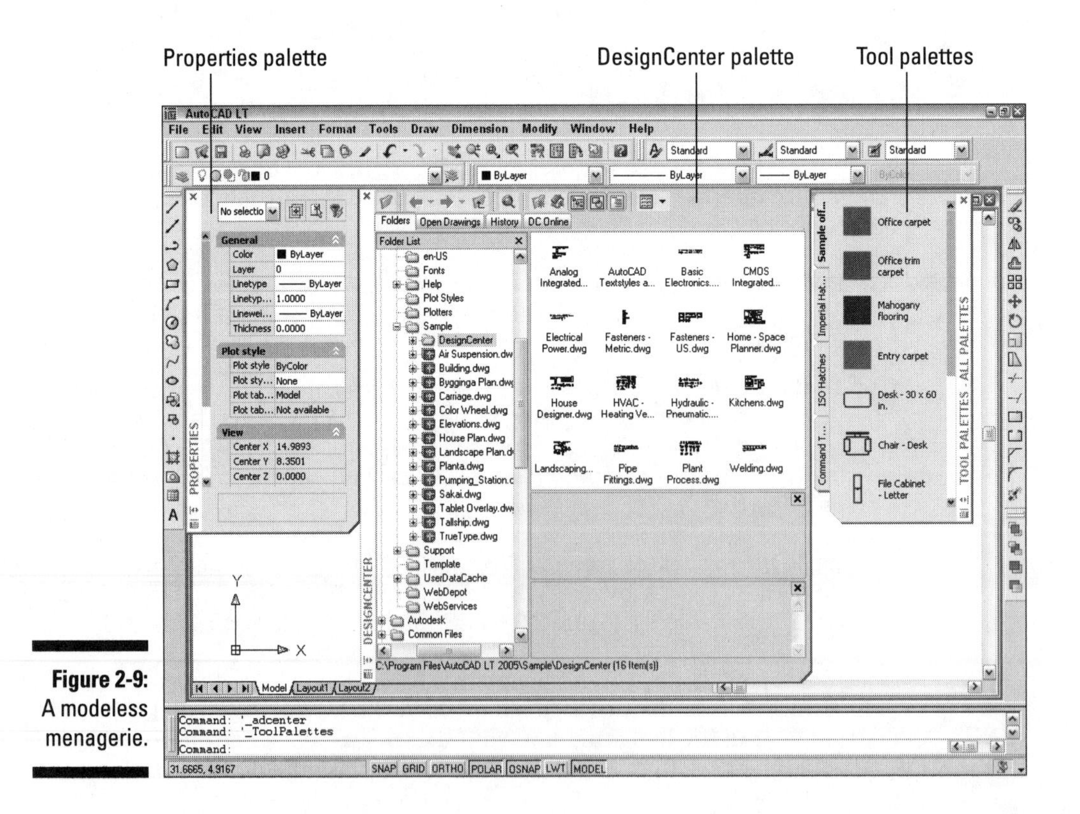

Figure 2-9: A modeless menagerie.

Another cool feature — for the Tool Palettes but not the Properties and DesignCenter palettes — is *transparency*. Right-click the Tool Palettes' title strip and choose Transparency to control this feature. With transparency turned on, you can see your drawing objects behind a faded version of the Tool Palettes. (According to my dictionary, that makes the palettes *translucent*, not transparent, but whatever.) If you combine transparency with auto-hide, you end up with Tool Palettes that have a low impact on your drawing area. And if you're bothered by the amount of screen space taken by the command line area, you can make it transparent, too: Undock it, right-click the title bar and turn off Allow Docking, and then right-click again and choose Transparency. After you set the transparency to your taste, click and drag the command line area to where you want it.

Under the LT Hood

Knowing how to use the command line, as described in the section, "Take an order: The command line area," is one of the secrets of becoming a competent AutoCAD LT user. In reading about and using LT, you frequently encounter two additional topics: *system variables,* which are AutoCAD's basic control levers, and *dialog boxes,* many of which put a friendlier face on the system variables.

Revving up with system variables

System variables are settings that AutoCAD LT checks before it decides how to do something. If you set the system variable SAVETIME to 10, LT automatically saves your drawing file every ten minutes; if you set SAVETIME to 60, the time between saves is one hour. Hundreds of system variables control AutoCAD LT's operations.

Of these hundreds of system variables, 70 control dimensioning alone. (*Dimensioning* is the process of labeling objects with their lengths, angles, or special notes. Different professions have different standards for presenting dimensions on their drawings. I describe dimensions in detail in Chapter 10.)

To change the value of a system variable, just type its name at the AutoCAD LT command prompt and press Enter. LT displays the current value of the system variable setting and prompts you for a new value. Press Enter to keep the existing setting, or type a value and press Enter to change the setting.

The procedure for entering a system variable is exactly the same as for entering a command name — type the name and press Enter. The only difference is what happens afterward:

- A system variable changes a setting.
- A command usually adds objects to the drawing, modifies objects, or changes your view of the drawing.

Being able to change system variables by typing their names at the command line is a boon to power users and occasionally a necessity for everybody else. The only problem is finding or remembering what the names are. In most cases, you're told what system variable name you need to type — by me in this book or by the local AutoCAD guru in your office.

To see a listing of all the system variables in AutoCAD LT and their current settings, use the following steps:

1. **Type** SETvar **at the LT command prompt and press Enter.**

   LT prompts you to type the name of a system variable (if you want to view or change just one) or question mark (if you want to see the names and current settings of more than one):

   ```
   Enter variable name or [?]
   ```

2. **Type** ? **(question mark) and press Enter.**

   LT asks which system variables to list:

   ```
   Enter variable(s) to list <*>:
   ```

3. **Press Enter to accept the default asterisk (which means "list all system variables").**

   LT displays the first screen of an alphabetical listing of variables and their settings:

   ```
   AFLAGS           0
   ANGBASE          0
   ANGDIR           0
   APBOX            0
   APERTURE         10
   AREA             0.0000                (read only)
   ATTDIA           0
   ATTMODE          1
   ATTREQ           1
   AUDITCTL         0
   AUNITS           0
   AUPREC           0
   AUTOSNAP         63
   BACKGROUNDPLOT   2
   ```

```
BACKZ            0.0000                (read only)
BLIPMODE         0
CDATE            20040304.10453569
CECOLOR          "BYLAYER"
CELTSCALE        1.0000
CELTYPE          "BYLAYER"
CELWEIGHT        -1
Press ENTER to continue:
```

4. **Press Enter repeatedly to scroll through the entire list, or press Esc to bail out.**

   LT returns to the naked command prompt:

   ```
   Command:
   ```

If you want to find out more about what a particular system variable controls, see the System Variables chapter in the Command Reference in the AutoCAD LT online help.

Three kinds of system variables exist:

- Those saved in the Windows Registry. If you change this kind of system variable, it affects all drawings when you open them with AutoCAD LT on your system.
- Those saved in the drawing. If you change this kind, the change affects only the current drawing.
- Those that aren't saved anywhere. If you change this kind, the change lasts only for the current drawing session.

The System Variables chapter in the Command Reference in the AutoCAD LT online help tells you which kind of system variable each one is.

The dialog box connection

Fortunately, you don't usually have to remember the system variable names. AutoCAD LT exposes most of the system variable settings in dialog boxes so that you can change their values simply by clicking check boxes or typing values in edit boxes. This approach is a lot more user-friendly than remembering an obscure name like "CELTSCALE."

For example, many of the settings on the tabs in the Options dialog box, shown in Figure 2-10, are in fact system variables. If you use the dialog box quick help (click the question mark in the Options dialog box's title bar, and then click an option in the dialog box), the pop-up description not only describes the setting, but also tells which system variable it corresponds to.

Figure 2-10: Options — a handy way to change some system variable settings.

Fun with F1

The AutoCAD LT 2005 Help menu, shown in Figure 2-11, offers several help options:

- **Help:** The main AutoCAD LT 2005 online Help system, shown in Figure 2-12, uses the same help engine as the Microsoft Office programs, Internet Explorer, and other modern Windows applications. Click the Contents tab to browse through the various online reference manuals, the Index tab to look up commands and concepts, and the Search tab to look for specific words. In this book, I sometimes direct you to the LT online Help system for information about advanced topics.

- **Info Palette:** This option opens a Quick Help Info Palette, which is the Autodesk version of the Microsoft paper clip guy who tries to tell you what to do in Word or Excel at each step along the way. Like the paper clip guy, Info Palette *seems* helpful — for 30 seconds. Then you get tired of the distraction and the wasted screen space.

- **New Features Workshop:** This workshop describes the new and enhanced features in AutoCAD LT 2005. It's especially useful for people who are upgrading from a previous AutoCAD or LT version.
- **Online Resources:** Most of the choices in the Online Resources submenu connect you to various parts of the Autodesk Web site. The most useful is Product Support. From the support Web page, you can search the Autodesk Knowledge Base, download software updates, and get help from Web- and newsgroup-based discussion groups.

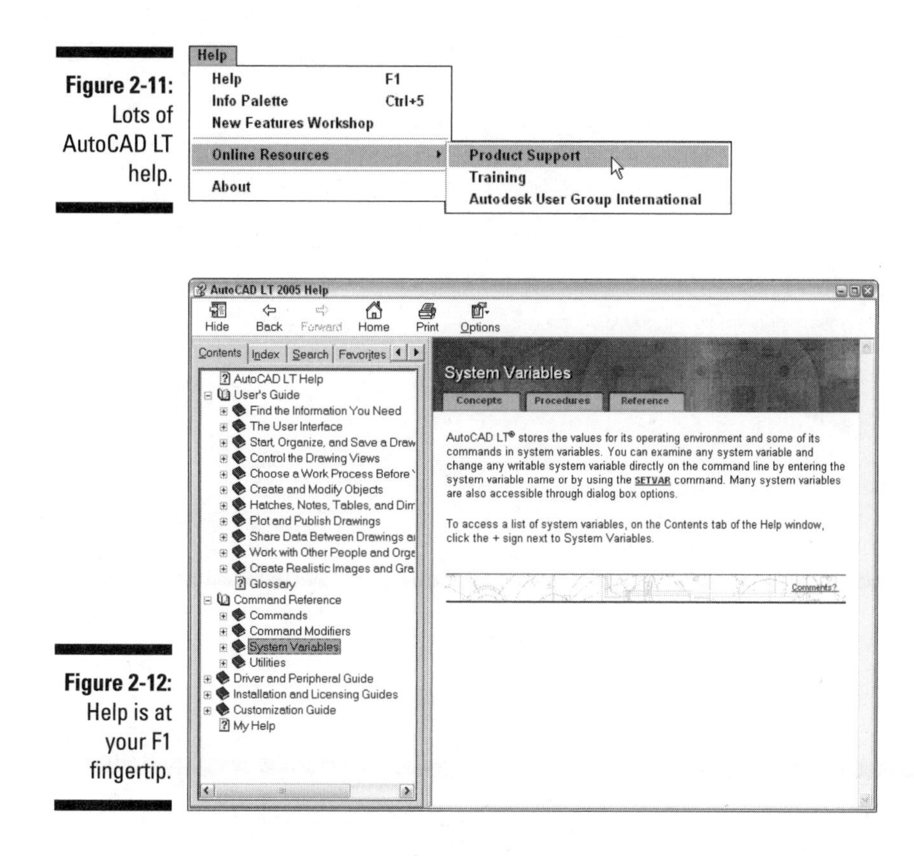

Figure 2-11: Lots of AutoCAD LT help.

Figure 2-12: Help is at your F1 fingertip.

AutoCAD LT is one program with which you really need to take advantage of the online help resources. LT contains many commands, options, and quirks, and everyone from the greenest beginner to the most seasoned expert can find out something by using the online help. Take a moment to peruse the Contents tab of the main Help system so that you know what's available. Throughout this book, I direct you to pages in the Help system that I think are particularly useful, but don't be afraid to explore on your own when you get stuck or feel curious.

Chapter 3

Before You Start Drawing

In This Chapter

- Managing layers
- Managing other object properties: color, linetype, and lineweight
- Copying layers and other named objects with DesignCenter
- Typing coordinates at the keyboard
- Snapping to object features
- Using other precision drawing and editing techniques

CAD programs are different from other drawing programs. You need to pay attention to little details, such as object properties and the precision of the points that you specify when you draw and edit objects. If you just start drawing objects without taking heed of these details, you end up with an unruly mess of imprecise geometry that's hard to edit, view, and plot.

This chapter introduces you to the AutoCAD LT tools and techniques that help you prevent making CAD messes. This information is essential before you start drawing objects and editing them, which I introduce you to in Chapter 4 and describe in detail in Chapters 6 and 7.

Drawing and Editing with LT

When you first start using AutoCAD LT, its most daunting requirement is the number of property settings and precision controls that you need to pay attention to — even when you draw a simple line. Unlike in many other programs, drawing a line in a more-or-less adequate location and then slapping some color on it is not enough. All those settings and controls can inspire the feeling that you're learning to pilot an airliner to make a trip down the street. (The advantage is that, after you *are* comfortable in the cockpit, LT takes you on the long-haul trips and gets you there faster.)

These are the three keys to good CAD drawing practice:

- Pay attention to and manage the *properties* of every object that you draw — especially the layer that each object is on.
- Pay attention to and manage the *named objects* in every drawing — the layers, text styles, block definitions, and other nongraphical objects that serve to define the look of all the graphical objects in the drawing.
- Pay attention to and control the *precision* of every point and distance that you use to draw and edit each object.

These things can seem like daunting tasks at first, but the following three sections help you cut them down to size.

Property Management

All the objects that you draw in AutoCAD LT are like good Monopoly players: They own *properties*. In LT, these properties aren't physical things; they're an object's characteristics, such as layer, color, linetype, and lineweight. You use properties to communicate information about the characteristics of the objects you draw, such as the kinds of real-world objects they represent, their materials, their relative location in space, or their relative importance. In CAD, you also use the properties to organize objects for editing and plotting purposes.

You can view — and change — all of an object's properties in the Properties palette. In Figure 3-1, the Properties palette shows properties for a line object.

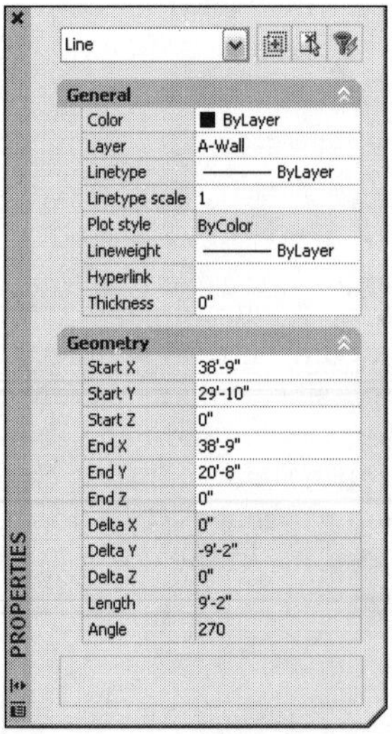

Figure 3-1: A line rich in properties.

To toggle the Properties palette on and off, click the Properties button on the Standard toolbar. Before you select an object, the Properties palette displays the *current properties* — properties that AutoCAD LT applies to new objects when you draw them. After you select an object, LT displays the properties for that object. If you select more than one object, LT displays the properties that they have in common.

Putting it on a layer

Every object has a *layer* as one of its properties. You may be familiar with layers — independent drawing spaces that stack on top of each other to create an overall image — from using drawing programs. AutoCAD LT, like most CAD programs, uses layers as the primary organizing principle for all the objects that you draw. Layers organize objects into logical groups of things that belong together; for example, walls, furniture, and text notes usually belong on three separate layers, for a couple of reasons:

- They give you a way to turn groups of objects on and off — both on the screen and on the plot.
- They provide the best way of controlling object color, linetype, and lineweight.

Looking at layers

If you spent any time "on the boards," as grizzled old-timers like to call paper-and-pencil drafting, you may be familiar with the manual drafting equivalent of layers. In *pin-bar drafting,* you stack a series of transparent Mylar sheets, each of which contains a part of the overall drawing — walls on one sheet, the plumbing system on another, the electrical system on another, and so on. You can get different views of the drawing set by including or excluding various sheets.

If you're too young to remember pin-bar drafting — or old enough to prefer not to — you may remember something similar from a textbook about human anatomy. The skeleton is on one sheet, the muscles on the next sheet that you laid over the skeleton, and so on until you built up a complete picture of the human body — that is, if your parents didn't remove some of the more grown-up sections.

CAD layers serve a similar purpose; they enable you to turn on or off groups of related objects. But layers do a lot more. You use them in AutoCAD LT to control other object display and plot properties, such as color, linetype, and lineweight. You also can use them to make some editing tasks more efficient and reduce the time that LT takes to load some drawings. Take the time to give each of your drawings a suitably layered look.

You create layers, assign them names, assign them properties such as color and linetype, and then put objects on them. When you draw an object, AutoCAD LT automatically puts it on the *current* layer, which appears in the drop-down list on the Layers toolbar.

Before you draw any object in AutoCAD LT, set an appropriate layer current — creating it first, if necessary, using the steps later in this section. If the layer already exists in your drawing, you can make it the current layer by choosing it on the Layers toolbar, as shown in Figure 3-2.

Make sure that no objects are selected before you use the Layer drop-down list to change the current layer. (Press the Esc key twice to be sure.) If objects are selected, the Layer drop-down list displays — and lets you change — those objects' layer. When no objects are selected, the Layer drop-down list displays — and lets you change — the current layer.

If you forget to set an appropriate layer before you draw an object, you can select the object and then change its layer by using the Properties palette or the Layer drop-down list.

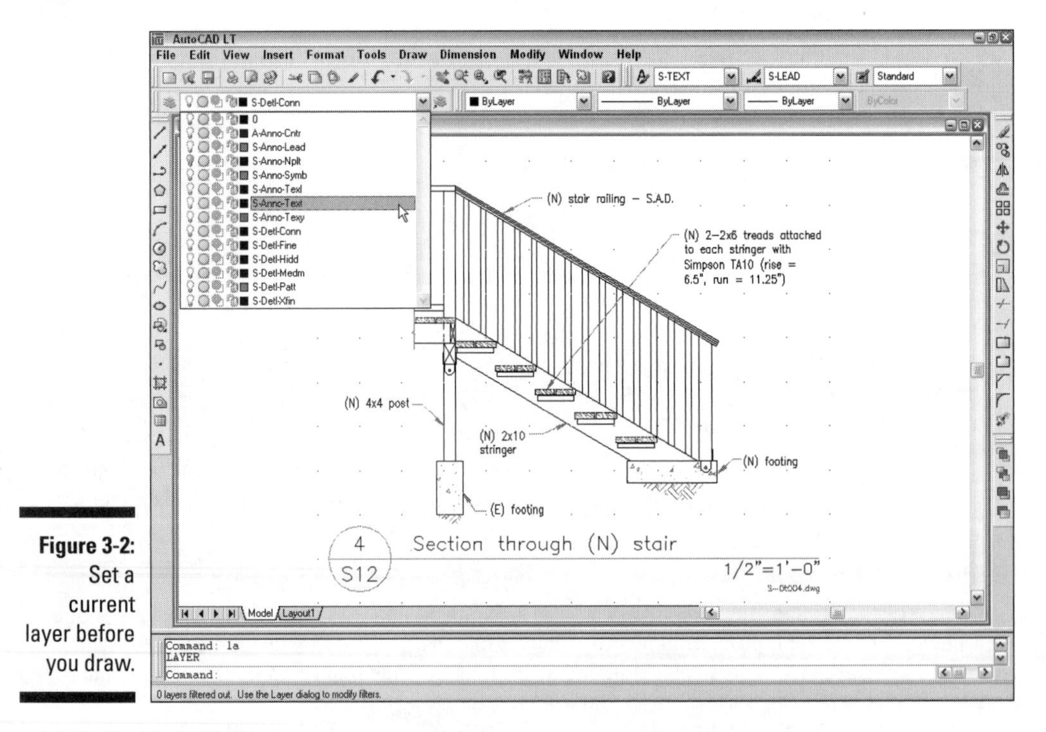

Figure 3-2: Set a current layer before you draw.

Stacking up your layers

How do you decide what to call your layers and which objects to put on them? Some industries have developed layer guidelines, and many offices have created documented layer standards. Some projects even impose specific layer requirements. (But be careful: If someone says, "You need a brick layer for this project," that can mean a couple of different things.) Ask experienced CAD drafters in your office or industry how they use layers in AutoCAD. If you can't find any definitive answer, create a chart of layers for yourself. List in each row in the chart the layer name, default color, default linetype, default lineweight, and what kinds of objects belong on that layer. Chapter 14 includes an example.

Accumulating properties

Besides layers, the remaining object properties that you're likely to want to use often are color, linetype, lineweight, and possibly plotstyle. Table 3-1 summarizes these four properties.

Table 3-1 Useful Object Properties

Property	*Controls*
Color	Displayed color and plotted color or lineweight (covered in this chapter)
Linetype	Displayed and plotted dash-dot line pattern (covered in this chapter)
Lineweight	Displayed and plotted line width (covered in this chapter)
Plotstyle	Plotted characteristics (see Chapter 12)

In AutoCAD LT 98 and older versions of LT (corresponding to Release 14 and older versions of AutoCAD), color also controlled the plotted lineweight of each object — strange, but now very common in the AutoCAD world. You may find yourself working this way even in AutoCAD LT 2005, for compatibility with drawings (and co-workers) that use the old way, as I describe in the "About colors and lineweights" sidebar.

About colors and lineweights

AutoCAD drafters traditionally have achieved different printed lineweights by mapping various on-screen display colors of drawing objects to different plotted lineweights. An AutoCAD-using company may decide to plot red lines thin, green lines thicker, and so on. This indirect approach sounds strange, but until AutoCAD and AutoCAD LT 2000, it was the only practical way to plot with a variety of lineweights. Also, not many people plotted in color until recently, so few folks minded the fact that color was used to serve a different master.

AutoCAD and AutoCAD LT 2000 added lineweight as an inherent property of objects and the layers that they live on. Thus, object display color can revert to being used for — surprise! — color. You can use display colors to control plot colors, of course. But even if you make monochrome plots, you can use color to help you distinguish different kinds of objects when you view them on-screen or to make jazzy on-screen presentations of drawings for others.

Lineweights are handy, but they have quirks. Watch for these problems as you work with them:

- Although lineweights are assigned to objects in a drawing that you open, you won't necessarily see them on-screen. You must turn on the Show/Hide Lineweight button on the AutoCAD LT status bar (the button labeled LWT).
- On a slow computer or a complex drawing, showing lineweights may cause LT to redraw the screen more slowly when you zoom and pan.
- You may need to zoom in on a portion of the drawing before the differing lineweights become apparent.

AutoCAD LT gives you two different ways of controlling object properties:

- **By layer:** Each layer has a default color, linetype, lineweight, and plot-style property. Unless you tell LT otherwise, objects inherit the properties of the layers on which they're created. AutoCAD LT calls this approach controlling properties *by layer.*
- **By object:** LT also enables you to override an object's layer's property setting and give the object a specific color, linetype, lineweight, or plot-style that differs from the layer's. AutoCAD LT calls this approach controlling properties *by object.*

If you've worked with other graphics programs, you may be used to assigning properties, such as color, to specific objects. If so, you'll be tempted to use the by object approach to assigning properties in AutoCAD LT. Resist the temptation. In almost all cases, creating layers, assigning properties to each layer, and letting the objects on each layer inherit that layer's properties is best. Here are some benefits of using the by layer approach:

- You can easily change the properties of a group of related objects that you put on one layer. You simply change the property for the layer, and not for a bunch of separate objects.
- Experienced drafters use the by layer approach, so if you work with drawings from other people, you'll be much more compatible with them if you do it the same way. You can also avoid getting yelled at by irate CAD managers, whose jobs include haranguing any hapless newbies who assign properties by object.

If you take my advice and assign properties by layer, all you have to do is set layer properties in the Layer Properties Manager dialog box, as shown in Figure 3-3. Before you draw any objects, make sure the Color Control, Linetype Control, Lineweight Control, and Plotstyle Control drop-down lists on the Properties toolbar are set to ByLayer, as shown in Figure 3-4.

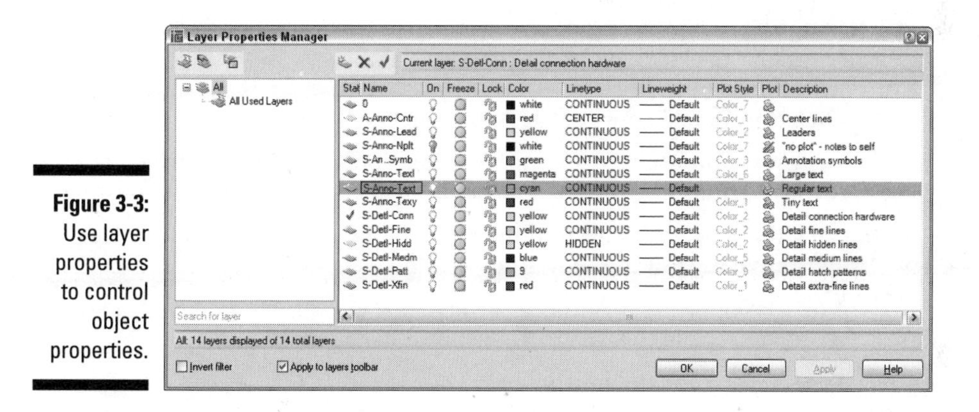

Figure 3-3: Use layer properties to control object properties.

If the drawing is set to use color-based plotstyles instead of named plotstyles (see Chapter 12), the Plotstyle Control drop-down list is inactive and displays `ByColor`. If the drawing is set to use named plotstyles, the Plotstyle Control is active and you should leave it set to ByLayer.

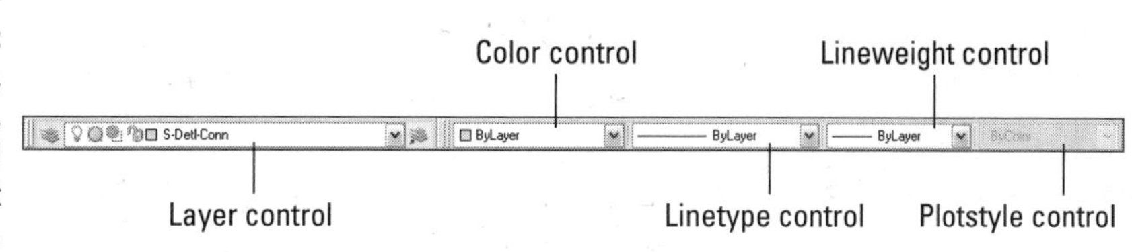

Figure 3-4: Color, Linetype, and Lineweight ByLayer.

If you don't like doing things the wrong way and getting yelled at by CAD managers, don't assign properties to objects in either of these ways:

- Don't choose a specific color, linetype, lineweight, or plotstyle from the appropriate drop-down list on the Properties toolbar, and then draw the objects.
- Don't draw the objects, select them, and then choose a property from the same drop-down lists.

If you prefer to do things the right way, assign these properties by layer, as I describe in this section.

Creating layers

If a suitable layer doesn't exist, you need to create one by using the Layer Properties Manager dialog box. Follow these steps:

1. **Click the Layer Properties Manager button on the Layers toolbar.**

   The Layer Properties Manager dialog box appears. A new drawing has only one layer, Layer 0. You need to add the layers you need for your drawing.

2. **Click the New Layer button (the sheet of paper with the yellow star just above the Status column) to create a new layer.**

   A new layer appears. AutoCAD LT names it Layer1, but you can easily type a new name to replace it, as shown in Figure 3-5.

3. **Type a name for the new layer.**

Figure 3-5: Adding a new layer in the Layer Properties Manager dialog box.

For the following reasons, type the layer name with *initial caps* (only the first letter of words in uppercase) if you can:

- Layer names written completely in uppercase are much wider, which means that they often get *truncated* in the Layers toolbar's Layer drop-down list.
- Uppercase layer names look like they're *SHOUTING*, which is not very polite.

4. **On the same line as the new layer, click the color block or color name (White) of the new layer.**

   The Select Color dialog box appears, as shown in Figure 3-6.

Figure 3-6: The Select Color dialog box. Magenta is selected from the Standard Colors list.

The normal AutoCAD and AutoCAD LT color scheme — AutoCAD Color Index (ACI) — provides 255 colors. So many choices are nice for rendering work but overkill for ordinary drafting.

If you see a color listed in the form "101,184,166" or "DIC 405," then you're looking at a drawing in which an AutoCAD user has taken advantage of AutoCAD's even more extravagant color options, which include True Color and PANTONE systems. AutoCAD LT displays the appropriate colors, but LT can't assign colors from these expanded palettes.

For now, stick with the first nine colors — the ones that appear in a single, separate row to the left of the ByLayer and ByBlock buttons on the Index Color tab of the Select Color dialog box.

- These colors are easy to distinguish from one another.
- Using a small number of colors makes configuring your plot parameters easier. (I describe the procedure in Chapter 12.)

5. **Click a color to select it as the color for this layer; then click OK.**

   The Layer Properties Manager dialog box reappears. In the Name list, the color for the new layer changes to either the name or the number of the color that you selected.

AutoCAD and AutoCAD LT's first seven colors are both assigned numbers and standard names: 1 = red, 2 = yellow, 3 = green, 4 = cyan, 5 = blue, 6 = magenta, and 7 = white (but it appears black when displayed on a white background). The remaining 248 colors have numbers only. You can play fashion designer and make up your own names for these colors. How about Overly Oxidized Ocher for color number 16?

6. **On the same line as the new layer, click the Linetype name of the new layer.**

   The default AutoCAD LT linetype is Continuous, which means no gaps in the line.

   The Select Linetype dialog box appears, as shown in Figure 3-7.

Figure 3-7: The Select Linetype dialog box.

If you already loaded the linetypes you need for your drawing, the Select Linetype dialog box displays them in the Loaded Linetypes list. If not, click the Load button to open the Load or Reload Linetypes dialog box. By default, AutoCAD LT displays linetypes from the standard LT linetype definition file — `Aclt.lin` for imperial units drawings or `Acltiso.lin` for metric units drawings. Load the desired linetype by selecting its name and clicking the OK button.

The linetypes whose names begin with ACAD_ISO are for people who use ISO (International Organization for Standardization) linetype patterns. If you don't follow ISO standards, you'll probably find using the linetypes with the more descriptive names easier: CENTER, DASHED, and so on.

7. **Click the desired linetype in the Loaded Linetypes list to select it as the linetype for the layer; then click OK.**

   The Select Linetype dialog box disappears, returning you to the Layer Properties Manager dialog box. In the Name list, the linetype for the selected layer changes to the linetype you just chose.

8. **On the same line as the new layer, click the new layer's lineweight.**

   The Lineweight dialog box appears, as shown in Figure 3-8.

9. **Select the lineweight you want from the scrolling list, and then click OK.**

Figure 3-8: The Lineweight dialog box.

The lineweight `0.00 mm` tells AutoCAD LT to use the thinnest possible lineweight on the screen and on the plot. I recommend that, for now, you leave lineweight set to Default and instead map screen color to plotted lineweight, as described briefly in the "About colors and lineweights" sidebar earlier in this chapter and in greater detail in Chapter 12.

The default lineweight for the current drawing is defined in the Lineweight Settings dialog box. After you close the Layer Properties Manager dialog box, choose Format➪Lineweight to change the default lineweight.

You use the plotstyle property to assign a named plotstyle to the layer, but only if you're using named plotstyles in the drawing (Chapter 12 explains why you probably don't want to — at least if you're exchanging drawings with veteran AutoCAD or AutoCAD LT users). The final property, Plot, controls whether the layer's objects appear on plots. Toggle this setting off for any layer whose objects you want to see on-screen but hide on plots.

10. **If you want to add a description to the layer, scroll the layer list to the right to see the Description column, click twice in the Description box corresponding to your new layer, and type a description.**

Layer descriptions are a new feature of AutoCAD LT 2005. If you choose to use them, stretch the Layer Properties Manager dialog box to the right so that you can see the descriptions without having to scroll the layer list.

11. **Repeat Steps 2 through 10 to create any other layers that you want.**
12. **Select the new layer that you want to make current and click the Set Current button (the green check mark).**

    The current layer is the one on which AutoCAD LT places new objects that you draw.

13. **Click OK to accept the new layer settings.**

    The Layer drop-down list on the Layers toolbar now displays your new layer as the current layer.

A load of linetypes

My layer creation steps demonstrate how to load a single linetype, but AutoCAD LT comes with a whole lot of linetypes, and you can work with them in other ways. You don't have to go through the Layer Properties Manager dialog box to load linetypes. You can perform the full range of linetype management tasks by choosing Format➪Linetype, which displays the Linetype Manager dialog box. This dialog box is similar to the Select Linetype dialog box I describe in the layer creation steps, but it includes some additional options.

After you click the Load button to display the Load or Reload Linetypes dialog box, you can load multiple linetypes in one fell swoop by holding down the Shift or Ctrl key while you click linetype names. As in most Windows dialog boxes, Shift+click selects all objects between the first and second clicks, and Ctrl+click enables you to select multiple objects, even if they aren't next to each other.

When you load a linetype, AutoCAD LT copies its *linetype definition* — a recipe for how to create the dashes, dots, and gaps in that particular linetype — from the `Aclt.lin` (imperial units) or `Acltiso.lin` (metric units) file into the drawing. The recipe doesn't automatically appear in other drawings; you have to load each linetype that you want to use into each drawing in which you want to use it. If you find yourself loading the same linetypes repeatedly into different drawings, consider adding them to your template drawings instead. (See Chapter 5 for information about templates and how to create them.) After you add linetypes to a template drawing, all new drawings that you create from that template start with those linetypes loaded automatically.

Don't go overboard on loading linetypes. For example, you don't need to load all the linetypes in the `Aclt.lin` file on the off chance that you may use them all someday. The resulting linetype list would be long and unwieldy. Most drawings require only a few linetypes, and most industries and companies settle on a half dozen or so linetypes for common use. Your industry, office, or project may have guidelines about which linetypes to use for which purposes.

If you're the creative type and don't mind editing a text file that contains linetype definitions, you can define your own linetypes. Choose Contents➪Customization Guide➪Custom Linetypes in the AutoCAD LT online Help system.

After you create layers, you can set any one of them to be the current layer. Make sure that no objects are selected, and then choose the layer name from the Layer drop-down list on the Layers toolbar.

After you create layers and drawn objects on them, you use the Layer Properties Manager dialog box to change layer properties. For example, you can turn a layer off or on to hide or show the objects on that layer.

If you find yourself using lots of layers, you can create *layer filters* to make viewing and managing the layer list easier. AutoCAD LT 2005 provides two kinds of layer filters: group and property. A *group filter* is simply a subset of layers that you choose (by dragging layer names into the group filter name or by selecting objects in the drawing). A *property filter* is a subset of layers that LT creates and updates automatically based on layer property criteria that you define (for example, all layer names whose names contain the text **Wall** or whose color is green). To find out more, click the Help button at the lower-right corner of the Layer Properties Manager dialog box and read about the New Property Filter and New Group Filter buttons.

Using AutoCAD DesignCenter

DesignCenter is a dumb name for a useful, if somewhat busy, palette. (Chapter 2 describes how to turn on and work with palettes.) The DesignCenter palette is handy for mining data from all kinds of drawings. Whereas the Properties palette, which I describe earlier in this chapter, is concerned with object properties, the DesignCenter palette deals primarily with named objects: layers, linetypes, block (that is, symbol) definitions, text styles, and other organizational objects in your drawings.

Named objects

Every drawing includes a set of *symbol tables,* which contain *named objects.* For example, the *layer table* contains a list of the layers in the current drawing, along with the settings for each layer (color, linetype, on/off setting, and so on). Each of these table objects, be it a layer or some other type, has a name, so Autodesk decided to call them *named objects* (duh!).

Neither the symbol tables nor the named objects appear as graphical objects in your drawing. They're like hardworking stagehands who keep the show running smoothly behind the scenes. The named objects include

- Layers (this chapter)
- Linetypes (this chapter)
- Text styles (Chapter 9)
- Dimension styles (Chapter 10)
- Block definitions and xrefs (Chapter 13)
- Layouts (Chapter 5)

When you use commands such as LAyer, LineType, and Dimstyle, you are creating and editing named objects. After you create named objects in a drawing, DesignCenter gives you the tools to copy them to other drawings.

Getting (Design) Centered

The DesignCenter palette (shown in Figure 3-9) consists of a toolbar at the top, a set of tabs below that, a navigation pane on the left, and a content pane on the right. The navigation pane displays a tree view with drawing files and the symbol tables contained in each drawing. The content pane usually displays the contents of the drawing or symbol table.

The four tabs just below the DesignCenter toolbar control what you see in the navigation and content panes:

- **Folders** shows the folders on your local and network disks, just like the Windows Explorer Folders pane does. Use this tab to copy named objects from drawings that you don't currently have open in AutoCAD LT.
- **Open Drawings** shows the drawings that are open in LT. Use this tab to copy named objects between open drawings.
- **History** shows drawings that you recently browsed in DesignCenter. Use this tab to jump quickly to drawings that you used recently on the Folders tab.

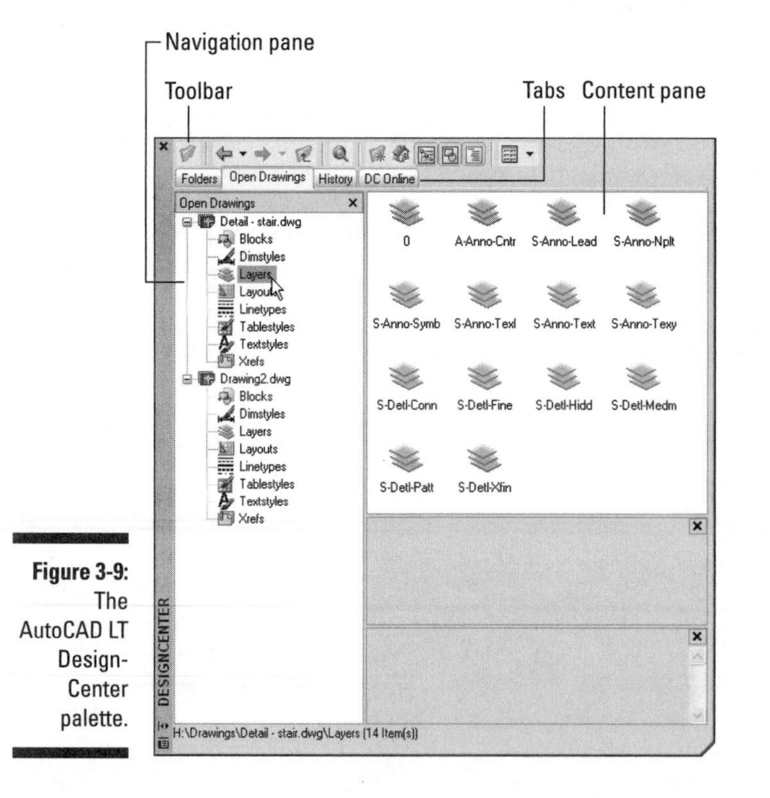

Figure 3-9: The AutoCAD LT DesignCenter palette.

- **DC Online** shows parts libraries that are available on Autodesk's and other companies' Web sites. This tab is essentially an advertising vehicle for software companies offering to sell you symbol libraries and manufacturers encouraging you to specify their products. Browse the offerings on this tab to see whether any of the online libraries can be useful in your work.

The toolbar buttons further refine what you see in the navigation and content panes. A few of these buttons toggle off and on different parts of the panes. If your DesignCenter palette is missing an area that appears in Figure 3-9, click each of the buttons until the missing part reappears.

Follow these steps to use DesignCenter:

1. **Load the drawing(s) whose content you want to view or use into the navigation pane on the left.**

   If a drawing doesn't appear on the Open Drawings tab, click the Load button — the first one on the DesignCenter toolbar — to load it into the navigation pane.

2. **Navigate the symbol tables (such as blocks and layers), viewing their individual named objects in the content pane on the right.**
3. **If you need them, drag or copy and paste individual named objects from the content pane into other open drawings.**

Copying layers between drawings

The following steps copy layers from one drawing to another, using DesignCenter. You can use the same technique to copy dimension styles, layouts, linetypes, and text styles.

1. **Toggle the DesignCenter palette on by choosing the DesignCenter button on the Standard toolbar.**
2. **Open or create a drawing containing named objects you want to copy.**

   You can also use the Folders tab, the Open button, or the Search button to load a drawing into DesignCenter without opening it in AutoCAD.

3. **Open or create a second drawing to which you want to copy the named objects.**
4. **Click the Open Drawings tab to display your two currently opened drawings in DesignCenter's navigation pane on the left.**

   If you used the Folders tab, the Open button, or the Search button in Step 2, skip this step; DesignCenter already displays the drawing you selected on the Folders tab.

5. **If DesignCenter doesn't display the symbol tables indented underneath the source drawing (the one you opened in Step 2), as shown in Figure 3-9, click the plus sign next to the drawing's name to display them.**
6. **Click the Layers table to display the source drawing's layers in the content pane.**
7. **Choose one or more layers in the content pane.**
8. **Right-click in the content pane and choose Copy from the menu to copy the layer(s) to the Windows Clipboard.**
9. **Click in the destination drawing's window (the drawing that you opened in Step 3).**
10. **Right-click and choose Paste from the menu.**

    DesignCenter copies the layers into the current drawing, using the colors, linetypes, and other settings from the source drawing.

You can copy layers from DesignCenter in two other ways: by dragging layers from the content pane to a drawing window, or by right-clicking in the content pane and then choosing Add Layer(s) from the menu, which adds layers to the current drawing. The copy-and-paste method in my example requires the least amount of manual dexterity and less guesswork about which drawing the layers get added to.

If the current drawing contains a layer whose name matches the name of one of the layers you're copying, DesignCenter doesn't change that layer's definition. For example, if you drag a layer named Doors whose color is red into a drawing that already includes a layer called Doors whose color is green, the target drawing's Doors layer remains green. Named objects from DesignCenter never overwrite objects with the same name in the destination drawing. AutoCAD LT always displays the Duplicate Definitions Will Be Ignored message even if no duplicates exist.

If you're repeatedly copying named objects from the same drawings or folders, add them to your DesignCenter favorites list. On the Folders tab, right-click the drawing or folder and choose Add to Favorites from the menu. This step adds another shortcut to your list of favorites.

- To see your favorites, click the DesignCenter toolbar's Favorites button.
- To return to a favorite, double-click its shortcut in the content pane.

Make Precision Your Passion

Drawing precision is vital to good CAD drafting practice, even more than for manual drafting. If you think CAD managers get testy when you assign properties by object instead of by layer, wait until they berate someone who doesn't use precision techniques when creating drawings in AutoCAD LT.

In CAD, lack of precision makes later editing, hatching, and dimensioning tasks much more difficult and time consuming:

- Small errors in precision in the early stages of creating or editing a drawing often have a big effect on productivity and precision later.
- Drawings may guide manufacturing and construction projects; drawing data may drive automatic manufacturing machinery. Huge amounts of money, even lives, can ride on a drawing's precision.

In recognition of this, a passion for precision permeates the profession. Permanently. Precision is one characteristic that separates CAD from ordinary illustration-type drawing work. The sooner you get fussy about precision in AutoCAD LT, the happier everyone is.

In the context of drawing objects, *precision* means specifying points and distances precisely, and AutoCAD LT provides a range of tools for doing so. Table 3-2 lists the more important LT precision techniques, plus the status bar buttons that you click to toggle some of the features off and on.

Precision is especially important when you're drawing or editing *geometry* — the lines, arcs, and so on that make up whatever you're representing in the CAD drawing. Precision placement usually is less important with notes, leaders, and other *annotations* that describe, not show.

Table 3-2 Precision Techniques

Technique	*Status Bar Button*	*Description*
Coordinate entry	—	Type exact X,Y coordinates.
Single point object snaps	—	Pick points on existing objects (lasts for one point pick).
Running object snaps	OSNAP	Pick points on existing objects (lasts for multiple point picks).
Snap	SNAP	Pick points on an imaginary grid of equally spaced "hot spots."
Ortho	ORTHO	Constrain the cursor to move at an angle of 0, 90, 180, or 270 degrees from the previous point.
Direct distance entry	ORTHO or POLAR	Point the cursor in a direction and type a distance.
Polar tracking	POLAR	Makes the cursor prefer certain angles.
Polar snap	—	Causes the cursor to prefer certain distances along polar tracking angles.

Before you draw objects, always check the status bar's SNAP, ORTHO, POLAR, and OSNAP buttons and set the buttons according to your precision needs.

- A button that looks *pushed in* indicates that the feature is *on.*
- A button that looks *popped up* indicates that the feature is *off.*

Keyboard capers: Coordinate entry

The most direct way to enter points precisely is to type numbers at the command line. AutoCAD LT uses these keyboard coordinate entry formats:

- Absolute rectangular coordinates in the form *X,Y* (for example: 7,4)
- Relative rectangular coordinates in the form @*X,Y* (for example: @3,2)
- Relative polar coordinates in the form @*distance<angle* (for example: @6<45)

AutoCAD LT locates *absolute rectangular coordinates* with respect to the 0,0 point of the drawing — usually its lower-left corner. LT locates *relative rectangular coordinates* and *relative polar coordinates* with respect to the previous point that you picked or typed. Figure 3-10 demonstrates how to use all three coordinate formats to draw a pair of line segments that start at absolute coordinates 2,1; go 3 units to the right and 2 units up; then go 4 units at an angle of 60 degrees.

CAD precision versus accuracy

We often use the words *precision* and *accuracy* interchangeably, but I think maintaining a distinction is useful. When I use the word *precision,* I mean controlling the placement of objects so that they lie exactly where you want them to lie in the drawing. For example, lines whose endpoints must meet exactly, and a circle that's supposed to be centered on the coordinates 0,0 must be drawn with its center exactly at 0,0. I use *accuracy* to refer to the degree to which your drawing matches its real-world counterpart. An accurate floor plan is one in which the dimensions of the CAD objects equal the dimensions of the as-built house.

CAD precision usually helps produce accurate drawings, but that's not always the case. You can produce a precise CAD drawing that's inaccurate because you started from inaccurate information (for example, the contractor gave you a wrong field measurement). Or you might deliberately exaggerate certain distances to convey the relationship between objects more clearly on the plotted drawing. Even where you must sacrifice accuracy, aim for precision.

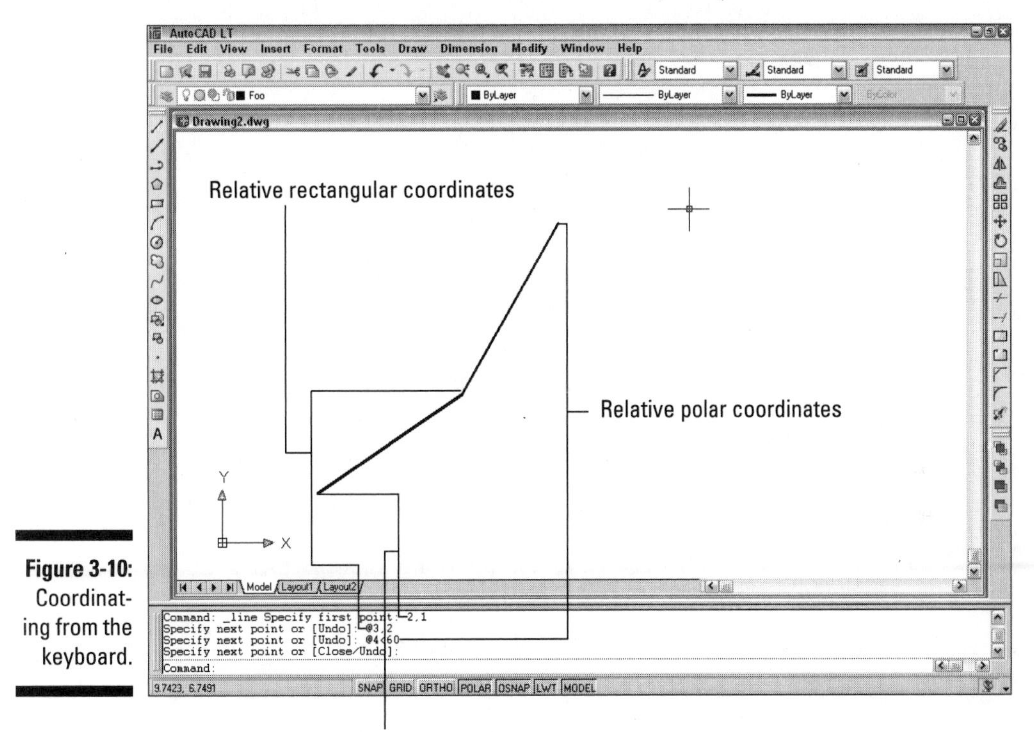

Figure 3-10: Coordinating from the keyboard.

You can view coordinate locations by moving the cursor around in the drawing area and reading the Coordinates area at the left of the status bar. The X,Y coordinates change as you move the cursor. If the coordinates don't change, click the Coordinates area until the command line says `<Coords on>`. Although not apparent at first, the status bar has two `<Coords on>` display modes: absolute coordinates and polar coordinates. If you start a command such as LINE, pick a point, and then click the Coordinates area a few times, the display changes from coordinates off to live absolute coordinates (X,Y position) to live polar coordinates (distance and angle from the previous point). The live polar coordinates display mode is the most informative most of the time.

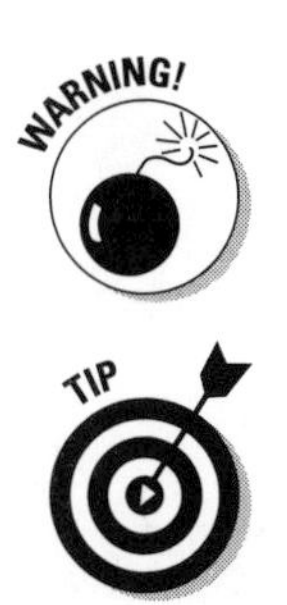

When you type coordinates at the command line, do *not* add any spaces because AutoCAD LT interprets them as though you pressed Enter. This "Spacebar = Enter" weirdness is a productivity feature that's been in AutoCAD and AutoCAD LT forever. Finding the spacebar is easier than the Enter key when you're entering lots of commands and coordinates in a hurry.

If you're working in architectural or engineering units, the default unit of entry is *inches,* not feet.

- To specify feet, you must enter the symbol for feet after the number, for example:

  6' for 6 feet.

- You can enter a dash to separate feet from inches, as architects often do:

  6'–6" is 6 feet, 6 inches.

- Both the dash and the inch mark are optional when you're entering coordinates and distances:

  AutoCAD LT understands **6'6"** and **6'6** as the same as **6'–6"**.

- If you're typing a coordinate or distance that contains fractional inches, you *must* enter a dash — not a space — between the whole number of inches and the fraction:

  6'6–1/2 (or **6'–6–1/2**) represents 6 feet, 6½ inches.

- If all this dashing about confuses you, enter partial inches using decimals instead:

  6'6.5 is the same as **6'6–1/2** to LT, whether you're working in architectural or engineering units.

- If you really want to keep things simple, you can stick with inches:

  78 is the same as **6'6"**, and **78.5** is the same as **6'6–1/2"**.

Grab an object and make it snappy

After you draw a few objects precisely in a new drawing, the most efficient way to draw more objects with equal precision is to grab *points,* such as endpoints, midpoints, or quadrants, on the existing objects. AutoCAD LT calls this *object snapping* because the program pulls, or *snaps*, the cursor to a point on an existing *object.* The object snapping feature in general and object snap points in particular often are called *osnaps*.

I'd like to make just one point

AutoCAD LT provides two kinds of object snapping modes:

- *Single point* (or *override*) object snaps

  A single point object snap lasts just while you pick one point.

- *Running* object snaps

  A running object snap stays in effect until you turn it off.

Here's how you draw precise lines by using single point object snaps:

1. **Open a drawing containing some geometry.**
2. **Turn on the Object Snap toolbar by right-clicking any toolbar button and choosing Object Snap from the list of available toolbars.**

   Figure 3-11 shows the Object Snap toolbar. If you want, you can move the toolbar or dock it along one side of the drawing area (see Chapter 2 for details).

Figure 3-11: The Object Snap toolbar.

3. **Turn off running osnap mode by clicking the OSNAP button on the status bar until the button appears to be pushed out and the words** `<Osnap off>` **appear on the command line.**

   Although you can use single point object snaps while running object snap mode is turned on, turn off running osnap mode while you're getting familiar with single point object snaps. After you have the hang of each feature separately, you can use them together.

4. **Start the Line command by clicking the Line button on the Draw toolbar.**

   The command line prompts you to select the first endpoint of the line:

   ```
   Specify first point:
   ```

5. **Choose an object snap mode, such as Endpoint, from the Object Snap toolbar.**

   The command line displays an additional prompt indicating that you've directed AutoCAD LT to seek out, for example, endpoints of existing objects:

   ```
   _endp of:
   ```

6. **Move the cursor slowly around the drawing, pausing over various lines and other objects without clicking yet.**

   When you move the cursor near an object with an endpoint, a colored square icon appears at the endpoint, indicating that AutoCAD LT can snap to that point. If you stop moving the cursor for a moment, a yellow ToolTip displaying the object snap mode (for example, `Endpoint`) appears to reinforce the idea.

7. **When the endpoint object snap square appears on the point you want to snap to, click.**

LT snaps to the endpoint, which becomes the first point of the new line segment that you're about to draw. The command line prompts you to select the other endpoint of the new line segment:

```
Specify next point or [Undo]:
```

When you move the cursor around the drawing, LT no longer seeks out endpoints because single point object snaps last only for a single pick.

8. **Repeat Step 5, but this time click another object snap mode, such as Midpoint, from the Object Snap toolbar.**

   The command line displays an additional prompt indicating that you've directed LT to seek, for example, midpoints of existing objects:

   ```
   _mid of:
   ```

   When you move the cursor near the midpoint of an object, a colored triangle appears at the snap point. Each object snap type (endpoint, midpoint, intersection, and so on) displays a different symbol. If you stop moving the cursor, the ToolTip text reminds you what the symbol means. Figure 3-12 shows what the screen looks like during this step.

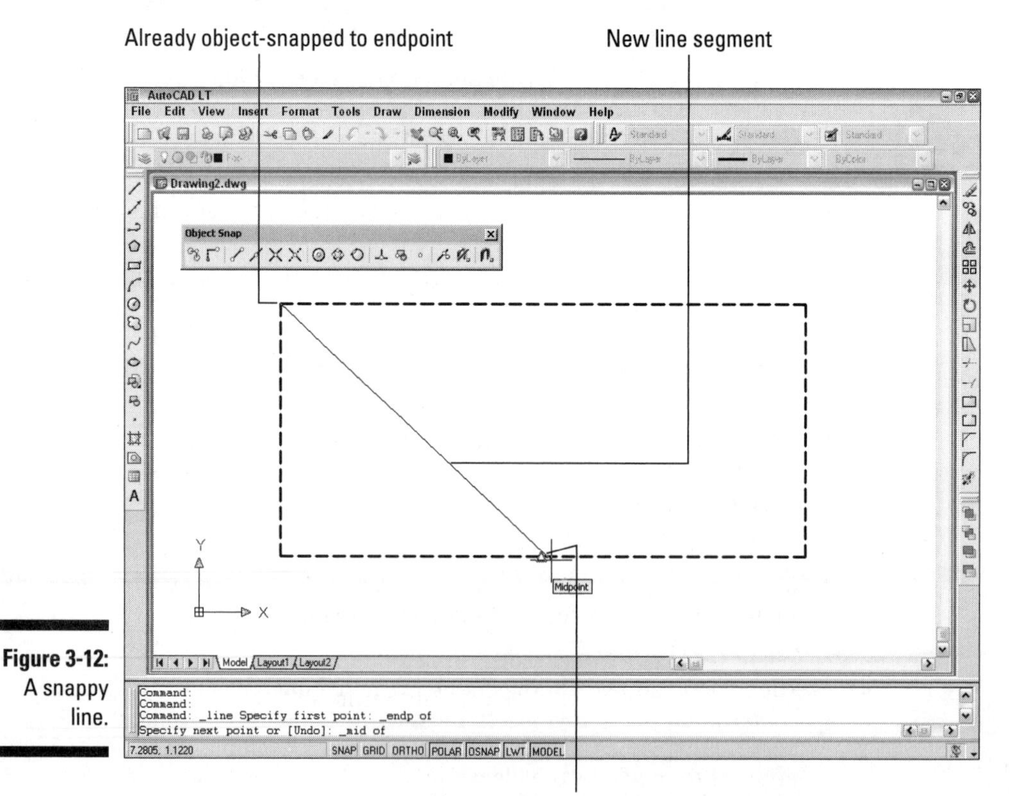

Figure 3-12: A snappy line.

9. **Draw additional line segments by picking additional points. Use the Object Snap toolbar to specify a single object snap type before you pick each point.**

   Try the Intersection, Perpendicular, and Nearest object snaps. If your drawing contains arcs or circles, try Center and Quadrant.

10. **When you finish experimenting with single point object snaps, right-click anywhere in the drawing area and choose Enter from the menu.**

The Object Snap toolbar is the easiest way to activate single point object snaps, but many AutoCAD and AutoCAD LT veterans prefer a different method: the Shift+right-click menu: When LT prompts you for a point, hold down the Shift key, right-click anywhere in the drawing area, and release the Shift key. When you perform this Shift+right-click sequence, AutoCAD LT pops up an object snap menu rather than the ordinary (unshifted) right-click menu. You choose an object snap mode from the menu and then continue as you do when using the toolbar. The advantage of this method is efficiency — you don't have to move the cursor all the way across the screen in order to get to the Object Snap toolbar; the object snap cursor menu, as its name suggests, appears right at your current cursor location. The disadvantage is that you must master the slightly awkward Shift+right-click, and then click sequence.

You find a difference between right-clicking and Shift+right-clicking in the drawing area:

- Right-clicking displays menu options for the current command (or common commands and settings when no command is active).
- Shift+right-clicking always displays the same object snap cursor menu, regardless of which command is active.

AutoCAD LT 2005 includes a new Mid Between 2 Points (**M2P**) object snap mode, which finds the point lying exactly halfway between two other points. You use precision techniques, such as other object snaps, to select the two points. The M2P object snap mode is not on the Object Snap toolbar. You must choose it from the Shift+right-click menu or type it at the command line.

Run with object snaps

Often, you use an object snap mode (such as Endpoint) repeatedly. Running object snaps address this need. These steps set a running object snap:

1. **Right-click the OSNAP button on the status bar.**
2. **Choose the Settings option.**

   The Object Snap tab on the Drafting Settings dialog box appears, as shown in Figure 3-13.

3. **Select one or more object snap modes by checking the appropriate boxes.**
4. **Click OK to close the dialog box.**

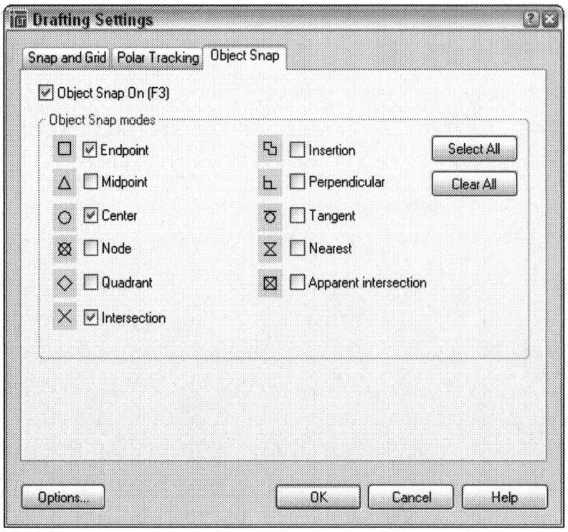

Figure 3-13: Grabbing multiple object features is an osnap.

You click the OSNAP button on the status bar to toggle running object snap mode off and on. After you turn on running object snap, AutoCAD LT hunts for points that correspond to the object snap modes you checked in the Drafting Settings dialog box. As with single point object snaps, LT displays a special symbol — such as a square for an Endpoint object snap — to indicate that it has found an object snap point. If you keep the cursor still, LT also displays a ToolTip that lists the kind of object snap point.

Use single point or running object snaps to enforce precision by making sure that new points you pick coincide *exactly* with points on existing objects. In CAD, points almost coinciding or looking like they coincide is not good enough. AutoCAD LT knows the difference between "looks the same" and "*is* the same," and causes you untold amounts of grief if you try to make do with "looks the same." You lose points, both figuratively and literally, if you don't use object snaps or one of the other precision techniques I cover in this chapter to enforce precision.

Other precision practices

The following are some other AutoCAD LT precision techniques (refer to Table 3-2, earlier in this chapter):

- **Snap:** If you turn on snap mode, AutoCAD LT constrains the cursor to an imaginary rectangular grid of points at the spacing that you specify. Follow these steps to turn on snap mode:

    1. **Right-click the SNAP button on the status bar.**
    2. **Choose the Settings option.**

The Snap and Grid tab in the Drafting Settings dialog box appears.

3. **Enter a snap spacing in the Snap X Spacing field and then click OK.**

Click the SNAP button on the status bar or press F9 to toggle snap mode off and on. To use snap effectively, change the snap spacing frequently — changing to a smaller spacing as you zoom in and work on smaller areas. You often need to toggle snap off and on, because selecting objects and some editing tasks are easier with snap off.

- **Ortho:** Ortho mode constrains the cursor to move at right angles (orthogonally) to the previous point. Click the ORTHO button on the status bar or press F8 to toggle ortho mode off and on. Because technical drawings often include lots of orthogonal lines, you use ortho mode a lot.
- **Direct distance entry:** This "point and type" technique is an easy and efficient way to draw with precision. You simply point the cursor in a particular direction, type a distance at the command line, and press Enter. AutoCAD LT calls it *direct distance entry* because it avoids the indirect command line method of specifying a distance by typing relative or polar coordinates. (I describe this older method earlier in this chapter.) You can use direct distance entry any time the crosshair cursor is anchored to a point and the command line prompts you for another point or a distance. You usually use direct distance entry with ortho mode turned on, to specify a distance in an orthogonal direction (0, 90, 180, or 270 degrees). You also can combine direct distance entry with polar tracking to specify distances in nonorthogonal directions (for example, in angle increments of 45 degrees).
- **Polar tracking:** When you turn on polar tracking, the cursor jumps to increments of the angle you select. When the cursor jumps, a ToolTip label starting with `Polar:` appears. Right-click the POLAR button on the status bar and choose the Settings option to display the Polar Tracking tab in the Drafting Settings dialog box. Select an angle from the Increment Angle drop-down list and then click OK. Click the POLAR button on the status bar or press F10 to toggle polar tracking mode off and on.
- **Polar snap:** You can force polar tracking to jump to specific incremental distances along the tracking angles by changing the snap type from grid snap to polar snap. For example, if you turn on polar tracking and set it to 45 degrees and turn on polar snap and set it to 2 units, polar tracking jumps to points that are at angle increments of 45 degrees and distance increments of 2 units from the previous point.

  To activate polar snap, follow these steps:

  1. **Right-click the SNAP button on the status bar.**
  2. **Choose the Settings option.**

     The Snap and Grid tab in the Drafting Settings dialog box appears.

3. **Click the Polar Snap radio button, type a distance in the Polar Distance edit box, and then click OK.**

When you want to return to ordinary rectangular snap, as I describe at the beginning of this list, select the Grid Snap radio button in the Drafting Settings dialog box.

If you're new to AutoCAD LT, its wide range of precision tools probably seems overwhelming at this point. Rest assured that there's more than one way to skin a cat precisely, and not everyone needs to understand all the ways. You can make perfectly precise drawings with a subset of LT's precision tools. I recommend these steps:

1. Get comfortable with typing coordinates, ortho mode, direct distance entry, and single point object snaps.
2. Become familiar with running object snaps and try snap.
3. After you have all these precision features under your belt, feel free to experiment with polar tracking and polar snap.

Confusing the names of the snap and object snap (osnap) features is easy. ***Remember:*** Snap limits the cursor to locations whose coordinates are multiples of the current snap spacing. Object snap (osnap) enables you to grab points on existing objects, whether those points happen to correspond with the snap spacing or not.

Chapter 4

Your (Drafting) Table Is Ready

In This Chapter

- Setting up a simple drawing
- Drawing some objects
- Zooming and panning in your drawing
- Editing some objects
- Plotting your drawing

The previous three chapters introduce you to the AutoCAD LT world, the LT interface, and the properties and techniques that underlie good drafting practice. By now you're probably eager to start moving the cursor around and draw something! This chapter takes you on a gentle tour of the most common CAD drafting functions: setting up a new drawing, drawing some objects, editing those objects, zooming and panning so that you can view those objects better, and plotting the drawing.

The example that I cooked up for this chapter is creating a drawing of a dining room table with some plates and napkins on it, shown in Figure 4-1. Planning the table arrangement for your next dinner party may not be the best and greatest use of AutoCAD LT, but it gives you some simple shapes to work with. And who knows — if the CAD thing doesn't work out, maybe you have a future as a restaurant design consultant.

Although the drafting example in this chapter is simple, the procedures that it demonstrates are real, honest-to-CADness, proper drafting practice. I emphasize from the beginning the importance of proper drawing setup, putting objects on appropriate layers, and drawing and editing with due concern for precision. Some of the steps in this chapter may seem a bit complicated at first, but they reflect the way that experienced AutoCAD LT users work. My goal is to help you develop good CAD habits and do things the right way from the very start.

The step-by-step procedures in this chapter, unlike those in most chapters of this book, form a sequence. You must do the steps in order. It's like baking a cake, except that here you're free to take breaks between steps.

Figure 4-1: Dinner is served.

If you find that object selection or editing functions work differently from how I describe them in this chapter, you or someone else probably changed the configuration settings on the Option dialog box's Selection tab. Chapter 7 describes these settings and how to restore the AutoCAD LT defaults.

A Simple Setup

During the remainder of this chapter, I walk you through creating, editing, viewing, and plotting a new drawing — refer to Figure 4-1 if you want to get an idea of what the goal looks like.

As Chapter 2 advises, make sure that you pay attention to the command line area. Glance at the command line area after each step so that you see the messages that AutoCAD LT is sending your way and so that you begin to get familiar with the names of commands and their options.

In this first set of steps, you create a new drawing from a template, change some settings to establish a 1:10 (1 to 10) scale, and save the drawing. As I describe in Chapter 5, drawing setup is not a simple task in AutoCAD LT. Nonetheless, drawing setup is an important part of the job, and if you don't get in the habit of doing it right, you run into endless problems later on — especially when you try to plot.

1. **Start AutoCAD LT by double-clicking its shortcut on the Windows desktop.**

   If you don't have an LT shortcut on your desktop, choose Start⇨Programs⇨Autodesk⇨AutoCAD LT 2005⇨AutoCAD LT 2005.

   The main AutoCAD LT screen appears with a new, blank drawing in it.

   If you see a Startup dialog box instead of just a new, blank drawing, click OK to dismiss the dialog box. Then choose Tools⇨Options, click the System tab, and change the Startup setting to `Do not show a startup dialog`.

2. **If the Tool Palettes and Info Palette appear as well, close them.**

3. **Click the New button on the Standard toolbar.**

   The Select Template dialog box appears with a list of drawing templates (DWT files), which you can use as the starting point for new drawings. Chapter 5 describes how to create and use drawing templates.

4. **Select the aclt.dwt template, as shown in Figure 4-2, and click the Open button.**

   LT creates a new, blank drawing with the settings in aclt.dwt. Aclt.dwt is LT's default, "plain Jane" drawing template for drawings in *imperial units* (that is, units expressed in inches and/or feet). Acltiso.dwt is the corresponding drawing template for drawings created in metric units. Chapter 5 contains additional information about these and other templates.

5. **Choose Format⇨Drawing Limits.**

   Drawing limits define your working area. LT prompts you at the command line:

   ```
   Specify lower left corner or [ON/OFF] <0.0000,0.0000>:
   ```

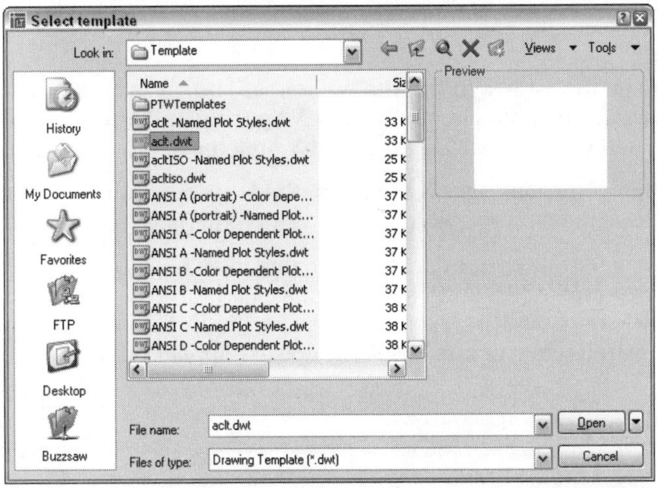

Figure 4-2: Starting a new drawing from a template.

6. **Press Enter to keep 0,0 as the lower-left corner value.**

   LT prompts you at the command line:

   ```
   Specify upper right corner <12.0000,9.0000>:
   ```

7. **Type** 100,75 **(no spaces) and press Enter.**

   100 x 75 corresponds to 10 inches by 7.5 inches (a little smaller than an 8.5 x 11 inch piece of paper turned on its side) times a drawing scale factor of 10 (because you're eventually going to plot at 1:10 scale). See Chapter 5 for more information about drawing scales.

8. **Right-click the SNAP button on the AutoCAD LT status bar and choose Settings.**

   The Snap and Grid tab of the Drafting Settings dialog box appears, as shown in Figure 4-3.

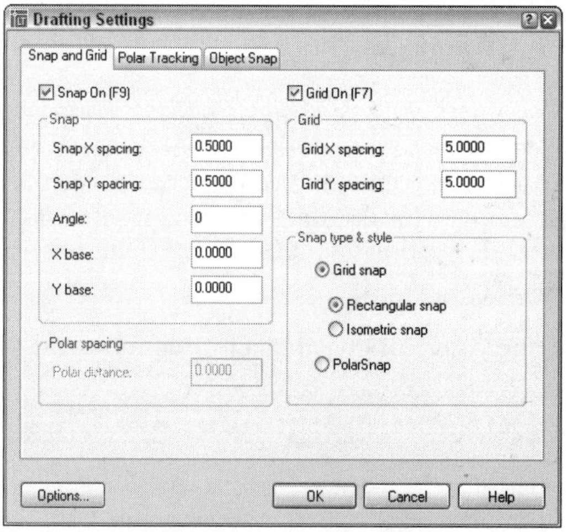

Figure 4-3: Snap and Grid settings.

9. **Change the values in the dialog box, as shown in Figure 4-3: Snap On checked, Grid On checked, Snap X Spacing and Snap Y Spacing set to 0.5, and Grid X Spacing and Grid Y Spacing set to 5.**

   (When you change the X spacings, the Y spacings automatically update to the same number, which saves you typing.)

   Snap constrains your cursor to moving in an invisible grid of equally spaced points (0.5 units apart in this case). *Grid* displays a visible grid of little dots on the screen (5 units apart in this case), which you can use as reference points. The grid doesn't appear on printed drawings.

10. **Click OK.**

    You see some grid dots, 5 units apart, in the drawing area. If you move your cursor around and watch the coordinate display area on the status bar, you notice that it moves in 0.5-unit jumps.

11. **Choose View⇨Zoom⇨All.**

    LT zooms out so that the entire area defined by the limits — as indicated by the grid dots — is visible.

12. **Type** LTScale **and press Enter.**

    When you see an AutoCAD LT command in mixed case, you can start the command by typing just the letters shown in upper case (LTS in this case) and press Enter. See the Introduction for more information.

    LTScale, or "linetype scale factor," is a system variable that controls the length of dashes and spaces in dash-dot (noncontinuous) linetypes. You must set it to a number that corresponds to your drawing scale — otherwise, the dashes and spaces don't look right.

    LT prompts you at the command line:

    ```
    Enter new linetype scale factor <1.0000>:
    ```

13. **Type** 5 **and press Enter.**

    The number 5 is half of your drawing scale factor (10). Based on experience, I know that an LTScale factor equal to about one half the drawing scale factor results in decent-looking dash-dot linetypes.

14. **Click the Save button on the Standard toolbar or press Ctrl+S.**

    Because you haven't saved the drawing yet, LT opens the Save Drawing As dialog box.

15. **Navigate to a suitable folder by choosing from the Save In drop-down list and/or double-clicking folders in the list of folders below it.**

16. **Type a name in the File Name edit box.**

    For example, type **Table** or **My Dinner With Andre**.

    Depending on your Windows Explorer settings, you may or may not see the `.dwg` extension in the File Name edit box. In any case, you don't need to type it. AutoCAD LT adds it for you.

17. **Click the Save button.**

    LT saves the new DWG file to the folder that you specify.

Whew — that was more work than scrubbing the oven — and all just to set up a simple drawing! Chapter 5 goes into more detail about drawing setup and describes why all these gyrations are necessary.

Set the Table

With a properly set up drawing, you're ready to draw some objects. In this example, you use the RECtang command to draw the top of a table, the Circle command to draw a plate, and the PLine command to draw a napkin that's folded into a triangular shape. (Both the RECtang and PLine commands create polylines — objects that contain a series of straight-line segments and/or arc segments.)

AutoCAD LT, like most CAD programs, uses *layers* as an organizing principle for all the objects that you draw. Chapter 3 describes layers and other object properties in detail. In this example, you create separate layers for the table, the plates, and the napkins, which may seem like layer madness. But when doing complex drawings, you need to use a lot of layers in order to keep things organized.

A rectangle on the right layer

The following steps demonstrate how to create and use layers, as well as how to draw rectangles. (Chapter 3 describes layers in detail and Chapter 6 covers the RECtang command.) Start by drawing a square tabletop on the Furniture layer.

1. **Make sure that you complete the drawing setup in the previous section of this chapter.**
2. **Click the Layers button on the Layers toolbar.**

   The LAyer command starts and LT displays the Layer Properties Manager dialog box.
3. **Click the New Layer button.**

   LT adds a new layer to the list and gives it the default name Layer1.
4. **Type a more suitable name for the layer on which you'll draw the table and press Enter.**

   In this example, type **Furniture**, as shown in Figure 4-4.
5. **Click the Set Current button (the green check mark).**

   Furniture becomes the current layer — that is, the layer on which LT places objects that you draw from this point forward.
6. **Click the color swatch or name ("White") in the Furniture layer row.**

   The Select Color dialog box appears.
7. **Click color 4 (cyan) in the single, separate row to the left of the ByLayer and ByBlock buttons, and then click OK.**

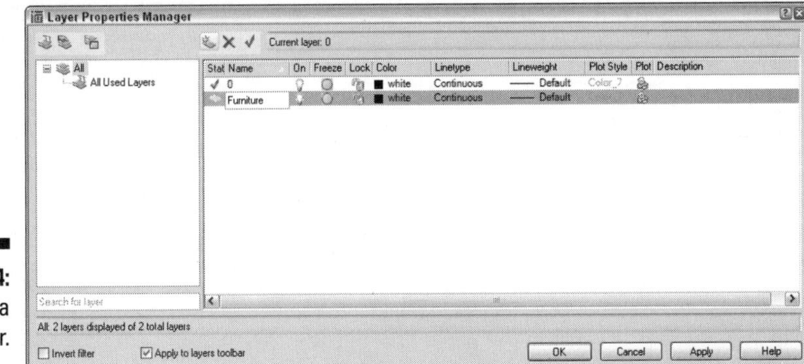

Figure 4-4: Creating a new layer.

The Standard Colors dialog box closes and LT changes the color of the Furniture layer to cyan.

8. **Click OK to close the Layer Properties Manager dialog box.**

   The Layer drop-down list on the Layers toolbar displays Furniture as the current layer.

   Now you can draw a rectangular table on the Furniture layer.

9. **Click the Rectangle button on the Draw toolbar.**

   The RECtang command starts and LT prompts you at the command line:

   ```
   Specify first corner point or
           [Chamfer/Elevation/Fillet/Thickness/Width]:
   ```

10. **Click a point in the drawing area at or near the point 20,20.**

    By watching the coordinate display area on the status bar, you can see the coordinates of the current cursor location. Because snap is set to 0.5 units, you land right on the point 20,20. Picking the point 20,20 instead of, say 21,19, isn't important but this general vicinity gives you enough room to work.

    If the status bar coordinates don't change when you move the cursor, click them until they do.

    LT prompts you at the command line:

    ```
    Specify other corner point or [Dimensions]:
    ```

11. **Type** @36,36 **(without any spaces) and press Enter.**

    The @ sign indicates that you're using a *relative* coordinate — that is, 36 units to the right and up from the point that you picked in the previous step. See Chapter 3 for more information about typing absolute and relative coordinates.

    LT draws the 36 x 36 rectangle, as shown in Figure 4-5. It's on the Furniture layer and inherits that layer's cyan color.

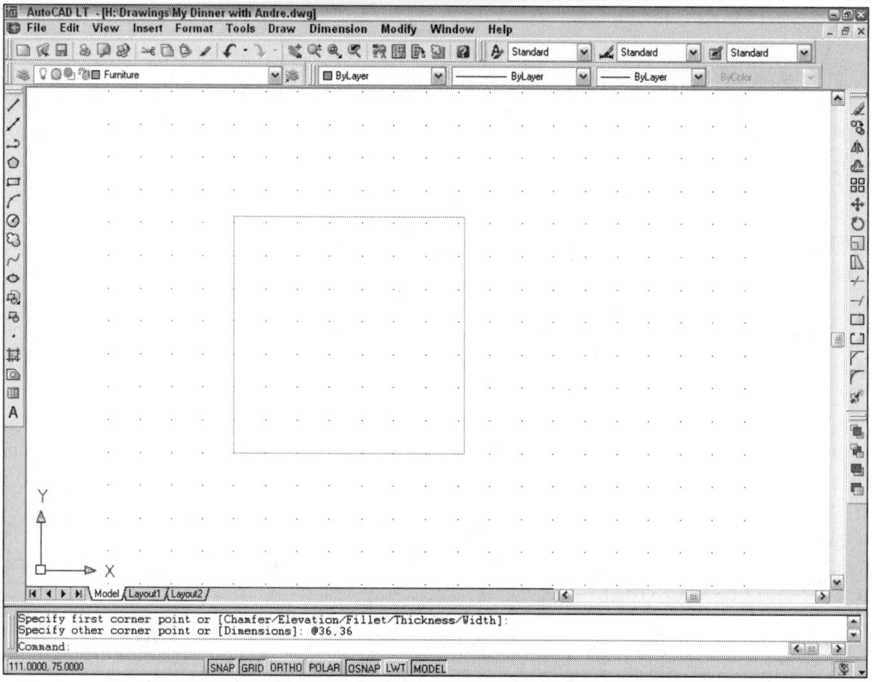

Figure 4-5: Your table is waiting.

12. **Press Ctrl+S to save the drawing.**

    LT saves the drawing, and renames the previously saved version *drawingname*.bak — for example, My Dinner With Andre.bak). BAK is AutoCAD's extension for a backup file; Chapter 16 describes `.bak` files and how to use them.

Circle around your plate

You can use the Circle command to draw an 11-inch diameter plate on the Plates layer.

1. **Repeat Steps 2 through 8 in the previous section to create a new layer for the plates and set it current. Give the layer the name Plates and assign it the color 3 (green).**

   The Layer drop-down list on the Layers toolbar displays Plates as the current layer.

2. **Click the Circle button on the Draw toolbar.**

   The Circle command starts and LT prompts you at the command line:

```
Specify center point for circle or [3P/2P/Ttr (tan tan
radius)]:
```

3. **Click a point in the drawing area at or near the point 38,27.**

   As in Step 10 of the table-drawing steps, the idea is not necessarily to land exactly on the point 38,27, but to pick a reasonable point for the center of the first plate.

   LT prompts you at the command line:

   ```
   Specify radius of circle or [Diameter]:
   ```

   You decide that you want 11-inch diameter plates. LT is asking for a radius. Although you probably can figure out the radius of an 11-inch circle, specify the Diameter option and let AutoCAD LT do the hard work.

4. **Type** D **and press Enter to select the Diameter option.**

   LT prompts you at the command line:

   ```
   Specify diameter of circle:
   ```

5. **Type** 11 **and press Enter.**

   LT draws the 11-inch diameter circle. It's on the Plates layer and inherits that layer's green color.

6. **Press Ctrl+S to save the drawing.**

Tuck in your polyline

This is a proper dinner, so adding a nicely folded napkin next to the plate is a good idea. Use the PLine command to draw a triangular polyline, and put it on the Linens layer. Besides showing you how to draw polylines, these steps introduce you to one of AutoCAD LT's more useful precision techniques: ortho.

1. **Repeat Steps 2 through 8 in the table-drawing steps to create a new layer for the napkins and set it current. Give the layer the name Linens and assign it the color 1 (red).**

   The Layer drop-down list on the Layers toolbar displays Linens as the current layer.

   You don't have to create a separate layer for every type of object that you draw. For example, you can draw both the plates and napkins on a layer called Table Settings. Layer names and usage depend on industry and office practices, in addition to a certain amount of individual judgment. However lumping two layers together is much easier, if you end up with too many, than dividing the objects on one layer into two layers, if you end up with too few.

2. **Click the Polyline button — the one that looks like a fishhook — on the Draw toolbar.**

   The PLine command starts and LT prompts you at the command line:

   ```
   Specify start point:
   ```

   Peek ahead to Figure 4-6 in order to get an idea of how the napkin will look after you draw it. As you move the cursor around near the plate, notice that LT tends to grab certain points briefly, especially on existing objects. This behavior is the result of running object snaps and tracking, which I discuss in Chapter 3.

3. **Turn off running object snaps by clicking the OSNAP button on the status bar until it looks popped out and you see** `<Osnap off>` **on the command line.**

   ```
   Specify start point:  <Osnap off>
   ```

4. **Click a point in the drawing area at or near the point 31,21.**

   LT prompts you at the command line:

   ```
   Specify next point or [Arc/Halfwidth/Length/Undo/Width]:
   ```

5. **Turn on Ortho mode by clicking the ORTHO button on the status bar until it looks popped in and you see** `<Ortho on>` **on the command line.**

   ```
   Specify next point or [Arc/Halfwidth/Length/Undo/Width]:
          <Ortho on>
   ```

6. **Move the cursor up about 12 inches — to just above the top of the plate — and click in order to draw a vertical segment approximately 12 inches long.**

   As you move the cursor, watch the coordinate display and use it to help guide you. If you click the coordinate display once or twice, you see an alternative *polar* coordinate display in the form 12.0000<90 (*distance<angle*), which is helpful in locating a point that lies a specific distance and angle from the previous point.

   LT draws the first segment and prompts you at the command line:

   ```
   Specify next point or
          [Arc/Close/Halfwidth/Length/Undo/Width]:
   ```

7. **Turn off Ortho mode by clicking the ORTHO button on the status bar until it looks popped out and you see** `<Ortho off>` **on the command line.**

   ```
   Specify next point or
          [Arc/Close/Halfwidth/Length/Undo/Width]: <Ortho
          off>
   ```

8. **Move the cursor down and to the left about 8 units and click to create the third point of the napkin.**

   LT draws the second segment and prompts you at the command line:

   ```
   Specify next point or
          [Arc/Close/Halfwidth/Length/Undo/Width]:
   ```

9. **Right-click in the drawing area and choose Close from the cursor menu.**

   LT draws the triangle by closing the polyline, as shown in Figure 4-6. It's on the Linens layer and inherits that layer's red color.

10. **Press Ctrl+S to save the drawing.**

This dinner is starting to look pretty lonely, but don't worry — I cover creating more place settings with editing commands later in this chapter. If your brain is feeling full, now is a good time to take a break and go check on that cake in the oven. If you exit AutoCAD LT, just restart LT and reopen your drawing when you're ready to continue.

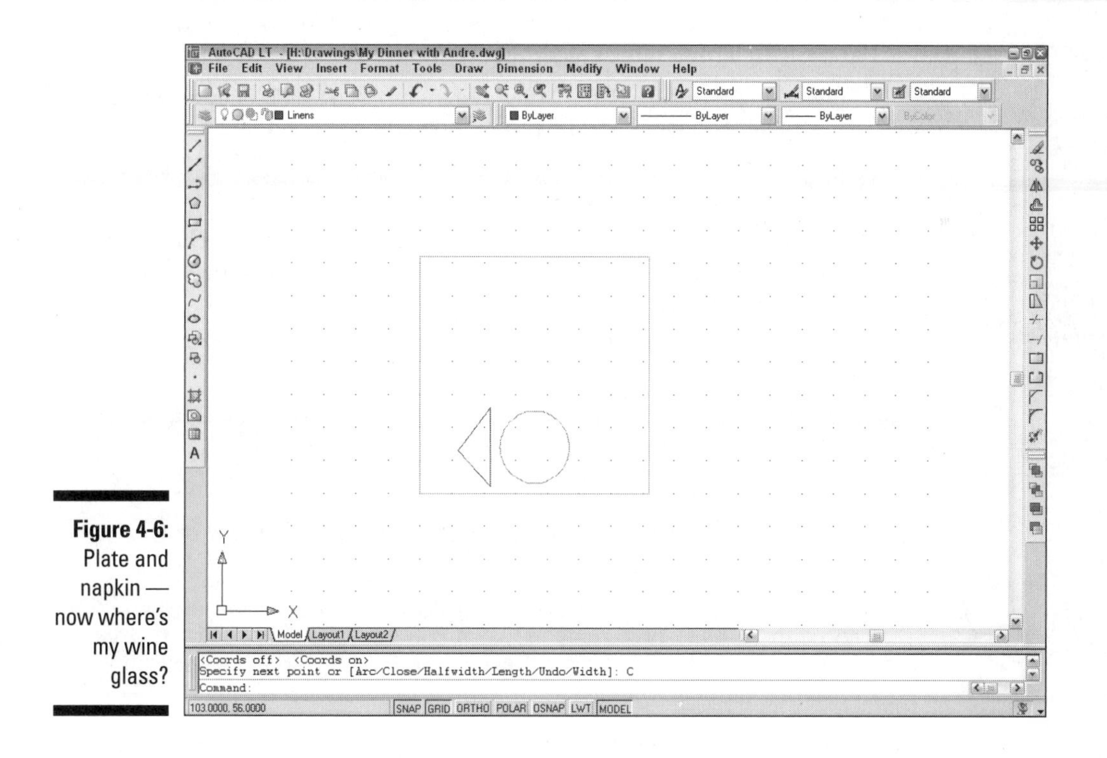

Figure 4-6: Plate and napkin — now where's my wine glass?

Get a Closer Look with Zoom and Pan

The example drawing in this chapter is pretty uncluttered and small, but most real CAD drawings are neither. Technical drawings usually are jampacked with lines, text, and dimensions. CAD drawings often get plotted on sheets of paper that measure two to three feet on a side — that's in the hundreds of millimeters, for you metric mavens. Anyone who owns a monitor that large probably can afford to hire a whole room of drafters and therefore isn't reading this book. The rest of us need to zoom and pan in our drawings — a lot. Zooming and panning frequently enables you to see the details better, draw more confidently (because you can see what you're doing), and edit more quickly (because object selection is easier when a zillion objects aren't on the screen).

Fortunately, zooming and panning in AutoCAD LT is as simple as it is necessary. The following steps describe how to use LT's Zoom and Pan Realtime feature, which is pretty easy to operate and provides a lot of flexibility. Chapter 8 covers additional zoom and pan options.

1. **Click the Zoom Realtime button (the one that looks like a magnifying glass with a plus/minus sign next to it) on the Standard toolbar.**

   The Realtime option of the Zoom command starts. The cursor changes to a magnifying glass and LT prompts you at the command line:

   ```
   Press ESC or ENTER to exit, or right-click to display
          shortcut menu.
   ```

2. **Move the cursor near the middle of the screen, press and hold the left mouse button, and drag the cursor up and down until the table almost fills the screen.**

   As you can see, dragging up increases the zoom magnification and dragging down decreases it.

3. **Right-click in the drawing area to display the Zoom/Pan Realtime menu, shown in Figure 4-7. Choose Pan from the menu.**

   The cursor changes to a hand.

4. **Click and drag to pan the drawing until the table is more or less centered in the drawing area.**

   You can use the right-click menu to toggle back and forth between Zoom and Pan as many times as you like. If you get lost, choose Zoom Original or Zoom Extents in order to return to a recognizable view. See Chapter 8 for more about zooming and panning.

5. **Right-click in the drawing area and choose Exit from the Zoom/Pan Realtime menu.**

   The cursor returns to the normal AutoCAD LT crosshairs.

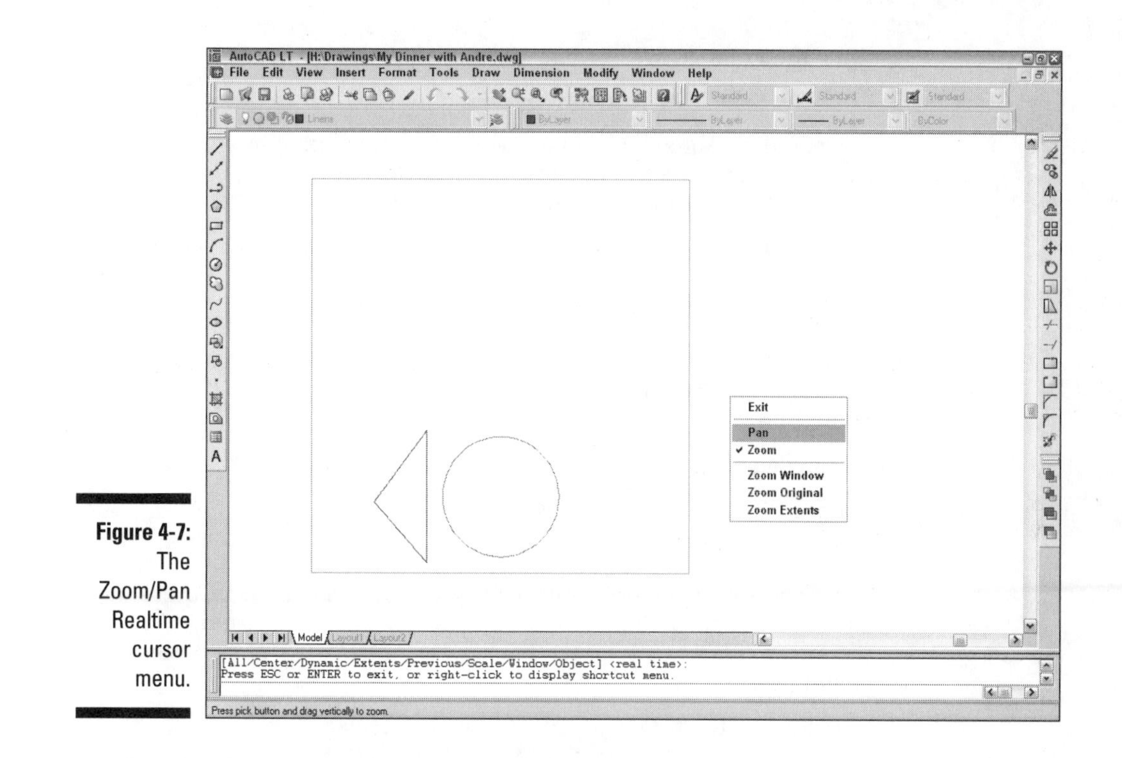

Figure 4-7: The Zoom/Pan Realtime cursor menu.

Modify to Make It Merrier

When you have a better view of your table, you can edit the objects on it more easily. In the following sections, you use the ARray command to add three more place settings, the Stretch command to add a leaf to the table, and the Move command to shove the plates and napkins around.

Hooray for Array

Using the ARray command is a great way to generate a bunch of new objects at regular spacings from existing objects. The array pattern can be either rectangular (that is, columns and rows of objects) or polar (in a circle around a center point, like the spokes of a wheel around its hub). In this example, you use polar array to create three additional place settings, with the center of the table as the hub of the array.

1. **Click the Array button — the one with four squares — on the Modify toolbar.**

   The ARray command starts and LT displays the Array dialog box.

2. **Click the Polar Array button.**
3. **Click the Select Objects button.**

   The standard AutoCAD LT object selection and editing sequence — start a command; then select objects — may seem backward to you until you get used to it. See Chapter 7 for more information.

   The Array dialog box temporarily disappears and LT prompts you at the command line:

   ```
   Select objects:
   ```

4. **Turn off Snap mode by clicking the SNAP button on the status bar until it looks popped out and you see `<Snap off>` on the command line.**

   Turning off Snap mode temporarily makes selecting objects easier.

   ```
   Select objects: <Snap off>
   ```

5. **Click the napkin and then click the plate.**

   If you encounter any problems while trying to select objects, press the Esc key a couple of times to cancel the command, and then restart the ARray command. Chapter **7** describes AutoCAD LT object selection techniques.

   LT continues to prompt you at the command line:

   ```
   Select objects: 1 found, 2 total
   ```

6. **Press Enter to end object selection.**

   The Array dialog box reappears.

7. **Click the Pick Center Point button (the one with a pointer and an X next to the Y text entry box).**

   LT prompts you at the command line:

   ```
   Specify center point of array:
   ```

   You want to specify the center point of the table. The new Mid Between 2 Points object snap option, combined with endpoint object snaps, helps you perform this feat. See Chapter 3 for more about object snaps.

8. **Right-click the OSNAP button on the status bar and choose Settings.**

   The Object Snap tab on the Drafting Settings dialog box appears, as shown in Figure 4-8.

9. **If the Object Snap On and Endpoint boxes aren't checked, click them until they are. Then click OK.**

   It's okay if other object snap modes — such as Center and Intersection — are checked as well. Just make sure that Endpoint is checked.

   ```
   Resuming ARRAY command.
   Specify center point of the array:
   ```

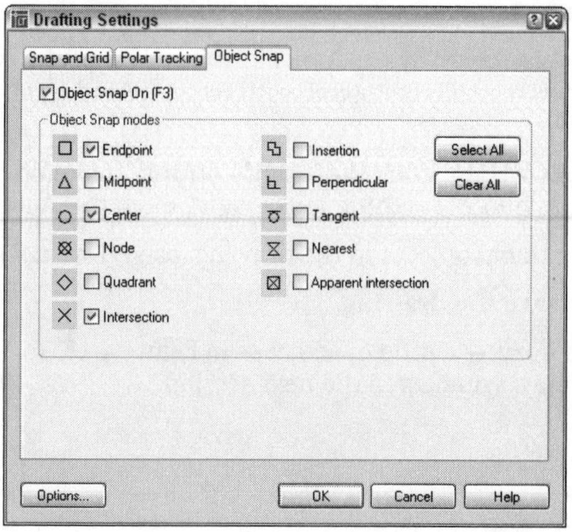

Figure 4-8: Setting running object snap points.

10. **Hold down the Shift key, right-click in the drawing, release the Shift key, and choose Mid Between 2 Points from the object snap menu.**

```
Specify center point of the array: _m2p First point of
        mid:
```

11. **Move the cursor to one corner of the table, and when you see the Endpoint Object Snap ToolTip, click.**

```
Second point of mid:
```

12. **Move the cursor to the diagonally opposite corner of the table, and when you see the Endpoint Object Snap ToolTip, click.**

    LT locates the point exactly midway between the corners of the table and then redisplays the Array dialog box, now showing the coordinates of that point in the Center Point edit boxes. The Array dialog box looks similar to Figure 4-9. (Your coordinates may be slightly different.)

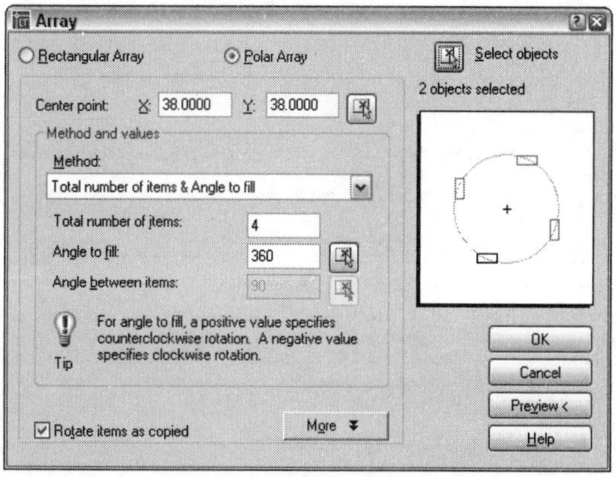

Figure 4-9: The Array dialog box, ready to set the table for you.

13. **Click the Preview button.**

    LT shows you what the array will look like if you accept the current settings and displays a small dialog box with Accept, Modify, and Cancel buttons.

14. **If anything looks wrong, click the Modify button, make changes, and preview again. When everything looks right, click the Accept button.**

    LT adds the additional objects to the drawing, as shown in Figure 4-10.

15. **Press Ctrl+S to save the drawing.**

    The table looks cozy — a little *too* cozy — in Figure 4-10, so stretch it out horizontally. I show you how in the next section.

Stretch out

The Stretch command is powerful but a little bit complicated — it can stretch or move objects, depending on how you select them. The key to using Stretch is specifying a *crossing selection box* properly. (Chapter 7 gives you more details about crossing boxes and how to use them with the Stretch command.)

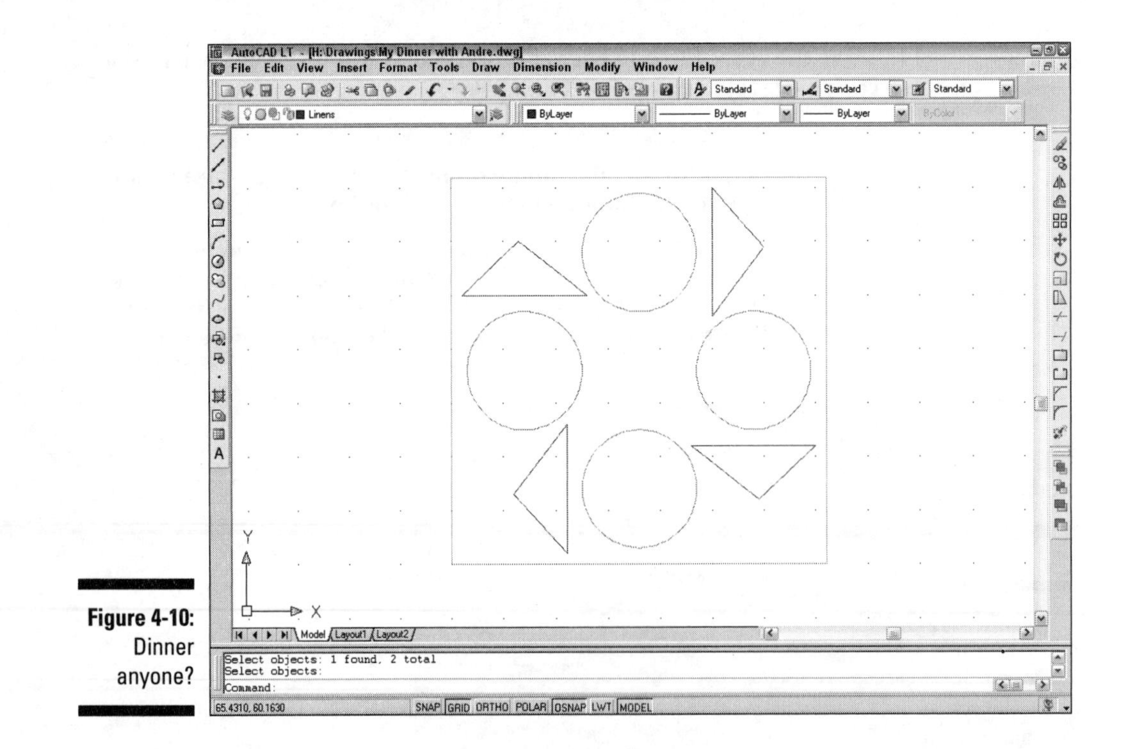

Figure 4-10: Dinner anyone?

Follow these steps to stretch the table:

1. **Click the Stretch button — the one with the corner of the rectangle being stretched — on the Modify toolbar.**

   The Stretch command starts and LT prompts you at the command line:

   ```
   Select objects to stretch by crossing-window or crossing-
           polygon...
   Select objects:
   ```

2. **Click a point above and to the right of the upper-right corner of the table (Point 1 in Figure 4-11).**
3. **Move the cursor to the left.**

   The cursor changes to a dashed rectangle, which indicates that you're specifying a crossing box. LT prompts you at the command line:

   ```
   Select objects: Specify opposite corner:
   ```

4. **Click a point below and to the left of the lower-right corner of the table (Point 2 in Figure 4-11).**

   The crossing box needs to enclose the plate and napkins on the right and approximately the right third of the table (refer to Figure 4-11).

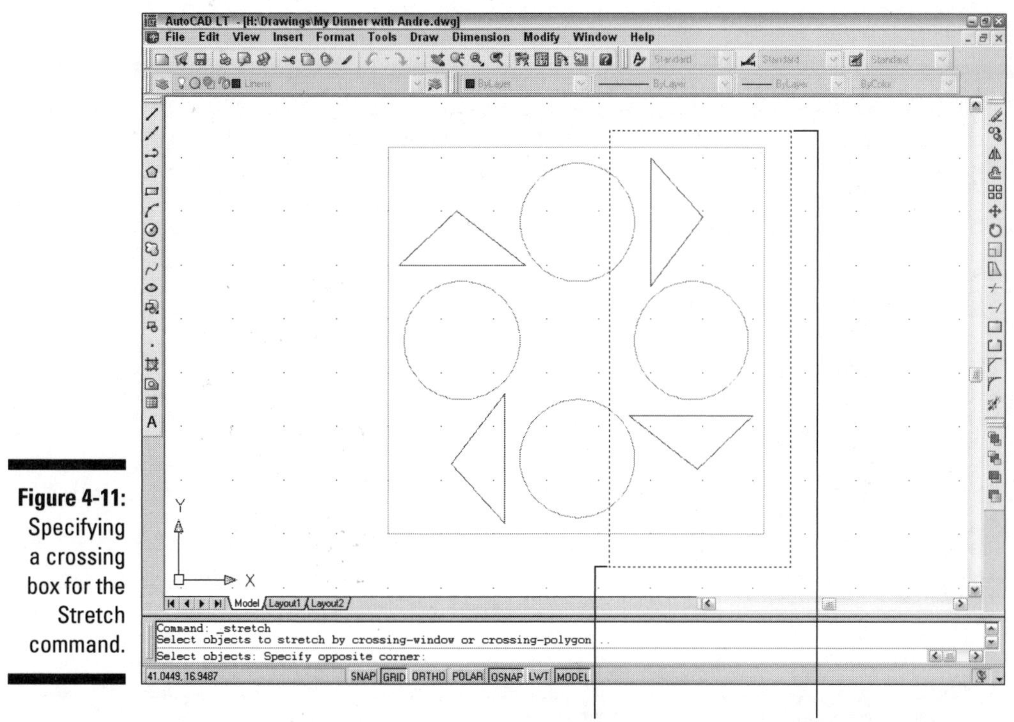

Figure 4-11: Specifying a crossing box for the Stretch command.

LT prompts you at the command line:

```
Select objects: Specify opposite corner: 6 found
Select objects:
```

5. **Press Enter to end object selection.**

   LT prompts you at the command line:

   ```
   Specify base point or displacement:
   ```

6. **Turn on Snap mode and Ortho mode by clicking the SNAP and ORTHO buttons on the status bar until they appear pushed in.**

7. **Click a point on or near the right edge of the table.**

   This point serves as the base point for the stretch operation. Chapter 7 describes base points and displacements in greater detail.

   LT prompts you at the command line:

   ```
   Specify second point of displacement or <use first point
          as displacement>:
   ```

8. **Move the cursor to the right about 18 units — use the coordinate display to guide you and then click.**

   LT stretches the table by the distance that you indicate and moves the plate and napkins that were inside the crossing window rectangle, as shown in Figure 4-12.

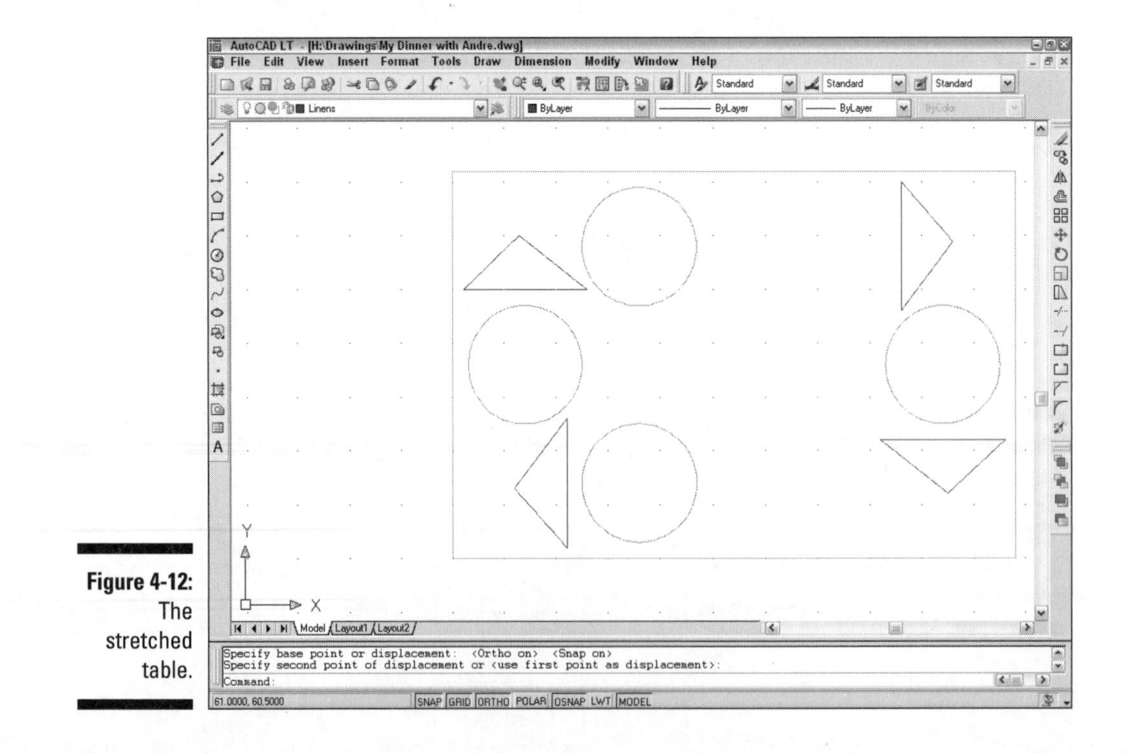

Figure 4-12: The stretched table.

If your first stretch didn't work right, click the Undo button on the Standard toolbar and try again. Stretch is an immensely useful command — one that makes you wonder how drafters used to do it all with erasers and pencils — but it does take some practice to get the hang of those crossing boxes.

9. **Press Ctrl+S to save the drawing.**

Move around

Your final editing task is to rearrange some of the plates and napkins so that the table looks tidy again. You can move objects in AutoCAD LT in lots of ways, but the Move command is one of the most useful and flexible. As a bonus, after you know the Move command, you pretty much know CoPy as well.

1. **Turn off running object snaps by clicking the OSNAP button on the status bar until it looks popped out.**
2. **Click the Move button — the one with the four-headed arrows — on the Modify toolbar.**

   The Move command starts and LT prompts you at the command line:

   ```
   Select objects:
   ```

3. **Click one or more of the objects that you want to move.**

   LT continues to prompt you at the command line:

   ```
   Select objects: 1 found, 2 total
   ```

4. **Press Enter to end object selection.**

   LT prompts you at the command line with the same prompt that you saw earlier with the Stretch command:

   ```
   Specify base point or displacement:
   ```

5. **Click a base point somewhere near the objects that you want to copy.**
6. **Move the cursor to the location where you want to place them and click.**
7. **Repeat Steps 2 through 6 until the table is set the way you like it. Figure 4-13 shows my arrangement.**

If you're feeling cocky about editing by now — or you're just expecting more company for dinner — try the Copy button on the Modify toolbar in addition to Move. Create a couple more place settings and then move them until everything looks good.

8. **Choose View➪Zoom➪All.**

   LT zooms out so that entire area defined by the limits is visible.

9. **Press Ctrl+S to save the drawing.**

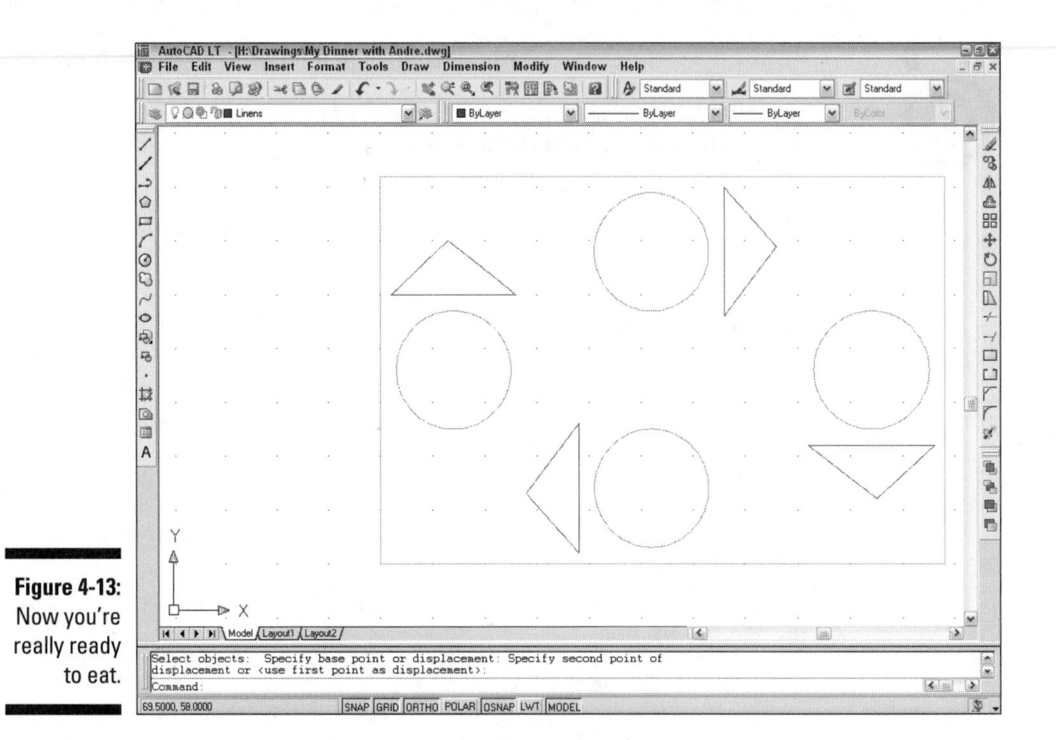

Figure 4-13: Now you're really ready to eat.

After some drawing and editing, you may wonder how you're supposed to know when to turn off or on the various status bar modes (Snap, Grid, Ortho, Osnap, and so on). You start to get an instinctive sense of when each mode is useful and when it gets in the way. In subsequent chapters of this book, I give you some more specific guidelines.

Follow the Plot

Looking at drawings on a computer screen and exchanging them with others via e-mail or Web sites is all well and good. But sooner or later someone — maybe you! — is going to want to see a printed version. Printing drawings — or *plotting*, as CAD geeks like to call it — is much more complicated than printing a word processing document or a spreadsheet. That's because you have to worry about things such as drawing scale, lineweights, title blocks, and weird paper sizes. I get into plotting in Chapter 12, but here's an abbreviated procedure that helps you generate a recognizable printed drawing.

The following steps show you how to plot the model space portion of the drawing. As Chapter 2 describes, AutoCAD LT includes a sophisticated feature called *paper space layouts* for creating arrangements of your drawing that you plot. These arrangements usually include a title block. Because I promised you a gentle tour of AutoCAD LT drafting functions, I left the paper space layout and title block issues for the next chapter. When you're ready for the whole plotting enchilada, turn to Chapter 5 for information about how to set up paper space layouts and Chapter 12 for full plotting instructions.

1. **Click the Plot button on the Standard toolbar.**

   LT opens the Plot dialog box.

2. **Click the More Options button (at the bottom-right corner of the dialog box, next to the Help button).**

   The Plot dialog box reveals additional settings, as shown in Figure 4-14.

Figure 4-14: The Plot dialog box, with the More Options area visible.

3. **In the Printer/Plotter area, select a printer from the Name list.**

4. **In the Paper Size area, select a paper size that's loaded in your printer or plotter.**

   Anything Letter size (8½ x 11) or larger works for this example.

5. **In the Plot Area, choose Limits.**

   This is the entire drawing area, which you specified when you set up the drawing earlier in this chapter.

6. **In the Plot Offset area, choose Center the Plot.**

   Alternatively, you can specify offsets of zero or other amounts in order to position the plot at a specific location on the paper.

7. **In the Plot Scale area, uncheck the Fit to Paper box and choose 1:10 from the Scale drop-down list.**

   1:10 is the scale used to set up the drawing (in the earlier section, "Follow the Plot").

8. **In the Plot Style Table area, click the Name drop-down list and choose monochrome.ctb.**

   The monochrome.ctb plotstyle table ensures that all your lines appear solid black, rather than as weird shades of gray. See Chapter 12 for information about plotstyle tables and monochrome and color plotting.

   A Question dialog box appears, asking, "Assign this plotstyle table to all layouts?"

9. **Click Yes.**

   You can leave the remaining settings on the Plot Device tab at their default values (refer to Figure 4-14).

10. **Point to the postage stamp-sized partial preview in the middle of the Plot dialog box and pause the cursor.**

    A ToolTip appears listing the Paper Size and Printable Area for the printer and paper size that you selected.

11. **Click the Preview button.**

    The Plot dialog box disappears temporarily and LT shows how the plot will look on paper. In addition, LT prompts you on the status bar:

    ```
    Press pick button and drag vertically to zoom, ESC or
            ENTER to exit, or right-click to display shortcut
            menu.
    ```

12. **Right-click in the preview area and choose Exit from the menu.**

13. **If the preview doesn't look right, adjust the settings in the Plot dialog box and look at the preview again until it looks right.**

14. **Click OK.**

    The Plot dialog box closes. AutoCAD LT generates the plot and sends it to the printer. After generating the plot, LT displays a Plot and Publish Job Complete balloon notification from the right end of the status bar. (A Click to view plot and publish details link displays more information about the plot job.)

15. **Click the X (close) button in the Plot and Publish Job Complete balloon notification.**

    The balloon notification disappears.

    If you're not happy with lineweights of the lines on your plot at this point, fear not. You can use the lineweights feature (Chapter 3) or plotstyles (Chapter 12) to control plotted lineweights.

16. **Press Ctrl+S to save the drawing.**

    When you make changes to the plot settings, LT saves them with the tab of the drawing that you plotted (the Model tab or one of the paper space layout tabs). Save the drawing after you plot if you want the modified plot settings to become the default plot settings the next time you open the drawing.

Congratulations! You successfully executed your first plot in AutoCAD LT. Chapter 12 tells you more — much more — about LT's highly flexible but occasionally perplexing plotting system.

Part II
Geometry Rules

"The funny thing is he's spent 9 hours organizing his computer desktop."

In this part . . .

Lines, circles, and other elements of geometry make up the heart of your drawing. Before you start drawing these objects, though, you need to set up your drawing for a suitable scale and sheet size, so this part starts there. With a properly set up drawing, you're ready to draw. AutoCAD LT offers many different drawing commands and many ways to use them to draw objects precisely. After you draw your geometry, you probably spend at least as much time editing it as your design and drawings evolve. And in the process, you need to zoom in and out and pan all around to see how the entire drawing is coming together. Drawing geometry, editing it, and changing the displayed view are the foundation of the drawing process; this part shows you how to make that foundation solid.

Chapter 5

A Big (Drawing) Setup

In This Chapter

- Developing a setup strategy
- Starting a new drawing
- Setting up model space
- Setting up paper space layouts
- Creating and using drawing templates

Surprisingly, drawing setup is one of the trickier aspects of using AutoCAD LT. It's an easy thing to do incompletely or wrong, and AutoCAD LT 2005 doesn't provide a dialog box or other simple, all-in-one-fell-swoop tool to help you do all of it right. And yet, drawing setup is a crucial thing to get right. Setup steps that you omit or don't do right can come back to bite you — or at least gnaw on your leg — later.

Sloppy setup really becomes apparent when you try to plot your drawing. Things that seemed more or less okay as you zoomed around on the screen suddenly are completely the wrong size or scale on paper. And nothing brands someone as a naive AutoCAD wannabe as quickly as the inability to plot a drawing at the right size and scale. Chapter 12 covers plotting procedures, but the information in this chapter is a necessary prerequisite to successful plotting. If you don't get this stuff right, there's a good chance you'll find that . . . the plot sickens.

This chapter describes the decisions you need to make before you set up a new drawing, shows the steps for doing a complete and correct setup, and demonstrates how to save setup settings for reuse.

Don't assume that you can just create a new blank DWG file and start drawing things. In other words, *do* read this chapter before you get too deeply into the later chapters in this book. Many AutoCAD LT drawing commands and concepts depend on proper drawing setup, so you have a much easier time of drawing and editing things if you do your setup homework. A few minutes invested in setting up a drawing well can save hours of thrashing around later on.

After you digest the detailed drawing setup procedures I describe in this chapter, use the Drawing Setup Roadmap on the Cheat Sheet at the front of this book to guide you through the process.

Setup Strategies

You need to set up AutoCAD LT drawings correctly, partly because LT is so flexible and partly because, well, you're doing *CAD* — computer-aided drafting (or design). The computer can't aid your drafting (or design) if you don't clue it in on things such as drawing scale, paper size, and units. In this context, the following reasons help explain why AutoCAD LT drawing setup is important:

- **Electronic paper:** The most important thing you can do to make using AutoCAD LT fun is to work on a correctly set up drawing so that your screen acts like paper, only smarter. When drawing on real paper, you constantly have to translate between units on the paper and the real-life units of the object you're drawing. But when drawing in LT, you can draw directly in real-life units — feet and inches, millimeters, or whatever you typically use on your projects. AutoCAD LT can then calculate distances and dimensions for you and add them to the drawing. You can make the mouse pointer jump directly to hot spots on-screen, and a visible, resizable grid gives you a better sense of the scale of your drawing. However, this smart paper function works well only if you tell LT some crucial parameters for your specific drawing. LT can't really do its job until you tell it how to work.
- **Dead-trees paper:** Creating a great drawing on-screen that doesn't fit well on paper is all too easy. After you finish creating your drawing on the smart paper AutoCAD LT provides on-screen, you usually must then plot it on the good, old-fashioned paper that people have used for thousands of years. At that point, you must deal with the fact that people like to use certain standard paper sizes and drawing scales. (Most people also like everything to fit neatly on one sheet of paper.) If you set up AutoCAD LT drawings correctly, good plotting results automatically; if not, plotting time can become one colossal hassle.
- **It ain't easy:** AutoCAD LT provides templates and setup wizards for you, but the templates don't work well unless you understand them, and some of the wizards don't work well even if you do understand them. This deficiency is one of the major weaknesses in AutoCAD LT. You must figure out on your own how to make the program work right. If you just plunge in without carefully setting it up, your drawing and printing efforts are likely to wind up a real mess.

Fortunately, setting up drawings correctly is a bit like cooking a soufflé: Although the steps for performing your setup are complex, you can master them with attention and practice. Even more fortunately, this chapter provides a detailed and field-tested recipe.

While you're working in AutoCAD LT, always keep in mind what your final output should look like on real paper. Even your first printed drawings should look just like hand-drawn ones — only without all those eraser smudges.

Before you start the drawing setup process, you need to make decisions about your new drawing. These three questions are absolutely critical. If you don't answer them, or you answer them wrong, you'll probably need to do lots of reworking of the drawing later:

- What drawing units will you use?
- At what scale — or scales — will you plot it?
- On what size paper does it need to fit?

In some cases, you can defer answering one additional question, but dealing with it upfront is usually best: What kind of border or title block does your drawing require?

If you're in a hurry, you may be tempted to find an existing drawing setup for the drawing scale and paper size that you want to use, make a copy of that DWG file, erase the objects, and start drawing. Use this approach with care, though. When you start from another drawing, you inherit any setup mistakes in that drawing. Also, drawings created in much older versions of AutoCAD or AutoCAD LT may not take advantage of current program features and CAD practices. If you can find a suitable drawing that was set up in a recent version of AutoCAD or LT by an experienced person who is conscientious about doing setup right, consider using it. Otherwise, you're better off setting up a new drawing from scratch.

Choosing your units

AutoCAD LT is extremely flexible about drawing units; it lets you have them *your* way. Usually, you choose the type of units that you normally use to talk about whatever you're drawing: feet and inches for a building in the United States, millimeters for a metric screw, and so on.

During drawing setup, you choose two units characteristics: a *type* of unit — Scientific, Decimal, Engineering, Architectural, and Fractional — and a *precision* of measurement in the Drawing Units dialog box, shown in Figure 5-1. (I show you how later in this chapter.) Engineering and Architectural units are in feet and inches; Engineering units use *decimals* to represent partial inches, and Architectural units use *fractions* to represent them. AutoCAD LT's other unit types — Decimal, Fractional, and Scientific — are *unitless* because LT doesn't know or care what the base unit is. If you configure a drawing to use Decimal units, for example, each drawing unit can represent a micron, millimeter, inch, foot, meter, kilometer, mile, parsec, the length of the king's forearm, or any other unit of measurement that you deem convenient. It's up to you to decide.

Figure 5-1: The Drawing Units dialog box.

After you specify a type of unit, you draw things on-screen full size in those units just as though you were laying them out on the construction site or in the machine shop. You draw an 8-foot-high line, for example, to indicate the height of a wall and an 8-inch-high line to indicate the cutout for a doggie door (for a Dachshund, naturally). The on-screen line may actually be only 2 inches long at a particular zoom resolution, but AutoCAD LT stores the length as 8 feet. This way of working is easy and natural for most people for whom CAD is their first drafting experience, but it seems weird to people who do a lot of manual drafting. If you're in the latter category, don't worry; you soon get the hang of it.

When you use dash-dot linetypes (see Chapter 3) and hatching (see Chapter 11) in a drawing, AutoCAD LT imposes one additional units consideration — whether the drawing uses an imperial (inches, feet, miles, and so on) or metric (millimeters, meters, kilometers, and so on) system of units. The MEASUREMENT system variable controls whether the linetype and hatch patterns that LT lists for you to choose from are scaled with inches or millimeters in mind as the plotting units. MEASUREMENT=0 means inches (that is, an imperial units drawing), whereas MEASUREMENT=1 means millimeters (that is, a metric units drawing). If you start from an appropriate template drawing, as I describe later in this chapter, the MEASUREMENT system variable is set correctly and you don't ever have to think about it.

Weighing your scales

The next decision you make before setting up a new drawing is choosing the scale at which you eventually plot the drawing. This decision gives you the *drawing scale* and *drawing scale factor* — two ways of expressing the same relationship between the objects in the real world and the objects plotted on paper.

Don't just invent some arbitrary scale based on your CD-ROM speed or camera's zoom lens resolution. Most industries work with a fairly small set of approved drawing scales that are related to one another by factors of 2 or 10. If you use other scales, you're at best branded a clueless newbie — and at worst have to redo all your drawings at an approved scale.

Table 5-1 lists some common architectural drawing scales, using both English and metric units. (Ratios such as 1:200 are unitless. Building plan and detail measurements often are expressed in millimeters, so you can think of 1:200 as meaning "1 millimeter on the plotted drawing equals 200 millimeters in actual building.") The table also lists the drawing scale factor corresponding to each drawing scale and the common uses for each scale. If you work in industries other than those listed here, ask drafters or co-workers what the common drawing scales are and for what kinds of drawings they're used.

Table 5-1 Common Architectural Drawing Scales

Drawing Scale	*Drawing Scale Factor*	*Common Uses*
1⁄16" = 1'–0"	192	Large building plans
1⁄8" = 1'–0"	96	Building plans
1⁄4" = 1'–0"	48	House plans
1⁄2" = 1'–0"	24	Plan details
1" = 1'–0"	12	Details
1:200	200	Large building plans
1:100	100	Building plans
1:50	50	House plans
1:20	20	Plan details
1:10	10	Details

After you choose a drawing scale, engrave the corresponding drawing scale factor on your desk, write it on your hand, and put it on a sticky note on your monitor. You need to know the drawing scale factor for many drawing tasks, as well as for some plotting. You should be able to recite the drawing scale factor of any drawing you're working on in AutoCAD LT without even thinking about it.

AutoCAD LT and paper

In other Windows programs, you can use any scaling factor you want to squeeze content onto paper. You've probably printed an Excel spreadsheet or Web page at some odd scaling factor, such as 82.5 percent of full size because that's what you had to do to squeeze the content onto a single sheet of paper while keeping the text as large as possible.

In drafting, your printout needs to use a specific, widely accepted scaling factor, such as ¼" = 1'–0", to be useful and understandable to others.

But the AutoCAD LT screen does not automatically enforce any one scaling factor or paper size. If you just start drawing stuff on the LT screen to fit your immediate needs, the final result unlikely fits neatly on a piece of paper at a desirable scale.

This chapter tells you how to start your drawing in such a way that you like how it ends up. With practice, this kind of approach becomes second nature.

Even if you use the Plot dialog box's Fit to Paper option, rather than a specific scale factor, to plot the drawing, you need to choose an artificial scale to make text, dimensions, and other annotations appear at a useful size. Choose a scale that's in the neighborhood of the Fit to Paper plotting factor, which AutoCAD LT displays in the Plot Scale area of the Plot dialog box. For example, if you determine that you need to squeeze your drawing down about 90 times to fit on the desired sheet size, choose a drawing scale of ⅛ inch = 1 foot – 0 inches (drawing scale factor = 96) if you're using architectural units or 1:100 (drawing scale factor = 100) for other kinds of units.

Thinking about paper

With knowledge of your industry's common drawing scales, you can choose a provisional scale based on what you're depicting. But you won't know for sure whether that scale works until you compare it with the size of the paper that you want to use for plotting your drawing. Here again, most industries use a small range of standard sheet sizes. Three common sets of sizes exist, as shown in Figure 5-2 and Table 5-2:

- ANSI (American National Standards Institute)
- Architectural
- ISO (International Organization for Standardization)

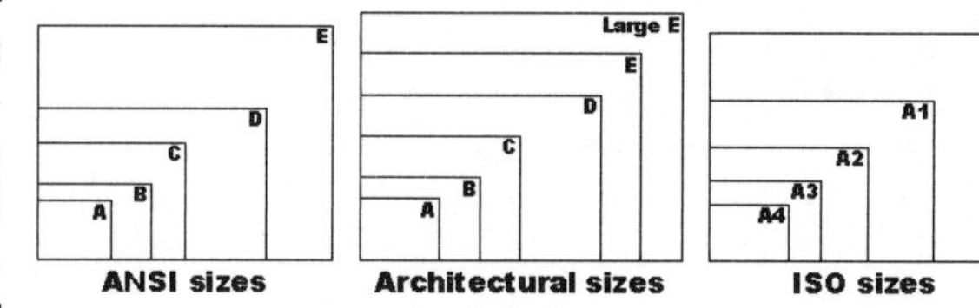

Figure 5-2: Relationships among standard paper sizes.

Table 5-2 Common Plot Sheet Sizes

Sheet Size	*Dimensions*	*Comment*
ANSI *E*	34 x 44"	
ANSI *D*	22 x 34"	*E* sheet folded in half
ANSI *C*	17 x 22"	*D* sheet folded in half
ANSI *B*	11 x 17"	*C* sheet folded in half
ANSI *A*	8½ x 11"	*B* sheet folded in half
Architectural Large *E*	36 x 48"	
Architectural *E*	30 x 42"	
Architectural *D*	24 x 36"	
Architectural *C*	18 x 24"	
Architectural *B*	12 x 18"	
Architectural *A*	9 x 12"	
ISO *A0*	841 x 1189 mm	
ISO *A1*	594 x 841 mm	*A0* sheet folded in half
ISO *A2*	420 x 594 mm	*A1* sheet folded in half
ISO *A3*	297 x 420 mm	*A2* sheet folded in half
ISO *A4*	210 x 297 mm	*A3* sheet folded in half

You select a particular set of sheet sizes based on the common practices in your industry. You then narrow down your choice based on the area required by what you're going to draw. For example, most architectural plans are plotted on Architectural D or E size sheets.

If you know the desired sheet size and drawing scale factor, you can calculate the available drawing area easily. Simply multiply each of the sheet's dimensions (X and Y) by the drawing scale factor. For example, if you choose an 11-x-17-inch sheet and a drawing scale factor of 96 (corresponding to a plot scale of ⅛" = 1'–0"), you multiply 17 times 96 and 11 times 96 to get an available drawing area of 1,632 inches x 1,056 inches (or 136 feet x 88 feet). If your sheet size is in inches but your drawing scale is in millimeters, you need to multiply by an additional 25.4 to convert from inches to millimeters. For example, with an 11-x-17-inch sheet and a scale of 1:200 (drawing scale factor = 200), you multiply 17 times 200 times 25.4 and 11 times 200 times 25.4 to get 86,360 x 55,880 mm or 86.36 x 55.88 m — not quite big enough for a football field (United States *or* European football).

Conversely, if you know the sheet size that you're going to use and the real-world size of what you're going to draw, and you want to find out the largest plot scale you can use, you have to divide, not multiply. Divide the needed real-world drawing area dimensions (X and Y) by the sheet's dimensions (X and Y). Take the larger number — either X or Y — and round up to the nearest real drawing scale factor (that is, one that's commonly used in your industry). For example, suppose you want to draw a 60-x-40-foot or, 720-x-480-inch, floor plan and print it on 11-x-17-inch paper. You divide 720 by 17 and 480 by 11 to get 42.35 and 43.64, respectively. The larger number, 43.64, corresponds in this example to the short dimension of the house and the paper. The nearest larger common architectural drawing scale factor is 48 (corresponding to ¼" = 1'–0"), which leaves a little room for the plotting margin and title block.

The Cheat Sheet at the front of this book includes two tables that list the available drawing areas for a range of sheet sizes and drawing scales. Use those tables to help you decide on an appropriate paper size and drawing scale, and revert to the calculation method for situations that the tables don't cover. (If you don't keep a favorite old calculator on your physical desktop, this time might be good to put a shortcut to the Windows Calculator on your virtual one.)

When you select a sheet size and drawing scale, always leave some extra room for the following two reasons:

- Most plotters and printers can't print all the way to the edge of the sheet — they require a small margin. For example, my trusty old Hewlett-Packard LaserJet III has a printable area of about 7.9 x 10.5 inches on an 8.5-x-11-inch ANSI A size (letter size) sheet. (You find this information in the ToolTip that pops up when you point to the postage stamp-sized preview that appears in the Plot dialog box; see Chapter 12 for details.) If you're a stickler for precision, you can use the printable area instead of the physical sheet area in the calculations I describe earlier in this section.

- Most drawings require some annotations — text, grid bubbles, and so on — outside the objects you're drawing, plus a title block surrounding the objects and annotations. If you don't leave some room for the annotations and title block, you end up having either to cram things together too much or to change to a different sheet size. Either way, you're slowed down later in the project when you can least afford it. Figure 5-3 shows an extreme example of selecting a sheet size that's too small or, conversely, a drawing scale that's too large. In this example, the building is too long for the sheet, and it overlaps the title block on both the right and left sides.

Some industries deal with the "sheet-is-too-small / drawing-scale-is-too-large" problem by breaking drawings up onto multiple plotted sheets.

Don't be afraid to *start* with paper. Experienced drafters often make a quick, throwaway pencil and paper sketch called a *cartoon*. A drawing cartoon usually includes a rectangle indicating the sheet of paper you intend to plot on, a sketch of the title block, and a very rough, schematic sketch of the thing you're going to draw. Scribbling down the dimensions of the sheet, the main title block areas, and the major objects you need to draw helps. By sketching out a cartoon, you often catch scale or paper size problems before you set up a drawing, when repairs only take a few minutes, and not after you create the drawing, when fixing the problem can take hours.

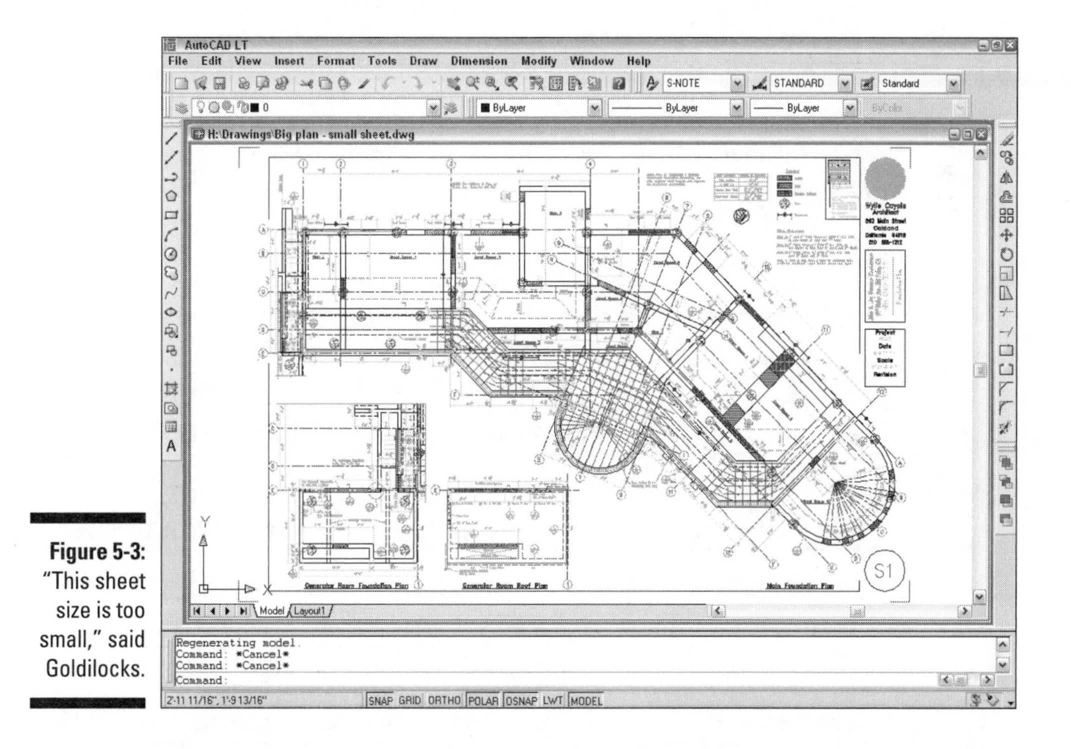

Figure 5-3: "This sheet size is too small," said Goldilocks.

Defending your border

The next decision to make is what kind of border your drawing deserves. The options include a full-blown title block, a simple rectangle, or nothing at all around your drawing. If you need a title block, do you have one, can you borrow an existing one, or do you need to draw one from scratch? Although you can draw title block geometry in an individual drawing, you save time by reusing the same title block for multiple drawings. Your company may already have a standard title block drawing ready to use, or someone else who's working on your project may have created one for the project.

The right way to draw a title block is in a separate DWG file at its normal plotted size (for example, 36 inches long by 24 inches high for an architectural D size title block). You then either insert or xref the title block drawing into each sheet drawing. Chapter 13 describes how to insert and xref separate DWG files.

All system variables go

As Chapter 2 describes, AutoCAD LT includes a slew of *system variables* that control the way your drawing and the LT program work. Much of the drawing setup process involves setting system variables based on the drawing scale, sheet size, and other desired properties of the drawing. You can set some system variables in AutoCAD LT dialog boxes, but a few require that you type at the command line. Table 5-3 shows the settings that you most commonly need to change — or at least check — during drawing setup, along with the names of the corresponding system variables. Later in the chapter, in the section "Master Model Space," I show you the procedure for changing these settings.

Table 5-3 System Variables for Drawing Setup

Setting	*Dialog Box*	*System Variables*
Linear units and precision	Drawing Units	LUNITS, LUPREC
Angular units and precision	Drawing Units	AUNITS, AUPREC
Grid spacing and visibility	Drafting Settings	GRIDUNIT, GRIDMODE
Snap spacing and on/off	Drafting Settings	SNAPUNIT, SNAPMODE
Drawing limits	None (use command line)	LIMMIN, LIMMAX
Linetype scale	Linetype Manager	LTSCALE, PSLTSCALE
Dimension scale	Dimension Style Manager	DIMSCALE

Drawing scale versus drawing scale factor

CAD users employ two different ways of talking about a drawing's intended plot scale: drawing scale and drawing scale factor.

Drawing scale is the traditional way of describing a scale — traditional in that it existed long before CAD came to be. Drawing scales are expressed with an equal sign or colon; for example ⅛" = 1'–0", 1 = 20, or 2:1. Translate the equal sign or colon as "corresponds to." In all cases, the measurement to the left of the equal sign or colon indicates a paper measurement, and the number to the right indicates a CAD drawing and real-world measurement. In other words, the architectural scale ⅛" = 1'–0" means "⅛" on the plotted drawing corresponds to 1'–0" in the CAD drawing and in the real world," assuming that the plot was made at the proper scale.

Drawing scale factor is a single number that represents a multiplier, such as 96, 20, or 0.5. The drawing scale factor for a drawing is the conversion factor between a measurement on the plot and a measurement in a CAD drawing and the real world.

Those of you who did your math homework in junior high realize that drawing scale and drawing scale factor are two interchangeable ways of describing the same relationship. The drawing scale factor is the multiplier that converts the first number in the drawing scale into the second number.

Starting with a Template

When you start AutoCAD LT with its desktop shortcut or from the Windows Start menu, LT creates a new, blank drawing based on the default template drawing — Aclt.dwt for imperial units or Acltiso.dwt for metric units. When you explicitly create a new drawing from within LT, the Select Template dialog box, shown in Figure 5-4, appears by default so that you can choose a template on which to base your new drawing.

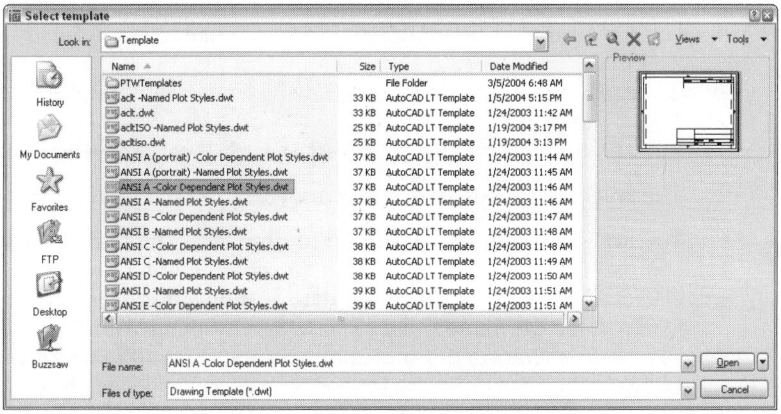

Figure 5-4: A plateful of templates to contemplate.

If you see a dialog box titled Startup instead of Select Template when you create a new drawing, click OK to dismiss the dialog box. Then choose Tools➪Options, click the System tab, and change the Startup setting to `Do not show a startup dialog`. This setting gives you more options for using templates, which you'll eventually need.

A *template* is simply a drawing whose name ends in the letters DWT, which you use as the starting point for another drawing. When you create a new drawing from a template, AutoCAD LT makes a copy of the template file and opens the copy in a new drawing editor window. The first time you save the file, you're prompted for a new filename to save to; the original template file stays unchanged.

You may be familiar with the Microsoft Word or Excel template documents, and AutoCAD LT template drawings work pretty much the same way — because Autodesk stole the idea from them! (Encouraged, of course, by Microsoft.)

Using a suitable template can save you time and worry because many of the setup options are already set correctly for you. You know the drawing will print correctly; you just have to worry about getting the geometry and text right. Of course, all this optimism assumes that the person who set up the template knew what he or she was doing.

The stock templates that come with AutoCAD LT are okay as a starting point, but you need to modify them to suit your purposes, or create your own from scratch. In particular, the stock LT templates aren't set up for the scales that you want to use. The instructions in the rest of this chapter tell you how to specify scale-dependent setup information.

So the only problems with templates are creating good ones and then later finding the right one to use when you need it. Later in this chapter, in the section "Making Your Own Templates," I show you how to create templates from your own setup drawings. Here I show you how to use an already created template, such as one of the templates that comes with AutoCAD LT or from one of your CAD-savvy colleagues. If you're lucky, someone in your office created suitable templates that you can use to get going quickly.

Follow these steps to create a new drawing from a template drawing:

1. **Run the New command by pressing Ctrl+N or choosing File➪New.**

   The Select Template dialog box appears.

   The first button on the Standard toolbar runs the QNEW ("Quick NEW") command instead of the ordinary New command. Unless you or someone else changed the Drawing Template Settings in the Options dialog box, QNEW does the same thing as New. See "Making Your Own Templates," later in this chapter, for information about how to take advantage of QNEW.

2. **Select the name of the template that you want to use as the starting point for your new drawing.**
3. **Click the Open button.**

   A new drawing window with a temporary name, such as `Drawing2.dwg`, appears. (The template you open remains unchanged on your hard drive.)

   Depending on which template you choose, your new drawing may open with a paper space layout tab, not the Model tab, selected. If that's the case, click the Model tab before changing the settings described in "Master Model Space." The section "A Layout Later?," later in this chapter, describes how to set up and take advantage of paper space layouts.

4. **Click the Save button on the Standard toolbar and save the file under a new name.**

   Take the time to save the drawing to the appropriate name and location now.

5. **Make needed changes.**

   For most of the templates that come with AutoCAD LT, you need to consider changing the units, limits, grid and snap settings, linetype scale, and dimension scale. See the section, "Master Model Space," for instructions.

6. **Consider saving the file as a template.**

   If you'll need other drawings in the future similar to the current one, consider saving your modified template as a template in its own right. See the section "Making Your Own Templates" later in this chapter.

   The simplest, no-frills templates are `Aclt.dwt` (for people who customarily work with sheet sizes expressed in inches) and `Acltiso.dwt` (for people who customarily work with sheet sizes expressed in millimeters). Most of the remaining templates that come with AutoCAD LT include title blocks for various sizes of sheets. In addition, most templates come in two versions — one for people who use color-dependent plotstyles and one for people who use namedplotstyles. You probably want the color-dependent versions. (Chapter 12 describes the two kinds of plotstyles and why you probably want the color-dependent variety.) I warned you that this drawing setup stuff is complicated!

If you dig around in the Options dialog box, you may discover a setting that turns on the old Startup dialog box, which offers several options other than starting with a template. Among these options are the enticingly named *Setup Wizards.* These so-called wizards were lame when they first appeared; they're no better now. Autodesk acknowledges as much by making them almost impossible to find in AutoCAD LT 2005.

Master Model Space

Most drawings require a two-part setup:

1. Set up the model space tab, where you create most of your drawing.
2. Create one or more paper space layout tabs for plotting.

After you decide on drawing scale and sheet size, you can perform model space setup as I describe in this section.

Setting your units

First, you set the linear and angular units that you want to use in your new drawing. The following steps describe how:

1. **Choose Format⇨Units from the menu bar.**

   The Drawing Units dialog box appears, as shown in Figure 5-5.

2. **Choose a linear unit type from the Length Type drop-down list.**

   Choose the type of unit representation that's appropriate for your work. Engineering and Architectural units display in feet and inches; the other types of units aren't tied to any particular unit of measurement. You decide whether each unit represents a millimeter, centimeter, meter, inch, foot, or something else. Decimal units usually are a good choice for metric drawings.

   AutoCAD LT can think in inches! If you're using Engineering or Architectural units (feet and inches), LT understands any coordinate you enter as a number of inches. You use the ' (apostrophe) character on your keyboard to indicate a number in feet instead of inches.

Figure 5-5: The default unitless units.

3. **From the Length Precision drop-down list, choose the degree of precision you want when AutoCAD LT displays coordinates and linear measurements.**

The precision setting controls how precisely LT displays coordinates, distances, and prompts in some dialog boxes. In particular, the Coordinates box on the status bar displays the current cursor coordinates, using the current precision. A *grosser* — that is, less precise — precision setting makes the numbers displayed in the status bar more readable and less jumpy. So be gross for now; you can always act a little less gross later.

The linear and angular precision settings only affect LT's *display* of coordinates, distances, and angles on the status bar, in dialog boxes, and in the command line area. For drawings stored as DWG files, AutoCAD LT always uses maximum precision to store the locations and sizes of all objects that you draw. In addition, LT provides separate settings for controlling the precision of dimension text — see Chapter 10 for details.

4. **Choose an angular unit type from the Angle Type drop-down list.**

   Decimal Degrees and Deg/Min/Sec are the most common choices.

   The Clockwise check box and the Direction button provide additional angle measurement options, but you rarely need to change the default settings: Measure angles counterclockwise and use east as the 0 degree direction.

5. **From the Angle Precision drop-down list, choose the degree of precision you want when AutoCAD LT displays angular measurements.**

6. **In the Drag-and-Drop Scale area, choose the units of measurement for this drawing.**

   Choose your base unit for this drawing — that is, the real-world distance represented by one AutoCAD LT unit.

7. **Click OK to exit the dialog box and save your settings.**

Telling your drawing its limits

The next model space setup task is to set your drawing's *limits*. You don't want it staying out all night and hanging out with just anybody, do you? The limits represent the rectangular working area that you draw on, which usually corresponds to the paper size. Setting limits correctly gives you the following advantages:

- When you turn on the grid (described in the section, "Making the drawing area snap-py (and grid-dy)," later in this chapter), the grid displays in the rectangular limits area. With the grid on and the limits set correctly, you always see the working area that corresponds to what you eventually plot, so you won't accidentally color outside the lines.

- The ZOOM command's All option zooms to the greater of the limits or the drawing extents. (The extents of a drawing consist of a rectangular area just large enough to include all the objects in the drawing.) When you set limits properly and color within the lines, ZOOM All gives you a quick way to zoom to your working area.
- If you plot from model space, you can choose to plot the limits area. This option gives you a quick, reliable way to plot your drawing, but only if you set limits correctly!

Many CAD drafters don't set limits properly in their drawings. After you read this section, you can smugly tell them why they should and how.

You can start the LIMITS command from a menu choice, but all subsequent action takes place on the command line; despite the importance of the topic, AutoCAD LT has no dialog box for setting limits.

The following steps show you how to set your drawing limits:

1. **Choose Format⇨Drawing Limits from the menu bar to start the LIMITS command.**

   The LIMITS command appears on the command line, and the command line displays the following prompt at the bottom of the screen:

   ```
   Command: limits
   Reset Model space limits:
   Specify lower left corner or [ON/OFF] <0.000,0.0000>:
   ```

   The value at the end of the last line of the prompt is the default value for the lower-left corner of the drawing limits. It appears according to the units and precision that you select in the Drawing Units dialog box — for example, `0'-0"` if you select Architectural units with precision to the nearest inch.

2. **Type the lower-left corner of the limits you want to use and press Enter.**

   The usual value to enter at this point is **0,0**. (Type a zero, a comma, and then another zero, with no spaces.) You can just press Enter to accept the default value.

   LT now prompts you for the upper-right corner of the limits:

   ```
   Specify upper right corner <12.0000,9.0000>:
   ```

   The initial units offered by AutoCAD LT correspond to an architectural A size sheet of paper in landscape orientation. (Almost no one uses Architectural A size paper; here's a classic example of a programmer choosing a silly default that no one has bothered to change in 22 years!)

3. **Type the upper-right corner of the limits you want to use and press Enter.**

   You calculate the usual setting for the limits upper-right corner by multiplying the paper dimensions by the drawing scale factor. For example, if you're setting up a ⅛" = 1'–0" drawing (drawing scale factor = 96) to be plotted on a 24-x-36-inch sheet in landscape orientation, the upper-right corner of the limits are 36 inches times 96, 24 inches times 96. Okay, pencils down. The correct answer is 3456,2304 (or 288 feet, 192 feet).

   TIP: Alternatively, you can cheat when specifying limits and read the limits from the tables on the Cheat Sheet.

   If you have the grid turned on, AutoCAD LT redisplays it in the new limits area after you press Enter.

   WARNING! If you're using Architectural or Engineering units and you want to enter measurements in feet and not inches, you must add the foot designator after the number, such as **6'**; otherwise, LT assumes that you mean inches.

4. **Choose View➪Zoom➪All.**

   LT zooms to the new limits.

Making the drawing area snap-py (and grid-dy)

AutoCAD LT's *grid* is a set of evenly spaced, visible dots that serve as a visual distance reference. (As I describe in "Telling your drawing its limits," earlier in this section, the grid also indicates how far the drawing limits extend.) LT's *snap* feature creates a set of evenly spaced, invisible hot spots, which make the cursor move in nice, even increments. Both grid and snap are like the intersection points of the lines on a piece of grid paper, but grid is simply a visual reference, whereas snap constrains the points that you can pick with the mouse. You can — and usually do — set the grid and snap spacing to different distances.

Set the grid and the snap intervals in the Drafting Settings dialog box with these steps:

1. **Right-click the Snap or Grid button on the status bar and choose Settings.**

   The Drafting Settings dialog box appears with the Snap and Grid tab selected, as shown in Figure 5-6.

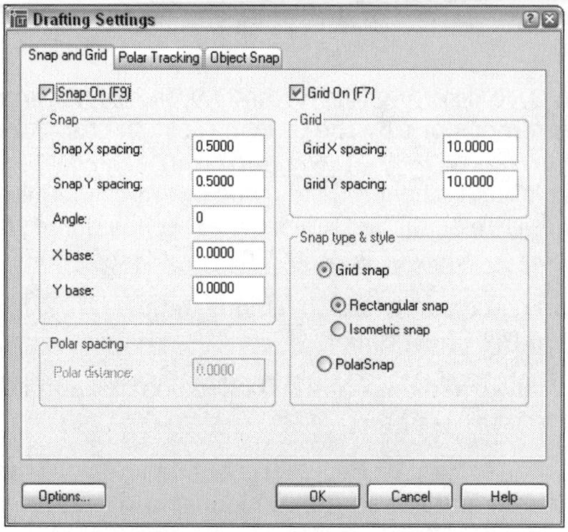

Figure 5-6: Get your Drafting Settings here!

The Snap and Grid tab has four parts, but the Snap and Grid sections are all you need to worry about for most drafting work.

2. **Select the Snap On check box to turn on snap.**

   This action creates default snaps half a unit apart.

3. **Enter the Snap X Spacing for the snap interval in the accompanying text box.**

   Use the information in the sections preceding this section to decide on a reasonable snap spacing.

   The Y spacing automatically changes to equal the X spacing, which is almost always what you want.

4. **Select the Grid On check box to turn on the grid.**
5. **Enter the Grid X Spacing for the grid in the accompanying text box.**

   Use the information in the sections preceding this section to decide on a reasonable grid spacing.

   The Y spacing automatically changes to equal the X spacing. As with the snap spacing, you usually want to leave it that way.

   X measures horizontal distance; Y measures vertical distance. The AutoCAD LT drawing area normally shows an X and Y icon in case you forget.

6. **Click OK to close the Drafting Settings dialog box.**

You also can click the SNAP button on the status bar to toggle snap on and off; the same goes for the GRID button and the grid setting.

Setting linetype and dimension scales

Even though you engraved the drawing scale factor on your desk and wrote it on your hand — not vice versa — AutoCAD LT doesn't know the drawing scale until you enter it. Keeping LT in the dark is fine as long as you're just drawing continuous lines and curves representing real-world geometry, because you draw these objects at their real-world size, without worrying about plot scale.

Making snap (and grid) decisions

You can set your grid spacing to work in one of two ways: to help with your drawing or to help you remain aware of how objects relate to your plot. For *a grid that helps with your drawing,* set the grid points a logical number of measurement units apart. For example, you might set the grid to 30 feet (10 yards) on a drawing of a (U.S.) football field. This kind of setting makes your work easier as you draw.

Another approach is to choose *a grid spacing that represents a specific distance,* such as 1 inch or 25 millimeters, on your final plot. If you want the grid to represent 1 inch on the plot and your drawing units are inches, enter the drawing scale factor. For example, in a ¼" = 1'–0" drawing, you enter the drawing scale factor of 48. A 48-inch grid interval in your drawing corresponds to a 1-inch interval on the plot when you plot to scale. If your drawing units are millimeters and you want the grid to represent 25 millimeters on the plot, enter the drawing scale factor times 25. For example, in a 1:50 drawing, you enter 25 x 50, or 1250.

In most cases, you want to set the snap interval considerably smaller than the grid spacing. A good rule is to start with a snap spacing in the range of the size of the smallest objects that you are drawing — 6 inches or 100 millimeters for a building plan, 0.5 inches or 5 millimeters for an architectural detail, ⅟16 inch or 1 millimeter for a small mechanical component, and so on.

Leaving the grid on in your drawing all the time is worthwhile because it provides a visual reminder of how far apart things are. This visual reference is especially useful as you zoom in and out.

You don't always want to leave snap turned on, however. Some drawings, such as contour maps, are made up mostly of objects with weird, uneven measurements. Even drawings with many objects that fall on convenient spacings have some unruly objects that don't. In addition, you sometimes need to turn off snap temporarily to select objects. Despite these caveats, snap is a useful tool in most drawings.

Setting the snap spacing to a reasonable value when you set up a new drawing is a good idea. Toggle snap off (by clicking the SNAP button on the status bar or pressing the F9 key) when you don't need it or find that it's getting in the way. Toggle snap on before drawing objects that align with specific spacings, including text and dimension strings that you want to align neatly.

To use snap effectively, you need to make the snap setting smaller as you zoom in and work on more detailed areas, and larger as you zoom back out. You are likely to find yourself changing the snap setting fairly frequently. The grid setting, on the other hand, can usually remain constant even as you work at different zoom settings; that keeps you oriented as to how far zoomed in you are in the drawing.

As soon as you start adding dimensions (measurements that show the size of the things you're drawing) and using dash-dot linetypes (line patterns that contain gaps in them), you need to tell AutoCAD LT how to scale the parts of the dimensions and the gaps in the linetypes based on the plot scale. If you forget this information, the dimension text and arrowheads can come out very tiny or very large when you plot the drawing, and dash-dot linetype patterns can look waaaay too big or too small. Figure 5-7 shows what I mean.

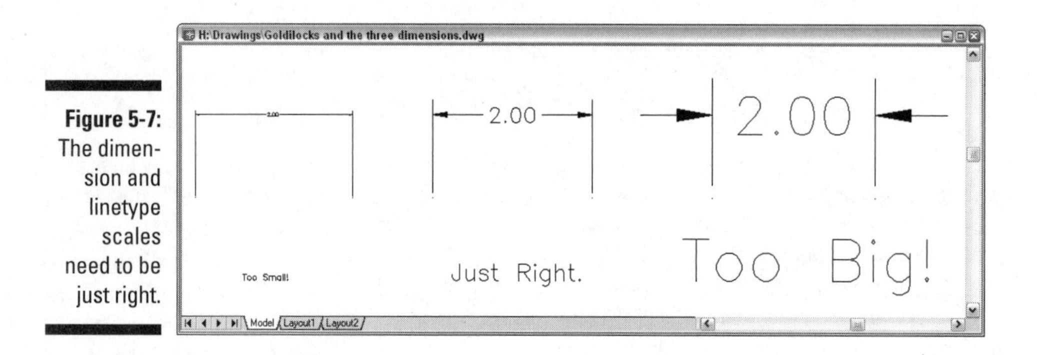

Figure 5-7: The dimension and linetype scales need to be just right.

You can find the scale factor that controls dash-dot linetypes in a system variable called *LTSCALE* (as in LineType SCALE). Find the scaling factor that controls dimensions in a system variable called *DIMSCALE.* You can change either of these settings at any time, but setting them correctly when you're setting up the drawing is best.

The following sequence includes directions for typing system variable and command names. When the names are mixed case (for example, LTScale), you can type the full name (**LTSCALE**) or just the letters shown in uppercase (**LTS**) before pressing Enter.

To set the linetype scale from the command line, follow these steps:

1. **Type** LTScale **on the command line and press Enter.**

   AutoCAD LT responds with a prompt, asking you for the scale factor. The value at the end of the prompt is the current linetype scale setting, as in the following example:

   ```
   Enter new linetype scale factor <1.0000>:
   ```

2. **Type the value you want for the linetype scale on the command line and press Enter.**

   The easiest choice is to set the linetype scale to the drawing scale factor. Some people (myself included) find that the dashes and gaps in dash-dot linetypes get a bit too long when they use the drawing scale factor. If you're one of those people, set LTSCALE to one-half of the drawing scale factor.

Alternatively, you can set LTSCALE in the Linetype Manager dialog box: Choose Format➪Linetype, click the Show Details button, and type your desired linetype scale in the Global Scale Factor text box.

To change the dimension scale, use the Dimension Style Manager dialog box. I describe dimensions in detail in Chapter 10, but you should get in the habit of setting the dimension scale during drawing setup. To do so, follow these steps:

1. **Choose Format➪Dimension Style from the menu bar, or click the Dimension Style Manager button on the Styles toolbar.**

   The Dimension Style Manager dialog box appears. New drawings contain the default dimension style named Standard (for English units drawings) or ISO-25 (for metric drawings).

2. **Click the Modify button.**

   The Modify Dimension Style dialog box appears.

3. **Click the Fit tab.**

   The Fit tab options appear, including a Scale for Dimension Features area.

4. **In the Scale for Dimension Features area, make sure that the Use Overall Scale Of radio button is selected.**

5. **In the Use Overall Scale Of text box, type the drawing scale factor for the current drawing.**

   I told you that you use that drawing scale factor a lot!

6. **Click OK to close the Modify Dimension Style dialog box.**

   The Dimension Style Manager dialog box reappears.

7. **Click Close.**

   The Dimension Style Manager dialog box closes. Now when you draw dimensions (see Chapter 10), AutoCAD LT scales the dimension text and arrowheads correctly.

Before you start creating dimensions, create your own dimension style(s) for the settings that you want to use. Chapter 10 explains why and how.

Entering drawing properties

You need to do one last bit of bookkeeping before you finish the model space drawing setup: Enter summary information in the Drawing Properties dialog box, as shown in Figure 5-8. Choose File➪Drawing Properties to open the Drawing Properties dialog box and then click the Summary tab. Enter the drawing scale you're using and the drawing scale factor, plus any other information you think useful.

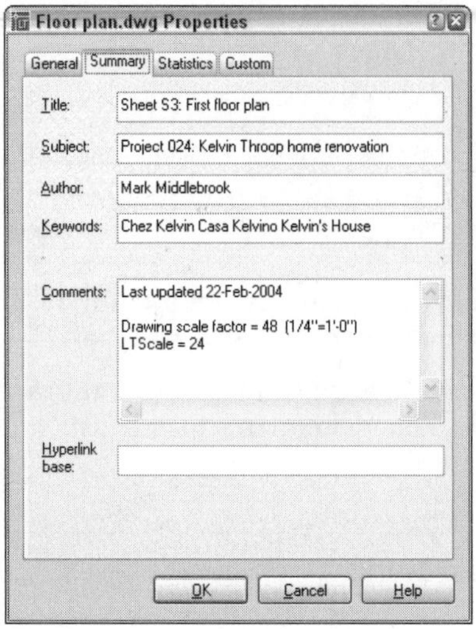

Figure 5-8: Surveying your drawing's properties.

A Layout Later?

As I describe in Chapter 2, *paper space* is a separate space in each drawing for composing a printed version of that drawing. You create the drawing itself, called the *model,* in *model space*. You then can create one or more plottable views, complete with title block. Each of these plottable views is called a *layout*. AutoCAD LT saves separate plot settings with each layout — and with the Model tab — so that you can plot each tab differently. In practice, you probably need to use only one of the paper space layout tabs.

A screen image is worth a thousand paper space explanations. If you haven't yet seen an example out in the wild, take a look at Figures 2-7 and 2-8 in Chapter 2. You also may want to open a few of the AutoCAD LT 2005 sample drawings and click the Model and layout tabs to witness the variety of ways in which AutoCAD LT uses paper space. A good place to start is `\Program Files\AutoCAD LT 2005\Sample\planta.dwg`.

At some point after you complete model space setup, you need to create a layout for plotting. You don't need to create the plotting layout right after you create the drawing and do model space setup; you can wait until after you draw some geometry. You should set up a layout sooner, not later, however. If any scale or sheet size problems exist, discovering them early is better.

In AutoCAD LT 2005, you can still ignore paper space layouts entirely and do all your drawing *and* plotting in model space. But you owe it to yourself to give layouts a try. You'll probably find that they make plotting more consistent and predictable. They certainly give you more plotting flexibility when you need it. And you'll certainly encounter drawings from other people that make extensive use of paper space, so you need to understand it if you plan to exchange drawings with anyone else.

Creating a layout

Creating a simple paper space layout is straightforward, thanks to the AutoCAD LT Create Layout Wizard, shown in Figure 5-9. (Yes! Finally, a useful LT wizard.) The command name is LAYOUTWIZARD, which is not to be confused with the WAYOUTLIZARD command for drawing geckos and iguanas! In any event, you can avoid a lot of typing by choosing Tools⇨Wizards⇨Create Layout.

Figure 5-9: The Create Layout Wizard.

Although the Create Layout Wizard guides you step by step through the process of creating a paper space layout from scratch, it doesn't eliminate the necessity of coming up with a sensible set of layout parameters. The sheet size and plot scale that you choose provide a certain amount of space for showing your model (see the information earlier in this chapter), and wizards aren't allowed to bend the laws of arithmetic to escape that fact. For example, a map of Texas at a scale of 1 inch = 1 foot doesn't fit on an 8½-x-11-inch sheet, no way, no how. In other words, garbage in, garbage (lay)out. Fortunately the Create Layout Wizard lends itself to experimentation, and you can easily delete layouts that don't work.

Follow these steps to create a layout:

1. **Choose Tools⇨Wizards⇨Create Layout.**
2. **Give the new layout a name and then click Next.**

   In place of the default name, Layout3, I recommend something more descriptive — for example, *D Size Sheet.*
3. **Choose a printer or plotter to use when plotting this layout, and then click Next.**

   Think of your choice as the *default* plotter for this layout. You can change to a different plotter later, or create page setups that plot the same layout on different plotters.

   Many of the names in the configured plotter list probably look familiar because they're your Windows printers (*system printers* in AutoCAD lingo). Names with a PC3 extension represent nonsystem (that is, AutoCAD LT-specific) printer drivers or configurations. See Chapter 12 for details.
4. **Choose a paper size and specify whether to use inches or millimeters to represent paper units, and then click Next.**

   The available paper sizes depend on the printer or plotter that you selected in Step 3.
5. **Specify the orientation of the drawing on the paper, and then click Next.**

   The icon showing the letter *A* on the piece of paper shows you which orientation is which.
6. **Select a title block or None (see Figure 5-10), and then click Next.**

   If you choose a title block, specify whether AutoCAD LT inserts it as a Block — which is preferable in this case — or attach it as an xref.

Figure 5-10: Title block options in the Create Layout Wizard.

Attaching a title block as an xref is a good practice if your title block DWG file is in the same folder as the drawing that you're working on. The Create Layout Wizard's title blocks live in the Template folder that's stored with the AutoCAD LT Application Data files under your Windows user profile, which isn't — or shouldn't be — where you keep your project files. Thus, in this case Block is a safer choice.

Choose a title block that fits your paper size. If the title block is larger than the paper, the Create Layout Wizard simply lets it run off the paper.

If you don't like any of the supplied title blocks, choose None. You can always draw, insert, or xref a title block later. See Chapter 13 for information about inserting or xrefing a title block.

The list of available title blocks comes from all the DWG files in your AutoCAD LT Template folder. You can add custom title block drawings to this directory (and delete ones that you never use). If you want to know where to put them, see "Making Your Own Templates," later in this chapter.

7. **Define the arrangement of viewports that AutoCAD LT creates, and the paper space to model space scale for all viewports. Then click Next.**

   A paper space layout viewport is a window into model space. You must create at least one viewport to display the model in your new layout. For most 2D drawings, a single viewport is all you need. 3D models often benefit from multiple viewports, each showing the 3D model from a different perspective.

   The default Viewport scale, Scaled to Fit, ensures that all of your model drawing displays in the viewport but results in an arbitrary scale factor. Most technical drawings require a specific scale, such as 1:10 or ⅛" = 1'–0".

8. **Specify the location of the viewport(s) on the paper by picking its corners. Then click Next.**

   After you click the Select Location button, the Create Layout Wizard displays the preliminary layout with any title block that you've chosen. Pick two points to define a rectangle that falls within the drawing area of your title block (or within the plottable area of the sheet, if you chose no title block in Step 6).

   AutoCAD LT represents the plottable area of the sheet with a dashed rectangle near the edge of the sheet. If you don't select a location for the viewport(s), the Create Layout Wizard creates a viewport that fills the plottable area of the sheet.

9. **Click Finish.**

   LT creates the new layout.

Copying and changing layouts

After you create a layout, you can delete, copy, rename, and otherwise manipulate it by right-clicking its tab. Figure 5-11 shows the right-click menu options.

The From Template option refers to layout templates. After you create layouts in a template (DWT) or drawing (DWG) file, you use the From Template option to import these layouts into the current drawing. For details, look up the LAYOUT command's Template option in the Command Reference section of the AutoCAD LT online help.

Many drawings require only one paper space layout. If you always plot the same view of the model and always plot to the same device and on the same size paper, a single paper space layout suffices. If you want to plot your model in different ways (for example, at different scales, with different layers visible, with different areas visible, or with different plotted line characteristics), you may want to create additional paper space layouts.

You can handle plotting the same model in a single paper space layout with different page setups in different ways. See Chapter 12 for details.

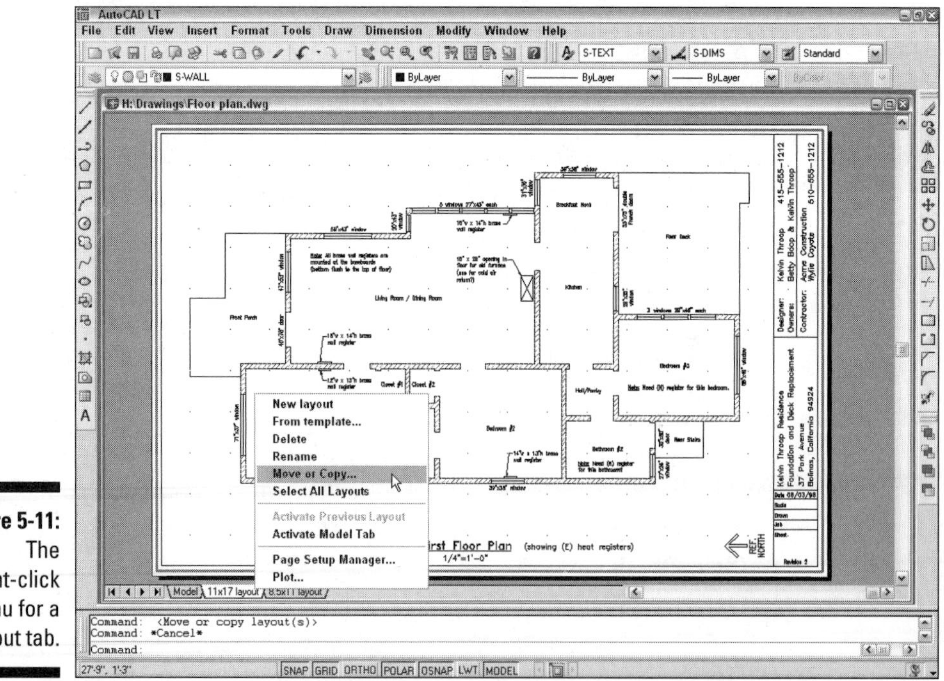

Figure 5-11: The right-click menu for a layout tab.

If you want to add another viewport to an existing layout, use the Viewports toolbar to create and scale it. (To turn on the Viewports toolbar, right-click a button on any toolbar and choose Viewports.) Click the Single Viewport button to create a viewport. Double-click inside the new viewport and then use the Viewport Scale Control drop-down list to scale the Viewport.

Where's my tab?

After you create a paper space layout, you suddenly have two views of the same drawing geometry: the view on your original Model tab and the new layout tab view (perhaps decorated with a handsome title block and other accoutrements of plotting nobility). You must realize that both views are of the *same* geometry. If you change the model geometry on one tab, you're changing it on all tabs because all tabs display the same model space objects. It's like seeing double after downing a few too many drinks — the duplication is in your head, not in the real world (or in this case, in the CAD world).

When you make a paper space layout current by clicking its tab, you can move the cursor between paper space (that is, drawing and zooming on the sheet of paper) and model space (drawing and zooming on the model, inside the viewport) in several ways, including:

- Clicking the PAPER/MODEL button on the status bar
- In the drawing area, double-clicking over a viewport to move the cursor into model space in that viewport, or double-clicking outside all viewports (for example, in the gray area outside the sheet) to move the cursor into paper space

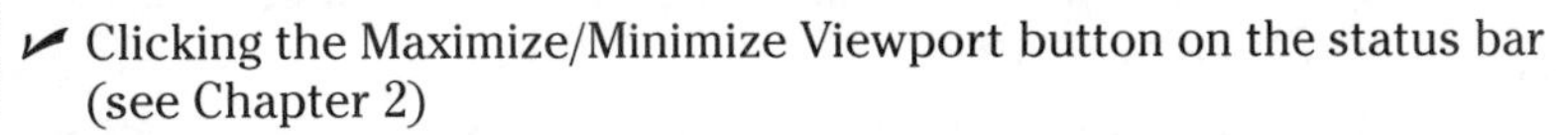

- Clicking the Maximize/Minimize Viewport button on the status bar (see Chapter 2)

When the cursor is in model space, anything you draw or edit changes the model (and thus appears on the Model tab and on all paper space layout tabs, assuming that the given paper space layout displays that part of the underlying model). When the cursor is in paper space, anything you draw appears only on that one paper space layout tab. It's as though you're drawing on an acetate sheet over the top of that sheet of plotter paper — the model beneath remains unaffected.

This distinction can be disorienting at first — even if you haven't had a few too many drinks. To avoid confusion, stick with the following approach (at least until you're more familiar with paper space):

- If you want to edit the model, switch to the Model tab first. (Don't try to edit the model in a paper space viewport.)
- If you want to edit a particular plot layout without affecting the model, switch to that layout's tab and make sure that the cursor is in paper space.

Making Your Own Templates

You can create a template from any DWG file by using the Save As dialog box. Follow these steps to save your drawing as a template:

1. **Choose File➪Save As from the menu bar.**

   The Save Drawing As dialog box appears, as shown in Figure 5-12.

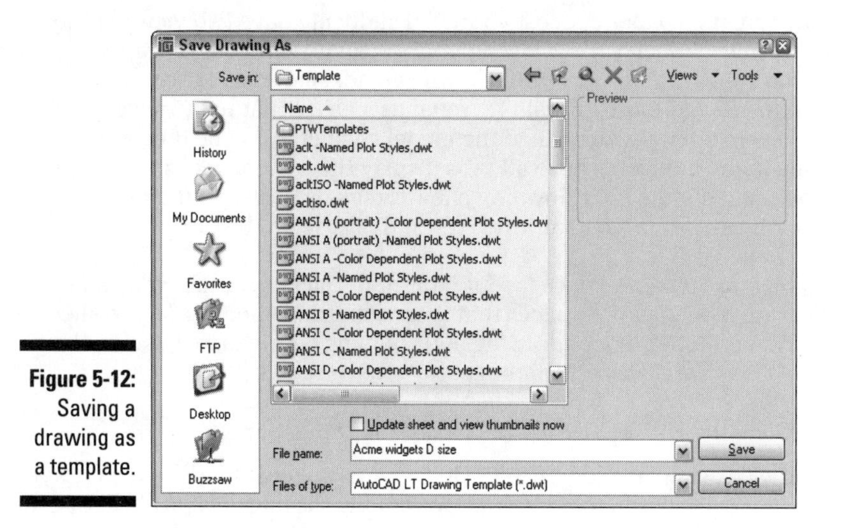

Figure 5-12: Saving a drawing as a template.

2. **From the Save As Type pull-down menu, choose AutoCAD LT Drawing Template (*.dwt).**
3. **Navigate to the folder where you want to store the drawing.**

   AutoCAD LT 2005's default folder for template drawings is called Template and is buried deep in the bowels of your Windows user profile. Save your templates there if you want them to appear in LT's Select Template list. You can save your templates in another folder, but if you want to use them later, you have to navigate to that folder each time to use them. See the Technical Stuff paragraph after these steps for additional suggestions.
4. **Enter a name for the drawing template in the File Name text box.**
5. **Click the Save button to save your drawing template.**

   The drawing is saved as a template. A dialog box for the template description and units appears.

6. **Enter the template's measurement units (English or Metric).**

   Enter the key info now; you can't do it later unless you save the template to a different name. Don't bother filling in the Description field. AutoCAD LT doesn't display it later in the Select Template dialog box.

7. **Click OK to save the file.**

8. **To save your drawing as a regular drawing, choose File➪Save As from the menu bar.**

   The Save Drawing As dialog box appears again.

9. **From the Save As Type pull-down menu, choose AutoCAD LT 2004/ AutoCAD 2004 Drawing (*.dwg).**

   AutoCAD and LT 2005 use the same DWG file format as AutoCAD and LT 2004, so the file type is listed that way.

10. **Navigate to the folder where you want to store the drawing.**

    Use a different folder from the one with your template drawings.

11. **Enter the name of the drawing in the File Name text box.**

12. **Click the Save button to save your drawing.**

    The file is saved. Now, when you save it in the future, the regular file, not the template file, gets updated.

AutoCAD LT includes a command called QNEW ("Quick NEW"), which, when properly configured, can bypass the Select Template dialog box and create a new drawing from your favorite template. The first button on the Standard toolbar — the one with the plain white sheet of paper — runs the new QNEW command instead of the old New command.

To put the Quick into QNEW, though, you have to tell AutoCAD LT which default template to use: Choose Tools➪Options➪Files➪Drawing Template Settings➪Default Template File for QNEW. AutoCAD LT's default setting for Default Template File for QNEW is None, which causes QNEW to act just like New (that is, QNEW opens the Select Template dialog box).

AutoCAD LT 2005 stores template drawings and many other support files under your Windows user folder. If you want to discover where your Template folder is, choose Tools➪Options➪Files➪Drawing Template Settings➪Drawing Template File Location. In all likelihood, your Template folder lives under a hidden folder, so you can't at first see it in Windows Explorer. If you want to find the template folder, choose Tools➪Folder Options➪View in Windows Explorer. Set the Hidden Files and Folders setting to Show Hidden Files and Folders, click the OK button, and then choose View➪Refresh. (After you snoop around, you'll probably want to switch back to Do Not Show Hidden Files and Folders.)

If you want to avoid this nonsense, create a folder where you can find it easily (for example, `C:\Acad-templates` or `F:\Acad-custom\templates` on a network drive). Put the templates that you actually use there and change the Drawing Template File Location so that it points to your new template folder.

As this chapter demonstrates, drawing setup in AutoCAD LT requires quite a bit. As with any other initially forbidding task, take it step by step and soon the sequence will seem natural. The Drawing Setup Roadmap on the Cheat Sheet helps you stay on track and avoid missing a step.

Chapter 6

Draw Once . . .

In This Chapter

- Drawing with the LT drawing commands
- Lining up for lines and polylines
- Closing up with rectangles and polygons
- Rounding the curves with circles, arcs, splines, and clouds
- Dabbling in ellipses and donuts
- Making your points

As you probably remember from your crayon and coloring book days, drawing stuff is *fun.* CAD imposes a little more discipline, but drawing objects in AutoCAD LT is still fun. In computer-aided drafting, you usually start by drawing *geometry* — shapes such as lines, circles, rectangles, and so on that represent the real-world object that you're documenting. This chapter shows you how to draw geometry.

After you create some geometry, you'll probably need to add some dimensions, text, and hatching, but those elements come later (in Part III). Your first task is to get the geometry right; then you can worry about labeling things.

Drawing geometry properly in AutoCAD LT depends on paying attention to object properties and the precision of the points that you specify to create the objects. I cover these matters in Chapter 3. If you eagerly jumped to this chapter to get right to the fun stuff, take a moment to review that chapter first.

Introducing the LT Drawing Commands

For descriptive purposes, this chapter divides the drawing commands into three groups:

- Straight lines and objects composed of straight lines
- Curves
- Points

Table 6-1 offers an overview of most of the drawing commands in AutoCAD LT. It describes the commands' major options and shows you how to access them from the command line, the Draw menu, and the Draw toolbar. (Don't worry if not all the terms in the table are familiar to you; they become clear as you read through the chapter and use the commands.)

Many of the choices on the AutoCAD LT Draw menu open submenus containing several variations on each drawing command.

The LT drawing commands depend heavily on your reading the command line area and sometimes typing things there. Don't worry; I remind you to do so. (If *command line area* sounds to you like a place to order cafeteria food, not an AutoCAD LT essential concept, see Chapter 2.) Many command options that you see in command line prompts are available as well by right-clicking in the drawing area.

So what's the best course: to enter drawing commands from the command line or to choose them from the menus or toolbars? I suggest that you start a drawing command the first few times — until you remember its command name — by clicking its button on the Draw toolbar. After you click the button, fasten your eyes on the command line area so that you see the name of the command and its command line options. Use the keyboard or the right-click menus to select options, depending on whether your hand is on the keyboard or the mouse at that moment. After you're acquainted with a drawing command and decide that you like it enough to use it often, memorize its keyboard shortcut (the uppercase letters in the command names in Table 6-1).

A few drawing commands, such as DOnut, aren't on the Draw toolbar; you have to type those or choose them from the Draw menu.

Table 6-1 AutoCAD LT Drawing Commands

Button	*Command*	*Major Options*	*Toolbar Button*	*Draw Menu*
	Line	Start, end points	Line	Line
None	RAY	Start point, point through which ray passes	None	Ray
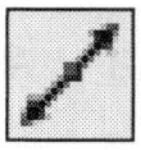	XLine	Two points on line	Construction line	Construction line
	PLine	Vertices	Polyline	Polyline
	POLygon	Number of sides, inscribed/ circumscribed	Polygon	Polygon
	RECtang	Two corners	Rectangle	Rectangle
	Arc	Various methods of definition	Arc	Arc; submenu for definition methods
	Circle	Three points, two points, tangent	Circle	Circle; submenu for definition methods
	REVCLOUD	Arc length	Revcloud	Revision Cloud
None	DOnut	Inside, outside diameters	None	Donut
	SPLine	Convert polyline or create new	Spline	Spline
	ELlipse	Arc, center, axis	Ellipse	Ellipse; submenu for definition methods
	POint	Point style	Point	Point; submenu for definition methods

The Straight Story: Lines, Polylines, and Polygons

As I harp on a bunch of times elsewhere in this book, CAD programs are for precision drawing, so you spend a lot of your time in AutoCAD LT drawing objects composed of straight line segments. This section covers these commands:

- **Line:** Draws a series of straight line segments; each segment is a separate object
- **PLine:** Draws a *polyline* — a series of straight- and/or curved line segments; all the segments remain connected to each other as a single object
- **RECtang:** Draws a polyline in the shape of a rectangle
- **POLygon:** Draws a polyline in the shape of a regular polygon (that is, a closed shape with all sides equal and all angles equal)

The following additional straight line drawing commands also are available in AutoCAD LT:

- **RAY:** Draws a *semi-infinite line* (a line that extends infinitely in one direction)
- **XLine:** Draws an *infinite line* (a line that extends infinitely in both directions)

The RAY and XLine commands are used to draw *construction lines* that guide the construction of additional geometry. Drawing construction lines is less common in AutoCAD LT than in some other CAD programs. LT's many precision techniques often provide more efficient methods of creating new geometry than what using construction lines offers.

Line it up

The Line command in AutoCAD LT draws a series of one or more connected line segments. Well, it *appears* to draw a series of connected segments. In fact, each *segment,* or piece of a line with endpoints, is a separate object. This construction doesn't seem like a big deal until you try to move or otherwise edit a series of segments that you drew with the Line command; you must select every piece separately. To avoid such a hassle, use polylines, which I describe later in this chapter, not lines and arcs, when you want the connected segments to be a single object.

If you're used to drawing lines in other programs, you may find it confusing at first that AutoCAD LT's Line command doesn't stop after you draw a single segment. LT keeps prompting you to specify additional points so that you can draw a series of (apparently) connected segments. When you finish drawing segments, just press the Enter key to finish the Line command and return to the command prompt.

Unlike a lot of LT drawing commands, Line doesn't offer a bunch of potentially confusing options. A Close option creates a closed polygon and an Undo option removes the most recent segment that you drew.

Like all drawing commands, Line puts the line segment objects that it draws on the current layer, and uses the current color, linetype, lineweight, and plotstyle properties. Make sure that you set these properties correctly before you start drawing. (I recommend that you set color, linetype, and lineweight to ByLayer.) See Chapter 3 for information on setting the current properties with the Properties toolbar.

When you're doing real drafting as opposed to just experimenting, make sure that you use one of LT's precision tools, such as object snaps, typed coordinates, or ortho to ensure that you specify each object point precisely. Chapter 3 also describes these tools.

Follow these steps to draw a series of line segments by using the Line command:

1. **Set object properties to the layer and other properties that you want applied to the line segments that you draw.**
2. **Click the Line button on the Draw toolbar.**

   AutoCAD LT starts the Line command and prompts you at the command line:

   ```
   Specify first point:
   ```
3. **Specify the starting point by clicking a point or typing coordinates.**

   Remember: Use one of the precision techniques I describe in Chapter 3 if you're doing real drafting. For the first point, object snap, snap, and typing coordinates all work well.

   LT prompts you at the command line to specify the other endpoint of the first line segment:

   ```
   Specify next point or [Undo]:
   ```
4. **Specify additional points by clicking or typing.**

   Again, use one of the AutoCAD LT precision techniques if you're doing real drafting. For the second and subsequent points, all the techniques I mention in Step 3 work well, plus ortho and direct distance entry.

   After you specify the third point, LT adds the Close option to the command line prompt:

   ```
   Specify next point or [Close/Undo]:
   ```

5. **When you finish drawing segments, end with one of these steps:**

   - Press Enter, or right-click anywhere in the drawing area and choose Enter (as shown in Figure 6-1) to leave the figure open.
   - Type C and press Enter, or right-click anywhere in the drawing area and choose Close from the cursor menu to close the figure.

   LT draws the final segment and returns to the command prompt, indicating that the Line command is finished:

   ```
   Command:
   ```

Connect the lines with polyline

The Line command is fine for some drawing tasks, but the PLine command is a better, more flexible choice in many situations. The PLine command draws a special kind of object called a *polyline*. You may hear CAD drafters refer to a polyline as a *pline* because of the command name. (By the way, PLine is pronounced to rhyme with "beeline" — in other words, it sounds like the place you stand when you've drunk a lot of beer at the ball game.)

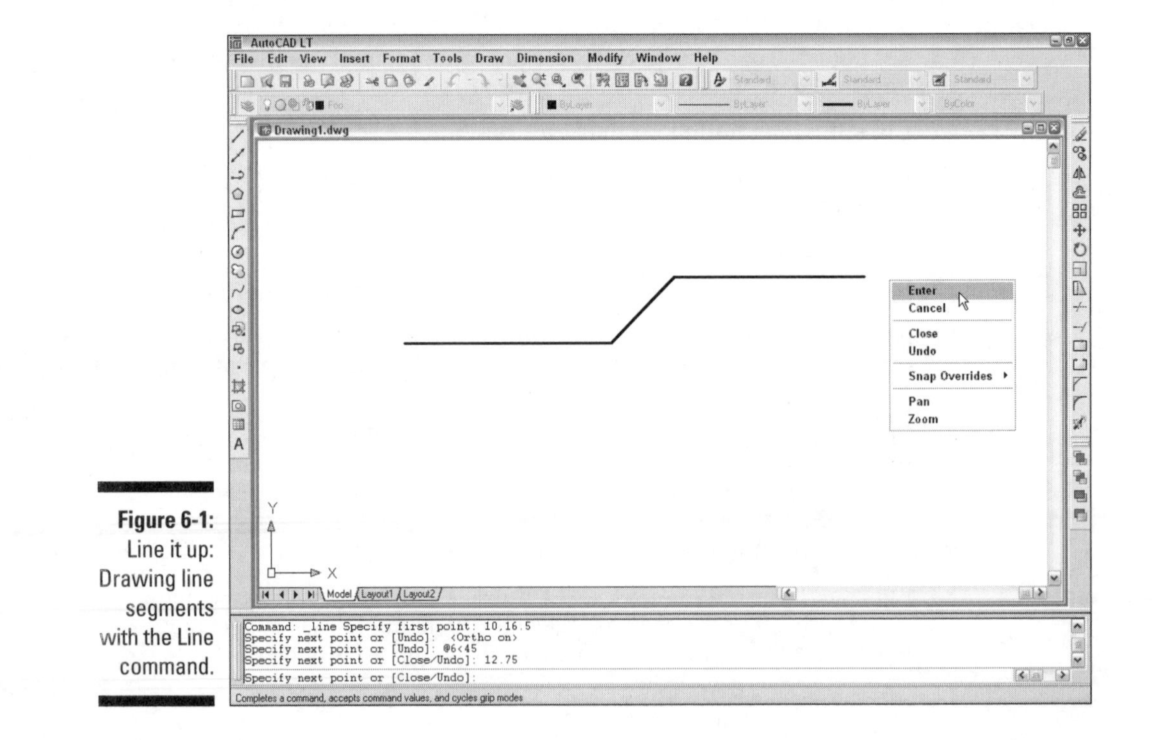

Figure 6-1: Line it up: Drawing line segments with the Line command.

The most important differences between the Line and PLine commands are these:

- The Line command draws a series of single line segment objects. Even though they appear to be linked on-screen, each segment is a separate object. If you move one line segment, the other segments that you drew at the same time don't move with it. The PLine command, on the other hand, draws a single, connected, multisegment object. If you select any segment for editing, your changes affect the entire polyline. Figure 6-2 shows how the same sketch drawn with the Line and the PLine commands responds when you select one of the objects.

Use the PLine command instead of Line in most cases where you need to draw a series of connected line segments. If you're drawing a series of end-to-end segments, there's a good chance that those segments are logically connected — for example, they might represent the outline of a single object or a continuous pathway. If the segments are connected logically, keeping them connected in your AutoCAD LT drawing makes sense. The most obvious practical benefit of grouping segments together into a polyline is that many editing operations are more efficient when you use polylines. If you move a single, disconnected line segment, the other segments that you drew at the same time don't move with it — likewise for other common editing operations, such as copying, erasing, rotating, and mirroring. When you select any segment in a polyline for editing, the entire polyline is affected.

- The PLine command can draw curved segments as well as straight ones.
- You can add width to each segment of a polyline. Polyline segment width is similar to lineweight, except that it can be uniform or tapered. The ability to create polyline segments with line widths was more important in the old days before AutoCAD LT had lineweight as an object property. People used to draw polylines with a small amount of width to show the segments as somewhat heavier than normal on plots. Nowadays, achieving this effect with object lineweights (as I describe in Chapter 3) or plotstyles (as I describe in Chapter 12) is easier and more efficient.

After you create a polyline, you can adjust its segments by grip editing any of the vertex points. (The little squares on the vertices in Figure 6-2 are called *grips.* To edit, you click on a grip to activate it, and then click on a different point — using LT's precision tools, of course — to move the grip there. See Chapter 7 for details on grip editing.) For more complicated polyline editing tasks, you can use the PEdit command to edit the polyline, or you can convert the polyline to a collection of line and arc segments by using the eXplode command — although you lose any width defined for each segment when you explode a polyline.

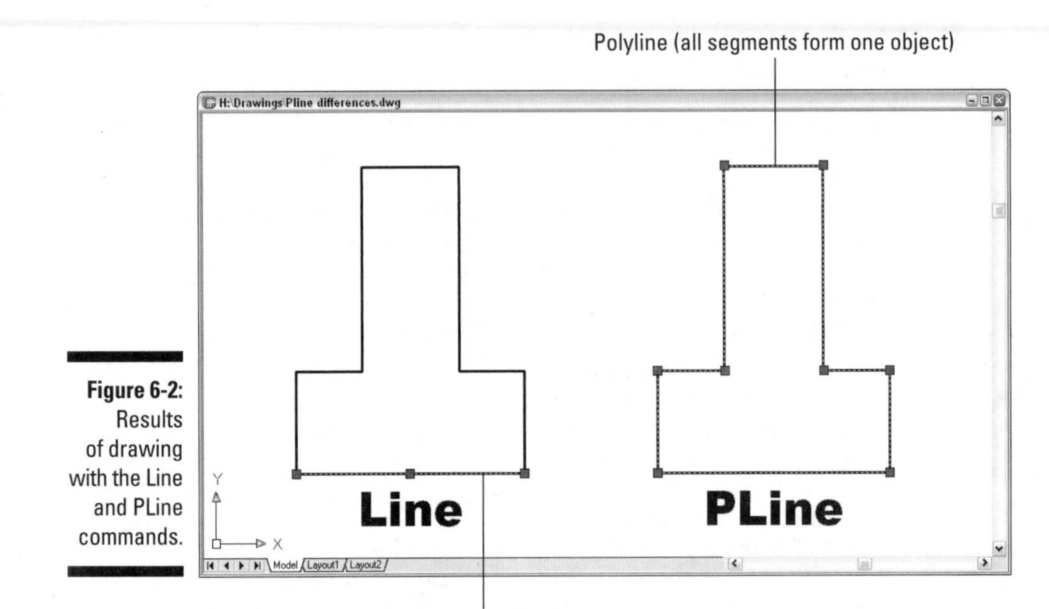

Figure 6-2: Results of drawing with the Line and PLine commands.

Drawing polylines composed of straight segments is pretty much like drawing with the Line command, as demonstrated in the following steps. Watch the command prompts carefully because the PLine command has a lot of options! ***Remember:*** You can right-click in the drawing area to select one of the options, but reading the command prompts is your ticket to knowing what the options are at any moment.

To draw a polyline composed of straight segments, follow these steps:

1. **Set object properties to the layer and other properties that you want applied to the polyline object that you draw.**
2. **Click the Polyline button — the one that looks like a fishhook — on the Draw toolbar.**

   AutoCAD LT starts the PLine command and prompts you at the command line:

   ```
   Specify start point:
   ```
3. **Specify the starting point by clicking a point or typing coordinates.**

   LT displays the current polyline segment line width and prompts you to specify the other endpoint of the first polyline segment:

   ```
   Current line-width is 0.0000
   Specify next point or [Arc/Halfwidth/Length/Undo/Width]:
   ```

4. **If the current line width isn't zero, change it to zero by typing** W, **Enter,** 0, **Enter,** 0 **(as shown in the following command line sequence).**

```
Specify next point or [Arc/Halfwidth/Length/Undo/Width]:
        W
Enter Specify starting width <0.0000>: 0
Enter Specify ending width <0.0000>: 0
Enter Specify next point or
        [Arc/Halfwidth/Length/Undo/Width]:
```

Despite what you may think, a zero width polyline segment is not the LT equivalent of writing with disappearing ink. *Zero width* means "display this segment, using the normal, thin line width on-screen." LT still applies object property or plotstyle lineweights when you plot.

5. **Specify additional points by clicking or typing.**

After you specify the second point, LT adds the Close option to the command line prompt:

```
Specify next point or
        [Arc/Close/Halfwidth/Length/Undo/Width]:
```

In addition, you can view and choose options from the right-click menu, as shown in Figure 6-3.

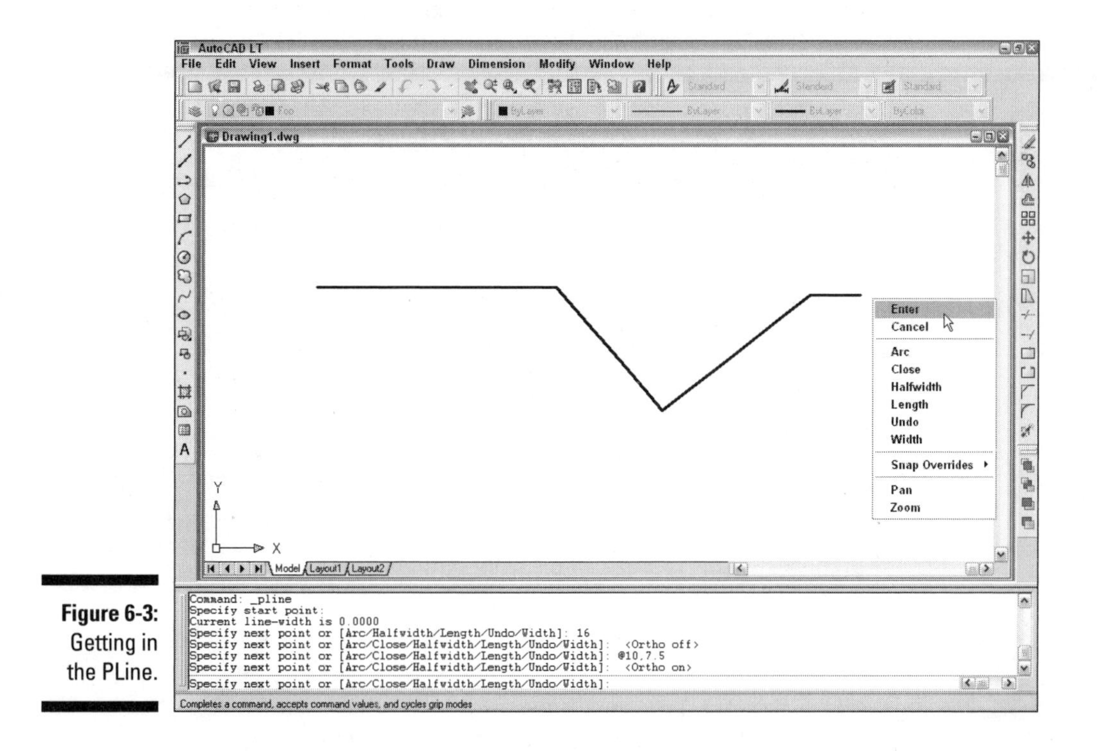

Figure 6-3: Getting in the PLine.

6. **After you finish drawing segments, either press Enter (to leave the figure open) or type** C **and press Enter (to close it).**

   LT draws the final segment and returns to the command prompt, indicating that the PLine command is finished:

   ```
   Command:
   ```

In the following steps, I spice things up a bit and give you a preview of coming (curvy) attractions by adding an arc segment to a polyline.

Just so you know, curved segments in polylines are *circular arcs* — pieces of circles that you can draw with the AutoCAD LT Arc command. LT can draw other kinds of curves, including ellipses and splines, but not within the PLine command.

To draw a polyline that includes curved segments, follow these steps:

1. **Repeat Steps 1 though 5 of the previous steps.**
2. **When you're ready to add one or more arc segments, type** A **and press Enter to select the Arc option.**

   The command line prompt changes to show arc segment options. Most of these options correspond to the many ways of drawing circular arcs in LT (see "Arc-y-ology," later in this chapter).

   ```
   Specify endpoint of arc or
           [Angle/CEnter/CLose/Direction/Halfwidth/Line/Radi
           us/Second pt/Undo/Width]:
   ```

3. **Specify the endpoint of the arc by clicking a point or typing coordinates.**

   LT draws the curved segment of the polyline. The command line prompt continues to show arc segment options.

   ```
   Specify endpoint of arc or
           [Angle/CEnter/CLose/Direction/Halfwidth/Line/Radi
           us/Second pt/Undo/Width]:
   ```

   Your options at this point include

   - Specifying additional points to draw more arc segments
   - Choosing another arc-drawing method (such as CEnter or Second pt)
   - Returning to drawing straight line segments with the Line option

   In this example, I return to drawing straight line segments.

   Perhaps the most useful of the alternative arc-drawing methods is Second pt. You can use it to gain flexibility in the direction of the arc, but at the cost of losing tangency of contiguous segments. Sometimes not going off on a tangent is best, anyway.

4. **Type** L **and press Enter to select the Line option.**

```
Specify endpoint of arc or
        [Angle/CEnter/CLose/Direction/Halfwidth/Line/Radi
        us/Second pt/Undo/Width]: L
```

The command line prompt changes back to showing straight line segment options.

```
Specify next point or
        [Arc/Close/Halfwidth/Length/Undo/Width]:
```

5. **Specify additional points by clicking or typing.**
6. **After you finish drawing segments, either press Enter or type** C **and press Enter.**

```
Command:
```

Figure 6-4 shows some of the things that you can draw with the PLine command by using straight segments, arc segments, or a combination of both.

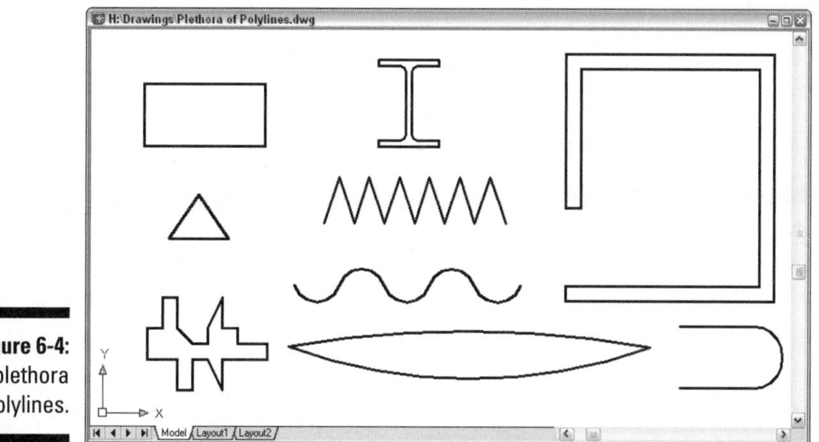

Figure 6-4: A plethora of polylines.

The Line and PLine commands work well for drawing a series of end-to-end single lines, but what if you want to draw a series of double lines to represent, for example, the edges of a wall or roadway? Here are two options:

- Use the DLine (Double Line) command to draw pairs of parallel line and/or arc segments. DLine works much like PLine (although it doesn't connect the line and arc segments together, as PLine does). Choose Draw⇨Double Line to launch the command, and look up "DLINE command" in the AutoCAD LT online help if you need more guidance about how to use it.
- Use the PLine command to draw a single set of connected line and/or arc segments, and then use the Offset command to create one or more sets of parallel segments. Chapter 7 covers the Offset command.

Square off with rectangle

You can use the PLine or Line command to draw a rectangle segment by segment. In most cases, though, you use the special-purpose RECtang command. The following steps demonstrate how:

1. **Set object properties to the layer and other properties that you want applied to the rectangle that you draw.**
2. **Click the Rectangle button on the Draw toolbar.**

   LT starts the RECtang command and prompts you at the command line to specify a point for one corner of the rectangle:

   ```
   Specify first corner point or
           [Chamfer/Elevation/Fillet/Thickness/Width]:
   ```

   You can add fancy effects with the additional command options. The default options work best for most purposes. Look up "RECTANG command" in the AutoCAD LT online help if you want to know more about the options.

3. **Specify the first corner by clicking a point or typing coordinates.**

   The command line prompts you to specify the other corner of the rectangle — the one that's diagonally opposite from the first corner:

   ```
   Specify other corner point or [Dimensions]:
   ```

4. **Specify the other corner by clicking a point or typing coordinates.**

   If you know the size of the rectangle that you want to draw (for example, 100 units long by 75 units high), type relative coordinates to specify the dimensions (for example, **@100,75**). (Chapter 3 describes how to type coordinates.)

   LT draws the rectangle.

The many sides of polygon

Rectangles and other closed polylines are types of *polygons*, or closed figures with three or more sides. The AutoCAD LT POLygon command provides a quick way of drawing *regular polygons* — polygons in which all sides and angles are equal. (If regular polygons seem a little square, maybe that's because a square is a special case of a regular polygon!)

The following procedure demonstrates the POLygon command:

1. **Set object properties to the layer and other properties that you want applied to the polygon that you draw.**
2. **Click the Polygon button on the Draw toolbar.**

   LT starts the POLygon command and prompts you at the command line to enter the number of sides for the polygon:

   ```
   Enter number of sides <4>:
   ```
3. **Type the number of sides in the polygon that you want to draw and press Enter.**

   The command line prompts you to specify the center point of the polygon:

   ```
   Specify center of polygon or [Edge]:
   ```

   You can use the Edge option to draw a polygon by specifying one side, instead of the center and radius of an imaginary inscribed or circumscribed circle. The imaginary circle method is much more common.
4. **Specify the center point by clicking a point or typing coordinates.**

   The command line prompts you to specify whether the polygon will be inscribed in or circumscribed about an imaginary circle whose radius you specify in the following step:

   ```
   Enter an option [Inscribed in circle/Circumscribed about
          circle] <I>:
   ```
5. **Type** I **or** C **and press Enter.**

   The command line prompts you to specify the radius of the imaginary circle:

   ```
   Specify radius of circle:
   ```
6. **Specify the radius by typing a distance or clicking a point.**

   LT draws the polygon.

   If you type a distance or you click a point with ortho mode turned on, the polygon aligns orthogonally, as shown in Figure 6-5. If you click a point with Ortho turned off, the polygon most likely isn't aligned orthogonally.

Figure 6-5 shows the results of drawing plenty of polygons — a practice known as "polygony," and which, as far as I know, remains legal in most states.

Rectangles and polygons in AutoCAD LT are really just polylines that you specify in a way that's appropriate to the shape you're creating. You'll notice this similarity when you grip edit a rectangle or polygon and move one of the vertexes: Only the selected vertex moves. LT doesn't make the entire rectangle or polygon larger or smaller. (See Chapter 7 for information about grip editing.)

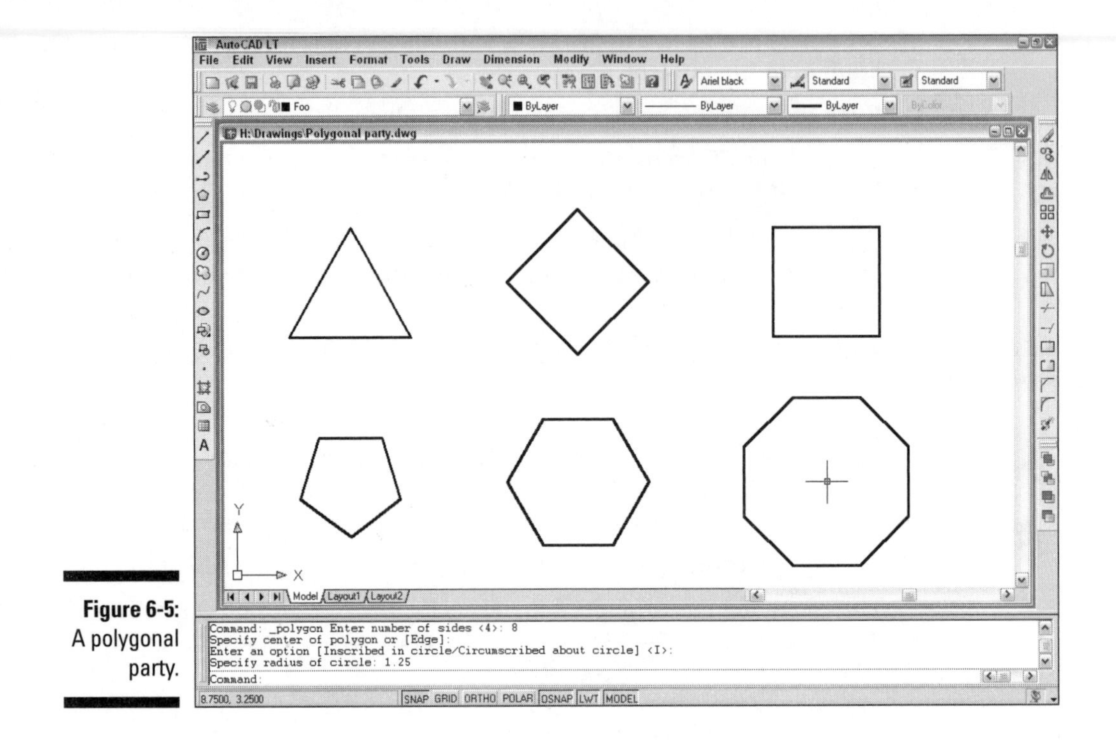

Figure 6-5: A polygonal party.

Carving Curves: Circles, Arcs, and Others

Although straight line segments predominate in many CAD drawings, even the most humdrum, rectilinear design is likely to have a few curves. And if you're drawing car bodies or Gaudí buildings, your drawings are almost nothing but curves! This section shows you how to use the following AutoCAD LT curve-drawing commands:

- **Circle:** Draws circles (you were expecting rectangles, maybe?)
- **Arc:** Draws circular arcs — arcs cut from circles, not from ellipses, parabolas, or some other complicated curve
- **ELlipse:** Draws ellipses and elliptical arcs
- **SPLine:** Draws smoothly flowing curves of a variety of shapes
- **DOnut:** Draws filled-in annular rings and circles
- **REVCLOUD:** Draws free-form "clouds," the most common application of which is to indicate revised areas in the drawing

The following sections describe each command.

A perfect circle

AutoCAD LT offers an easy way to draw circles, and it also offers . . . *other* ways. The easy way is to define the center point of the circle and then to define the radius or diameter. You can also define a circle by entering one of the following options of the command (for those "other" ways):

- **3P (3-Point):** Specify any three points on the circumference.
- **2P (2-Point):** Specify the endpoints of a diameter of the circle.
- **Ttr (Tangent-Tangent-Radius):** Specify two lines or other objects that are tangent to the circle, and then specify its radius.
- **Tan, Tan, Tan (Tangent-Tangent-Tangent; available only from the menu):** Specify three lines or other objects that are tangent to the circle.

Whether these additional circle-drawing methods are useful or superfluous depends on the kinds of drawings that you make and how your industry defines geometry. Get familiar with the default center point/radius method and then try the other methods to see whether they may be helpful to you. If you find yourself going around in circles, you can always draw them the default way and move them into position with other geometry.

1. **Set object properties to the layer and other properties that you want applied to the circle that you draw.**
2. **Click the Circle button on the Draw toolbar.**

   LT starts the Circle command and prompts you at the command line to specify the center point of the circle:

   ```
   Specify center point for circle or [3P/2P/Ttr (tan tan
   radius)]:
   ```

   The prompt shows the methods other than "center point plus radius" that you can use to draw circles in AutoCAD. (No, "tan tan radius" is not a mathematician's dance.) Look up "CIRCLE command" in the online help if you think you may have a use for these less common circle-drawing methods.

3. **Specify the center point by clicking a point or typing coordinates.**

   Use one of the precision techniques I describe in Chapter 3 if you're doing real drafting. Object snap, snap, and typing coordinates all work well for specifying the center point.

   The command line then prompts you to specify the circle's radius:

   ```
   Specify radius of circle or [Diameter]:
   ```

Type **D** and press Enter if you prefer to enter the diameter rather than the radius and you've forgotten your twos tables — or, more seriously, if the diameter is easier to specify with the cursor or type exactly than the radius is.

4. **Specify the radius by typing a distance or clicking a point.**

   LT draws the circle, as shown in Figure 6-6.

Arc-y-ology

Arcs in AutoCAD LT are, quite simply, pieces of circles. As with circles, LT offers you an easy way to define arcs. Just specify three points on-screen to define the arc, easy as one-two-three. These points tell LT where to start the arc, how much to curve it, and where to end it.

Sounds pretty easy, right? So where's the problem? The trouble is that you often must specify arcs more exactly than is possible by using this method. AutoCAD LT helps you specify such arcs, too, but the procedure ain't easy.

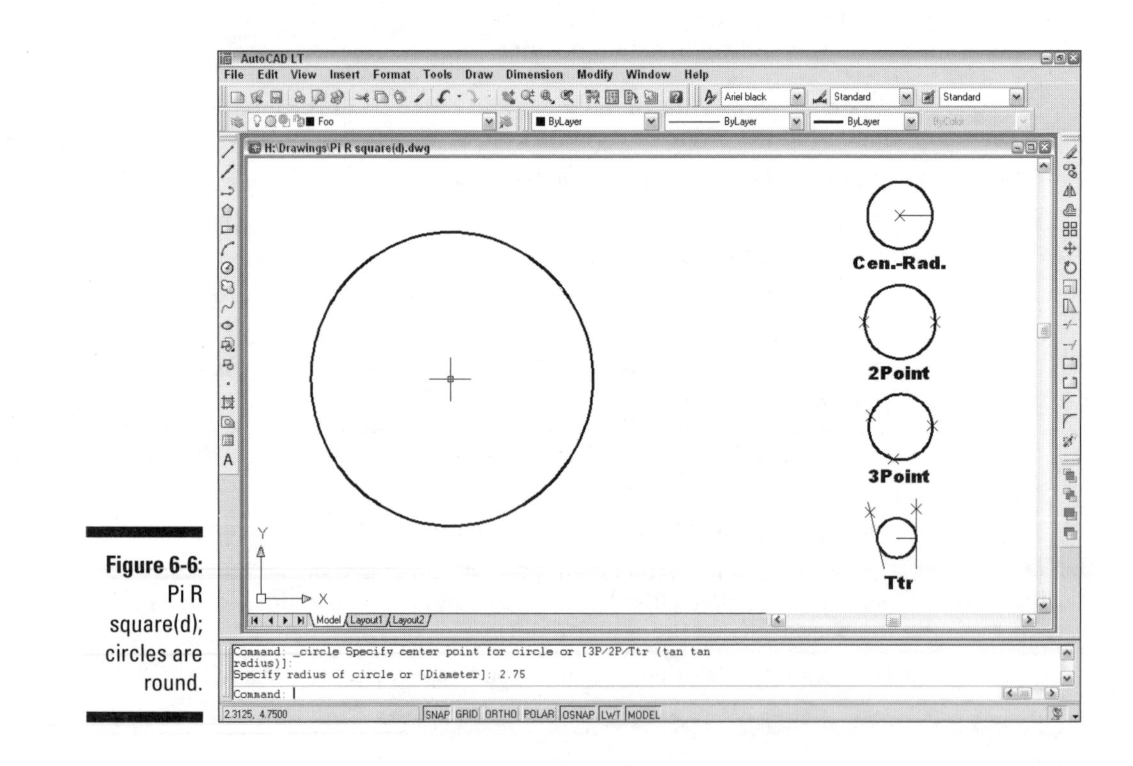

Figure 6-6: Pi R square(d); circles are round.

You can start your arc by specifying the center of the arc or the start point. If you choose the Center option, LT prompts you for the center point first and the start point second. LT defines arcs counterclockwise, so pick a start point in a clockwise direction from the endpoint. After you specify the center and start point, LT presents several options you can choose, including the following:

- **Angle:** This option specifies the included angle that the arc sweeps out. A 180-degree angle, for example, is a semicircle.
- **Length of chord:** This option specifies the length of an imaginary straight line connecting the endpoints of the arc. Most people use this option seldom or never.
- **Endpoint:** This option specifies where the arc ends. It's the default option and is often the easiest to use.

If you specify the start point as the first option, you can choose among the following three command line options as well:

- **Center:** This option prompts you for the arc's center point and then finishes with the three preceding options.
- **End:** This option specifies the endpoint of the arc. You then need to define the angle the arc covers, its direction, its radius, or its center point.
- **Second point:** This option is the default. The second point you choose is not the endpoint; instead, it's a point on the arc that, along with the start and endpoints, defines the arc's *curvature* — that is, how much it curves. After you enter the second point, you must specify an endpoint to complete the arc.

To get a feel for how these permutations can be strung together to create different arc-drawing methods, choose Draw⇨Arc and look at the impressive submenu that unfurls, as shown in Figure 6-7.

The following example shows how you draw an arc using the default start point/second point/endpoint method:

1. **Set object properties to the layer and other properties that you want applied to the arc that you draw.**
2. **Click the Arc button on the Draw toolbar.**

   LT starts the Arc command and prompts you at the command line to specify the first endpoint of the arc:

   ```
   Specify start point of arc or [Center]:
   ```

3. **Specify the start point by clicking a point or typing coordinates.**

   The command line prompts you to specify a second point on the arc:

   ```
   Specify second point of arc or [Center/ENd]:
   ```

4. **Specify a second point on the arc by clicking a point or typing coordinates.**

   The second point lies somewhere along the curve of the arc. LT determines the exact curvature of the arc after you choose the final endpoint in the following step. To align the second point with an existing object, use an object snap mode.

   The command line prompts you to specify the other endpoint of the arc; as you move the cursor around, LT shows how the arc will look:

   ```
   Specify end point of arc:
   ```

5. **Specify the other endpoint of the arc by clicking a point or typing coordinates.**

   LT draws the arc (refer to Figure 6-7).

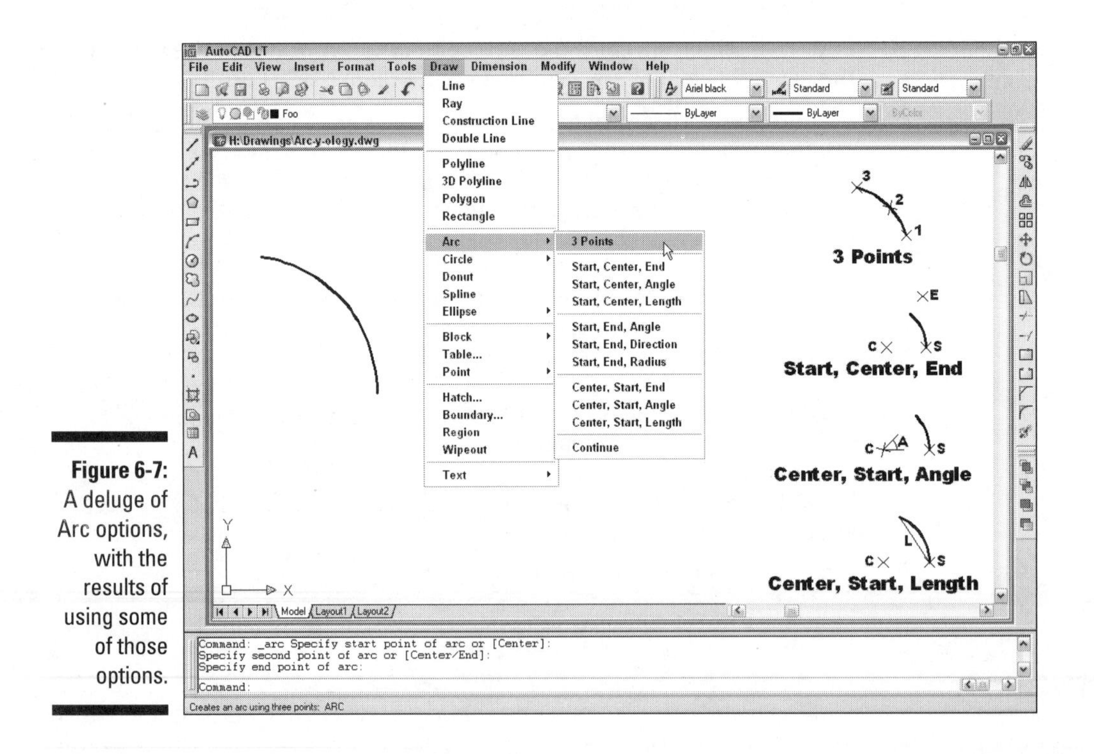

Figure 6-7: A deluge of Arc options, with the results of using some of those options.

Orbit with ellipse

An *ellipse* is like a warped circle with a *major* (long) axis and a *minor* (short) axis. These axes determine the ellipse's length, width, and degree of curvature. An *elliptical arc* is an arc cut from an ellipse. Some kinds of drawing geometry require ellipses or elliptical arcs, but many people use AutoCAD LT happily for years without ever drawing an ellipse. If you think you could be one of those people, skip this section.

The LT ELlipse command provides a straightforward way of drawing an ellipse: You specify the two endpoints of one of its axes and then specify an endpoint on the other axis. But like the Arc command, the ELlipse command offers a bunch of other options on the command line:

- **Arc:** This option generates an elliptical arc, not a full ellipse. You define an elliptical arc just as you do a full ellipse. The following methods for creating an ellipse apply to either.
- **Center:** This option requires that you define the center of the ellipse and then the endpoint of an axis. You can then either enter the distance of the other axis or specify that a rotation around the major axis defines the ellipse. If you choose the latter, you can enter (or drag the ellipse to) a specific rotation for the second axis that, in turn, completely defines the ellipse.
- **Rotation:** With this option, you specify an angle, which defines the curvature of the ellipse — small angles make fat ellipses (0 degrees creates a circle, in fact), and large angles make skinny ellipses. The name of the option, Rotation, has something to do with rotating an imaginary circle around the first axis. If you can figure out the imaginary circle business, then you have a better imagination than I do.

The following example creates an ellipse by using the default endpoints of the axes method. Figure 6-8 shows an ellipse and an elliptical arc.

```
Command: ELlipse Enter
Specify axis endpoint of ellipse or [Arc/Center]: pick or
          type the first endpoint of one axis
Specify other endpoint of axis: pick or type the other
          endpoint of one axis
Specify distance to other axis or [Rotation]: pick or type
          the endpoint of the other axis
```

You can create elliptical arcs (as opposed to the circular arcs that the AutoCAD LT Arc command draws) by using the Arc option of the ELlipse command; it's perfect for drawing those cannonball trajectories! Alternatively, you can draw a full ellipse and then use the TRim or BReak command to cut a piece out of it.

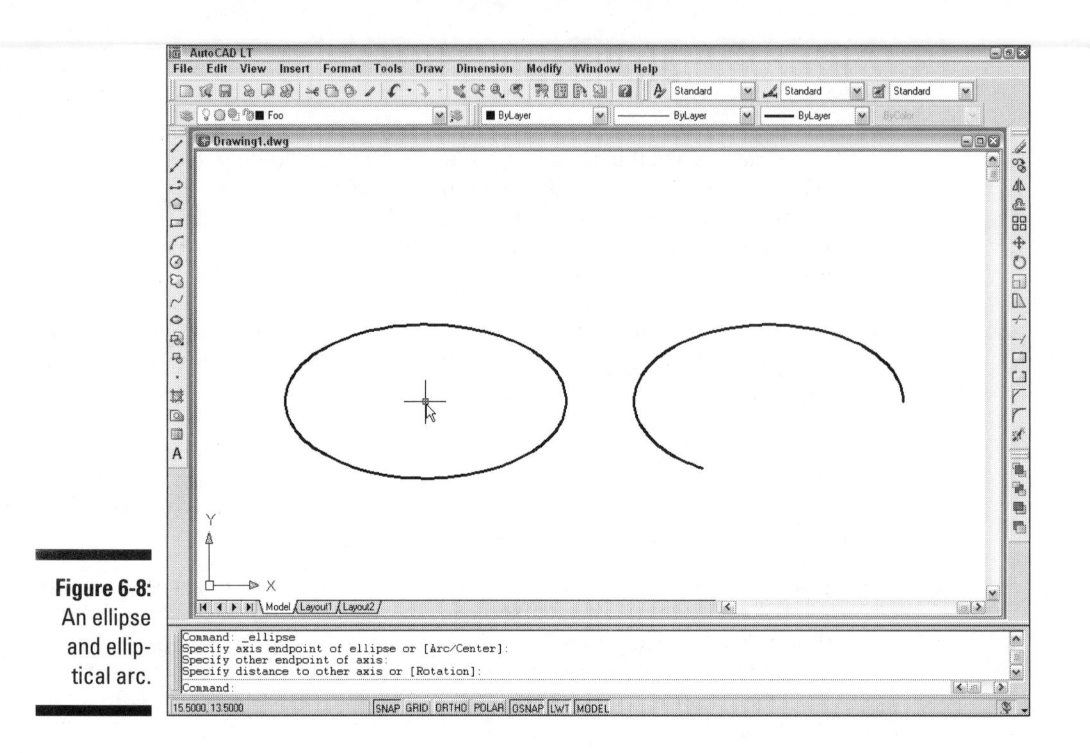

Figure 6-8: An ellipse and elliptical arc.

Spline: The sketchy, sinuous curve

Most people use CAD programs for precision drawing tasks: straight lines, carefully defined curves, precisely specified points, and so on. AutoCAD LT is not the program to free your inner artist — unless your inner artist is Mondrian. Nonetheless, even meticulously created CAD drawings sometimes need free-form curves. The AutoCAD LT *spline object* is just the thing for the job.

Although PLine is pronounced to rhyme with "beeline," SPLine rhymes with "vine." If you liked my earlier pronunciation comment, you might want to think about beer before you say "PLine" and about wine before you say "SPLine.")

You can use AutoCAD LT splines in two ways:

- Eyeball the location and shape of the curve and don't worry too much about getting it just so. That's the free-form, sketchy, not-too-precise approach that I describe here.
- Specify their control points and curvature characteristics precisely. Beneath their easy-going, informal exterior, AutoCAD LT splines are really highly precise, mathematically defined entities called *NURBS*

curves (Non-Uniform Rational B-Spline curves). Mathematicians and some mechanical and industrial designers care a lot about the precise characteristics of the curves they work with. For those people, the LT SPLine and SPlinEdit commands include a number of advanced options. Look up "spline curves" in the AutoCAD LT online help if you need precision in your splines.

Drawing splines is straightforward, if you ignore the advanced options. The following steps draw a free-form curve with the SPLine command:

1. **Set object properties to the layer and other properties that you want applied to the spline that you draw.**
2. **Click the Spline button on the Draw toolbar.**

   LT starts the SPLine command and prompts you at the command line to specify the first endpoint of the spline:

   ```
   Specify first point or [Object]:
   ```
3. **Specify the start point by clicking a point or typing coordinates.**

   The command line prompts you to specify additional points:

   ```
   Specify next point:
   ```
4. **Specify additional points by clicking or typing coordinates.**

   After you pick the second point, the command line prompt changes to show additional options:

   ```
   Specify next point or [Close/Fit tolerance] <start tan-
           gent>:
   ```

   Because you're drawing a free-form curve, you usually don't need to use object snaps or other precision techniques when picking spline points.
5. **Press Enter after you choose the final endpoint of your spline.**

   LT prompts you to specify tangent lines for each end of the spline:

   ```
   Specify start tangent:
   Specify end tangent:
   ```

   The `Specify start tangent` and `Specify end tangent` prompts can control the curvature of the start and endpoints of the spline. In most cases, just pressing Enter at both prompts to accept the default tangents works fine.
6. **Press Enter twice to accept the default tangent directions.**

   LT draws the spline.

Figure 6-9 shows some examples of splines.

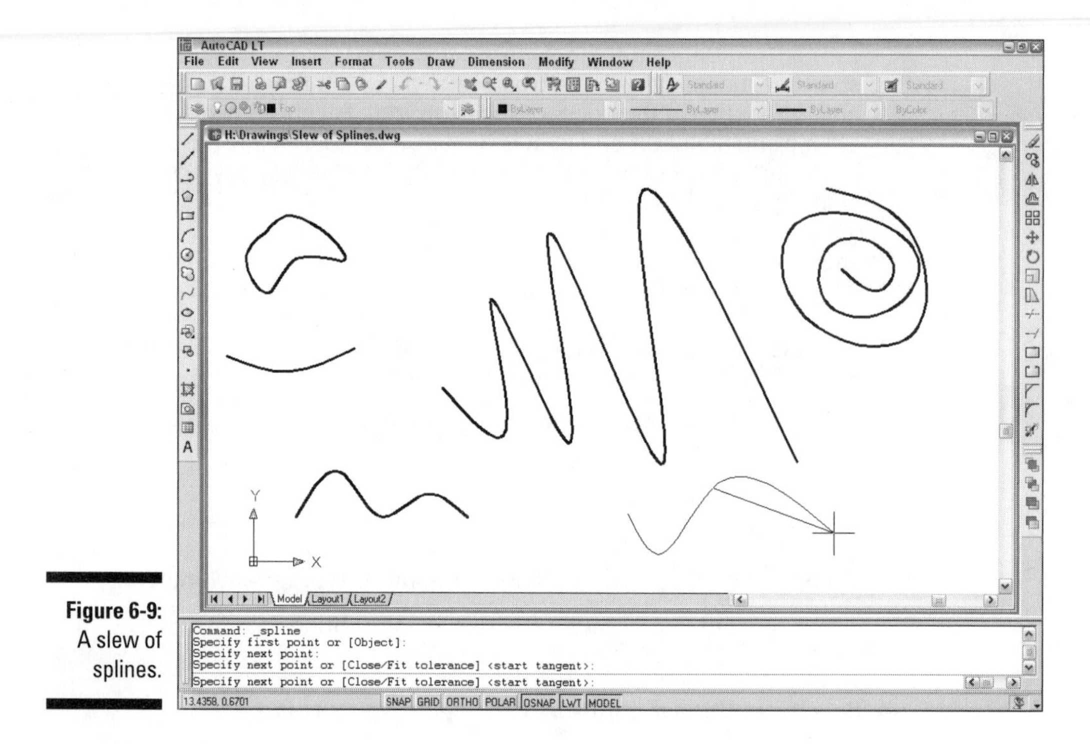

Figure 6-9: A slew of splines.

After you draw a spline, you can grip edit it to adjust its shape. See Chapter 7 for information about grip editing. If you need finer control over spline editing, look up the SPlinEdit command in the AutoCAD LT online help.

Donuts: Plain and jelly-filled

Creating a *donut* is a simple way to define a single object that consists of two concentric circles with the space between them filled.

When you start the DOnut command, LT prompts you for the inside diameter and the outside diameter — the size of the hole and the size of the donut, as measured across their widest points. After you enter these values, LT prompts you for the center point of the donut. But one donut is rarely enough, so LT keeps prompting you for additional center points until you press Enter (the AutoCAD LT equivalent of saying, "no, really, I'm full now!").

The following example draws a regulation-size donut, with a 1.5" hole and 3.5" outside diameter. Figure 6-10 shows several kinds of donuts.

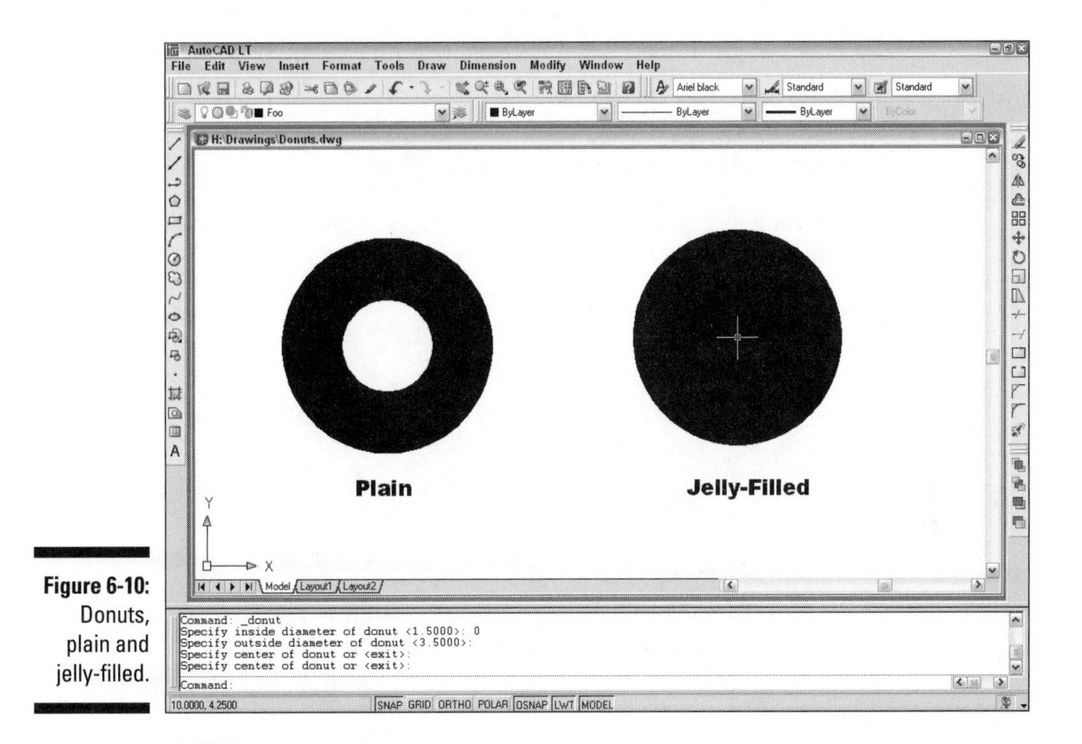

Figure 6-10: Donuts, plain and jelly-filled.

```
Command: DOnut Enter
Specify inside diameter of donut <0.5000>: 1.5 Enter
Specify outside diameter of donut <1.0000>: 3.5 Enter
Specify center of donut or <exit>: pick or type the center
          point of one or more donuts
Specify center of donut or <exit>: Enter
```

You can use the DOnut command to create a filled circle — also known as a jelly-filled donut. Just specify an inside diameter of zero.

Revision clouds on the horizon

Submitting a set of drawings at an intermediate stage of completion and then submitting them again later with *revisions* — corrections, clarifications, and requested changes is customary. Often, the recipients like to locate changed stuff easily. A common drafting convention in many industries is to call attention to revised items by drawing free-form clouds around them. The REVCLOUD command makes quick work of drawing such clouds.

Drawing revision clouds is easy, if you understand that you click with the mouse only once in the drawing area. That one click defines the starting point for the cloud's perimeter. After that, you simply move the cursor around and the cloud takes shape. When you return to near the point that you clicked in the beginning, LT automatically closes the cloud.

The following example shows you how to draw a revision cloud. Figure 6-11 shows what revision clouds look like.

```
Command: REVCLOUD
Minimum arc length: 0.5000  Maximum arc length: 0.5000
         Style: Normal
Specify start point or [Arc length/Object/Style] <Object>:
         pick a point along the perimeter of your future
         cloud
Guide crosshairs along cloud path... sweep the cursor around
         to define the cloud's perimeter
```

You don't need to click again. Simply move the cursor around without clicking. LT draws the next *lobe* of the cloud when your cursor reaches the `Minimum arc length` distance from the end of the previous lobe.

Continue moving the cursor around until you return to the point that you clicked at first.

```
Revision cloud finished.
```

Here are a few tips for using revision clouds:

- Putting revision clouds on their own layer so that you can choose to plot with or without the clouds visible is a good idea.
- You'll probably find controlling the shape of revision clouds easier if you turn off ortho mode before you start the command.
- You may need to add a triangle and number to indicate the revision number (refer to Figure 6-11). A block with an attribute is a good way to handle this requirement; Chapter 13 covers blocks and attributes.

If the revision cloud's lobes are too small or too large, erase the cloud, restart the REVCLOUD command, and use the command's Arc length option to change the minimum and maximum arc lengths. The default minimum and maximum lengths are 0.5 (or 15 in metric drawings) multiplied by the DIMSCALE (DIMension SCALE) system variable setting. If you make the minimum and maximum lengths equal (which is the default), the lobes are approximately equal in size. If you make them unequal, more variation is in lobe size — you get "fluffier" clouds. Fortunately, all these options are more than most non-meteorologists need. If you set DIMSCALE properly during your drawing setup procedure (see Chapter 5), REVCLOUD does a pretty good job of guessing reasonable default arc lengths.

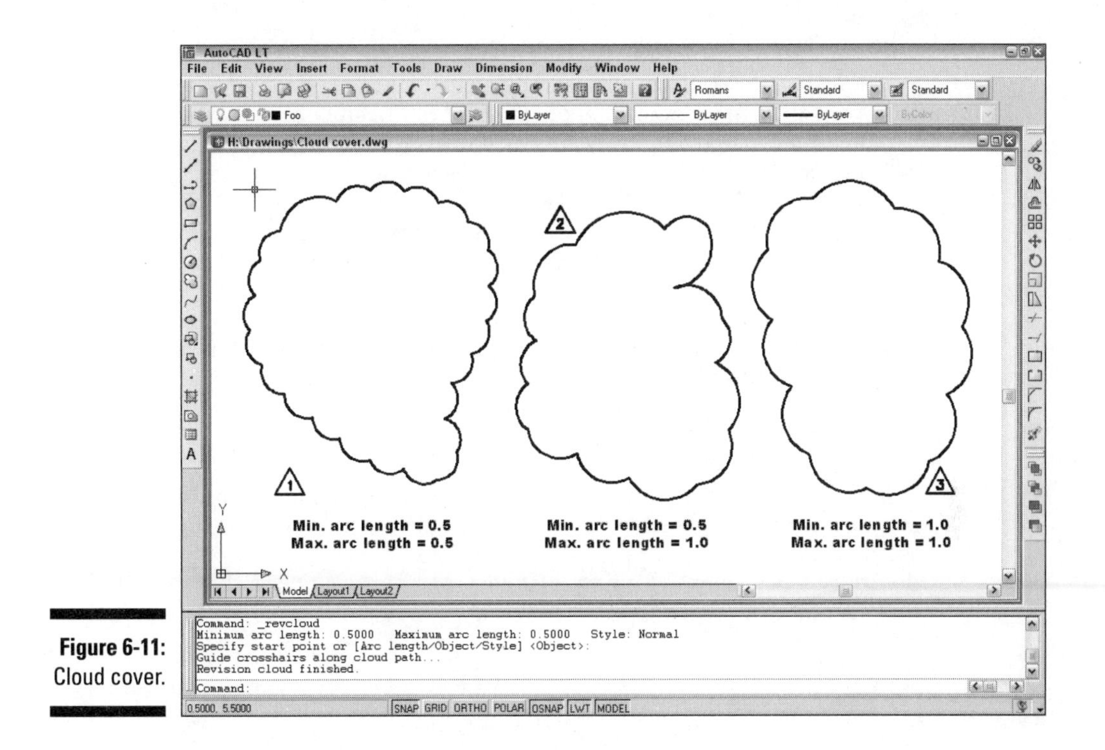

Figure 6-11: Cloud cover.

Making Your Point(s)

I thought about not covering points in this book, but I didn't want you complaining that *AutoCAD LT 2005 For Dummies* is pointless.

The word *point* describes two different things in AutoCAD LT:

- A *location* in the drawing that you specify (by typing coordinates or clicking with the mouse)
- An *object* that you draw with the POint command

Throughout this chapter and most of the book, I tell you to specify points — that's the location meaning. This section tells you how to draw point objects.

A *point object* can serve two purposes in an AutoCAD LT drawing.

- **Points often identify specific locations in your drawing to other people who look at the drawing.** A point can be something that displays onscreen, either as a tiny dot or as another symbol, such as a cross with a circle around it.

- **You can use points as precise object snap locations.** Think of them as construction points. For example, when you're laying out a new building, you might draw point objects at some of the engineering survey points and then snap to those points as you sketch the building's shape with the polyline command. You use the NODe object snap mode to snap to AutoCAD LT point objects. In this guise, points usually are for your use in drawing and editing precisely. Other people who view the drawing probably won't even be aware that the point objects are there.

What makes AutoCAD LT point objects complicated is their almost limitless range of display options, provided to accommodate the two different kinds of purposes just described (and possibly some others that I haven't figured out yet). You use the Point Style dialog box, shown in Figure 6-12, to specify how points look in the current drawing.

DDPTYPE is the command that opens the Point Style dialog box. You can access it from the menus by choosing Format➪Point Style. The top portion of the dialog box shows the available point display styles. Most of the choices do pretty much the same thing. Just click one of the squares that says "hey, that's a point!" to you.

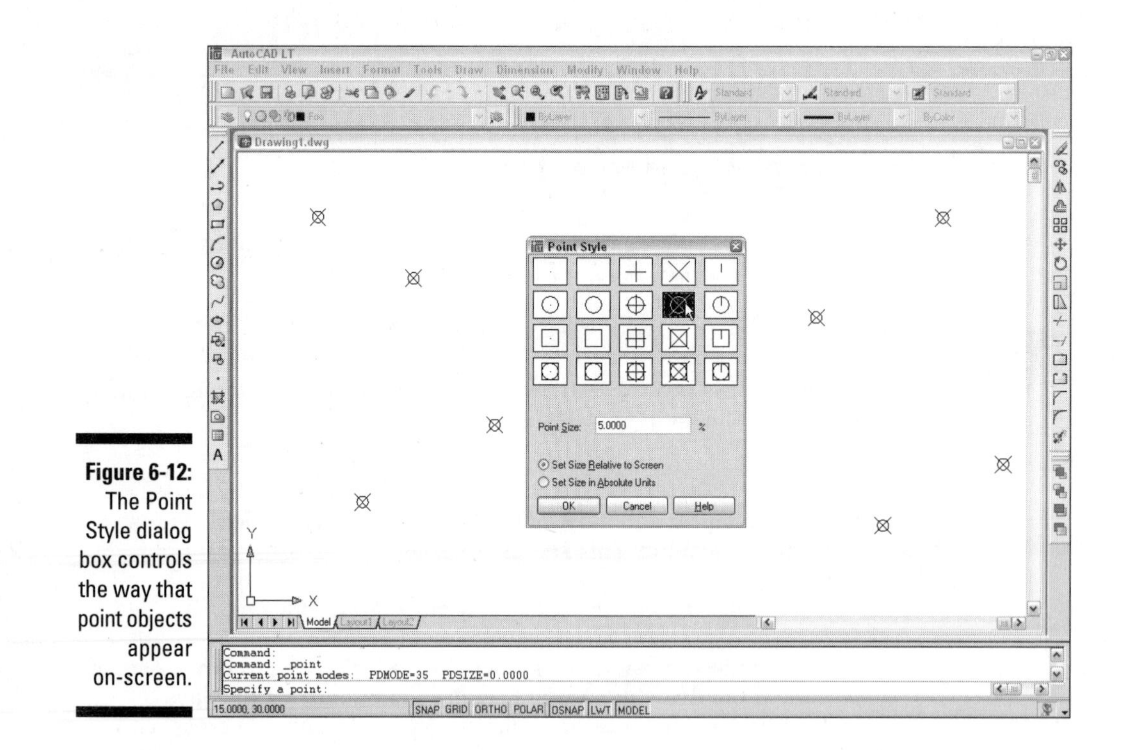

Figure 6-12: The Point Style dialog box controls the way that point objects appear on-screen.

The first choice, a single-pixel dot, is hard to see on-screen, and the second choice, invisible (a stealth point?), is impossible to see. Avoid these choices if you want your point objects to show up on-screen and on plots. The single-pixel dot, which is the default display style, works well if you use point objects as object snap locations and don't want the points obtrusive on plots.

The remaining settings in the Point Style dialog box control the size at which points appear on-screen at different zoom resolutions. The default settings often work fine, but if you're not satisfied with them, click the Help button to find out how to change them.

After you specify the point style, placing points on-screen is easy; the following example shows you how.

This example is of the command-line commands to create a point:

```
Command: POint Enter
Current point modes: PDMODE=0 PDSIZE=0.0000
Specify a point:  pick or type the coordinates of a location
        in the drawing
```

`PDMODE` and `PDSIZE` in the command prompt are system variables that correspond to the point display mode and display size options in the Point Style dialog box. If you want to know exactly how the system variables correspond to the dialog box choices, you have all the makings of a successful CAD nerd. Click the Help button in the Point Style dialog box to find out more (about the system variables — not about yourself).

If you start the POint command from the Draw toolbar or the Draw➪Point➪Multiple Point menu, it repeats automatically — that is, it prompts you repeatedly to `Specify a point`. When you finish drawing points, press Esc to finish the command for good. If the command doesn't repeat automatically and you want to draw more points, press the Enter key to repeat the POint command and pick another location on the screen. Repeat as required: Enter, pick, Enter, pick, Enter pick . . . by now you should've gotten the point.

Chapter 7

. . . Edit Often

In This Chapter

- Using command-first editing
- Selecting objects with maximum flexibility
- Moving, copying, and stretching objects
- Manipulating whole objects
- Changing pieces of objects
- Editing with grips
- Editing object properties

Editing objects is the flip side of creating them. In AutoCAD LT, you spend a lot of time editing — far more than drawing objects from scratch. That's partly because the design and drafting process is by its nature iterative, and also because CAD programs enable you to easily edit objects cleanly.

When you edit objects in AutoCAD LT, you need to be just as concerned about specifying precise locations and distances as you are when you originally create the objects. Make sure that you're familiar with the precision techniques I describe in Chapter 3 before you apply the editing techniques from this chapter to real drawings.

Commanding and Selecting

AutoCAD LT offers two main styles of editing:

- Command-first editing
- Selection-first editing

Within the selection-first editing style, you have an additional choice of editing that uses actual, named commands and *direct manipulation* of objects without named commands. The following sections cover these editing styles.

Command-first editing

With *command-first editing,* you enter a command and then click the objects on which the command works. This style of editing may seem backwards to you at first unless you've worked with AutoCAD or LT before or are a veteran of command-line operating systems (where you typically type the name of a command and then the names of the files or other objects to which you want to apply the command). Command-first editing works well for power users who are in a hurry and who are willing to memorize most of the commands they need to do their work. It's no surprise that command-first editing is the default style of editing in AutoCAD — and AutoCAD LT.

Selection-first editing

In *selection-first editing*, you perform the same steps — in the same order — as in most Windows applications: Select the object first, and then choose the command.

Selection-first editing tends to be easier to master, which is why Windows and the Macintosh are easier for most people to use for a variety of tasks than DOS ever was. Selection-first editing makes AutoCAD LT more approachable for new and occasional users.

Direct manipulation is a refinement of selection-first editing in which you perform common editing operations by using the mouse to grab the selected object and perform an action on it, such as moving all or part of it to a different place in the drawing. No named command is involved; the act of moving the mouse and clicking the mouse buttons in certain ways causes the editing changes to happen. AutoCAD LT supports direct manipulation through a powerful but somewhat complicated technique called *grip editing.* Grips are the little square handles that appear on an object when you select it. You can use the grips to stretch, move, copy, rotate, or otherwise edit the object. These grip-editing techniques can make selection-first editing almost as powerful as command-first editing. The complications arise from the fact that you can do so many things with an object after you select it.

Choosing an editing style

This chapter emphasizes command-first editing. (I also discuss grip editing at the end of the chapter.) AutoCAD LT, like its big brother AutoCAD, is fundamentally a command-first program. AutoCAD started out offering *only* command-first editing and later added selection-first methods; AutoCAD LT 2005 inherits this ancestral trait. I emphasize command-first editing for the following reasons:

- It's the default AutoCAD LT editing style.
- It works consistently with all editing commands — some editing commands remain command-first only.
- It provides added object selection flexibility, which is useful when you work on complicated, busy drawings.

After you know how to do command-first editing, you can simply reverse the order of *many* editing operations to do them selection-first style instead. But if you don't get familiar with command-first editing in the beginning, you can be completely bewildered by some very useful AutoCAD LT commands that work only in the command-first style, such as TRim and EXtend. (Commands such as these ignore any already selected objects and prompt you to select objects.)

Much of the information in this chapter assumes that you're using the default AutoCAD LT selection settings. If object selection or grip editing works differently from what I describe in this chapter, check the settings on the Option dialog box's Selection tab. Turn on these five check box settings (be sure all other check box settings are turned off):

- Noun/Verb Selection
- Implied Windowing
- Object Grouping
- Enable Grips
- Enable Grip Tips

Grab It

Part of AutoCAD LT's editing flexibility comes from its object selection flexibility. For example, command-first editing offers 16 selection modes! (I describe the most useful ones in this chapter.) Don't worry though; you can get by most of the time with just three selection modes:

- Selecting a single object
- Enclosing objects in a selection box, which AutoCAD LT calls *Window* (pick left corner, and then right corner)
- Including part or all the objects in a crossing selection box, which LT calls *Crossing* (pick right corner, and then left corner)

One by one selection

The most obvious way to select objects is to pick (by clicking) them one at a time. You can build up a selection set cumulatively with this "pick one object at a time" selection mode. This cumulative convention may be different from what you're used to. In most Windows programs, if you select one object and then another, the first object is deselected, and the second one selected. Only the object you select last remains selected. In AutoCAD LT, *all* the objects you select, one at a time, remain selected and are added to the set, no matter how many objects you pick. (You can change this behavior to make LT work like Windows does by turning on the Use Shift to Add to Selection option on the Option dialog box's Selection tab, but I suggest you not change it.) Most editing commands affect the entire group of selected objects.

Selection boxes left and right

Selecting objects one at a time works great when you want to edit a small number of objects, but many CAD editing tasks involve editing lots of objects. Do you really want to pick 132 lines, arcs, and circles one at a time?

Like most Windows graphics programs, AutoCAD LT provides a selection window feature for grabbing a bunch of objects in a rectangular area. As you may guess by now, the LT version of this feature is a bit more powerful than the analogous feature in other Windows graphics programs and, therefore, slightly confusing at first. AutoCAD LT calls its version *implied windowing.*

If you click a blank area of the drawing — that is, not on an object — you're *implying* to LT that you want to specify a selection window, or box. If you move the cursor to the right before picking the other corner of the selection box, you're further implying that you want to select all objects that reside completely within the selection box. If you instead move the cursor to the left before picking the other corner of the selection box, you're implying that you want to select all objects that reside completely *or partially* within the selection box.

The AutoCAD LT terminology for these two kinds of selection boxes gets a little confusing:

- The move-to-the-right, only-select-objects-completely-within-the-box mode is called *Window* object selection.
- The move-to-the-left, select-objects-completely-or-partially-within-the-box mode is called *Crossing* object selection.

You might think of these modes as *bounding box* (to the right) and *crossing box* (to the left). Fortunately, LT gives you a visual cue that there's a difference. As you move to the right, the bounding box appears as a solid rectangle. As you move to the left, the crossing box appears as a ghosted, or dashed, rectangle.

Figures 7-1 and 7-2 show a bounding box and a crossing box, respectively, in action.

You can mix and match selecting individual objects, specifying a bounding box, and specifying a crossing box. Each selection adds to the current selection set, allowing you to build up an enormously complicated selection of objects and then operate on them with one or more editing commands.

You can press the Shift key in combination with any of the three standard selection modes — single object, bounding box (Window), and crossing box (Crossing) — to *remove* already selected objects from the selection set. This feature is especially useful when you're building a selection set in a crowded drawing; you can select a big batch of objects using Window or Crossing, and then hold down the Shift key while selecting to remove the objects that you want to exclude from the editing operation.

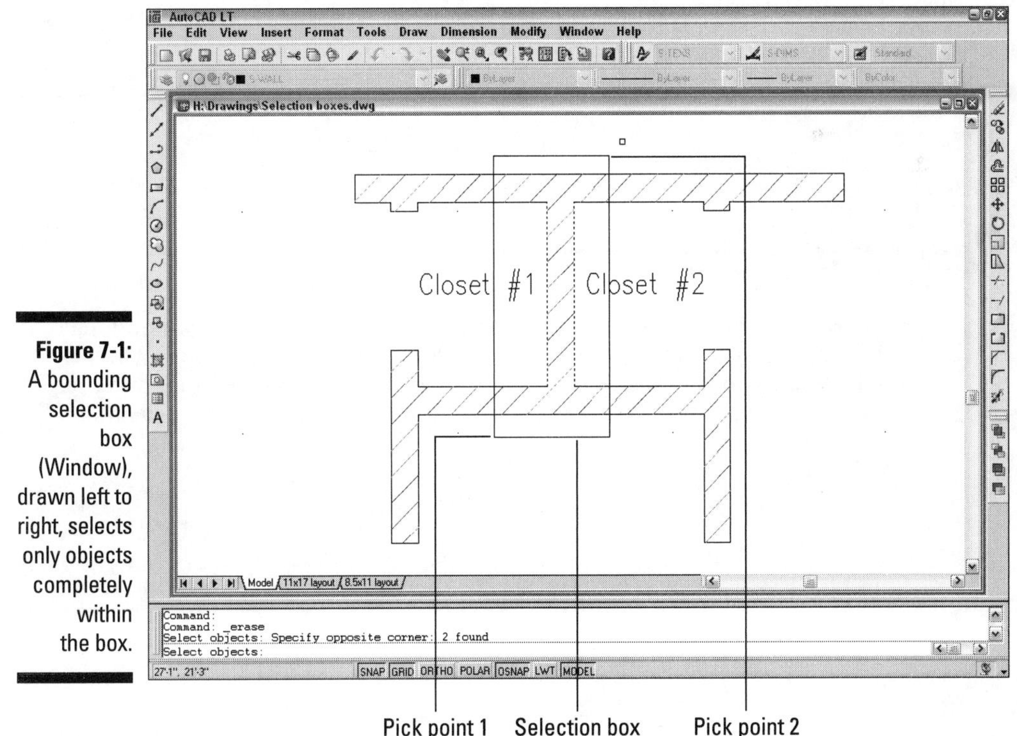

Figure 7-1: A bounding selection box (Window), drawn left to right, selects only objects completely within the box.

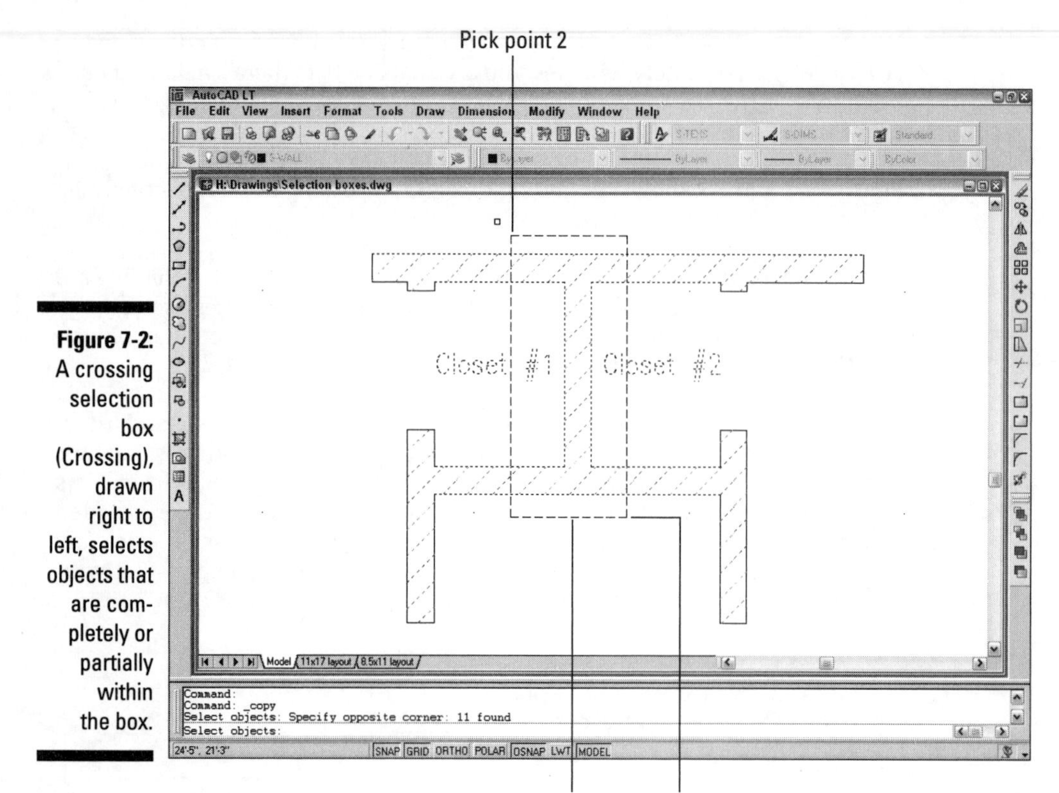

Figure 7-2: A crossing selection box (Crossing), drawn right to left, selects objects that are completely or partially within the box.

Perfecting Selecting

When you edit in command-first mode, you have all the selection options that I describe in the previous section — single object, bounding box (Window), and crossing box (Crossing) — plus a slew of others. If you type **?** and press Enter at any `Select objects` prompt, AutoCAD LT lists all the selection options:

```
Window/Last/Crossing/BOX/ALL/Fence/WPolygon/CPolygon/Group/
        Add/Remove/Multiple/Previous/Undo/AUto/SIngle
```

Table 7-1 summarizes the most useful command-first selection options.

Table 7-1 Some Useful Command-First Selection Options

Option	*Description*
Window	All objects within a rectangle that you specify by picking two points
Last	The last object you drew that's still visible in the drawing area
Crossing	All objects within or crossing a rectangle that you specify by picking two points
ALL	All objects on layers that aren't frozen and that are in the current space (model space or paper space)
Fence	All objects touching an imaginary polyline whose vertices you specify by picking points
WPolygon	All objects within a polygonal area whose corners you specify by picking points
CPolygon	All objects within or crossing a polygonal area whose corners you specify by picking points
Previous	The previous selection set that you specified

To use any of the command-first selection options at the `Select objects` prompt, type the uppercase letters corresponding to the option and press Enter. After you finish selecting objects, you must press Enter again to tell LT that you're finished selecting objects and want to start the editing operation.

The following example demonstrates how to use the Erase command in command-first mode with several different selection options. The selection techniques used in this example apply to most AutoCAD LT editing commands:

1. **Press Esc to make sure that no command is active and no objects are selected.**

   If any objects are selected when you start an editing command, the command, in most cases, operates on those objects (selection-first editing) instead of prompting you to select objects (command-first editing). For the reasons that I describe earlier in this chapter, use the command-first editing style until you're thoroughly familiar with it. Later, you can experiment with selection-first editing if you like. (Just reverse the sequence of commanding and selecting that I describe in this chapter.)

2. **Click the Erase button on the Modify toolbar.**

   The command line displays the `Select objects` prompt.

3. **Select two or three individual objects by clicking each one.**

   LT adds each object to the selection set. All the objects you select remain ghosted. The command line displays the `Select objects` prompt.

4. **Specify a bounding selection box (Window) that completely encloses several objects.**

   Move the cursor to a point below and to the left of the objects, click, release the mouse button, move the cursor above and to the right of the objects, and click again.

   All objects that are completely within the box are selected.

5. **Specify a crossing selection box (Crossing) that encloses a few objects and cuts through several others.**

   Move the cursor to a point below and to the right of some of the objects, click, release the mouse button, move the cursor above and to the left of some of the objects, and click and release again.

   All objects that are completely within or cross through the box are selected.

6. **Type** F **and press Enter to activate the Fence selection option.**

   The command line prompts you to pick points that define the selection fence — that is, a series of straight line segments cutting across objects that you want to select.

7. **Pick a series of points and press Enter.**

   Figure 7-3 shows an example. After you press Enter, LT selects all objects that are crossed by the selection fence.

8. **Press Enter to end object selection.**

   LT erases all the selected objects.

Notice how you are able to use a combination of object selection methods to build up a selection set and then press Enter to execute the command on them. Most AutoCAD LT editing commands work this way in command-first mode.

If, after erasing a selection set, you immediately realize that you didn't really mean to do away with so many objects, you can use the Undo button on the Standard toolbar to restore all of them. But LT has one additional un-erase trick up its sleeve — the aptly named OOps command. When you type **OOps** and press Enter, LT restores the last selection set that you erased — even if you ran other commands after Erase.

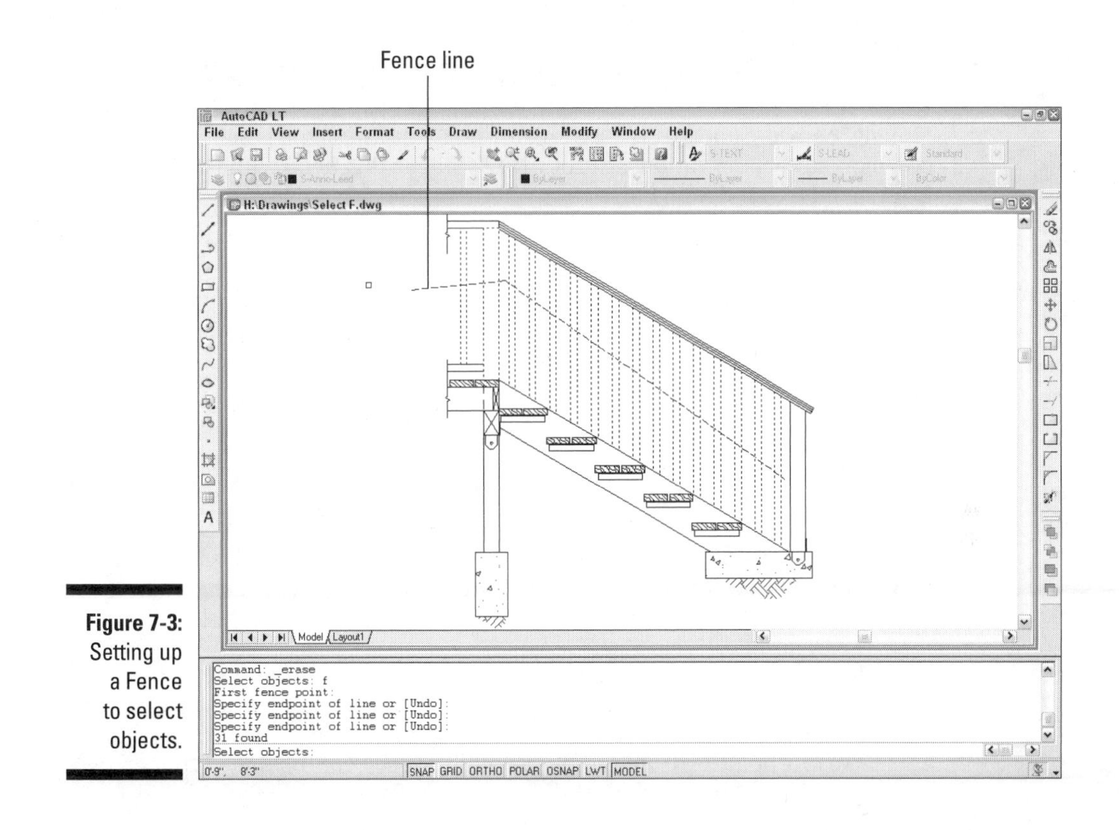

Figure 7-3: Setting up a Fence to select objects.

Ready, Get Set, Edit!

The following sections cover the most important AutoCAD LT editing commands, using command-first editing mode.

Whether you start an LT editing command by clicking a toolbar button, choosing a pull-down menu command, or typing a command name, in almost all cases the command prompts you for points, distances, and options at the command line. Read the command line prompts during every step of the command, especially when you're figuring out how to use a new editing command. Otherwise, you're unlikely to complete the command successfully.

As I describe in Chapter 3, maintaining precision when you draw and edit is crucial to good CAD work. If you've used a drawing program and are accustomed to moving, stretching, and otherwise editing objects by eye, you need to suppress that habit when you edit in LT. Nothing ruins a drawing faster than approximate editing, in which you shove objects around until they look okay, without worrying about precise distances and points.

The big three: Move, Copy, and Stretch

Moving, copying, and stretching are, for many drafters, the three most common editing operations. AutoCAD LT obliges this need with the Move, CoPy, and Stretch commands.

Base points and displacements

The Move, CoPy, and Stretch commands all require that you specify how far and in what direction you want to move, copy, or stretch the objects. After you select the objects to edit and start the command, AutoCAD LT prompts you for two pieces of information:

```
Specify base point or displacement:
Specify second point of displacement or <use first point as
          displacement>:
```

In a not-so-clear way, these prompts say that two possible methods exist for you to specify how far and in what direction you want to copy, move, or stretch the objects:

- **The most common way is to pick or type the coordinates of two points that define a displacement vector.** LT calls these points the *base point* and the *second point* (hence, it's called the *base point method*). Imagine an arrow pointing from the base point to the second point — that arrow defines how far and in what direction to copy, move, or stretch the objects.
- **The other way is to type an X,Y pair of numbers that represents a distance rather than a point.** This distance is the absolute displacement that you want to copy, move, or stretch the objects (thus it's called the *displacement method*).

How does AutoCAD LT know whether your response to the first prompt is a base point or a displacement? It depends on how you respond to the second prompt. (Is that confusing, or what?) First, you pick a point on-screen or enter coordinates at the `Base point` prompt. Next, you have a couple of possibilities:

- If you then pick or type the coordinates of a point at the second point prompt, LT says to itself, "Aha — displacement vector!" and moves the objects according to the imaginary arrow pointing from the base point to the second point.
- If you press Enter at the second prompt (without having typed anything), LT says, "Aha — displacement distance," and uses the X,Y pair of numbers that you typed at the first prompt as an absolute displacement distance.

What makes this displacement business even more confusing is that AutoCAD LT lets you pick a point at the first prompt and press Enter at the second prompt. LT still says, "Aha — displacement distance," but now it treats the coordinates of the point you picked as an absolute distance. If the point you picked has relatively large coordinates, the objects can get moved way outside the normal drawing area as defined by the limits. The objects fly off into space, which you probably won't notice at first because you're zoomed into part of your normal drawing area; it just looks to you like the objects have vanished! In short, be careful when you press Enter during the Move, CoPy, and Stretch commands. Press Enter in response to the second prompt only if you want LT to use your response to the first prompt as an absolute displacement. If you make a mistake, click the Undo button to back up and try again. You can use Zoom Extents (described in Chapter 8) to look for objects that have flown off into space.

Move

The following steps demonstrate command-first editing with the Move command, using the base point method of indicating how far and in what direction to move the selected objects. This example also gives detailed recommendations on how to use precision techniques when you edit:

1. **Press Esc to make sure that no command is active and no objects are selected.**
2. **Click the Move button on the Modify toolbar.**

   The command line displays the `Select objects` prompt.
3. **Select one or more objects.**

   You can use any of the object selection techniques that I describe in the "Perfecting Selecting" section, earlier in this chapter.
4. **Press Enter when you finish selecting objects.**

   LT displays the following prompt:

   ```
   Specify base point or displacement:
   ```
5. **Specify a base point by clicking a point or typing coordinates.**

   This point serves as the tail end of your imaginary arrow indicating how far and in what direction you want to move the objects. After you pick a base point, seeing what's going on is fairly easy because LT displays a temporary image of the object that moves around as you move the cursor. Figure 7-4 shows what the screen looks like.

   Specify a base point somewhere on or near the object(s) that you're moving. You can use an object snap mode to choose a point exactly on one of the objects.

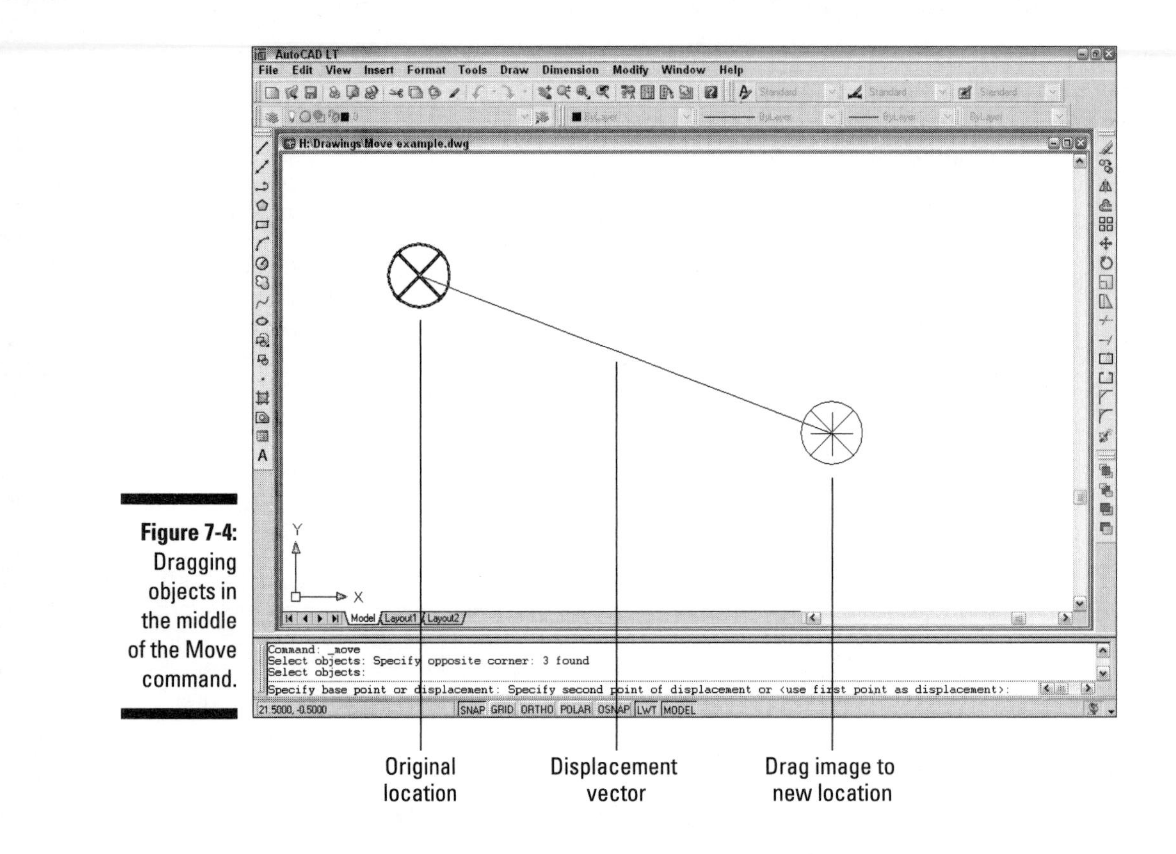

Figure 7-4: Dragging objects in the middle of the Move command.

LT displays the following prompt:

```
Specify second point of displacement or <use first point
         as displacement>:
```

6. **Specify the second point by clicking a point or typing coordinates.**

   The second point serves as the arrow end of your imaginary displacement arrow. After you specify the second point, LT moves the objects.

   Don't press Enter alone at this prompt! If you do, LT treats the X,Y coordinates of the first point you picked as an absolute displacement, and the objects fly off in an unpredictable fashion.

These are common precision techniques for specifying the second point:

- Use an object snap mode to pick a second point exactly on another object in the drawing.
- Type a relative or polar coordinate, as I describe in Chapter 3. For example, if you type **@6,2**, LT moves the objects 6 units to the right and 2 units up. If you type **@3<45**, LT moves the objects 3 units at an angle of 45 degrees.
- Use direct distance entry to move objects in an orthogonal or polar tracking direction. See Chapter 3 for instructions.

Copy

The CoPy command works almost identically to the Move command, except that AutoCAD LT leaves the selected objects in place and moves new copies of them to the new location. The CoPy command also includes a Multiple option for making multiple copies of the same set of objects. You activate the Multiple option by typing **M** and pressing Enter after you finish the object selection. As always, you must watch the command line prompts to find out what you can do and when to do it!

Copy between drawings

You can't copy objects from one drawing to another by using the CoPy command. Instead, you use the COPYCLIP command, together with its companion command, PASTECLIP. Follow these steps:

1. **Open two drawings that contain geometry you want to copy from one to the other. Arrange the two drawings so that you can see both of them, as shown in Figure 7-5.**

   If you don't have enough screen real estate to arrange the two drawings side by side, you can leave them overlapped and change between the two drawing windows by using the Window menu or by pressing Ctrl+Tab.

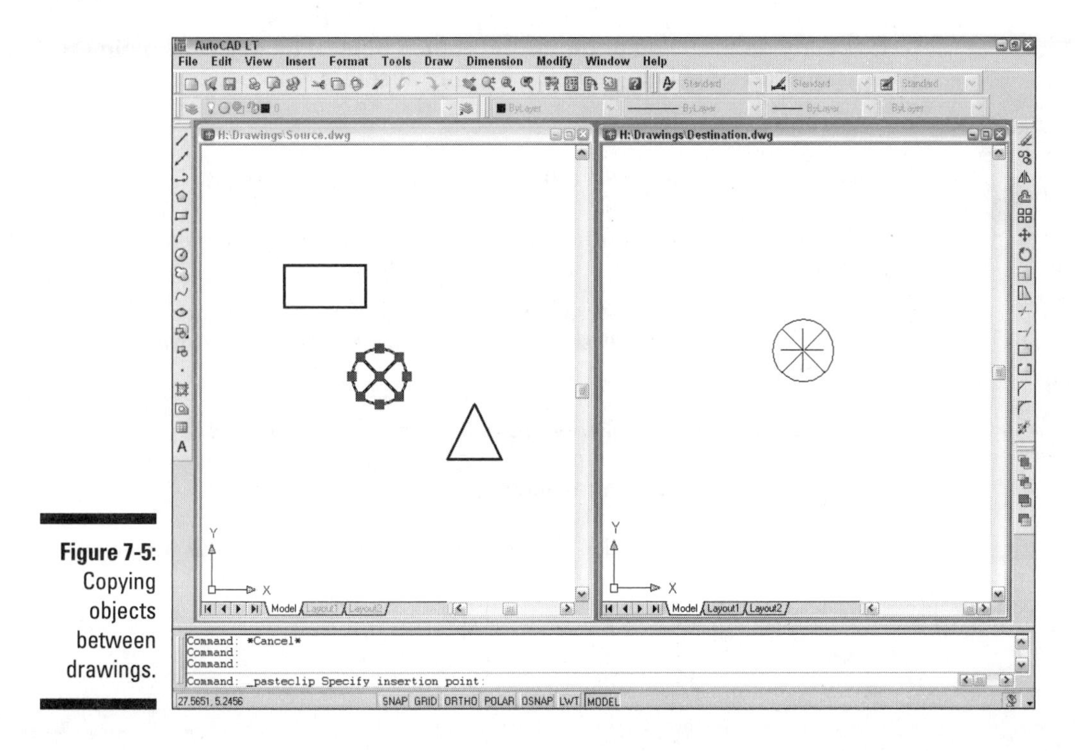

Figure 7-5: Copying objects between drawings.

2. **In the first drawing, right-click in the drawing area and choose Copy from the menu.**

   Choose Cut if you want to move rather than copy the objects to the other drawing. Choose Copy with Base Point if you want to choose a specific base point rather than let AutoCAD LT choose a base point.

   The base point that LT chooses is the lower-left corner of an imaginary rectangle that just barely encloses all the objects you've selected.

3. **If you chose Copy with Base Point in Step 2, pick a base point to use for the copy operation.**

   The base point is like a base point for a block definition, as I describe in Chapter 13. Choose a useful point such as the endpoint of a line, the lower-left corner of a rectangle, or the center of a circle.

4. **Select the objects that you want to copy and then press Enter to end object selection.**

5. **Click in the second drawing's window to make it current.**

6. **Right-click in the second drawing's window and choose Paste from the menu.**

   Choose Paste to Original Coordinates if you want to copy the objects so that they land at the same point (with respect to 0,0) in the second drawing as they were located in the first drawing.

7. **Specify an insertion point for the copied objects by object snapping to a point on an existing object or typing absolute X,Y coordinates.**

   LT copies the objects.

Confusing the CoPy and COPYCLIP commands is easy:

- CoPy is AutoCAD LT's primary command for copying objects within a drawing.
- COPYCLIP — along with related commands like CUTCLIP and PASTECLIP — is LT's version of copy-and-paste via the Windows Clipboard.

(You can use the Windows Clipboard cut-and-paste method to copy or move objects within a single drawing, but using the LT CoPy and Move commands usually gives you better control and precision.)

Table 7-2 summarizes AutoCAD LT's Clipboard-related commands, along with the equivalent choices on the Edit menu and the Standard toolbar.

Table 7-2 AutoCAD LT Clipboard Commands

Edit Menu Choice	*Command Name*	*Toolbar Button Name*
Cut	CUTCLIP	Cut to Clipboard (Ctrl+X)
Copy	COPYCLIP	Copy to Clipboard (Ctrl+C)
Copy with Base Point	COPYBASE	None
Paste	PASTECLIP	Paste from Clipboard (Ctrl+V)
Paste as Block	PASTEBLOCK	None
Paste to Original Coordinates	PASTEORIG	None

Stretch

The Stretch command is superficially similar to CoPy and Move; it has the same inscrutable base point and displacement prompts, and it shifts objects (or parts of objects) to other locations in the drawing. But it also has important differences that often confound new AutoCAD LT users to the point where they give up trying to use Stretch. That's a mistake because Stretch is a valuable command. With it, you can perform editing operations in seconds that take many minutes with other commands. Here are the things you need to know to make Stretch your friend:

- To use Stretch, you must select objects by using a crossing selection box (or crossing polygon), as described in the section "Perfecting Selecting," earlier in this chapter. See Figure 7-6.
- Stretch operates on the defining points of objects — endpoints of a line, vertices of a polyline, the center of a circle, and so on — according to the following rule: If a defining point is within the crossing selection box that you specify, LT moves the defining point and updates the object accordingly.

  For example, if your crossing selection box surrounds one endpoint of a line but not the other endpoint, Stretch moves the first endpoint and redraws the line in the new position dictated by the first endpoint's new location. It's as though you have a rubber band tacked to the wall with two pins, and you move one of the pins. See Figure 7-7.
- Stretch can make lines longer or shorter, depending on your crossing selection box and displacement vector. In other words, the Stretch command really combines stretching and compressing.
- You usually want to turn on ortho or polar tracking mode before stretching. Otherwise, you end up stretching objects in strange directions, as shown in Figure 7-8.

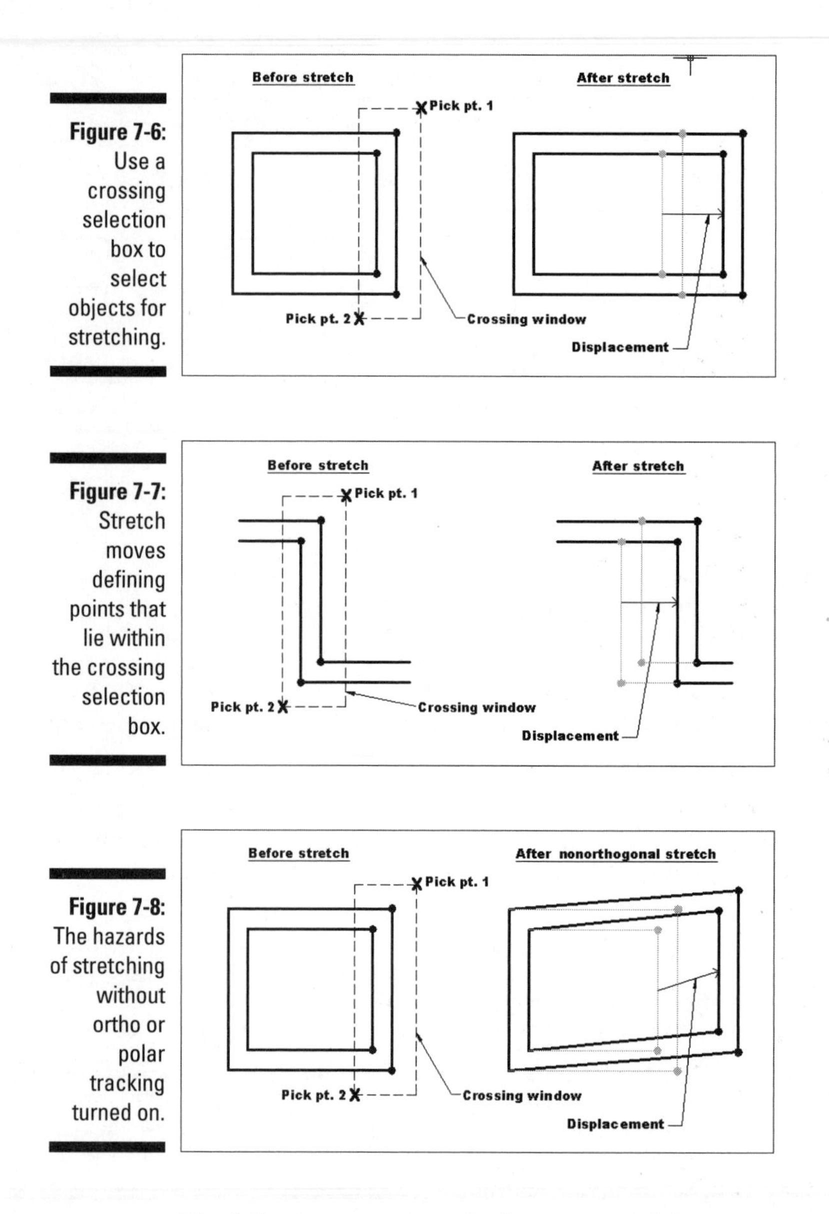

Figure 7-6: Use a crossing selection box to select objects for stretching.

Figure 7-7: Stretch moves defining points that lie within the crossing selection box.

Figure 7-8: The hazards of stretching without ortho or polar tracking turned on.

The following steps describe how to stretch lines:

1. **Draw some lines in an arrangement similar to the dark lines shown in Figure 7-9.**

   Start your stretching with simple objects. You can work up to more complicated objects — polylines, circles, arcs, and so on — after you limber up with lines.

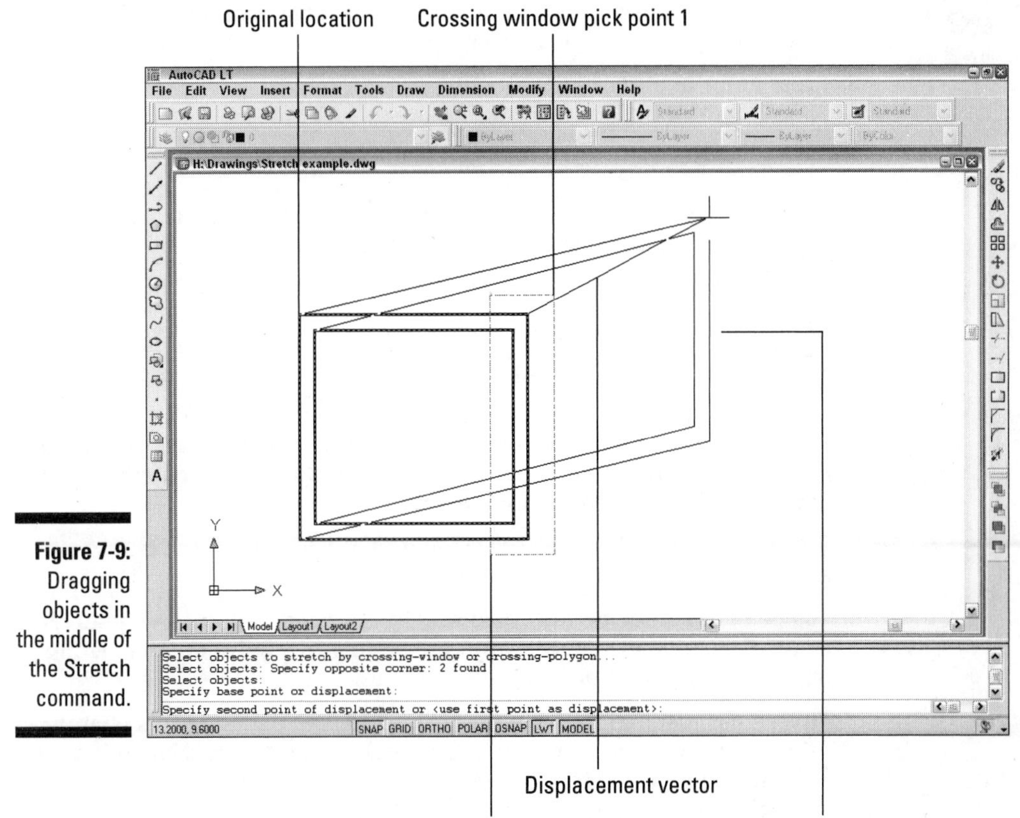

Figure 7-9: Dragging objects in the middle of the Stretch command.

2. **Press Esc to make sure that no command is active and no objects are selected.**
3. **Click the Stretch button on the Modify toolbar.**

   The command line displays the `Select objects` prompt, with a warning to use the Crossing or CPolygon object selection mode:

   ```
   Select objects to stretch by crossing-window or crossing-
         polygon...
   Select objects:
   ```
4. **Specify a crossing selection box that encloses some, but not all, endpoints of the lines.**

   Figure 7-9 shows a sample crossing selection box that completely encloses the two vertical lines on the right side of the figure. This crossing selection box cuts through the four horizontal lines, enclosing only one endpoint of each.

You specify a crossing selection box by picking a point, moving your mouse to the *left*, and picking a second point.

5. **Press Enter to end object selection.**

   LT displays the following prompt.

   ```
   Specify base point or displacement:
   ```

6. **Specify a base point by object snapping to a point on an existing object or by typing absolute X,Y coordinates.**

   This step is just like Step 5 in the "Move" section earlier in this chapter.

   LT displays the following prompt:

   ```
   Specify second point of displacement or <use first point
         as displacement>:
   ```

7. **Toggle ortho mode on and then off by clicking the ORTHO button on the status bar; try moving the cursor around first with ortho mode on and then with it off to see the difference.**

   Figure 7-9 shows what the screen looks like as you move the cursor around with ortho off.

8. **Toggle ortho mode on and then specify the second point — usually by using direct distance entry, object snapping to a point on an existing object, or typing relative X,Y coordinates.**

   This step is just like Step 6 in the "Move" section earlier in this chapter. After you pick the second point, LT stretches the objects. Notice that the Stretch command moved the two vertical lines because the crossing selection box contains both endpoints of both lines. Stretch lengthens or shortens the four horizontal lines because the crossing selection box encloses only one endpoint of each.

The Stretch command takes some practice, but it's worth the effort. Draw some additional kinds of objects and practice stretching with different crossing selection box locations as well as different base points and second points.

More manipulations

The commands in this section — ROtate, SCale, MIrror, ARray, and Offset — provide other ways (in addition to Move, CoPy, and Stretch) of manipulating objects or creating new versions of them. The procedures for each command assume that you're familiar with the object selection and editing precision techniques presented in the Move, CoPy, and Stretch procedures (see the previous sections in this chapter).

Rotate

The ROtate command "swings" one or more objects around a point that you specify. Follow these steps to use the ROtate command:

1. **Press Esc to make sure that no command is active and no objects are selected.**
2. **Click the Rotate button on the Modify toolbar.**
3. **Select one or more objects and then press Enter to end object selection.**

   LT prompts you for the base point for rotating the selected objects:

   ```
   Specify base point:
   ```
4. **Specify a base point by clicking a point or typing coordinates.**

   The base point becomes the point about which LT rotates the objects. You also have to specify a rotation angle:

   ```
   Specify rotation angle or [Reference]:
   ```
5. **Specify a rotation angle by typing an angle measurement and pressing Enter.**

   Alternatively, you can indicate an angle on-screen by moving the cursor until the Coordinates section of the status bar indicates the desired angle and then clicking. If you choose this alternative, you need to use ortho mode or polar tracking to indicate a precise angle (for example, 90 or 45 degrees) or an object snap to rotate an object so that it aligns precisely with other objects.

   After you specify the rotation angle by typing or picking, LT rotates the objects into their new position.

Scale

If you read all my harping on drawing scales and drawing scale factors in Chapter 5, you might think that the SCale command performs some magical scale transformation on your entire drawing. No such luck. It merely scales one or more objects up or down by a factor that you specify. Here's how it works:

1. **Press Esc to make sure that no command is active and no objects are selected.**
2. **Click the Scale button on the Modify toolbar.**
3. **Select one or more objects and then press Enter to end object selection.**

   LT prompts you for the base point about which it scales all the selected objects:

   ```
   Specify base point:
   ```

LT does not scale each object individually around its own base point (because most AutoCAD LT drawing objects don't have individual base points). Instead, LT uses the base point that you specify to determine how to scale *all* objects in the selection set. For example, if you select a circle to scale, pick a point outside the circle as the base point, and then specify a scale factor of 2, LT not only makes the circle twice as big, but also moves the circle twice as far away from the base point that you specify.

4. **Specify a base point by picking a point or typing coordinates.**

   The base point becomes the point about which the objects are scaled. LT prompts you for the scale factor:

   ```
   Specify scale factor or [Reference]:
   ```

5. **Type a scale factor and press Enter.**

   LT then scales the objects by the factor that you type, using the base point that you specify. Numbers greater than one increase the objects' size. Numbers smaller than one decrease the objects' size.

Changing the drawing scale factor of a drawing after you draw it is a tedious and complicated process in AutoCAD LT. In brief, you need to change the scale-dependent system variables described in Chapter 5, and then scale some, but not all, drawing objects. You don't scale the real-world geometry that you draw because its measurements in the real world remain the same. You do scale objects such as text and hatching that have a fixed height or spacing regardless of drawing scale factor. (The SCALETEXT command can help with this operation. See Chapter 9 for more information.) Because of these complications, try to make sure that you choose a proper scale and set up the drawing properly for that scale before you begin drawing. See Chapter 5 for details.

Mirror

The MIrror command creates a mirror image — that is, a flipped-around version — of one or more objects. The MIrror command can move *or* copy the original objects; in other words, you can direct MIrror to leave the original, unflipped version in place along with the flipped version or to make the original version vanish and leave only the flipped version. Follow these steps to use the MIrror command:

1. **Press Esc to make sure that no command is active and no objects are selected.**
2. **Click the Mirror button on the Modify toolbar.**
3. **Select one or more objects and then press Enter to end object selection.**

   LT prompts you for the first endpoint of an imaginary line about which MIrror will flip the objects:

   ```
   Specify first point of mirror line:
   ```

4. **Specify a point by clicking a point or typing coordinates.**

   LT prompts you for the second endpoint of the imaginary mirror line:

   ```
   Specify second point of mirror line:
   ```

5. **Specify a second point.**

   The length of the imaginary mirror line doesn't matter — only its orientation and distance from the original objects. If you want the flipping to occur about a vertical or horizontal mirror line, turn on ortho mode before you specify the second point.

   After you specify the second point, LT asks whether you want to delete the original objects or leave them in place:

   ```
   Delete source objects [Yes/No] <N>:
   ```

6. **Press Enter to leave the original objects in place, or type** Y **and press Enter to delete them.**

   LT creates the mirrored objects. If you answered No to the `Delete source objects` prompt, LT creates the mirrored objects as copies of the original objects. If you answered Yes, LT replaces the original objects with the mirrored ones.

The MIRRTEXT system variable controls whether mirrored text appears normally — the way most people write and read it — or as though you were reading the letters and words themselves in a mirror — the way that Leonardo da Vinci wrote some of the time. The default setting, MIRRTEXT=0, causes the MIrror command to reflip mirrored text so that it reads normally, and that's almost certainly what you want. If you prefer da Vinci style, you can set MIRRTEXT=1 before running the MIrror command.

Array

The ARray command is like a supercharged CoPy: You use it to create a rectangular grid of objects at regular X and Y spacings or a polar wheel of objects at a regular angular spacing. For example, you can use rectangular arrays to populate an auditorium with chairs or a polar array to draw bicycle spokes.

The following steps describe how to create a rectangular array, which you'll probably do more often than creating a polar array:

1. **Press Esc to make sure that no command is active and no objects are selected.**

   Alternatively, you can select objects before starting the ARray command and thereby skip Step 3.

2. **Click the Array button on the Modify toolbar.**

   The Array dialog box appears, as shown in Figure 7-10.

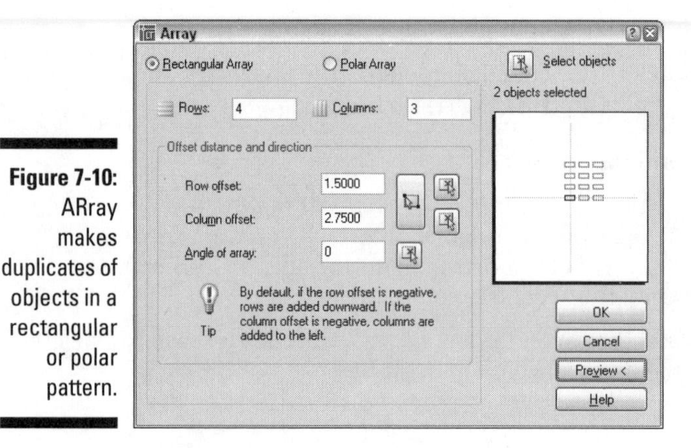

Figure 7-10: ARray makes duplicates of objects in a rectangular or polar pattern.

3. **Click the Select Objects button, and then select one or more objects. Press Enter to end object selection and return to the Array dialog box.**
4. **Make sure that the Rectangular Array radio button is selected.**

   If rectangular arrays seem too square, choose the cool Polar Array radio button instead and experiment with the other array option.
5. **Fill in the five edit boxes: Rows, Columns, Row Offset, Column Offset, and Angle of Array.**

   The Rows and Columns numbers include the row and column of the original objects themselves. In other words, entries of 1 don't create any new objects in that direction. The Row Offset and Column Offset measurements are the distances between adjacent rows and columns.
6. **Click Preview.**

   LT shows what the array will look like by using your current settings and displays a dialog box with Accept, Modify, and Cancel buttons.
7. **Click the Accept button if you're satisfied with the array, or the Modify button if you want to change the array parameters.**

Offset

You use the Offset command to create parallel copies of lines, polylines, circles, arcs, or splines. Follow these steps to use Offset:

1. **Click the Offset button on the Modify toolbar.**

   LT prompts you for the *offset distance* — the distance from the original object to the copy you're creating:

   ```
   Specify offset distance or [Through] <Through>:
   ```
2. **Type an offset distance and press Enter.**

Alternatively, you can indicate an offset distance by picking two points on-screen. If you choose this method, you normally use object snaps to specify a precise distance from one existing object to another.

A third alternative is to use the Through option, after which you specify one or more points through which you want the offset lines to run. (See Steps 3 and 4.)

LT prompts you to select the object from which you want to create an offset copy:

```
Select object to offset or <exit>:
```

3. **Select a single object, such as a line, polyline, or arc.**

   Note: You can select only one object at a time with the Offset command. LT asks where you want the offset object:

   ```
   Specify point on side to offset:
   ```

   If you specified the Through option in Step 2, LT prompts you with the following instead:

   ```
   Specify through point:
   ```

4. **Point to one side or the other of the object and then click.**

   If you typed or pointed to a distance in Step 2, then how far away from the object the cursor is when you click doesn't matter. You're simply indicating a direction.

   If you specified the Through option in Step 2, then how far away from the object the cursor is when you click *does* matter. Use object snap or another precision tool to specify a point through which you want the offset object to run.

   In either case, LT repeats the `Select object` prompt, in case you want to offset other objects by the same distance:

   ```
   Select object to offset or <exit>:
   ```

5. **Go back to Step 3 if you want to offset another object, or press Enter if you're finished offsetting objects for now.**

Figure 7-11 shows the Offset command in progress.

If you want to offset a series of connected lines (for example, a rectangular house plan outline or one side of a pathway on a map), make sure that you either draw it as a polyline or convert the individual line and/or arc segments into a polyline with the PEdit command. If you draw a series of line segments with the Line command and then try to offset it, you have to pick each segment and offset it individually. Even worse, the corners usually aren't finished off in the way that you expect because AutoCAD LT doesn't treat the segments as connected. You avoid all of these problems by offsetting a polyline, which LT does treat as a single object. See Chapter 6 for more information about the differences between lines and polylines.

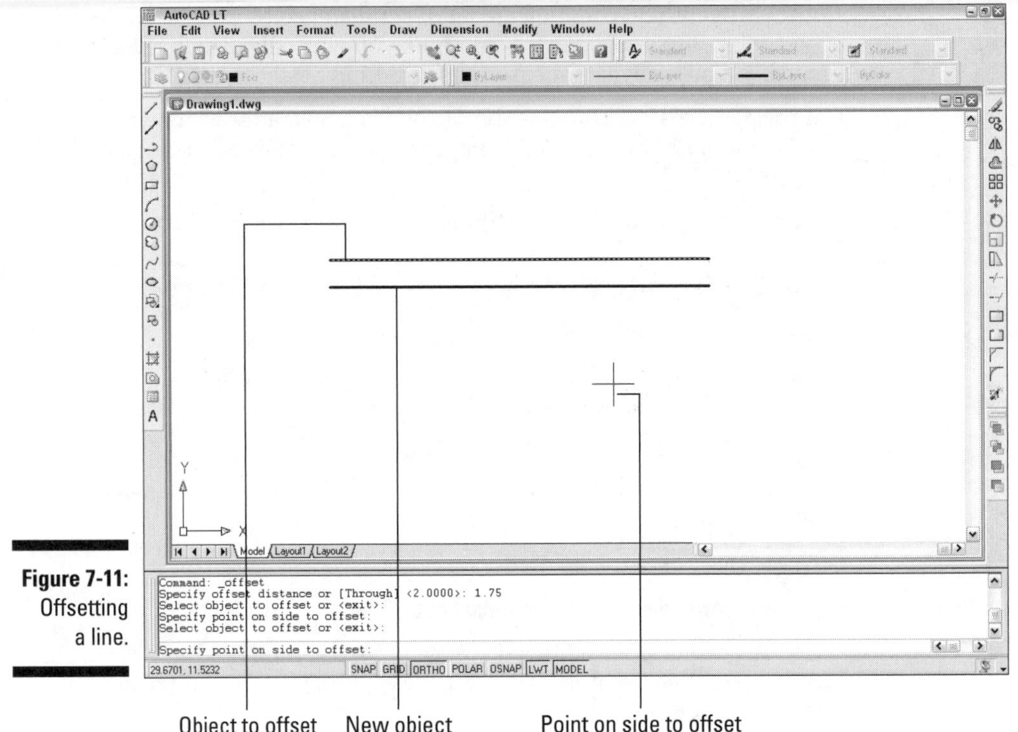

Figure 7-11: Offsetting a line.

Slicing and dicing

The commands in this section — TRim, EXtend, BReak, Fillet, and CHAmfer — are useful for shortening and lengthening objects and for breaking them in two.

Trim and Extend

TRim and EXtend are the twin commands for making lines, polylines, and arcs shorter and longer. They're the yin and yang, the Laurel and Hardy, the Jack Sprat and his wife of the AutoCAD LT editing world. The two commands and their prompts are almost identical, so the following steps cover both. I show the prompts for the TRim command; the EXtend prompts are similar:

1. **Click the Trim or Extend button on the Modify toolbar.**

   LT prompts you to select cutting edges that do the trimming (or, if you choose the EXtend command, boundary edges for extending to):

   ```
   Current settings: Projection=UCS, Edge=None
   Select cutting edges ...
   Select objects:
   ```

2. **Select one or more objects that act as the knife for trimming objects or the wall to which objects extend. Press Enter to end object selection.**

   Figure 7-12 shows a cutting edge (for TRim) and a boundary edge (for EXtend).

   LT prompts you to select objects that you want to trim or extend:

   ```
   Select object to trim or shift-select to extend or
           [Project/Edge/Undo]:
   ```

3. **Select a single object to trim or extend. Choose the portion of the object that you want LT to trim away or the end of the object that's closer to the extend-to boundary.**

   LT trims or extends the object to one of the objects that you selected in Step 2. If LT can't trim or extend the object — for example, if the trimming object and the object to be trimmed are parallel — the command line displays an error message such as `Object does not intersect an edge.`

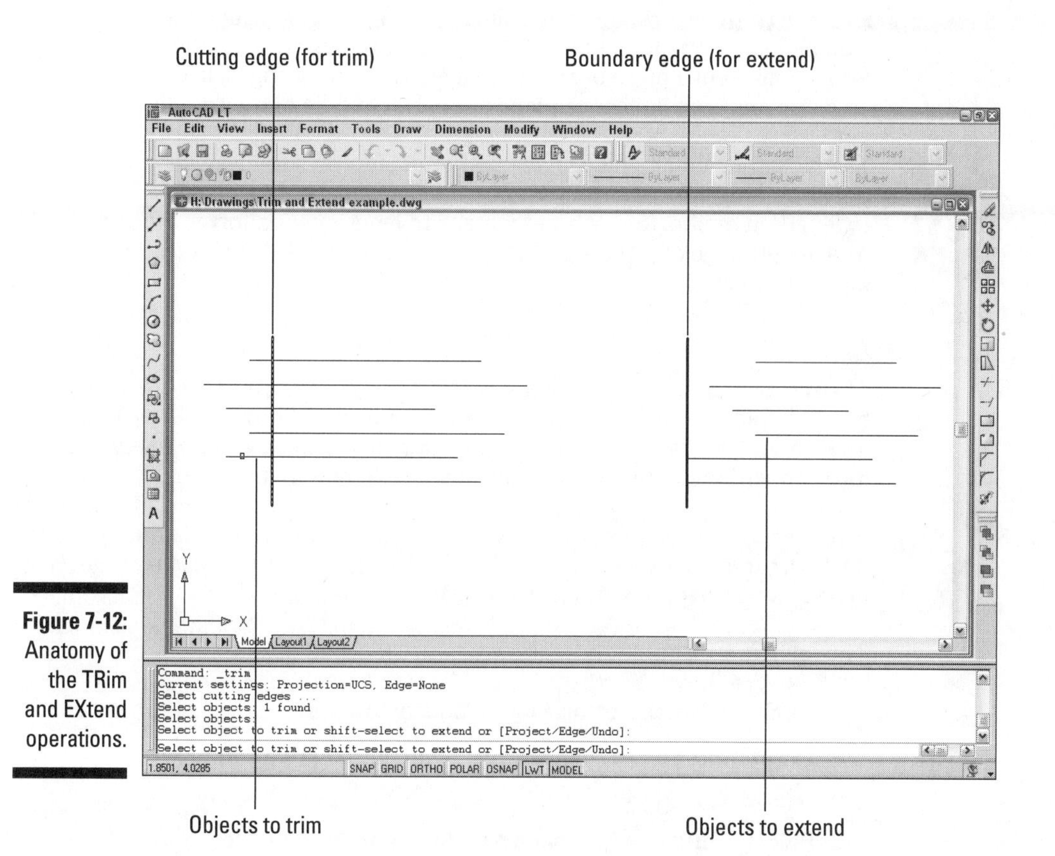

Figure 7-12: Anatomy of the TRim and EXtend operations.

TRim and EXtend normally allow you to select only one object at a time for trimming or extending. The one exception is that you can type **F** and press Enter to use the Fence object selection mode (refer to Table 7-1 and the selection example in the "Perfecting Selecting" section earlier in this chapter). Fence is useful for trimming or extending a large group of objects in one fell swoop.

The command line continues to prompt you to select other objects to trim or extend:

```
Select object to trim or shift-select to extend or
        [Project/Edge/Undo]:
```

4. **Choose additional objects, or press Enter when you're finished trimming or extending.**

If you accidentally trim or extend the wrong object and you're still in the TRim or EXtend command, type **U** and press Enter to undo the most recent trim or extend.

Figure 7-12 shows trimming to a single cutting edge, in which the end of the trimmed lines gets lopped off. Another common use of the TRim command is for trimming out a piece of a line between two cutting edges. In the two-cutting-edges scenario, TRim cuts a piece out of the middle of the trimmed line.

The LENgthen command provides other useful ways to make lines, arcs, and polylines longer (or shorter). You can specify an absolute distance (or "delta") to lengthen or shorten by, a percentage to lengthen or shorten by, or a new total length. Look up "LENGTHEN command" in AutoCAD LT's online help for more information.

Break

The BReak command isn't what you use before heading out for coffee. It's for breaking pieces out of — that is, creating gaps in — lines, polylines, circles, arcs, or splines. BReak also comes in handy if you need to split one object into two without actually removing any visible material.

If you want to create regularly spaced gaps in an object — so that it displays dashed, for instance — don't use BReak. Use an AutoCAD LT dash-dot linetype instead. See Chapter 3 for more linetype information.

The following example shows how you to BReak an object:

1. **Click the Break button on the Modify toolbar.**

   LT prompts you to select a single object that you want to break:

   ```
   Select object:
   ```

2. **Select a single object, such as a line, polyline, or arc.**

The point you pick when selecting the object serves double-duty: It selects the object, of course, but it also becomes the default first break point (that is, it defines one side of the gap that you're creating). Thus, you either use one of the AutoCAD LT precision techniques, such as an object snap, to pick the object at a precise point, or use the `First point` option (described in the next step) to re-pick the first break point.

LT prompts you to specify the second break point, or to type **F** and press Enter if you want to re-specify the first break point:

```
Specify second break point or [First point]:
```

3. **If the point that you picked in the preceding step doesn't also correspond to a break point (see the previous tip), type** F **and press Enter to re-specify the first break point, and then pick the point by using an object snap or other precision technique.**

   If you do type **F** and press Enter and then re-specify the first break point, LT prompts you now to select the second break point:

   ```
   Specify second break point:
   ```

4. **Specify the second break point by picking a point or typing coordinates.**

   LT cuts a section out of the object, using the first and second break points to define the length of the gap.

If you want to cut an object into two pieces without removing anything, click the Break at Point button on the Modify toolbar. You first select the object and then choose a second point that defines where LT breaks the object into two. You can then move, copy, or otherwise manipulate each section of the original object as a separate object.

Fillet and Chamfer

Whereas TRim, EXtend, and BReak alter one object at a time, the Fillet and CHAmfer commands require a pair of objects. As Figure 7-13 shows, Fillet creates a curved corner between two lines, whereas CHAmfer creates an angled, straight corner. In case you wondered, it's pronounced "fill-et," not "fill-eh." Saying that you know how to "fill-eh" may get you a job in a butcher shop, but it gets you strange looks in a design office.

The following steps describe how to use the Fillet command:

1. **Click the Fillet button on the Modify toolbar.**

   LT displays the current Fillet settings and prompts you to select the first object for filleting or specify one of three options:

   ```
   Current settings: Mode = TRIM, Radius = 0.0000
   Select first object or [Polyline/Radius/Trim/mUltiple]:
   ```

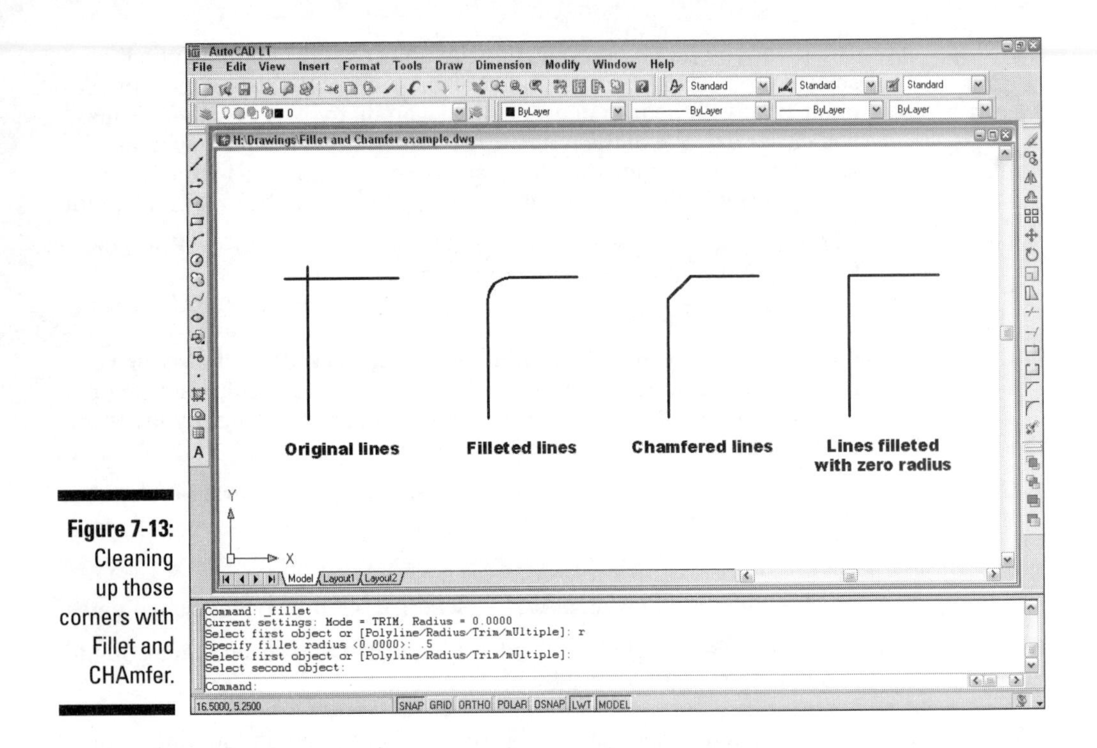

Figure 7-13: Cleaning up those corners with Fillet and CHAmfer.

2. **Type** R **and press Enter to set the fillet radius.**

   LT prompts you to specify the fillet radius that it uses for future fillet operations:

   ```
   Specify fillet radius <0.0000>:
   ```

3. **Type a fillet radius and press Enter.**

   The number you type is the radius of the arc that joins the two lines.

   ```
   Select first object or [Polyline/Radius/Trim/mUltiple]:
   ```

4. **Select the first line of the pair that you want to fillet.**

   LT prompts you to select the second object for filleting:

   ```
   Select second object:
   ```

5. **Select the second line of the pair that you want to fillet.**

   LT fillets the two objects, drawing an arc of the radius that you specified in Step 3.

You can fillet two lines and specify a radius of zero to make them meet at a point. If you have lots of lines to fillet, whether with a zero or nonzero radius, use the Fillet command's mUtliple option to speed the process. And finally, you can use the Fillet command's Polyline option to fillet all the vertices of a polyline in one fell swoop.

The CHAmfer command works similarly except that, instead of specifying a fillet distance, you specify either two chamfer distances or a chamfer length and angle.

Get a Grip

Although command-first editing is the most flexible and widespread editing style in AutoCAD LT, it's not the only way. *Grip editing* is a useful adjunct to command-first editing, especially when you want to modify just one or two objects. You may have encountered grip editing when using other kinds of graphics programs. Even if you're an experienced user of other graphics programs, you've never seen grips used in quite the way that AutoCAD LT uses them.

Anything that you can do with grip editing can be done with command-first editing as well. In some situations, grip editing is a little more efficient or convenient than command-first editing, but command-first editing always gets the job done. If you master only one style of editing, make it command-first style. In other words, feel free to skip this section — at least until you're comfortable with command-first editing.

Polishing those properties

When you think of editing objects, you probably think first about editing their geometry: moving, stretching, making new copies, and so on. That's the kind of editing I cover in this chapter.

Another kind of editing is changing objects' properties. As I describe in Chapter 3, every object in an AutoCAD LT drawing has a set of nongeometrical properties, including layer, color, linetype, and lineweight. Sometimes, you need to edit those properties — when you accidentally draw something on the wrong layer, for example. Three common ways of editing objects properties in AutoCAD LT are

- **The Properties palette:** This palette is the most flexible way to edit properties. Select any object (or objects), right-click in the drawing area, and choose Properties from the menu. The Properties palette displays a tabular grid that lists the names and values of all properties. Click in the value cell to change a particular property.
- **Layers and Properties toolbars:** Another way to change properties is to select objects and then choose from the drop-down lists (Layer, Color, and so on) on the Layers and the Properties toolbars. See Chapter 3 for more information.
- **Match Properties:** You can use the Match Properties button on the Standard toolbar — the button with the paintbrush on it — to paint properties from one object to another. Match Properties works similarly to the Format Painter button in Microsoft applications. Match Properties works even when the objects reside in different drawings.

About grips

Grips are little square handles that appear on an object after you select it.

In their simplest guise, AutoCAD LT grips work similar to the little squares on graphical objects in other Windows programs. But in LT, instead of clicking and dragging a grip, you must click, move the cursor, and click again at the new location. (By separating the selection of beginning and ending points into two different operations, AutoCAD LT allows you to use different techniques — such as different object snap modes — to select each point.)

AutoCAD LT grips are, for sophisticated users, better than the grips you find in most other programs because you can do so much more with them. You can, for example, use LT grips to move, stretch, or copy an object. You also can use them to rotate an object, scale it to a different size, or *mirror* an object — that is, create one or more backwards copies. Grips also act as *visible object snaps,* or little magnets that draw the cursor to themselves.

A gripping example

The following sections cover in detail the five grip-editing modes — Stretch, Move, Rotate, Scale, and Mirror. Follow these steps to explore the grip-editing modes:

1. **Press Esc to make sure that no command is active and no objects are selected.**

   LT displays the naked command prompt — that is, no command is currently active:

   ```
   Command:
   ```

2. **Click an object on-screen to select it and display its grips.**

   Grips — solid blue squares on the selected object — appear at various points on the object. Note that the LT command prompt remains naked; you haven't started a command or grip-editing operation yet.

3. **Click another object.**

   Both the newly selected object and the object that you selected previously display grips.

4. **Click one of the grips on either object.**

   The blue square turns to a red square. This grip is now *hot,* or ready for a grip-editing operation.

   Grip-editing options now appear on the command line. The first option to appear is STRETCH.

5. **Press the Enter key (or spacebar) repeatedly to cycle through the five grip-editing options on the command line:**

```
** STRETCH **
Specify stretch point or [Base point/Copy/Undo/eXit]:
** MOVE **
Specify move point or [Base point/Copy/Undo/eXit]:
** ROTATE **
Specify rotation angle or [Base
        point/Copy/Undo/Reference/eXit]:
** SCALE **
Specify scale factor or [Base
        point/Copy/Undo/Reference/eXit]:
** MIRROR **
Specify second point or [Base point/Copy/Undo/eXit]:
```

The grip-editing option displayed on the command line changes as you press the Enter key or spacebar. If you move the cursor (without picking) in between each key press, the appearance of your selected object changes as you display each option. As you can see, each of the grip-editing operations resembles the ordinary AutoCAD LT command of the same name. Choosing STRETCH, for example, causes a stretched version of the object to appear on-screen.

TIP

Pressing Enter or spacebar a bunch of times is a good way to become familiar with the grip-editing modes, but a more direct way is to choose a particular mode. After you click a grip to make it hot, right-click to display the grip-editing menu. That menu contains all the grip-editing options plus some other choices, as shown in Figure 7-14.

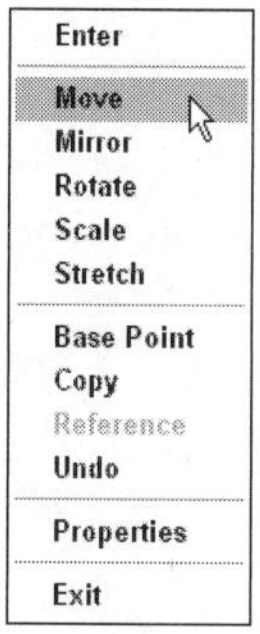

Enter
Move
Mirror
Rotate
Scale
Stretch
Base Point
Copy
Reference
Undo
Properties
Exit

Figure 7-14: The grip-editing menu.

6. **Press the spacebar until STRETCH (or the option you want) reappears as the grip-editing option.**

7. **Move the hot grip in the direction in which you want to stretch (or otherwise manipulate) your object.**

   LT dynamically updates the image of the object to show you what the modified object will look like before you click the final location.

8. **Click again to finish the grip-editing operation.**

   The selected object with the hot grip updates. The object with the cold grips doesn't change.

9. **Click the same grip that you chose in Step 4 (now in a different location) to make it hot.**

10. **This time, move the cursor near one of the grips on the other object. When you feel the magnetic pull of the grip on the other object, click again to connect the hot grip with the other grip.**

    The object point represented by the hot grip now coincides exactly with the grip on the other object.

11. **Press Esc to deselect all objects and remove all grips.**

Figure 7-15 shows a hot (red) endpoint grip of a line being connected to the cold (blue) endpoint grip of another line. The ghosted line shows the original position of the line being edited, and the continuous line shows the new position. Using a grip in this way as a visible object snap offers the same advantage as using single point object snaps, which I describe in Chapter 3: It ensures precision by making sure that objects meet exactly.

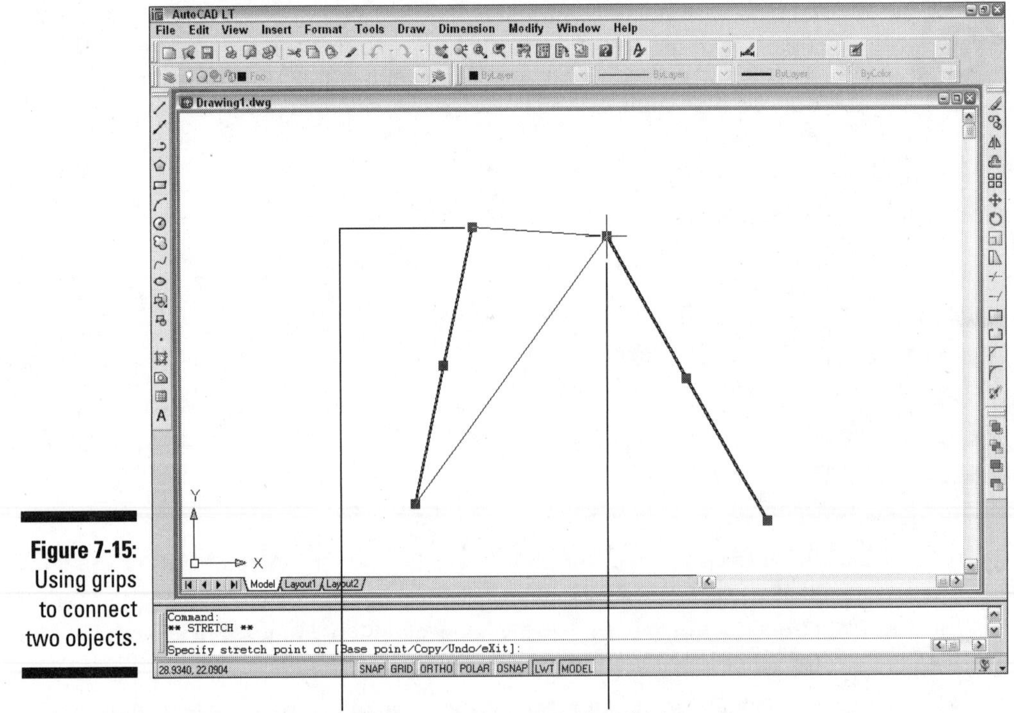

Figure 7-15: Using grips to connect two objects.

You can experiment with all the grip-editing options to find out how they affect a selected object.

Because MOVE and STRETCH are the most useful grip-editing modes, I cover them more specifically.

Move it!

Back in the days of manual drafting, moving objects was a big pain in the eraser. You had to erase the stuff you wanted to move and redraw the objects in their new location. In the process, you usually ended up erasing parts of other stuff that you didn't want to move and left smudged lines and piles of eraser dust everywhere. CAD does away with all the fuss and muss of moving objects, and AutoCAD LT grip editing is a great way to make it happen. The following steps describe how to move objects:

1. **Select one or more objects.**

   Use any combination of the three editing modes — single object, bounding box, or crossing box — described in the section, "Grab It," earlier in this chapter.

2. **Click one of the grips to make it hot.**

   At this point in your editing career, which grip you click doesn't matter. As you become more familiar with grip editing, you'll discover that certain grips serve as better reference points than others for particular editing operations.

3. **Right-click anywhere in the drawing area and choose Move from the menu.**

4. **Move the cursor to a different location and click.**

   As you move the cursor around, LT displays the tentative new positions for all the objects, as shown in Figure 7-16. After you click, the objects assume their new positions.

5. **Press Esc to deselect all objects and remove all grips.**

Copy, or a kinder, gentler move

If you were paying attention during "A gripping example," earlier in the chapter, you may have noticed while pressing the spacebar that COPY was not among the five grip-editing modes. Why not? Because every grip mode includes a copy option (as the command line prompts shown in "A gripping example," earlier in this chapter indicate). In other words, you can STRETCH with copy, MOVE with copy, ROTATE with copy, SCALE with copy, and MIRROR with copy.

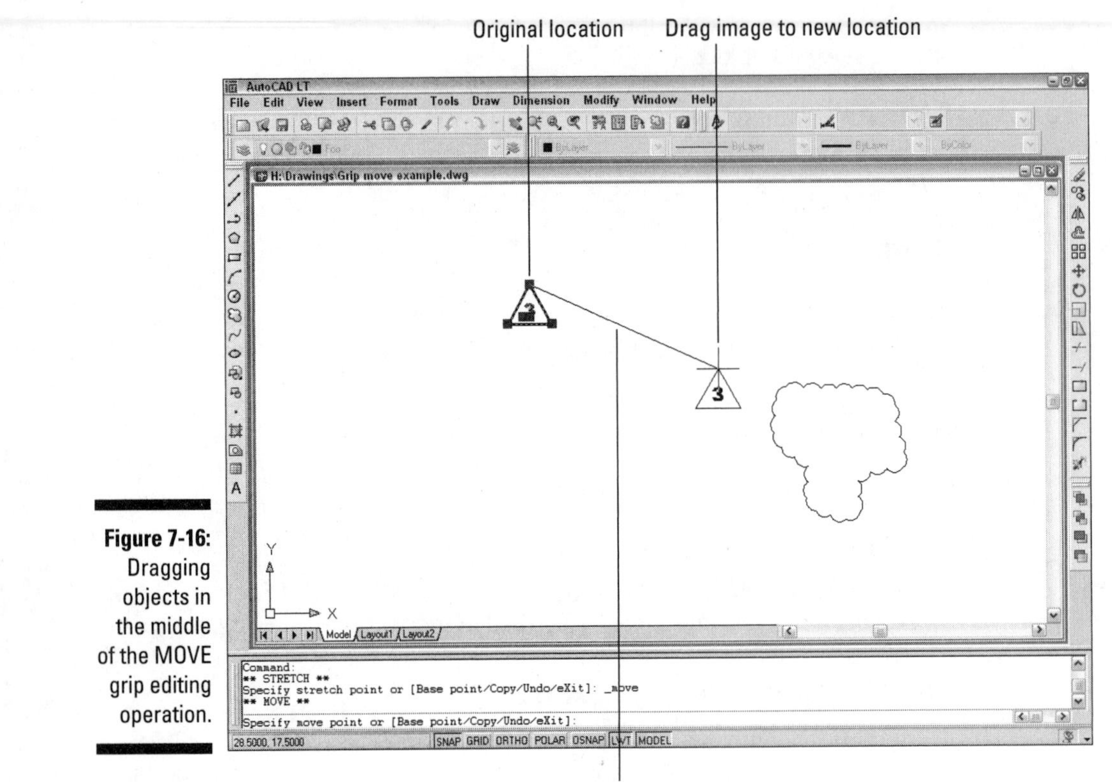

Figure 7-16: Dragging objects in the middle of the MOVE grip editing operation.

The copy option leaves the selected objects in place and does the editing operation on a new copy of the objects.

By far the most common use for the copy option is with the MOVE grip-editing mode. If you think about "MOVE with copy" for about two seconds, you'll realize that it's just a complicated way of saying "copy." The following steps show how to copy objects quickly by using grip editing:

1. **Select one or more objects.**
2. **Click any one of the grips to make it hot.**
3. **Right-click anywhere in the drawing area and choose Move from the menu.**

If you want to copy objects in the normal sense of the word "copy," you must choose the MOVE grip-editing mode first. Otherwise, you're copying with the STRETCH grip-editing mode.

4. **Right-click again and choose Copy from the menu.**
5. **Move the cursor to a different location and click.**

   New objects appear in the new location.
6. **Move the cursor to additional locations and click there if you want to make additional copies.**
7. **Press Esc twice — once to end the copying operation and once to deselect all objects and remove all grips.**

A warm-up stretch

In AutoCAD LT, stretching is the process of making objects longer *or* shorter. The STRETCH grip-editing operation is really a combination of stretching and compressing, but the programmers probably realized that STRETCHAND-COMPRESS didn't exactly roll off the tongue.

The STRETCH grip-editing mode works differently from the other modes. By default, it affects only the object with the hot grip on it, not all objects with grips on them. You can override this default behavior by using the Shift key to pick multiple hot grips. Follow these steps to get acquainted with using the STRETCH grip-editing mode to stretch one or more objects:

1. **Turn off ortho mode by clicking the ORTHO button on the status bar until the button appears to be pushed out and the words** `<Ortho off>` **appear on the command line.**

   Ortho mode forces stretch displacements to be orthogonal — that is, parallel to lines running at 0 and 90 degrees. During real editing tasks, you often want to turn on ortho mode, but while you get acquainted with stretching, leaving ortho mode off makes things clearer.
2. **Select several objects, including at least one line.**
3. **On one of the lines, click one of the endpoint grips to make it hot.**

   All the objects remain selected, but as you move the cursor, only the line with the hot grip changes. Figure 7-17 shows an example.
4. **Click a new point for the hot endpoint grip.**

   The line stretches to accommodate the new endpoint location.
5. **On the same line, click the midpoint grip to make it hot.**

   As you move the cursor, the entire line moves. Using the STRETCH grip-editing mode with a line's midpoint "stretches" the entire line to a new location.

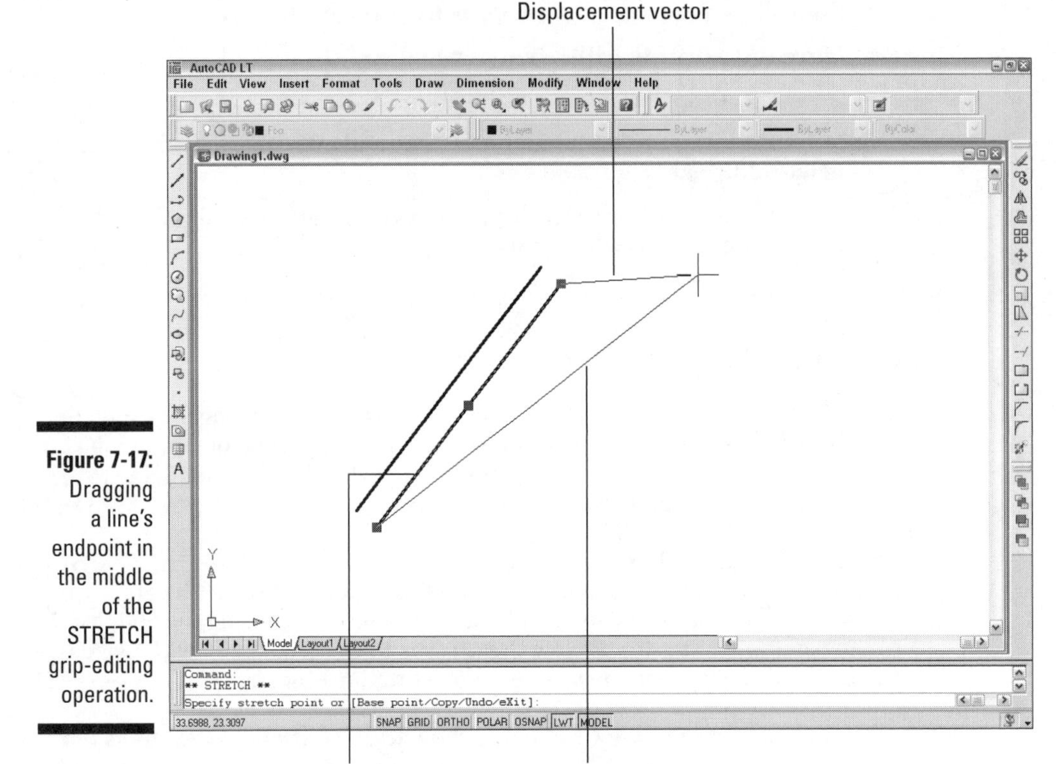

Figure 7-17: Dragging a line's endpoint in the middle of the STRETCH grip-editing operation.

6. **Click a new point for the hot midpoint grip.**

   The line moves to the new midpoint location.

7. **On one of the lines, click one of the endpoint grips to make it hot.**
8. **Hold down the Shift key, and then click one of the endpoint grips on a different line to make it hot.**

   Two grips on two different lines are now hot because you held down the Shift key and clicked the second grip.

   You can create more hot grips by holding down the Shift key and clicking more grips.

9. **Release the Shift key and re-pick any one of the hot grips.**

   Releasing the Shift key signals that you're finished making grips hot. Re-picking one of the hot grips establishes it as the base point for the stretch operation (see Figure 7-18).

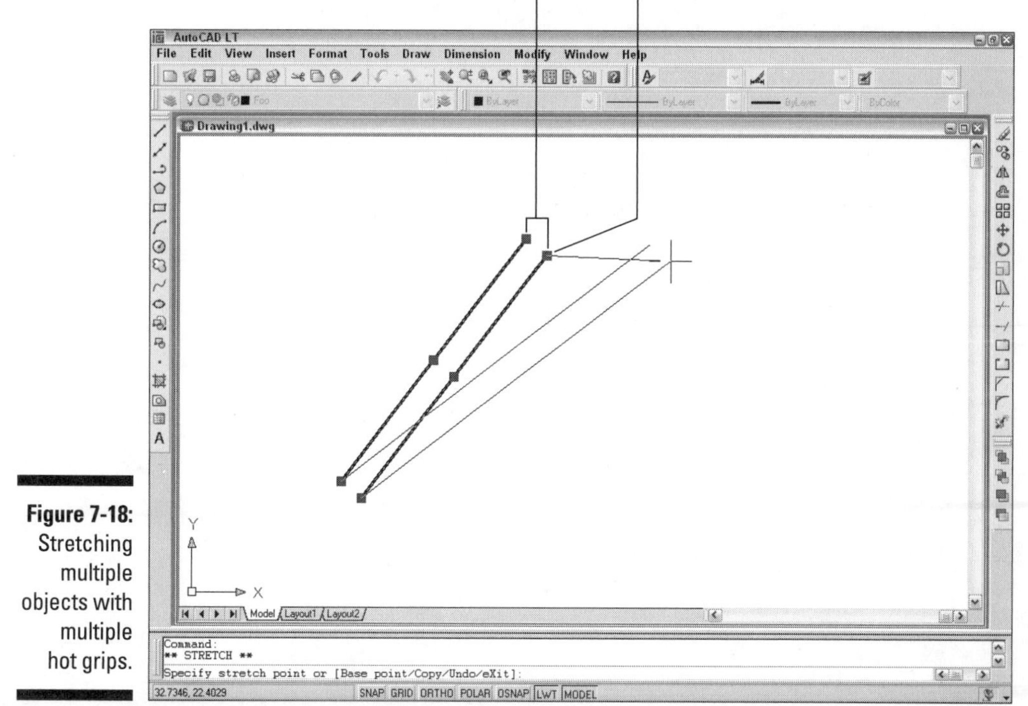

Figure 7-18: Stretching multiple objects with multiple hot grips.

10. **Click a new point for the grip.**

    All the objects with hot grips stretch based on the displacement of the grip that you clicked in Step 9.

11. **Turn on ortho mode by clicking the ORTHO button on the status bar until the button appears to be pushed in and the words `<Ortho on>` appear on the command line. Repeat Steps 2 through 10 to see the effect of ortho mode on stretching.**

For most real-world editing situations, I recommend turning on ortho or polar tracking mode before stretching. Ortho mode is good for all kinds of drawing and editing tasks because it enforces a nice, rectilinear orderliness on your drawing. Chapter 3 describes how to use ortho mode to draw orthogonal lines.

Chapter 8

Zoom It In, Zoom It Out — and Pan It All About

In This Chapter

- Zooming and panning
- Naming and restoring views
- Zooming and panning in paper space layouts
- Regenerating the display

One of the advantages of CAD over manual drawing is its capability of giving you different ways to view your drawing. You can zoom in close, zoom out to a great distance, and pan around. In fact, not only *can* you zoom and pan in your drawing, but in most kinds of drawings, you *must* do it frequently to draw, edit, and view effectively.

Technical drawings are jam-packed with lines, text, and dimensions. Zooming and panning frequently enables you to see the details better, draw more confidently (because you can see what you're doing), and edit more quickly (because object selection is easier when a zillion objects aren't on-screen). This chapter covers AutoCAD LT's most useful display control features.

Zoom and Pan with Glass and Hand

Moving your viewpoint in to get a closer view of your drawing data is called *zooming in;* moving your viewpoint back to get a more expansive view is called *zooming out.*

Zooming in and out of your drawing is one of the big advantages that AutoCAD LT offers over manual drawing. You can do detailed work on tiny objects and then zoom out and move around rooms, houses, or neighborhoods from an Olympian perspective.

Panning is closely related to zooming. If you zoom in enough that some of your drawing no longer shows up on-screen, you're going to want to pan around — move left, right, up, and down in your drawing — without zooming in and out. AutoCAD LT makes panning easy with scroll bars and *realtime* panning.

Both panning and zooming change what is known as the *view*. The view is the current location and magnification of the AutoCAD LT depiction of your drawing. Each time you zoom or pan, you establish a new view. You can give a name to a specific view to make returning to that view easy, as I demonstrate later in this chapter.

Fortunately, zooming and panning in AutoCAD LT is as simple as it is necessary. The following steps describe how to use LT's Zoom and Pan Realtime feature, which is easy to operate and provides a lot of flexibility:

1. **Click the Zoom Realtime button (the one that looks a magnifying glass with a plus/minus sign next to it) on the Standard toolbar.**

   The Realtime option of the Zoom command starts. The cursor changes to a magnifying glass, and LT prompts you at the command line:

   ```
   Press ESC or ENTER to exit, or right-click to display
           shortcut menu.
   ```

2. **Move the cursor near the middle of the screen, press and hold down the left mouse button, and drag the cursor up and down.**

   Dragging up increases the zoom magnification and dragging down decreases it.

3. **Right-click in the drawing area and choose Pan from the Zoom/Pan Realtime menu that appears, as shown in Figure 8-1.**

   The cursor changes to a hand.

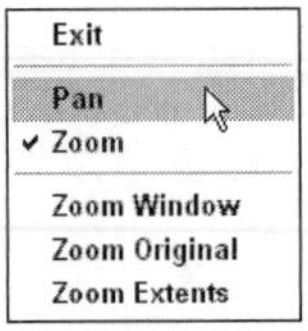

Exit
Pan
✓ Zoom
Zoom Window
Zoom Original
Zoom Extents

Figure 8-1: The Zoom/Pan Realtime menu.

4. **Click and drag to pan the drawing in any direction.**

   You can use the right-click menu to toggle back and forth between Zoom and Pan as many times as you like. If you get lost, choose Zoom Original or Zoom Extents to return to a recognizable view.

5. **Right-click in the drawing area and choose Exit.**

   The cursor returns to the normal AutoCAD LT crosshairs.

In the preceding example, you start with zooming and end with panning. You also have the option of doing the reverse: Click the Pan Realtime button (the one showing a hand), and after you pan, use the right-click menu to switch to zooming. However you start it, the important thing to realize is that Zoom and Pan Realtime is a single AutoCAD LT function. At any time, you can switch between panning and zooming (or switch to a related function, such as Zoom Window) by using the right-click menu.

You also can pan and zoom by using your mouse's *scroll wheel* (if it has one) or the *middle button* of a three-button mouse:

- To zoom in and out, roll the scroll wheel forward (in) or backward (out).
- To zoom to the extents of your drawing, double-click the scroll wheel or the middle button.
- To pan, hold down the scroll wheel or the middle button as you move the mouse.

The scroll wheel or middle mouse button zoom and pan operations described in the preceding paragraph depend on an obscure AutoCAD LT system variable named MBUTTONPAN. (See Chapter 2 for a description of what system variables are and how to change them.) When MBUTTONPAN is set to 1 — the default value — you can use the middle button to pan and zoom, as I describe in the preceding tip. If you change MBUTTONPAN to 0, clicking the middle mouse button displays an object snap menu, as it did in older AutoCAD LT versions. If you're not able to zoom or pan with your middle mouse button, set MBUTTONPAN back to 1. (With MBUTTONPAN set to 1, you use Shift+right-click to display the object snap menu. See Chapter 3 for more information about this menu.)

Realtime zooming and panning is the easiest, most interactive way to get around in your drawings. In some situations, though, this method is less efficient or precise than the old-fashioned methods, the most important of which I describe in the next section.

A pan-oply of methods

Another way to pan in AutoCAD LT is familiar from other Windows programs — the scroll bars in the drawing area. Scrolling is the same in LT as in any other Windows program; click the arrows in the right and bottom borders of the drawing window to scroll, or pan, a step at a time; or click and drag the little square "thumbs" in those borders to pan as little or as much as you want to.

Believe it or not, the realtime and scrollbar panning methods are relatively recent enhancements in AutoCAD and LT's long history. These methods have pretty much replaced the less-intuitive two-point method of panning in older versions of the program. If you want to see how Grandpa used to pan, enter **–Pan** (with the leading dash) at the command line and then follow the prompts. This older method remains useful in special situations where you need to pan *orthogonally* by a specific distance — that is, move the display precisely horizontally without wavering up and down or precisely vertically without wavering side to side. This situation sometimes occurs in advanced paper space viewport setup, which I don't cover in this book.

Zoom faster

Because zooming is such a frequent necessity in AutoCAD LT, knowing some alternative ways of doing it is worth the effort.

The Zoom command has different options, the most important of which are the following:

- **All and Extents:** Zoom Extents zooms out just far enough to show all the objects in the current drawing. Zoom All does the same thing, unless the drawings limits are larger than the extents, in which case Zoom All zooms to show the entire rectangular area defined by the limits. If you define your limits properly (see Chapter 5), Zoom All is a good way to see your whole drawing area. These two options are especially useful when you zoom in too small or pan off into empty space and want to see your entire drawing again.

  It's a good idea to Zoom All or Zoom Extents and then save before you close a drawing. By performing these steps, you ensure the following:

  - The next person who opens the drawing — whether it's you or someone else — can see the full drawing from the very beginning.
  - The drawing preview that displays in the Select File dialog box displays the full drawing, instead of just a tiny, unidentifiable corner of it.

- **Window:** This option is great for zooming in quickly and precisely. It zooms to a section of your drawing that you specify by clicking two points. The two points define the diagonal of a window around the area you want to look at. (***Note:*** The Zoom command's Window option is not a click-and-drag operation — unlike in some other Windows programs and, confusingly, unlike in the Zoom/Pan realtime Zoom Window option. With the Zoom command's Window option, you click one corner, release the mouse button, and then click the other corner.)
- **Scale (X/XP):** The X option zooms by a percentage of the current display; values less than 1 cause you to zoom in, values greater than 1 cause you to zoom out. You can also think of the value as a scaling factor: 0.5X causes the screen image to shrink to half its apparent size, and 2X causes the screen image to double its apparent size. (The XP option after a number is for zooming model space objects in a viewport relative to paper space; see Chapter 5 for information about paper space.)
- **Realtime:** Realtime zooming, the technique described previously, enables you to zoom in and out by starting a realtime zoom and then moving the cursor up to zoom in or down to zoom out.
- **Previous:** This option undoes the last zoom and/or pan sequence. It's like going back in time but without the funny costumes!

Some of the zoom options take some getting used to. I recommend that you use realtime zoom and pan for most of your zooming and panning. Supplement it with Zoom Window to move quickly into a precise area, Zoom Previous to back up in zoom/pan time, and Zoom All or Zoom Extents to view your whole drawing.

Improve Your View

If you find yourself repeatedly zooming and panning to the same area, you probably can get there faster with a named view. A *named view* is a name that you assign to a particular region of your drawing. After you create a named view, you can return to that region quickly by restoring the view. You use the View command, which displays the View dialog box, to create and restore named views. Follow these steps to create a named view:

1. **Zoom and pan until you find the view that you want to assign a name to.**
2. **Choose View➪Named Views.**

   The View dialog box appears.

3. **Click the New button.**

   The New View dialog box appears, as shown in Figure 8-2.

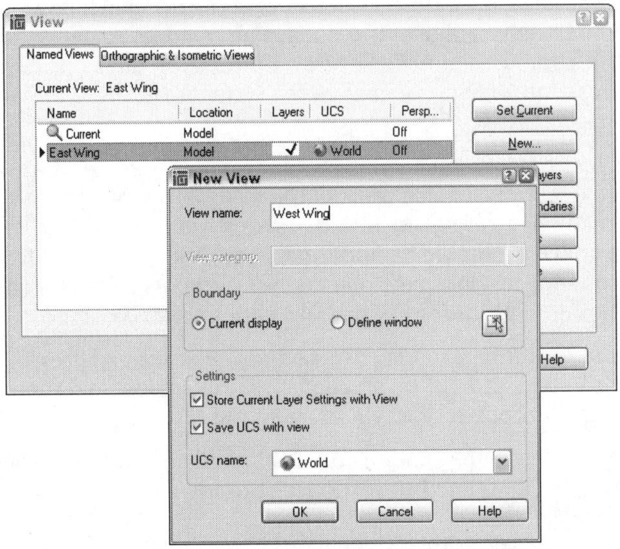

Figure 8-2: Create a new view for you.

4. **Type a name in the View Name text box.**

   The grayed-out View Category option corresponds to a new view property in AutoCAD 2005. AutoCAD LT 2005 doesn't include the view category feature.

5. **Select the Current Display radio button, if it's not selected already.**

   If you want to name a region other than the currently displayed view, select the Define Window radio button instead, click the Define View Window button to the right of it, and pick two corners of the region's rectangle (as though you were zooming windows).

6. **Confirm or change the choices in the Settings area.**

   The Store Current Layer Settings with View option is new in AutoCAD LT 2005. If you leave this setting turned on, when you later restore the view, LT also restores the layer visibility settings (on/off and freeze/thaw) that were in effect when you created the view. (Chapter 3 describes the layer visibility settings.) The two UCS-related settings are primarily for 3D drawings. If you're creating 2D drawings, which you probably are in AutoCAD LT, you can ignore the UCS settings.

7. **Click OK.**

   The New View dialog box disappears, and you see your new named view in the list in the View dialog box.

8. **Click OK.**

   The View dialog box disappears.

To restore a named view, choose View➪Named Views or enter **View** at the command line to display the View dialog box. Click the name of the view that you want to restore, click the Set Current button, and then click OK to close the dialog box.

With the new Update Layers and Edit Boundaries buttons in the main View dialog box, you can change the layer visibility settings that AutoCAD LT associates with an existing view and revise the view's boundary.

You also can plot the area defined by a named view. See Chapter 12 for instructions on plotting views.

Looking Around in Layout Land

All the zoom, pan, and view operations I describe in this chapter apply to paper space layouts as well as to model space. (Chapter 5 describes the difference between model space and paper space and how to navigate between the two.) One little complication exists, though: In a *paper space layout* — that is, any drawing area tab except for the Model tab — it's possible for the cursor to be either in paper space or in model space inside a viewport. Zooming and panning have a different effect depending on which space your cursor is in at the moment. Experiment with the different effects by following these steps:

1. **Open a drawing that contains at least one paper space layout with a title block and one or more viewports.**

   If you don't have any such drawings handy, try using this sample drawing:

   ```
   \Program Files\AutoCAD LT
           2005\Sample\pumping_station.dwg.
   ```

2. **Click one of the layout tabs — that is, any tab other than the Model tab.**

   LT displays the paper space layout for that tab, including any title block and viewports.

3. **Click the PAPER/MODEL button on the status bar until it says PAPER.**

   Alternatively, you can double-click in the gray part of the drawing area outside of the layout.

   The cursor is now in paper space, so zooming and panning changes the display of all the objects in the layout, including the title block.

4. **Choose View⇨Zoom⇨All.**

   LT displays the entire layout, as shown in Figure 8-3.

5. **Zoom and pan by using any of the techniques described in this chapter.**

   Zooming and panning change the appearance of the title block, as shown in Figure 8-4. The effect is similar to moving a plotted sheet in and out and all around in front of your face.

6. **Choose View⇨Zoom⇨All.**

   LT displays the entire layout again.

7. **Click the PAPER/MODEL button on the status bar until it says MODEL.**

   Alternatively, you can double-click with the cursor over a viewport.

   The cursor is now in model space, inside the viewport, so zooming and panning change only the display of the objects that are visible in the viewport. The display of the title block doesn't change.

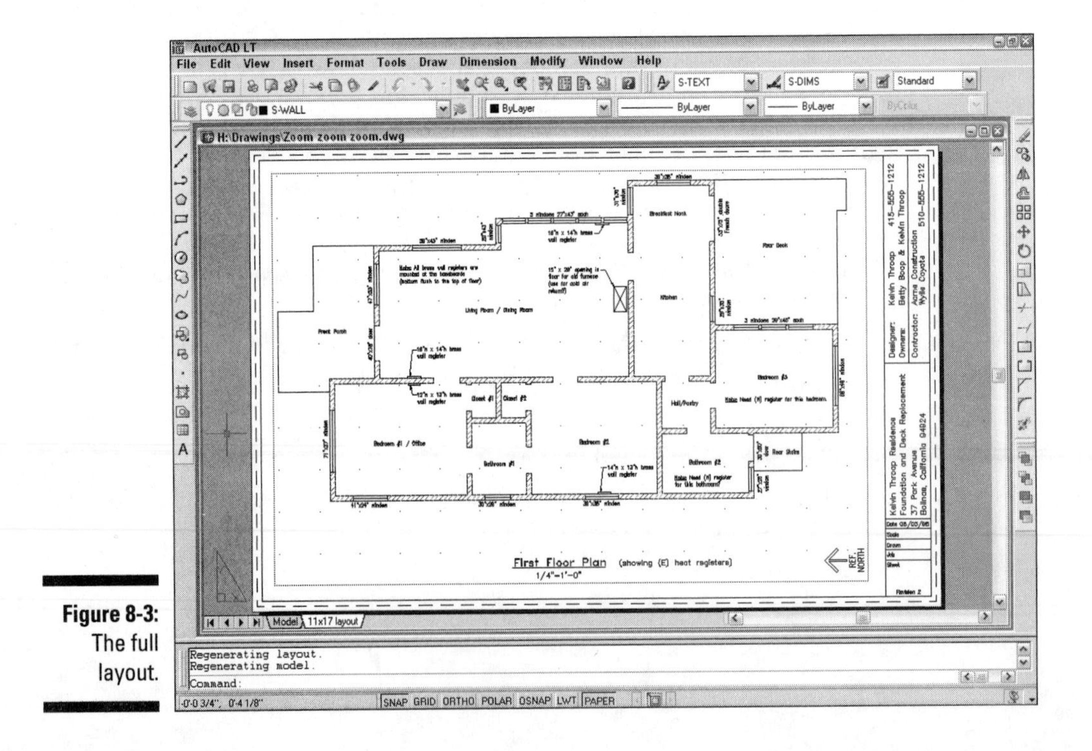

Figure 8-3: The full layout.

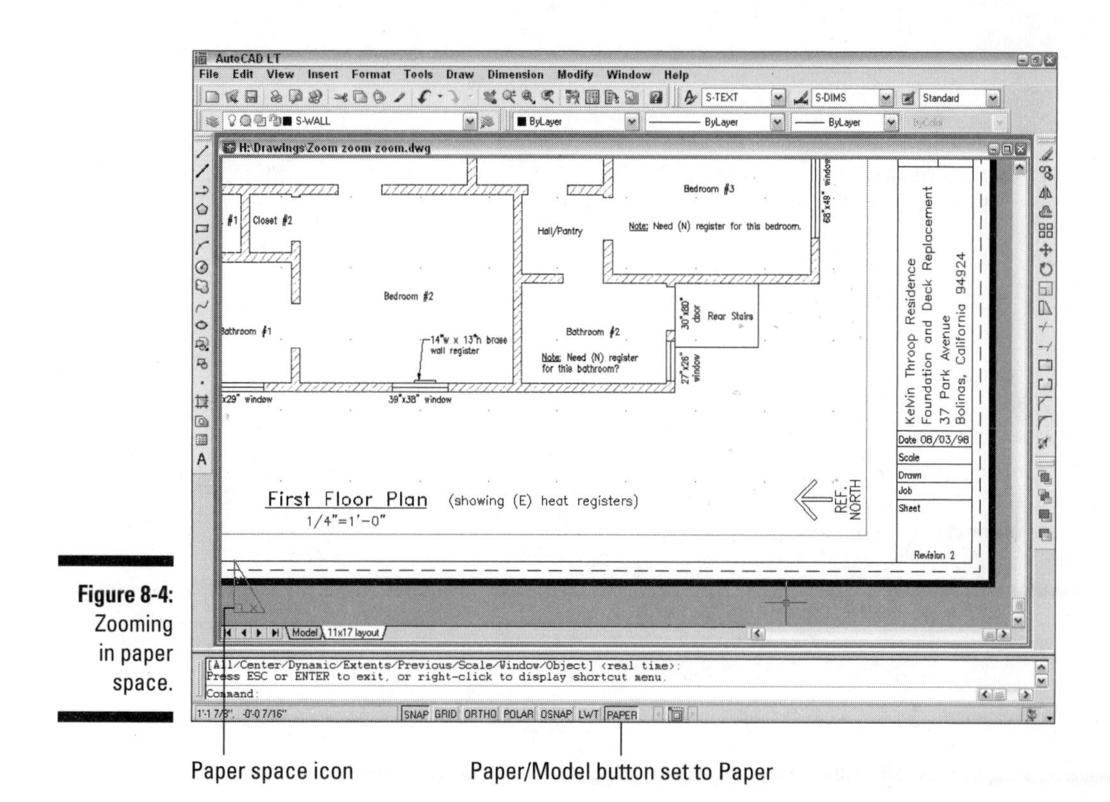

Figure 8-4: Zooming in paper space.

8. **Zoom and pan by using any of the techniques described in this chapter.**

   Zooming and panning don't change the appearance of the title block, as shown in Figure 8-5. The result looks as if you're moving a picture of the model space geometry in and out and all around behind a frame.

   In real drawings, you usually don't zoom and pan inside viewports after they're set up (see Chapter 5). Doing so changes the scale of the viewport, which messes up plotting. I'm asking you to do it here to illustrate the difference between zooming in paper space and zooming in a model space viewport.

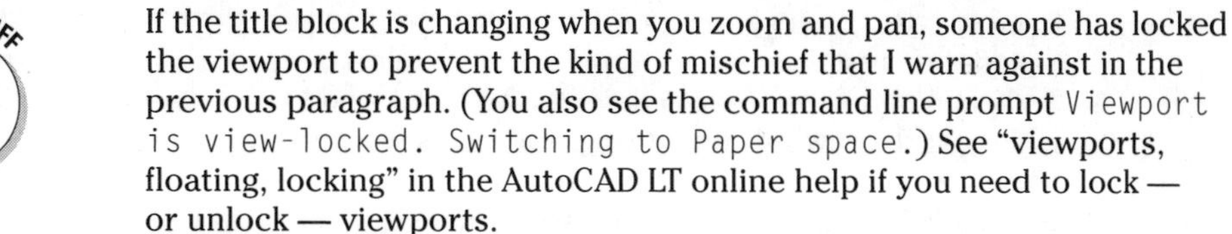

   If the title block is changing when you zoom and pan, someone has locked the viewport to prevent the kind of mischief that I warn against in the previous paragraph. (You also see the command line prompt `Viewport is view-locked. Switching to Paper space.`) See "viewports, floating, locking" in the AutoCAD LT online help if you need to lock — or unlock — viewports.

9. **Choose View➪Zoom➪Previous one or more times until you restore the original view.**

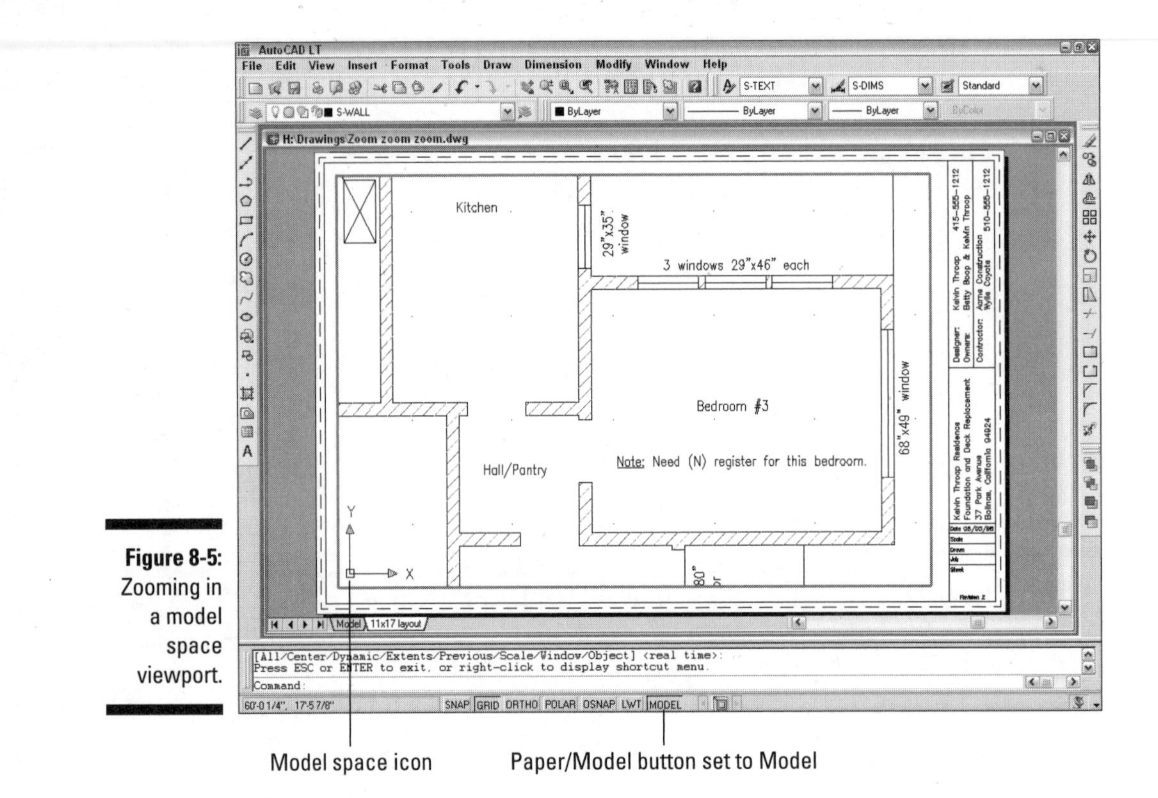

Figure 8-5: Zooming in a model space viewport.

10. **Click the PAPER/MODEL button on the status bar until is says PAPER.**

    Always leave the cursor in paper space when you finish. Doing so ensures that future zooming or panning on this tab — whether by you or by someone else who opens the drawing — takes place in paper space rather than inside a viewport.

11. **Choose File⇨Close and click the No button to close the drawing without saving changes.**

    In this example, I have you close the drawing without saving changes, just in case you did mess up the viewport zoom scale.

In most cases, you set up a paper space layout once, as described in Chapter 5, and then just return to it to plot. You shouldn't spend a lot of time zooming and panning in paper space layouts. You zoom and pan to get a better view of what you're drawing and editing, and that's what the Model tab is for. But if you do want to zoom in paper space — to get a better look at part of your title block, for example — make sure that you're doing it with the PAPER/MODEL button set to PAPER.

AutoCAD LT 2005 includes new VPMAX and VPMIN commands for maximizing and minimizing a viewport in the current layout. These commands provide an alternative to switching between the Model and Layout tabs without the potential problems of zooming inside of paper space viewports. The easiest way to run VPMAX or VPMIN is to click the new Maximize Viewport/Minimize Viewport button located on the status bar, just to the right of the PAPER button.

Degenerating and Regenerating

As you zoom and pan around your drawing, you may wonder how the image that you see on-screen is related to the DWG file that AutoCAD LT saves on the hard drive. Well, maybe you don't wonder about that, but I'm going to tell you anyway!

When you draw and edit objects, AutoCAD LT stores all their geometrical properties (that is, location and size) in a highly precise form — technically, *double floating-point precision*. The program always maintains that precision when you save the DWG file. For computer performance reasons, however, LT does *not* use that high-precision form of the data to display your drawing on-screen. Instead, the program converts the highly precise numbers in the DWG file into slightly less precise *integers* in order to create the view that you see on-screen.

The happy consequence of this conversion is that zooming, panning, and other display changes are a lot faster than they are otherwise. The unhappy consequence is that the conversion, which is called a *regeneration* (or *regen* for short), occasionally leaves you with some artifacts to deal with.

In most cases, AutoCAD LT performs regenerations automatically when it needs to. You sometimes see command line messages like `Regenerating model` or `Regenerating layout`, which indicate that LT is taking care of regens for you.

If, on the other hand, you see the command line message `Regen queued`, then AutoCAD LT is warning you that it's *not* performing a regeneration, even though one might be advisable now. In addition, you might see a warning dialog box with the message `About to regen -- proceed?` These messages are LT's way of saying, "What your drawing looks like on-screen at the moment may not exactly match the real version of the drawing database that gets stored when you save the drawing. I'll update the display version at the next regeneration."

The REGENMODE system variable controls whether or not AutoCAD LT performs most regenerations automatically (see Chapter 2 if you're unfamiliar with system variables or how to change them):

- The default REGENMODE setting in new drawings, 1, tells LT to regenerate your drawing automatically if it's required to synchronize the screen display with the drawing database.
- The other REGENMODE setting, 0 (Off), tells LT not to regenerate automatically, but instead to display `Regen queued` on the command line and let you force a regeneration with the REgen command if you want to.

The REGENMODE=0 option is for the most part a holdover from much slower computers and older versions of AutoCAD and LT. You probably don't need to subject yourself to the mental contortion of trying to avoid regens unless you work on huge drawings and/or use a painfully slow computer.

Don't confuse the REgen command with the Redraw command. REgen (View⇨Regen) forces the synchronization process described in this section. Redraw (View⇨Redraw) simply repaints the screen, without attempting to synchronize the screen with the drawing database. The Redraw command was useful in the days of very slow computers and older versions of AutoCAD and LT, which didn't handle the display as effectively, but it's essentially a useless command now.

The REgenAll command (View⇨Regen All) regenerates all viewports in a paper space layout. If you run the REgenAll command in model space, it has the same effect as the ordinary REgen command.

Part III

Annotation for Communication

In this part . . .

Text, dimensions, and hatching have long been important clarifying elements in drafting. In AutoCAD LT, these elements are flexible almost to a fault, and you can edit and update them quickly as you change the geometry beneath them. The text, dimension, and hatching annotations that you add "speak" about the geometry so that others can understand exactly what, how big, and how far.

After you make some drawings that talk, you probably send the message around by printing — or what CAD users call *plotting* — them. AutoCAD LT 2005 introduces a redesigned, streamlined Plot dialog box that makes the often-complex task of plotting a little less daunting. Chapter 12 in this section is your passport to navigating the revised plot process, understanding how the legacy of AutoCAD plotting influences current practice, and most of all getting a good-looking, properly scaled plot onto paper.

Chapter 9

Get Specific with Text

In This Chapter

- Using text styles to control text appearance
- Creating single-line and multiline text
- Using background masks with text
- Making hanging indents
- Editing text contents and properties
- Creating tables
- Checking spelling

Although the saying "a picture is worth a thousand words" is often true, adding a few words to your drawing can save you from having to draw a thousand lines and arcs is also true. Writing "Simpson A35 framing clip" next to a simple, schematic representation of a clip is a lot easier than drawing one in photorealistic detail and hoping that the contractor can figure out what it is!

Most CAD drawings include some text in the form of explanatory notes, objects labels, and titles. This chapter demonstrates how to add text to drawings and shows you how to take advantage of AutoCAD LT text styles and the spell checker. Chapter 10 covers text that's connected with dimensions and leaders.

In most cases, adding text, dimensions, and other descriptive symbols is something that you do later in the drafting process, after you draw at least some of the geometry. In CAD drawings, text and other annotations usually are intended to complement the geometry, not to stand alone. Thus, you generally need to have the geometry in place before you annotate it. Many drafters find that drawing as much geometry as possible first, and then adding text labels and dimensions to all the geometry at the same time is most efficient. In this way, you develop a rhythm with the text and dimensioning commands, instead of bouncing back and forth between drawing geometry and adding annotations. (It helps if you hum "I've got rhythm . . ." while sliding the mouse back and forth in time.)

Getting Ready to Write

In AutoCAD LT, adding text to a drawing is only slightly more complicated than adding it to a word processing document. Here are the steps:

1. **Create a new AutoCAD LT text style, or select an existing style, that includes the font and other text characteristics you want to use.**
2. **Make an appropriate text layer current.**
3. **Run *one* of these commands to draw text:**
   - mText draws paragraph (also called multiline) text.
   - TeXt draws single-line text.
4. **Specify the text alignment points, justification, and height.**
5. **Type the text.**

You're probably familiar with most of these steps already — especially if you've ever used a word processor. In the next few sections of this chapter, I review the particularities of AutoCAD LT text styles, the two kinds of text, and ways of controlling height and justification.

Simply stylish text

AutoCAD LT assigns text properties to individual lines or paragraphs of text based on *text styles*. These text styles are similar to the paragraph styles in Microsoft Word: They contain font and other settings that determine the look and feel of text. An AutoCAD LT text style includes

- The font
- A font height, which you can set or leave at 0 for later flexibility
- Special effects such as italic
- *Really* special effects such as vertical and upside down, which almost nobody uses

Before you add text to a drawing, use the Text Style dialog box to select an existing style or create a new one with settings appropriate to your purpose. Your AutoCAD LT notes may generate strange responses (or no response at all) if they appear in Old Persian Cuneiform or the Cyrillic alphabet.

Most drawings require very few text styles. You can create one style for all notes, object labels, and annotations, and another one for special titles. A title block may require one or two additional fonts, especially if you want to mimic the font used in a company logo or project logo.

As with layers, your office may have its own text style standards. If so, you'll make everyone happy by following those standards. One of the best ways to make your use of text styles efficient and consistent is to create them in a template drawing that you use to start new drawings. (If your office is well organized, it may already have a template drawing with the company-approved styles defined in it.) See Chapter 5 for information about creating and using templates. Another handy technique is to copy existing text styles from one drawing to another by using the DesignCenter palette. See Chapter 3 for instructions.

Font follies

When you create a text style in AutoCAD LT, you have a choice of a huge number of fonts. LT can use two different kinds of fonts: native AutoCAD SHX (compiled SHape) fonts and Windows TTF (TrueType) fonts:

- **SHX:** In the Text Style dialog box, SHX font names appear with a drafting compass to the left of the name. SHX fonts usually provide better performance because they're optimized for AutoCAD's and LT's use.
- **TTF:** In the Text Style dialog box, TrueType font names appear with a TT symbol to the left of name. TrueType fonts give you more and fancier font options, but they slow down AutoCAD LT when you zoom, pan, and select and snap to objects. TrueType fonts also can cause greater complication when you exchange drawings with other AutoCAD or LT users. Chapter 15 describes the special procedure that you need to use in order to install custom TrueType fonts.

Using a TrueType font sparingly is okay for something like a title block logo, but in general, stick with standard AutoCAD SHX fonts whenever possible.

The most popular AutoCAD font is ROMANS.SHX (Roman Simplex). (You may also run into SIMPLEX.SHX, an older version of Roman Simplex.) ROMANS.SHX is a good, general-purpose font for drafting in AutoCAD and LT. Avoid complicated, thick fonts. They can slow down the program, and they're usually more difficult to read than the simpler fonts. Remember, you're doing CAD here — not fancy graphic design or reproduction of medieval manuscripts!

Whenever possible, avoid *custom fonts,* which are font files that don't come with AutoCAD or LT (both programs come with the same fonts). AutoCAD LT installs its standard SHX fonts into the `C:\Program Files\AutoCAD LT 2005\Fonts folder` — as long as you haven't added any custom fonts to that folder, you can refer to it for a list of standard fonts. If you use a custom font, exchanging your drawings with other people is more complicated. If you're compelled to use a custom font, make a note of it and remember either to send it whenever you send the DWG file (assuming that the font isn't copyrighted, which many custom fonts are) or to warn the recipients that the text will appear differently on their systems. Eschewing custom fonts altogether is far less hassle. See Chapter 15 for additional information about how to deal with fonts when you send and receive drawings.

Get in style

The following steps describe how to select an existing text style or create a new one before you enter text into a drawing. (If you want to experiment with an existing drawing that contains a variety of text styles, you can use `\Program Files\AutoCAD LT 2005\Sample\house plan.dwg`.)

1. **Choose Format➪Text Style.**

   The Text Style dialog box appears, as shown in Figure 9-1.

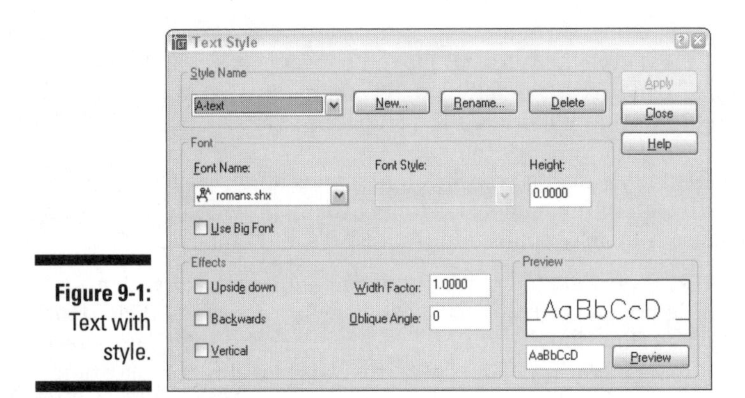

Figure 9-1: Text with style.

2. **In the Style Name drop-down list, select each style in turn to see what text styles have been created in this drawing.**

   Note the font name and look at the Preview panel to get a feel for what the different fonts look like.

3. **If you find a suitable text style, select it in the Style Name drop-down list and then skip to Step 9.**

   What constitutes a suitable text style depends on industry practices, office standards, and personal preferences about how the text needs to look. The information in the preceding sections may help you decide. If not, ask an experienced drafter in your office or look at some printed drawings and try to match the text on those.

   The selected text style name becomes the current style.

4. **If you don't find a suitable text style, or if you prefer to create your own text style, click New.**

   The New Text Style dialog box appears, with an edit box for you to type a name.

5. **Type a name for your new text style and then click OK.**

   Your new text style is added to the Style Name list and becomes the current style.

6. **Choose a font from the Font Name list.**

   ROMANS.SHX is the best all-purpose font for most drafting work. If you want to use a different font, review the font suggestions and warnings in the previous section.

   The font that you choose becomes the font that's assigned to your new text style.

7. **Set the remaining text style settings as shown in Figure 9-1: Height = 0.0, Width Factor = 1.0, Oblique Angle = 0.0, and all four check boxes unchecked.**

   A text style height of 0.0 makes the style *variable height,* which means that you can specify the height separately for each single-line text object. Assigning a *fixed* (that is, nonzero) height to a text style forces all single-line text using the style to be the same height. Variable height styles are more flexible, but fixed height styles usually make drawing text of consistent height easier. The decision to use variable height versus fixed height styles is another aspect of text that depends on office practice, so if you work with other AutoCAD or LT users, ask around.

8. **Click Apply.**

9. **Click Close.**

   The Text Style dialog box closes, and the text style that you selected or created is now the current style for new text objects.

Taking your text to new heights

In Chapter 5, I describe the importance of choosing an appropriate drawing scale when you set up a drawing. I warn you that you need to know the drawing scale factor for tasks described in other chapters of this book. This chapter is one of those, and I'm about to explain one of those tasks!

Drawing scale is the traditional way of describing a scale with an equal sign or colon — for example ¼" = 1'–0", 1:20, or 2:1. The *drawing scale factor* represents the same relationship with a single number such as 48, 20, or 0.5. The drawing scale factor is the multiplier that converts the first number in the drawing scale into the second number.

One of the things that distinguishes knowledgeable CAD users is that they *always* know the drawing scale factor of any drawing they're working on. Make a point of determining the drawing scale factor of a drawing before you add text to it.

Attack of the giant text strings

"Why do I need to know the drawing scale factor in order to draw text?," you may ask — especially if you've spent time "on the boards," as we grizzled old-timers like to call manual drafting. You need to know the drawing scale factor because you handle scaling of objects and text in CAD opposite from the way you do in manual drafting.

In manual drafting, you squeeze real-world objects (the building, widget, or whatever) down by a specific scale factor, like 10 or 48, so that they fit nicely on a sheet of paper. Naturally, you always draw text the size that you want it to appear on the paper (for example, ⅛ inch or 3 mm high), regardless of the scale of the drawing.

In CAD drafting, you draw objects as if they were at their actual size. Then, when you plot, you shrink (or, if you make drawings of tiny things such as microprocessor circuitry, expand) the entire drawing by that same scale factor (for example, 10 or 48) to fit on the paper. When you shrink the whole drawing to fit on the paper, text shrinks, too. To avoid indecipherably small text, or incredibly large text, you must create text at a size that's scaled appropriately by the drawing scale factor. (If you're an architect, imagine that your text is neon lettering on the side of the building. If you're a mechanical designer, think of a brand name stamped on the side of a screw.)

For example, assume that someone has drawn a widget at a scale of 1:20 (corresponding to a drawing scale factor of 20), and you want your notes to appear 3 mm high when the drawing is plotted to scale. You need to create text that's 20 times 3 mm, or 60 mm, high. In a building plan drawn at a scale of ¼" = 1'–0" (drawing scale factor equals 48), text that appears ⅛ inch when plotted needs to be ⅛ inch times 48, or 6 inches, high.

This "tiny text" / "enormous text" approach seems peculiar at first, especially if you are schooled in manual drafting. But CAD's ability lets you draw and measure the geometry in real-world units. After all, the geometry of what you're representing, not the ancillary notes, usually is the main point of the drawing.

Plotted text height

Most industries have plotted text height standards. A plotted text height of ⅛ inch or 3 mm is common for notes. Some companies use slightly smaller heights (for example, 3⁄32 inch or 2.5 mm) to squeeze more text into small spaces.

Calculating CAD text height

To calculate CAD text height, you need to know the drawing scale factor, the desired plotted text height, and the location of the multiplication button on your calculator. Use the following steps to figure out text height:

1. **Determine the drawing's drawing scale factor.**

   If you set up the drawing, you know its drawing scale, as described in Chapter 5. If someone else set up the drawing, try the suggestions in the sidebar, "Figuring out a drawing's scale factor."

2. **Determine the height that you want your notes to appear when you plot the drawing to scale.**

   See the "Plotted text height" section for suggestions.

3. **Multiply the numbers that you figured out in Steps 1 and 2.**

Table 9-1 lists some common drawing scales and text heights for drawings in imperial and metric units. You need to know how to calculate the drawing scale factors and text heights, but you're allowed to use the table to check your work. (***Hint:*** Multiply the number in the second column by the number in the third column to get the number in the fourth column!) The Cheat Sheet tables include some additional drawing scales and text heights.

Table 9-1 Common Drawing Scales and Text Heights

Drawing Scale	*Drawing Scale Factor*	*Plotted Text Height*	*CAD Text Height*
⅛" = 1'–0"	96	⅛"	12"
¼" = 1'–0"	48	⅛"	6"
¾" = 1'–0"	16	⅛"	2"
1" = 1'–0"	12	⅛"	1½"
1 = 100 mm	100	3 mm	300 mm
1 = 50 mm	50	3 mm	150 mm
1 = 20 mm	20	3 mm	60 mm
1 = 10 mm	10	3 mm	30 mm

After you know the CAD text height, you can use it to define the height of a text style or of an individual text object. If you assign a nonzero height to a text style (Step 7 in the "Get in style" section, earlier in this chapter), all single-line text strings that you create with that style use the fixed height. If you leave the text style's height set to zero, AutoCAD LT asks you for the text height when you draw each single-line text object.

This discussion of text height assumes that you're adding text in model space, which is the most common practice. You may want to add text to a paper space layout — for example, when you draw text in a title block or add a set of sheet notes that doesn't directly relate to the model space geometry. When you create text in paper space, you specify the actual, plotted height, instead of the scaled-up height.

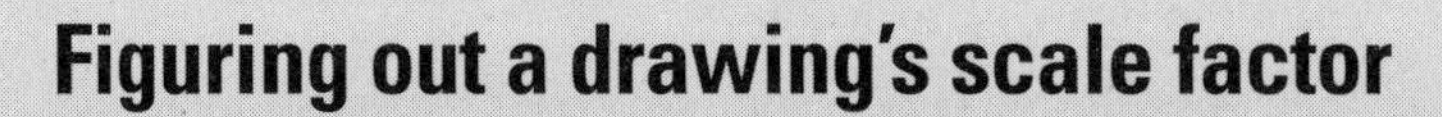

Figuring out a drawing's scale factor

If you're adding text to a drawing that someone else created, you may not immediately know its drawing scale factor. In some cases, making the determination is trivial, whereas in other cases it's tricky indeed. Here are some methods you can use:

- Ask the creator of the drawing.
- Look for text or a scale bar on the drawing that indicates the scale.
- Use an architectural or engineering scale to measure distances on the plotted drawing, if you have one.
- Check the value of the DIMSCALE (DIMension SCALE) system variable, as described in Chapter 10.

None of these methods is infallible by itself, but by comparing the evidence, you usually can figure out the drawing scale factor with reasonable certainty.

One line or two?

For historical reasons (namely, because the AutoCAD and LT text capabilities used to be much more primitive than they are now), LT offers two different kinds of text objects and two corresponding text-drawing commands. Table 9-2 explains the two options.

Table 9-2 The Two Kinds of AutoCAD LT Text

Text Object	*Command*	*Comments*
Paragraph text	mText	Designed for multiple lines, with word-wrapping. AutoCAD LT keeps the multiple lines together as a single object. Other special formatting, such as hanging indents, is possible.
Single-line text	TeXt	Designed for creating single lines. Although you can press Enter to create more than one line of text, each line becomes a separate text object.

Although you may be inclined to ignore the older single-line text option, it's worth knowing how to use both kinds of text. The TeXt command is a bit simpler than the mText command, so it's still useful for entering short, single-line pieces of text such as object labels and one-line notes. And it's the command of choice for CAD comedians who want to document their one-liners!

Your text will be justified

Both the TeXt and mText commands offer a bewildering array of text *justification* options — in other words, which way the text flows from the justification point or points that you pick in the drawing. For most purposes, the default Left justification for single-line text or Top Left justification for paragraph text works fine. Occasionally, you may want to use a different justification, such as Center for labels or titles. Both commands provide command-line options for changing text justification. I point out these options when I demonstrate the commands later in this chapter.

Using the Same Old Line

Despite its limitations, the TeXt command is useful for labels and other short notes for which mText can be overkill. The following steps show you how to enter text by using the AutoCAD LT TeXt command.

You can use TeXt for multiple lines of text: Just keep pressing Enter after you type each line of text, and TeXt puts the new line below the previous one. The problem is that TeXt creates each line of text as a separate object. If you later want to add or remove words in the multiple lines, LT can't do any word-wrapping for you; you have to edit each line separately, cutting words from one line and adding them to the adjacent line.

The AutoCAD LT 2005 TeXt command was called DTEXT (Dynamic TEXT) in older versions of LT (AutoCAD LT 98 and earlier). You may hear AutoCAD old-timers refer to the DTEXT command instead of TeXt. In addition, LT's Draw⇨Text⇨Single Line Text menu choice enters DTEXT at the command line, as Figure 9-2, later in this chapter, shows. (And you thought they called it DTEXT because it wasn't good enough to be A, B, or C text. . . .)

The TeXt command does all its prompting on the command line, so be sure to read the command line prompts at each step along the way.

Here's how you enter text with the TeXt command:

1. **Set an appropriate layer current, as I describe in Chapter 3.**
2. **Set an appropriate text style current, as described in the section "Simply stylish text," earlier in this chapter.**
3. **Use the OSNAP button on the status bar to turn off running object snap mode.**

   You usually don't want to snap text to existing objects.

4. **Choose Draw⇨Text⇨Single Line Text from the menu bar to start the TeXt command.**

   The Text button on the Draw toolbar starts the multiline text command, mText, which I cover in the next section.

   LT tells you the current text style and height settings and prompts you to select a starting point for the text, or to choose an option for changing the text justification or current text style first:

   ```
   Current text style: "Standard" Text height: 0.2000
   Specify start point of text or [Justify/Style]:
   ```

5. **If you want to change justification from the default (lower left), type** J**, press Enter, and choose one of the other justification options.**

   Look up "single-line text, aligning" in the online help if you need help with the justification options.

6. **Specify the insertion point for the first text character.**

   You can enter the point's coordinates from the command line, use the mouse to click a point on-screen, or press Enter to locate new text immediately below the most recent single-line text object that you created.

   LT prompts you at the command line for the text height:

   ```
   Specify height <0.2000>:
   ```

7. **Specify the height for the text.**

   This prompt doesn't appear if you're using a text style with a fixed (that is, nonzero) height. See "Simply stylish text," earlier in this chapter, for information about fixed versus variable text heights.

   LT prompts you at the command line for the text rotation angle:

   ```
   Specify rotation angle of text <0>:
   ```

8. **Specify the text rotation angle by entering the rotation angle from the command line and pressing Enter or by rotating the line on-screen with the mouse.**

   LT prompts you at the command line to type the text:

   ```
   Enter text:
   ```

9. **Type the first line of text and press Enter.**

10. **Type additional lines of text, pressing Enter at the end of each line.**

    Figure 9-2 shows text appearing on-screen as you type it.

11. **To complete the command, press Enter at the start of a blank line.**

    LT adds the new line text object — or objects, if you type more than one line — to the drawing.

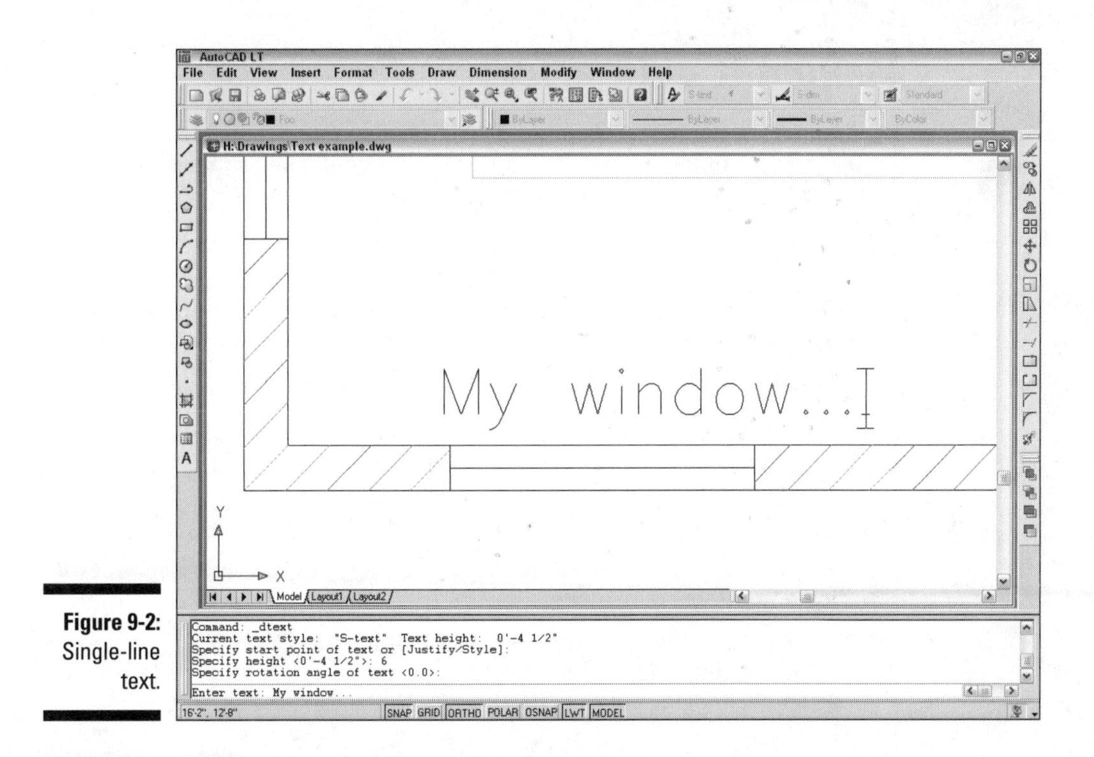

Figure 9-2: Single-line text.

To align lines of text exactly, make sure that you type in all the lines in one invocation of the TeXt command, pressing Enter after each line to make the next line appear just after it. Otherwise, aligning different lines of text precisely is harder to do (unless you set your snap just right or use a complicated combination of object snaps and point filters).

To edit single-line text after you create it, double-click the text string (or select it, right-click, and choose Text Edit). The Edit Text dialog box appears, enabling you to edit the contents of the text string. If you want to edit other text properties, such as text height, select the text, right-click, and choose Properties to display the Properties palette. Use the Properties palette to change parameters as needed.

Saying More in Multiline Text

When you just can't shoehorn your creative genius into one or more one-line pieces of text, the AutoCAD LT multiline text object gives you room to go on and on and on. The following procedure shows you how to create text paragraphs with the mText (multiline Text) command.

Making it with mText

The first part of the mText command prompts you for various points and options on the command line. The order is a bit confusing, so read these steps and the command line prompts carefully.

Here's how you use the mText command:

1. **Set an appropriate layer and text style current and turn off running object snaps, as in Steps 1 through 3 in the previous section.**
2. **Click the Multiline Text button on the Draw toolbar.**

   The command line displays the current text style and height settings and prompts you to select the first corner of an imaginary rectangle that determines the word-wrapping width for the text object:

   ```
   Current text style:  "S-NOTES"  Text height:  0.125
   Specify first corner:
   ```
3. **Pick a point in the drawing.**

   The command line prompts you for the opposite corner of the text rectangle that determines the word-wrapping width and gives you the option of changing settings first:

   ```
   Specify opposite corner or [Height/Justify/Line
           spacing/Rotation/Style/Width]:
   ```
4. **Type** H **and press Enter to change the default text height.**

   The command line prompts you for a new default text height:

   ```
   Specify height <0.2000>:
   ```
5. **Type an appropriate text height.**

   See the "Taking your text to new heights" section, earlier in this chapter, for information. If you're adding text in model space, remember to use the scaled CAD text height, not the plotted text height.

   The command line prompt for the opposite corner of the mText rectangle reappears:

   ```
   Specify opposite corner or [Height/Justify/Line
           spacing/Rotation/Style/Width]:
   ```
6. **If you want to change justification from the default (top left), type** J**, press Enter, and choose one of the other justification options.**

   Look up "multiline text, aligning, Justify Multiline Text" in the online help if you want an explanation of the other justification options.

7. **Pick another point in the drawing.**

Don't worry about the height of the rectangle that you create by choosing the second point; the width of the rectangle is all that matters. LT adjusts the height of the text rectangle to accommodate the number of lines of word-wrapped text. Don't worry too much about the width, either; you can adjust it later.

The Multiline Text Editor frameless window appears with the tab and indent ruler above it and the Text Formatting toolbar above that, as shown in Figure 9-3.

If you want to see multiline text at its final height as you type it, zoom to a reasonable magnification before you start the mText command. If the text is very small (because you're zoomed way out) or very large (because you're zoomed way in), LT temporarily adjusts the size of the text in the frameless editor to show what you're typing. When you finish entering the text (as in Step 11), LT places it in the drawing at the height that you specify.

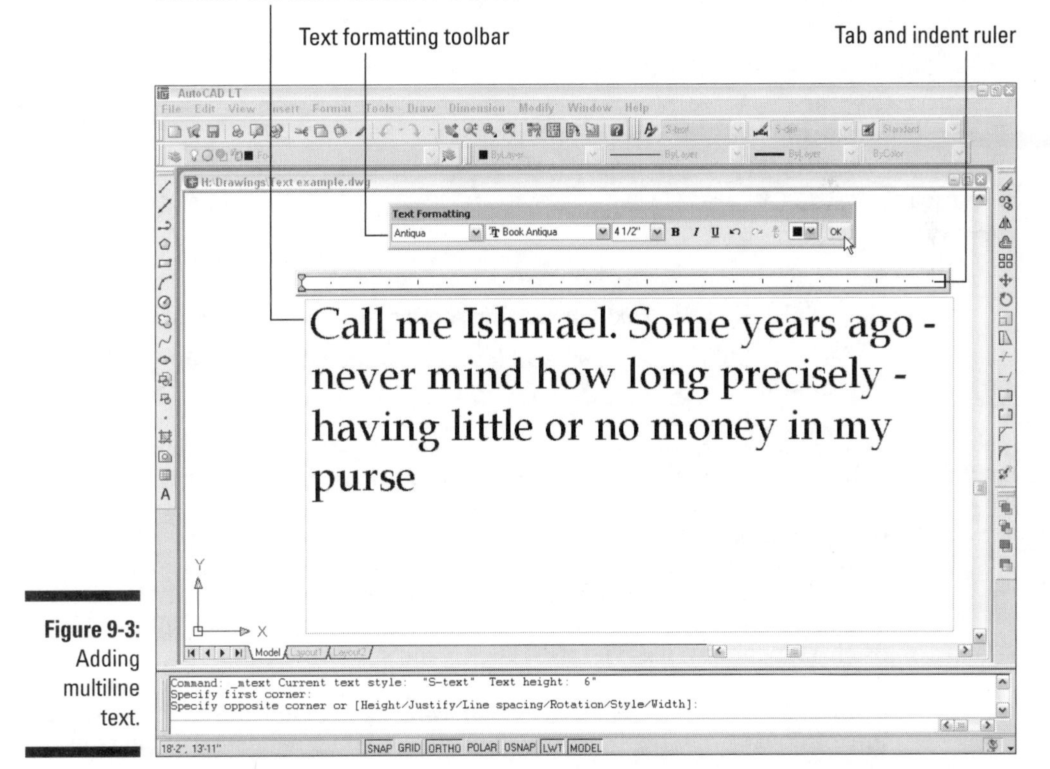

Figure 9-3: Adding multiline text.

8. **Verify the text font and height.**

   The text font and height is right if you correctly performed Steps 1, 4, and 5. If not, you can change these settings in the Font drop-down list and the Font Height edit box in the Text Formatting toolbar.

9. **Type text into the text area of the window.**

   LT word wraps multiline text automatically. If you want to force a line break at a particular location, press Enter.

10. **If you want other formatting, select the text, right-click, and select the appropriate option from the menu (as in Figure 9-4).**

Undo	Ctrl+Z
Redo	Ctrl+Y
Cut	Ctrl+X
Copy	Ctrl+C
Paste	Ctrl+V
Indents and Tabs...	
Justification	▸
Find and Replace...	Ctrl+R
Select All	Ctrl+A
Change Case	▸
AutoCAPS	
Remove Formatting	Ctrl+Space
Combine Paragraphs	
Symbol	▸
Import Text...	
Background Mask...	
Help	
Character Set	▸

Figure 9-4: More multiline text formatting options in the right-click menu.

11. **Click OK in the Text Formatting toolbar (or press Ctrl+Enter).**

    The Multiline Text Editor window closes, and LT adds your text to the drawing.

As you can tell by looking at the Text Formatting toolbar and multiline text right-click menu, the mText command gives you plenty of other options. The Text Formatting toolbar includes a Stack/Unstack button for fractions. The right-click menu includes access to the Indents and Tabs feature, a Find and Replace utility, tools for changing between lower- and uppercase, a special Symbol submenu (including some new symbols in AutoCAD LT 2005), and an Import Text option for importing text from a TXT (ASCII text) file or RTF (Rich Text Format) file. The right-click menu's AutoCAPS setting ensures that all the multiline text you type is uppercase (a common convention on technical drawings). If you think you may have a use for these additional features, choose Contents➪Command Reference➪Commands➪M Commands➪MTEXT in AutoCAD LT's online help.

mText dons a mask

AutoCAD LT 2005 adds one more option to the multiline text right-click menu: Background Mask. When you turn on background masking, LT hides the portions of any objects that lie underneath the text. Use these steps to turn on and control this feature:

1. **Right-click in the Multiline Text Editor window and choose Background Mask from the menu.**
2. **Click the Use Background Mask check box so that this option is turned on.**
3. **Either click the Use Background option (to make the mask the same color as the drawing area's background color) or choose a color from the drop-down list (to make the text appear in a solid rectangle of the specified color).**
4. **Click OK to return to the Multiline Text Editor window.**

If you turn on background masking but it isn't having the desired effect, use the DRaworder or TEXTTOFRONT command to move text "on top of" other objects.

Figure 9-5 shows background masking in action.

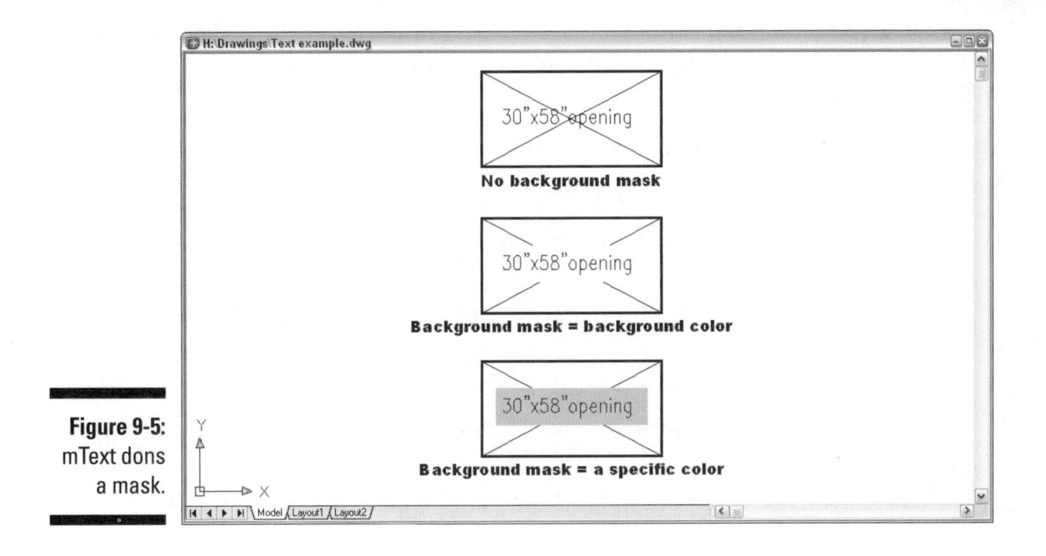

Figure 9-5: mText dons a mask.

Keeping tabs (and indents) on your mText

Another advantage of mText is that it supports tabs and indents. This feature is especially useful for creating hanging indents — the kind of indents that push an entire paragraph to the right of a number or bullet, as shown in Figure 9-6. (Before AutoCAD and LT 2004, you had no straightforward way of performing this feat.) These steps aren't as straightforward as in most word processing programs, but at least you *can* create numbered and bulleted lists with hanging indents. Here's how:

1. **Follow Steps 1 through 8 in the preceding section, "Making it with mText."**
2. **In the tab and indent ruler, drag the lower slider (the triangle pointing up) to the right a small distance.**

   The lower slider controls the indentation of the second and subsequent lines in each paragraph. (The upper slider controls the indentation of the first line in each paragraph.) An indent of two to four of the short, vertical tick marks usually works well.
3. **Click in the ruler just above the lower slider.**

   A small *L* appears above the lower slider. The L shows the tab stop.

   Make sure that the corner of the *L* aligns horizontally with the point of the lower slider triangle. If not, click and drag the *L* until it aligns.
4. **Type a number followed by a period or parenthesis (for example,** 1.) **or a character that represents a bullet (for example,** *).
5. **Press the Tab key.**

   The cursor jumps to the tab stop that you added in Step 3.
6. **Type the text corresponding to the current number or bullet.**

   As LT wraps the text, the second and subsequent lines align with the beginning of the text in the first line, as in Figure 9-6.
7. **Press Enter to finish the current numbered or bulleted item.**
8. **Press Enter again if you want to leave a blank line between numbered or bulleted items.**
9. **Repeat Steps 4 through 8 for each subsequent numbered or bulleted item.**

   If you find that your indents aren't quite the right size, select all the text and adjust the lower slider and tab stop.
10. **Resume with Step 9 in the section, "Making it with mText."**

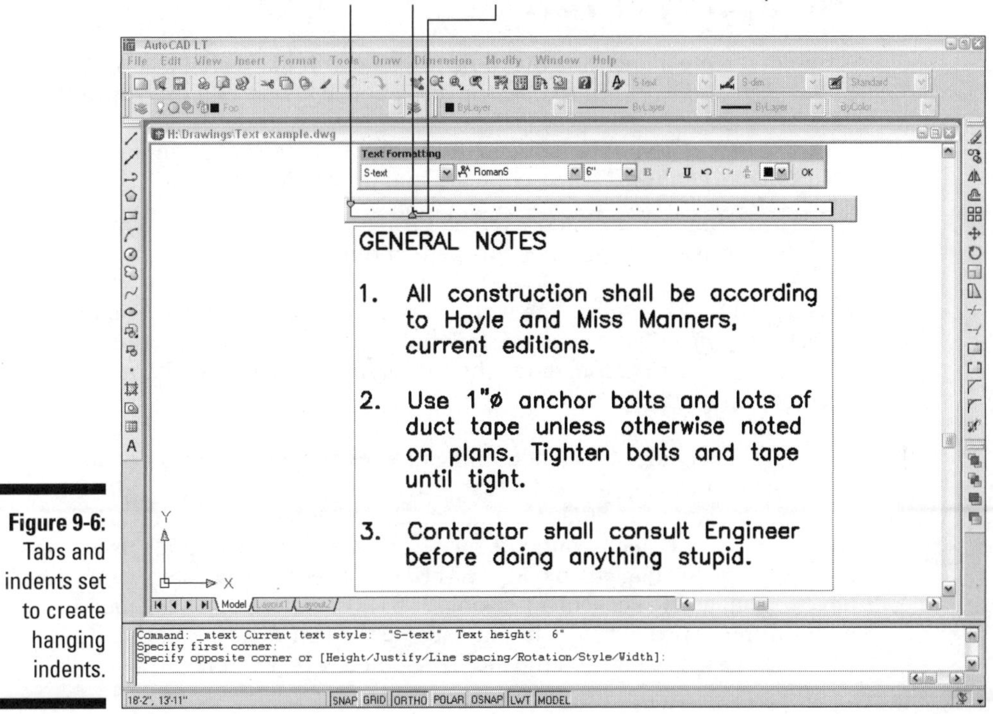

Figure 9-6: Tabs and indents set to create hanging indents.

If you prefer to type tab and indent distances, not adjust them with the cursor, use the Indents and Tabs choice on the mText right-click menu. Whichever way you do it, if you select text first, the tab and indent changes apply to the selected text. If you don't select text first, the changes apply to new text from that point in the multiline text object forward.

The AutoCAD LT text commands are designed for the kinds of text that most people add to drawings: short, single-line notes or longer blocks of a paragraph or two. If you want sophisticated formatting or long stretches of text, you're likely to bump up against the fact that LT lacks the capabilities of even the most basic word processing programs. If you're contemplating adding pages of text or fancy text formatting to a drawing, consider putting the text in a separate word processing document instead. If you absolutely must place the text from a long document on a drawing (on a general notes sheet, for example), you have to break it up into several columns, each of which is a separate mText object. Get the text right in a word processor first and then copy and paste it into AutoCAD LT. If you're tempted to circumvent my warning by pasting a word processing document directly into an AutoCAD LT drawing, please read Chapter 17 first.

Modifying mText

After you create a multiline text object, you edit it like a single-line text object: Select the object, right-click, and choose mText Edit or Properties.

- The mText Edit option opens the Multiline Text Editor window so that you can change the text contents and formatting.
- The Properties option opens the Properties palette, where you can change overall properties for the text object.

The easiest way to change the word-wrapping width of a paragraph text object is to *grip edit* it. Select the text object, click one of the corner grips, release the mouse button, move the cursor, and click again. Chapter 7 describes grip editing in detail.

AutoCAD LT includes two text modification commands that may be useful to you when you become an LT textpert. SCALETEXT scales a group of text objects, similar to the SCale command. The difference is that SCALETEXT scales each text object around its own base point, whereas SCale uses a single base point for scaling all objects. SCALETEXT is especially useful when you have to change the scale of a drawing. JUSTIFYTEXT changes the justification of one or more text strings without causing the text to move. Both of these commands are available on the Modify➪Object➪Text submenu.

Setting the Text Table

My vote for the best new feature in AutoCAD LT 2005 without a doubt goes to tables. You don't know the meaning of the word "tedious" unless you've tried to create a column-and-row data table in previous versions of AutoCAD LT with the Line and TeXt commands. AutoCAD LT 2005's new table object and the TableStyle and TaBle commands for creating it make the job almost fun.

Tables have style, too

You control the appearance of tables — both the text and the gridlines — with *table styles* (just as you control the appearance of standalone text with text styles). Use the TableStyle command to create and modify table styles. Follow these steps to create a table:

1. **Choose Format➪Table Style.**

   The Table Style dialog box appears.

2. **In the Styles list, select the existing table style whose settings you want to use as the starting point for the settings of your new style.**

   For example, select the default Standard table style.

3. **Click the New button to create a new table style that's a copy of the existing style.**

   The Create New Table Style dialog box appears.

4. **Enter a New Style Name and click Continue.**

   The New Table Style dialog box appears as shown in Figure 9-7.

5. **On the Data tab, specify settings for the data text and gridlines (that is, for all cells except the column heads and the table title).**

   The settings you are likely to want to change are Text Style, Text Height, and perhaps either Text Color or Grid Color. (If you leave colors set to ByBlock, the text and grid lines inherit the color that's current when you create the table. That color is the current layer's color, if you follow my advice in the "Accumulating properties" section of Chapter 3.)

6. **Repeat Step 5 for the Column Heads tab and the Title tab.**

7. **Click OK to close the New Table Style dialog box.**

   The Table Style dialog box reappears.

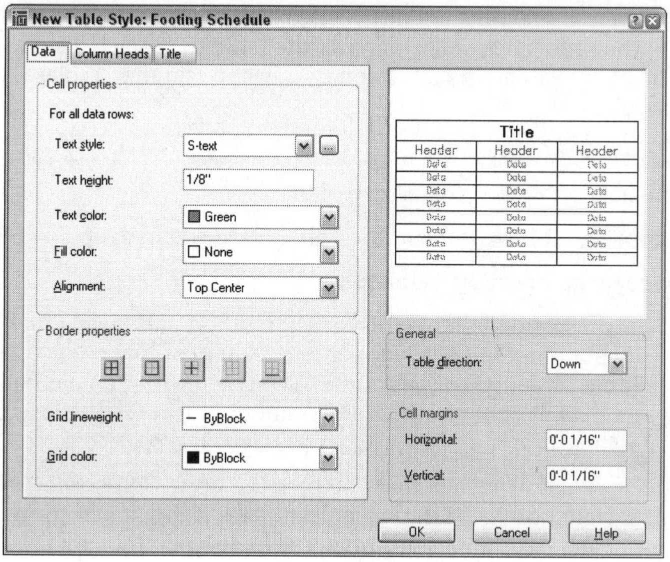

Figure 9-7: Setting the table.

8. **(Optional) Select your new table style from the Styles list, and then click Set Current.**

   Your new table style becomes the current table style that LT uses for future tables in this drawing.

9. **Click Close.**

   The Table Style dialog box closes. Now you're ready to create a table, as I describe in the next section.

AutoCAD LT stores table styles in the DWG file, so a style that you create in one drawing isn't immediately available in others. You can copy a table style from one drawing to another with DesignCenter. (Use the "Borrowing existing dimension styles" steps in Chapter 10, but substitute Table Styles for DimStyles.)

Creating and editing tables

After you create a suitable table style, adding a table to your drawing is easy with the TaBle command. Here's how:

1. **Set an appropriate layer current.**

   Assuming that you leave the current color, linetype, and lineweight set to ByLayer, as I recommend in Chapter 3, the current layer's properties control the properties of any parts of the table that you left set to ByBlock when you defined the table style. (See Step 5 in the "Tables have style, too" section.)

2. **Choose Draw⇨Table.**

   The Insert Table dialog box appears.

3. **Choose a table style from the Table Style Name drop-down list.**

4. **Choose an Insertion Behavior.**

   Specify Insertion Point is the easiest method and means that you pick the location of the table's upper-left corner (or lower-left corner if you set Table Direction to Up in the table style). With this method, you specify the default column width and number of rows in the Insert Table dialog box.

   Specify Window means that you pick the upper-left corner and then the lower-right corner. With this method, LT automatically scales the column widths and determines how many rows to include.

5. **Specify Column & Row Settings.**

If you chose Specify Window in Step 4, LT sets the Column Width and number of Data Rows to Auto, which means that AutoCAD LT figures them out based on the overall size of the table that you specify in Steps 7 and 8.

6. **Click OK.**

   LT prompts you to specify the insertion point of the table.

7. **Click a point or type coordinates.**

   If you chose Specify Insertion Point in Step 4, LT draws the table grid lines, places the cursor in the title cell, and displays the Text Formatting toolbar.

8. **If you chose Specify Window in Step 4, specify the diagonally opposite corner of the table.**

   LT draws the table. Based on the table size that you indicated, LT chooses the column width and number of rows.

9. **Type a title for the table.**

10. **Press the arrow keys or Tab key to move among cells, and type values in each cell.**

    The cell right-click menu offers many other options, including copying contents from one cell to another, merging cells, inserting rows and columns, changing formatting, and inserting a block (that is, a graphical symbol — see Chapter 13 for information about blocks).

11. **Click OK on the Text Formatting toolbar.**

    Figure 9-8 shows a completed table, along with the Insert Table dialog box.

You can edit cell values later simply by double-clicking in a cell. To change column width or row height, click in the table grid and then click and move the blue grips. (To change the width of one column without altering the overall width of the table, hold down the Ctrl key while you move the grip.) If you want to change other aspects of a table or individual cells in it, select the table or cell and use the Properties palette to make changes.

You can import tables from Microsoft Excel instead of using the Insert Table dialog box. To import Excel data, select the desired cells and then choose Edit⇨Copy from the Excel menu bar. Then in AutoCAD LT, choose Edit⇨Paste Special and choose AutoCAD LT Entities in the Paste Special dialog box. LT attempts to copy the Excel spreadsheet's formatting along with the cell data, but you probably have to adjust column widths and perform other cleanup on the imported table.

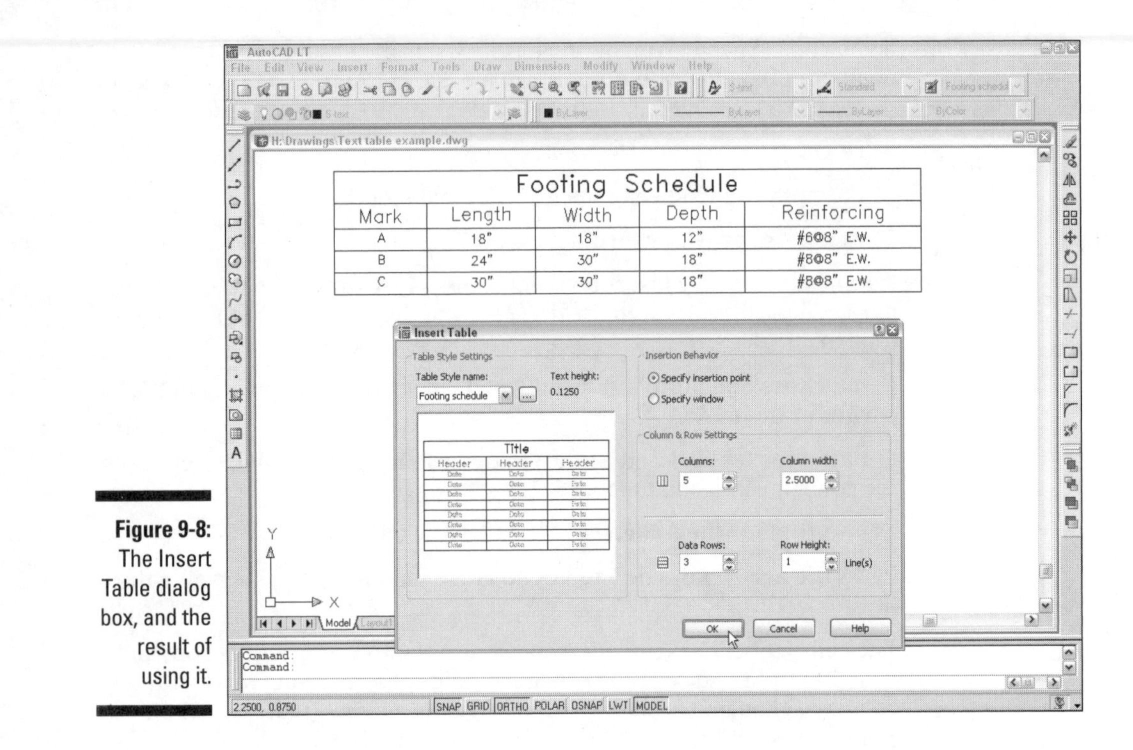

Figure 9-8: The Insert Table dialog box, and the result of using it.

You can go the other direction — from AutoCAD LT to Excel or another program — via a CSV (Comma Separated Value) file. Look up "TABLEEXPORT command" in AutoCAD LT's online help to do so.

Checking Out Your Spelling

AutoCAD LT, like almost every other computer program on this planet — and possibly on other planets and moons in our solar system — has a spell checker.

Unlike Microsoft Word, AutoCAD LT's spell checker doesn't make those little red squiggles under your errors, but it does let you search for spelling errors in most of the text objects in your drawing. This feature checks single-line text, paragraph text, and attribute text (described in Chapter 13), but not dimension text (described in Chapter 10). The following steps demonstrate how to use the spell checker:

1. **Press the Esc key to deselect any selected objects.**
2. **Choose Tools⇨Spelling to start the SPell command.**

   This is text spell checking, not casting a spell. (That's the EYEOFNEWT command.) The command line prompts you to select objects.

3. **Select the objects you want to check.**

   You can use any of the standard AutoCAD LT object selection methods to select text to check. (See Chapter 7 if you're unfamiliar with object selection.) Type **ALL** and press Enter if you want to check the spelling of all text in the drawing. Don't worry if you select objects other than text; the spell checker ignores any objects that aren't text. When you finish selecting objects, press Enter to start the spell check.

   If LT finds a misspelling, the Check Spelling dialog box appears with the first misspelled or unrecognized word. Figure 9-9 shows an example.

4. **Click the dialog box buttons to tell LT how to handle a misspelling.**

   You probably know which buttons to click from having used other spell checkers. If not, use the dialog box help to find out: Click the question mark on the Check Spelling dialog box's title bar, and then click the button that you want to know more about.

   LT continues with spell checking until it checks all the selected text objects. When it finds no further misspellings, the dialog box disappears, and the `Spelling check complete` alert appears.

Figure 9-9: It's good to sue your spell checker.

Every industry has its own abbreviations and specialized vocabulary. At first, AutoCAD LT complains about perfectly good words (from a drafter's point of view) such as *thru* and *S.A.D.* (which stands for See Architectural Drawing). Be prepared to click the Add button frequently during the first few weeks to tell LT which words and abbreviations are acceptable in your industry and office. If you're patient with it, AutoCAD LT, like an errant puppy, gradually becomes more obedient. Then you'll be thru feeling S.A.D.

Chapter 10

Dimension This!

In This Chapter

- Understanding dimension parts and types
- Using dimension styles from other drawings
- Creating and modifying your own dimension styles
- Drawing and editing dimensions
- Drawing leaders

In drafting — either CAD or manual drafting — *dimensions* are special text labels with attached lines that together indicate unambiguously the size of something. Although drawing all the pieces of each dimension with AutoCAD LT commands such as Line and mText is theoretically possible, dimensioning is so common a drafting task that LT provides special commands for doing the job more efficiently. These dimensioning commands group the parts of each dimension into a convenient, easy-to-edit package. Even better, as you edit an object — by stretching it for example — LT automatically updates the measurement displayed in the dimension text label to indicate the object's new size, as shown in Figure 10-1.

AutoCAD LT controls the look of dimensions by means of *dimension styles*, just as it controls the look of text with text styles. (LT also uses text styles to control the appearance of the text in dimensions.) But dimension styles are much more complicated than text styles, because dimensions have so many more pieces that you need to control. After you find or create an appropriate dimension style, you use one of several dimensioning commands to draw dimensions that point to the important points on an object (the two endpoints of a line, for example).

AutoCAD LT dimensioning is a big, complicated subject. (It's so complicated, in fact, that Autodesk has an especially wise person in charge of dimensioning in AutoCAD and LT — this person is called the "DimWit.") Every industry has its own dimensioning conventions, habits, and quirks. As usual, AutoCAD and LT try to support them all and, in so doing, make things a bit convoluted for everyone. This chapter covers the essential concepts and commands that you need to know to start drawing dimensions. Be prepared to spend some additional time studying how to create any specialized types of dimensions that your industry uses.

You may be able to avoid getting too deeply into the details of dimensioning just by copying dimension styles from existing drawings in your office. (I show you how later in this chapter.) Now may also be a good time to get some advice and coaching from the AutoCAD geek in the cubicle across from yours.

You add dimensions to a drawing *after* you draw at least some of the geometry; otherwise, you don't have much to dimension! Your dimensioning and overall drafting efficiency improve if you add dimensions in batches, rather than draw a line, draw a dimension, draw another line, draw another dimension. . . .

Why dimensions in CAD?

You may think that CAD had rendered text dimensions obsolete. After all, you comply with all my suggestions about using AutoCAD LT precision techniques when you draw and edit, and you're careful to draw each object at its true size, right? The contractor or machinist can just use AutoCAD or LT to query distances and angles in the CAD DWG file, right? Sorry, but no (to the last question, anyway). Here are a few reasons why the traditional dimensioning that CAD drafting has inherited from manual drafting is likely to be around for a while:

- **Some people need to or want to use paper drawings when they build something.** We're still some time away from the day when contractors haul computers around in their tool belts (never mind mousing around a drawing while hanging from scaffolding).
- **In many industries, paper drawings still rule legally.** Your company may supply both plotted drawings and DWG files to clients, but your contracts probably specify that the plotted drawings govern in the case of any discrepancy. The contracts probably also warn against relying on any distances that the recipient of the drawings measures — using measuring commands in the CAD DWG file or a scale on the plotted drawing. The text dimensions are supposed to supply all the dimensional information that's needed to construct the object.
- **Dimensions sometimes carry additional information besides the basic length or angle.** For example, dimension text can indicate the allowable construction tolerances or show that a particular distance is typical of similar situations elsewhere on the drawing.
- **Even conscientious CAD drafters rarely draw *every* object at its true size.** Drafters sometimes exaggerate distances for graphical clarity. For example, they may draw a small object larger than its true size so that it shows up clearly on a scaled plot. In addition, drafters sometimes settle for approximate distances because time pressures (especially late in a project) make being completely accurate difficult.

So remember the old rule of drafting prowess: "It's not the size of the drawn object that matters, but the dimensions that are on it."

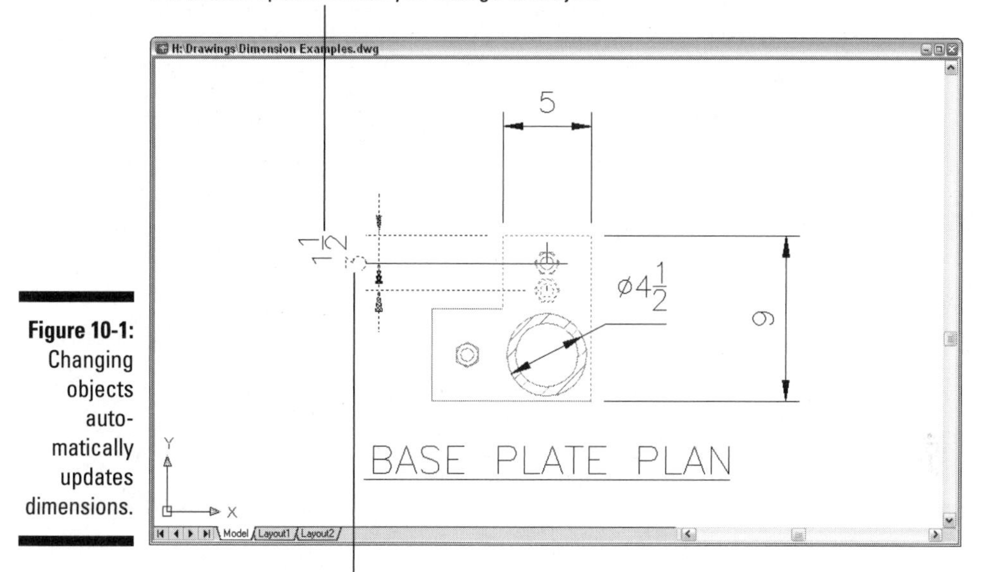

Figure 10-1: Changing objects automatically updates dimensions.

Discovering New Dimensions

Before digging into the techniques that you use to create dimension styles and dimensions, I review some AutoCAD LT dimensioning terminology. If you're already familiar with CAD dimensioning lingo, just skim this section and look at the figures in it. Otherwise, read on.

Anatomy of a dimension

AutoCAD LT uses the names shown in Figure 10-2 and I describe in the following list to refer to the parts of each dimension:

- **Dimension text:** Dimension text usually is the number that indicates the actual distance or angle. Dimension text can also include other text information in addition to or instead of the number. For example, you can add a suffix such as `TYP.` to indicate that a dimension is typical of several similar configurations, or you can insert a description such as `See Detail 3/A2`.
- **Dimension lines:** The dimension lines go from the dimension text outward (parallel to the direction of the object being measured), to indicate the extent of the dimensioned length. AutoCAD LT's default dimension style settings center the dimension text vertically and horizontally on

the dimension lines (see Figure 10-2), but you can change those settings to cause the text to appear in a different location — riding above an unbroken dimension line as shown in Figure 10-1, for example. See the section "Adjusting style settings," later in this chapter, for instructions.

- **Dimension arrowheads:** The dimension arrowheads appear at the ends of the dimension lines and clarify the extent of the dimensioned length. AutoCAD LT's default arrowhead style is the closed, filled type shown in Figure 10-2, but you can choose other symbols, such as tick marks, to indicate the ends of the dimension lines. (Don't get ticked off, but LT calls the line ending an *arrowhead* even when, as in the case of a tick mark, it doesn't look like an arrow.)
- **Extension lines:** The extension lines extend outward from the extension line origin points that you select (usually by snapping to points on an object) to the dimension lines. By drafting convention, a small gap usually exists between the extension line origin points and the beginning of the extension lines. The extension lines usually extend just beyond where they meet the dimension lines.

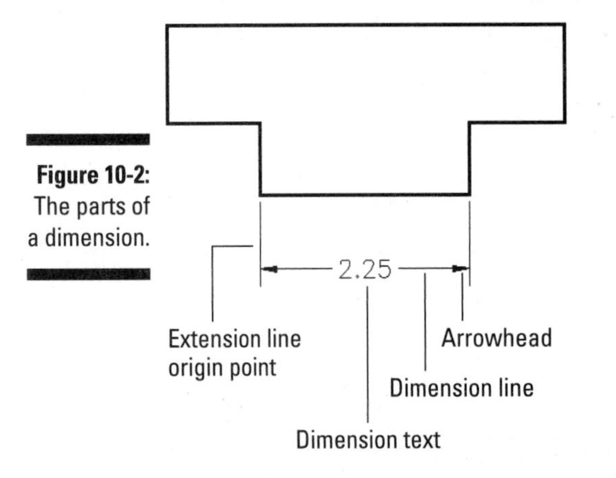

Figure 10-2: The parts of a dimension.

A field guide to dimensions

AutoCAD LT provides several types of dimensions and commands for drawing them. Figure 10-3 shows the most common types, and the following list describes them:

- **Linear dimensions:** A linear dimension measures the linear extent of an object or the linear distance between objects. Most linear dimensions are either *horizontal* or *vertical,* but you can draw dimensions that are *rotated* to other angles, too. An *aligned* dimension is similar to a linear dimension, but the dimension line tilts to the same angle as a line drawn through the origin points of its extension lines.

- **Radial dimensions:** A *radius* dimension calls out the radius of a circle or arc, and a *diameter* dimension calls out the diameter of a circle or arc. You can position the dimension text inside or outside the curve, as shown in Figure 10-3. If you position the text outside the curve, AutoCAD LT by default draws a little cross at the center of the circle or arc.
- **Angular dimensions:** An *angular* dimension calls out the angular measurement between two lines, the two endpoints of an arc, or two points on a circle. The dimension line appears as an arc that indicates the sweep of the measured angle.

Other types of AutoCAD LT dimensions include ordinate, tolerance, center mark, and leader dimensions. See the "Pointy-Headed Leaders" section at the end of this chapter for instructions on how to draw leaders. Look up "dimensions, creating" on the Index tab in the AutoCAD LT online help for more information about other kinds of dimensions.

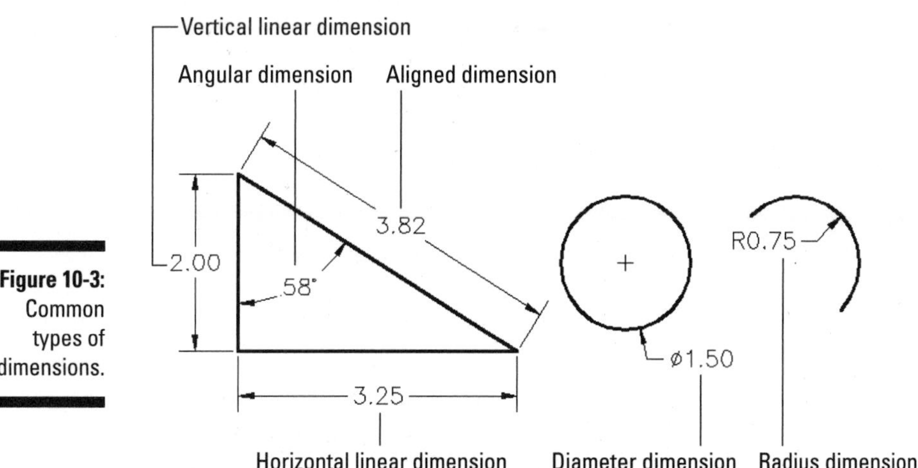

Figure 10-3: Common types of dimensions.

Dimension associativity

By default, AutoCAD LT groups all the parts of each dimension — the extension lines, dimension lines, arrowheads, and text — into a special *associative dimension* object. *Associative* means two things:

- The different parts of the dimension function as a single object. When you click any part of the dimension, LT selects all its parts.
- The dimension is connected with the points on the object that you specified when you drew the dimension. If you change the size of the object (for example, stretch a line), the dimension updates appropriately — the lines and arrows move, and the text changes to reflect the line's new size.

I call dimensions with both of these characteristics *geometry-driven associative dimensions* because the geometry "drives" the location of the parts of the dimension and what the text says.

For historical reasons, AutoCAD and LT also are capable of creating dimensions that possess just the first type of associativity — that is, the dimension functions as a single, grouped object but isn't directly connected with the object whose size it shows. Autodesk now calls these kinds of dimensions *nonassociative,* which is pretty confusing to AutoCAD veterans, because Autodesk used to call them *associative!* AutoCAD and LT also are capable of creating dimensions that possess no type of associativity at all — no grouping of the bits and pieces and no connection to the dimensioned object. Autodesk now calls these *exploded* dimensions, but before AutoCAD and LT 2002, they were called *nonassociative!*

I mention the conflicting use of associative and nonassociative in case you find yourself discussing dimensions with AutoCAD veterans, most of whom use the terms in their older sense. To avoid confusion, I always use the term *geometry-driven associative dimensions* (or simply *geometry-driven dimensions*) in this book to refer to dimensions that possess both types of associativity. For more information about how to determine which kind of dimension AutoCAD LT draws, see "Controlling and editing dimension associativity," later in this chapter.

Pulling out your dimension tools

The AutoCAD LT Dimension menu provides access to dimensioning commands. If you find yourself adding dimensions in batches, the Dimension toolbar is more efficient because the dimensioning commands are more accessible. You toggle the Dimension toolbar off and on by right-clicking any LT toolbar icon and choosing Dimension from the menu. As with other toolbars, you can move the Dimension toolbar to a different location on-screen or dock it on any margin of the drawing area.

All dimensioning commands have long command names (such as DIMLINEAR and DIMRADIUS) and corresponding shortened abbreviations (DLI and DRA) that you can type at the command prompt. If you do lots of dimensioning and don't want to toggle the Dimension toolbar on and off repeatedly, memorize the abbreviated forms of the dimension commands that you use frequently. You find a list of the long command names on the Contents tab in the AutoCAD LT online help. Choose Command Reference⇨Commands⇨D Commands. The short names are the first, fourth, and fifth letters of the long names. (In other words, take the first five letters of the long name and remove *IM.*)

Doing Dimensions with Style(s)

Creating a usable dimension style that gives you the dimension look you want is the biggest challenge in using AutoCAD LT's dimensioning features. Each drawing contains its own dimension styles, so changes you make to a dimension style in one drawing affect only that drawing. However, after you get the dimension styles right in a drawing, you can copy them to other drawings with DesignCenter, as I describe in the next section. (Alternatively, you can create a template — that is, a DWT file — from a drawing containing useful dimension styles and use the template, complete with its dimension styles, to create new drawings. Chapter 5 describes this procedure.)

A dimension style is a collection of drawing settings called *dimension variables,* which are a special class of the *system variables* that I introduce in Chapter 2.

If you want to see a list of the dimension variable names and look up what each variable controls, see Contents⇨Command Reference⇨System Variables⇨D System Variables in the AutoCAD LT online help. All the system variables that begin with DIM are dimension variables.

AutoCAD and LT users, like all computer nerds, like to shorten names. You may hear them refer to dimstyles and dimvars instead of dimension styles and dimension variables. You can tell them that doing so makes you think of them as dimwits — which is actually an honorable title at Autodesk, as I mention earlier in this chapter.

Borrowing existing dimension styles

If you're lucky enough to work in an office where someone has set up dimension styles that are appropriate for your industry and project, you can skip the pain and strain of creating your own dimension styles. If the ready-made dimension style that you need lives in another drawing, you can use the DesignCenter palette to copy it into your drawing, as in the following steps:

1. **Open the drawing that contains the dimension style you want to copy (the *source* drawing).**
2. **Open the drawing to which you want to copy the dimension style (the *destination* drawing).**

   If you already have both drawings open, make sure that you can see the destination drawing. If you can't, choose the Window menu and then choose the destination drawing in order to bring it to the foreground.

3. **Click the DesignCenter button on the Standard toolbar.**

   The DesignCenter palette appears. (Chapter 3 describes this palette in detail.)

4. **In the DesignCenter palette, click the Open Drawings tab.**

   DesignCenter's navigation pane displays a list of drawings that you currently have open in AutoCAD LT.

5. **In the left pane of the DesignCenter palette, click the plus sign next to the name of the drawing that you opened in Step 1, and then click on Dimstyles.**

   A list of copyable objects, including Dimstyles, appears.

6. **Click and drag the desired dimension style from the right pane of the DesignCenter palette into the window containing the drawing that you opened in Step 2, as shown in Figure 10-4.**

   If the name of the dimension style that you copy duplicates the name of an existing dimension style in the destination drawing, LT refuses to overwrite the existing dimension style. In that case, you must first rename the existing dimension style in the destination drawing by using the information in the following section ("Creating and managing dimension styles").

7. **Change the Use Overall Scale Of factor on the Fit tab of the Modify Dimension Style dialog box so that it matches the drawing scale factor of the current drawing.**

   The next section describes the Dimension Style dialog box. Chapter 5 includes detailed instructions on how to use this dialog box to modify the Use Overall Scale Of setting.

If you want a dimension style to be available in new drawings, copy the style to a template drawing and use that template to create your new drawings. See Chapter 5 for more information about template drawings.

Creating and managing dimension styles

If you *do* need to create your own dimension styles, or you want to tweak ones that you copy from another drawing, you use the Dimension Style Manager dialog box, shown in Figure 10-5.

Every drawing comes with a default dimension style named Standard (for nonmetric drawings) or ISO-25 (for metric drawings). Although you can use and modify the Standard or ISO-25 style, I suggest that you leave it as is and create your own dimension style(s) for the settings that are appropriate to your work. This approach ensures that you can use the default style as a reference. More important, it avoids a potential naming conflict that can change the way your dimensions look if the current drawing gets inserted into another drawing. (Chapter 13 describes this potential conflict.)

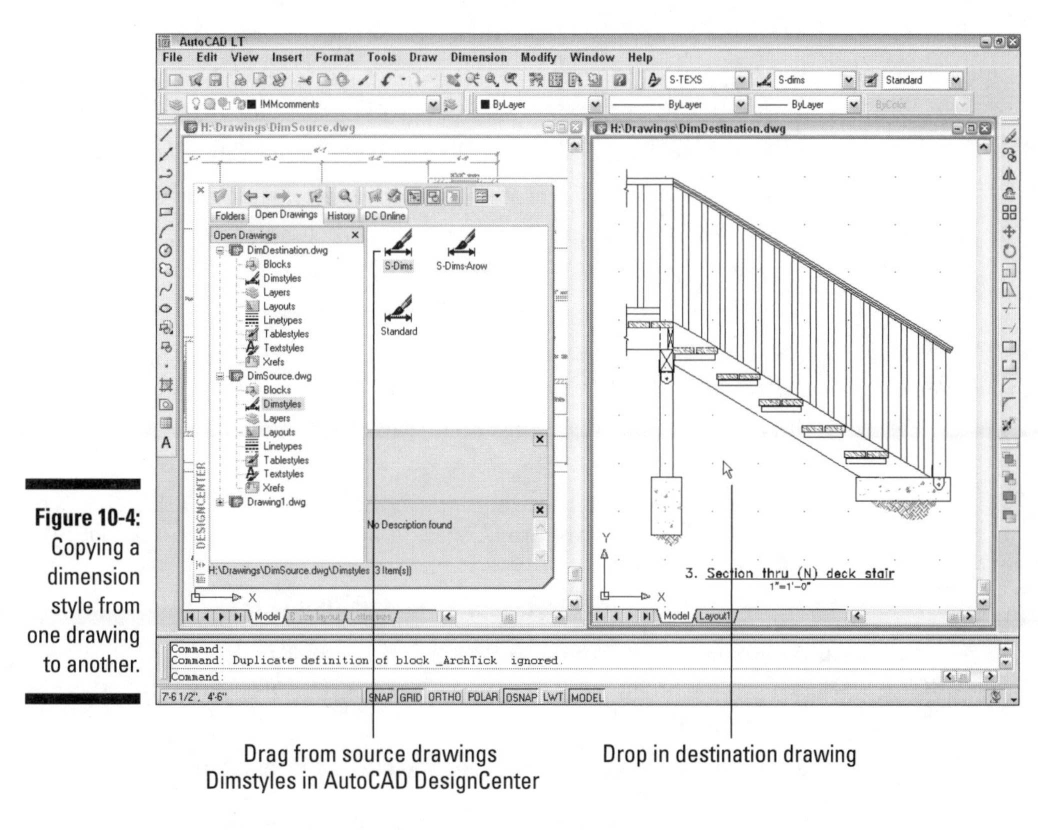

Figure 10-4: Copying a dimension style from one drawing to another.

Figure 10-5: Yet another manager, this one for dimension styles.

The following steps describe how to create your own dimension style(s):

1. **Choose Format➪Dimension Style from the menu bar, or click the Dimension Style Manager button on the Styles toolbar.**

   The Dimension Style Manager dialog box appears (refer to Figure 10-5).

2. **In the Styles list, select the existing dimension style whose settings you want to use as the starting point for the settings of your new style.**

   For example, select the default dimension style named Standard or ISO-25.

3. **Click the New button to create a new dimension style that's a copy of the existing style.**

   The Create New Dimension Style dialog box appears.

4. **Enter a New Style Name and click Continue.**

   The New Dimension Style dialog box appears, which is the same as the Modify Dimension Style dialog box shown in Figure 10-6.

5. **Modify the dimension settings on any of the six tabs in the New Dimension Style dialog box.**

   See the descriptions of these settings in the next section of this chapter. In particular, be sure to set the Use Overall Scale Of factor on the Fit tab to set the drawing scale factor.

6. **Click OK to close the New Dimension Style dialog box.**

   The Dimension Style Manager dialog box reappears.

7. **Select your new dimension style from the Styles list, and then click the Set Current button.**

   Your new dimension style becomes the current dimension style that LT uses for future dimensions in this drawing.

8. **Click Close.**

   The Dimension Style Manager dialog box closes.

9. **Draw some dimensions to test your new dimension style.**

Avoid changing existing dimension styles that you didn't create, unless you know for sure what they're used for. When you change a dimension style setting, all dimensions that use that style change to reflect the revised setting. Thus, one small dimension variable setting change can affect a large number of existing dimensions! When in doubt, ask the dimension style's creator what the dimension style is for and what the consequences of changing it are. If that's not possible, instead of modifying an existing dimension style, create a new style by copying the existing one, and then modify the new one.

A further variation on the already baroque dimension style picture is that you can create dimension *secondary styles* (also called *substyles* or *style families*) — variations of a main style that affect only a particular type of dimension, such as radial or angular. You probably want to avoid this additional complication if you can, but if you open the Dimension Style Manager dialog box and see names of dimension types indented beneath the main dimension style names, be aware that you're dealing with secondary styles. Look up "dimension styles, secondary styles" on the Index tab in the AutoCAD LT online help for more information.

Adjusting style settings

After you click New or Modify in the Dimension Style Manager dialog box, AutoCAD LT displays a tabbed New/Modify Dimension Style subdialog box with a mind-boggling — and potentially drawing-boggling, if you're not careful — array of settings. Figure 10-6 shows the settings on the first tab, which I modified from the LT defaults to conform to one office's drafting standards.

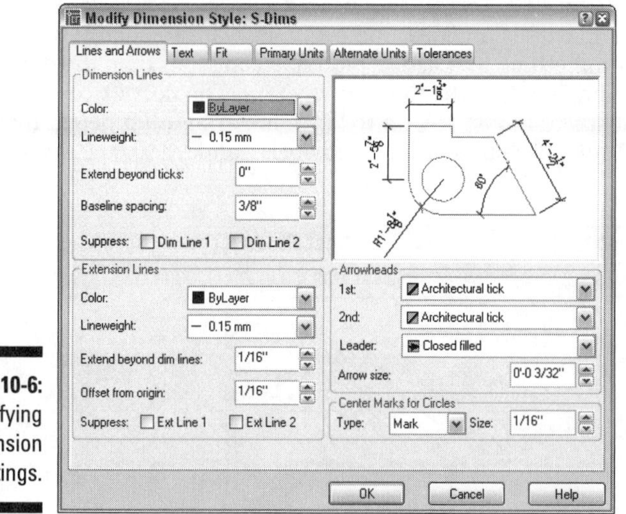

Figure 10-6: Modifying dimension settings.

Fortunately, the dimension preview that appears on all tabs — as well as on the main Dimension Style Manager dialog box — immediately shows the results of most setting changes. With the dimension preview and some trial-and-error changing of settings, you usually can home in on an acceptable group of settings. For more information, use the dialog box help: Click the question mark button on the title bar and then click the setting that you want to know more about.

Before you start messing with dimension style settings, you need to know what you want your dimensions to look like when they're plotted. If you're not sure how it's done in your industry, ask others in your office or profession or look at a plotted drawing that someone in the know represents as being a good example.

The following sections introduce you to the more important New/Modify Dimension Style tabs and highlight useful settings. ***Note:*** Whenever you specify a distance or length setting, enter the desired *plotted* size. AutoCAD LT scales all these numbers by the overall scale factor that you enter on the Fit tab.

Following Lines and Arrows

The settings on the Lines and Arrows tab control the basic look and feel of all parts of your dimensions except text. Use this tab to change the type and size of arrowheads or the display characteristics of the dimension and extension lines.

Tabbing to Text

Use the Text tab to control how your dimension text looks — the text style and height to use (see Chapter 9) and where to place the text with respect to the dimension and extension lines. You probably want to change the Text Style setting to something that uses a more pleasing font than the dorky default Txt.shx font, such as the Romans.shx font. The default Text Height is too large for most situations — set it to ⅛", 3mm, or another height that makes sense. Figure 10-7 shows one company's standard text settings.

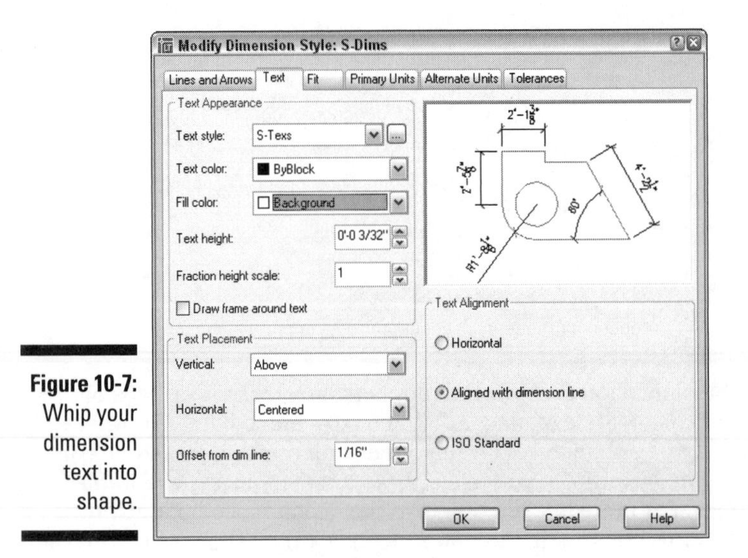

Figure 10-7: Whip your dimension text into shape.

The text style that you specify for a dimension style must be a variable height style — that is, the height that you specify in the Text Style dialog box must be zero. (See Chapter 9 for more information about variable height and fixed height text styles.) If you specify a fixed height text style for a dimension style, the text style's height overrides the Text Height setting in the New/Modify Dimension Style subdialog box. This behavior is confusing at best and unacceptable at worst. Use a variable height style to avoid the problem.

Enter the desired *plotted* text height. Don't multiply it by the drawing scale factor, as you do for ordinary text.

Industry or company standards usually dictate the size of dimension text. (For example, ⅛ inch is common in the U.S. architectural industry.) In any case, make sure you pick a height that's not too small to read on your smallest check plot.

AutoCAD LT 2005's new background mask feature, described in Chapter 9, works for dimension text, too. To turn on masking, choose either Background or a specific color from the Fill Color drop-down list. When you do, LT hides the portions of any objects that lie underneath dimension text. (To ensure that dimension text lies on top of other objects, use the DRaworder or TEXTTOFRONT command — see Chapter 9 for more information.)

Getting Fit

The Fit tab includes a bunch of confusing options that control when and where AutoCAD LT shoves the dimension text if it doesn't quite fit between the dimension lines. The default settings leave LT in "maximum attempt at being helpful mode" — that is, LT moves the text, dimension lines, and arrows around automatically so that things don't overlap. If these guesses seem less than satisfactory to you, try the modified settings shown in Figure 10-8: Select the Over the Dimension Line, without a Leader radio box in the Text Placement section and the Always Draw Dim Line between Ext Lines check box in the Fine Tuning section. (You can always move the text yourself by grip editing it, as I describe later in this chapter.) Most important, the Fit tab includes the Use Overall Scale Of setting, as noted in Figure 10-8. This setting acts as a global scaling factor for all the other length-related dimension settings. Always set Use Overall Scale Of to the drawing scale factor of the current drawing.

If your drawing includes areas of different scales, you can create multiple dimension styles, one for each scale. Alternatively, you can turn on the Scale Dimensions to Layout (Paperspace) setting (which changes the Use Overall Scale Of setting to 0.0) and draw dimensions in a paper space layout, rather than in model space. See the "Trans-spatial dimensioning" section, later in this chapter, for another alternative.

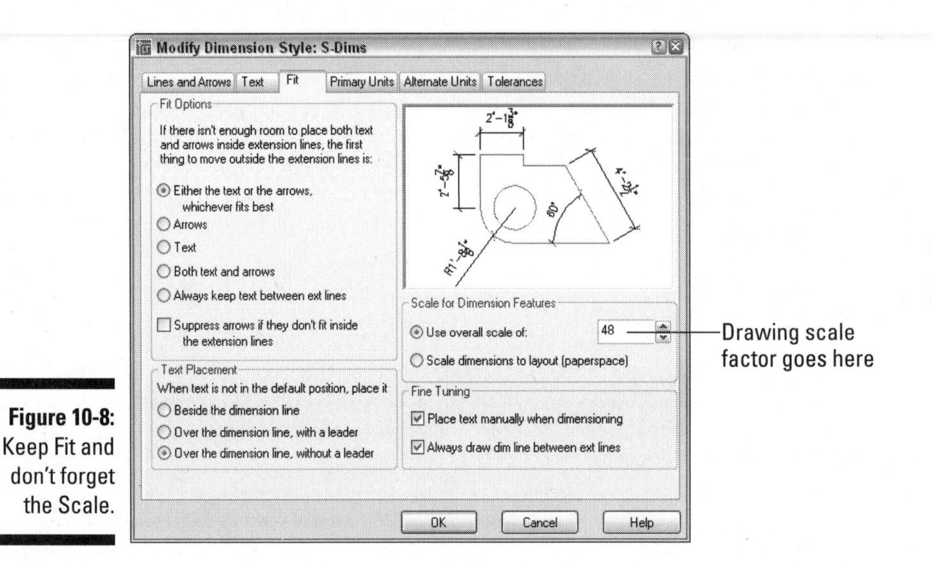

Figure 10-8: Keep Fit and don't forget the Scale.

The Use Overall Scale Of setting corresponds to the DIMSCALE system variable, and you hear AutoCAD drafters refer to it as such. AutoCAD and LT accept zero as a special DIMSCALE setting for dimensioning in paper space layouts. Look up the DIMSCALE system variable in the AutoCAD LT online help for more information about additional dimension scale options.

Using Primary Units

The Primary Units tab gives you incredibly — or maybe overly — detailed control over how AutoCAD LT formats the characters in the dimension text string. You usually want to set the Unit format and Precision and maybe specify a suffix for unitless numbers, such as **mm** for millimeters. You may also change the Zero Suppression settings, depending on whether you want dimension text to read 0.5000, .5000, or 0.5. ("Zero Suppression!" also makes a great rallying cry for organizing your fellow AutoCAD LT drafters.)

Other style settings

If your work requires that you show dimensions in two different units (such as inches and millimeters), use the Alternate Units tab to turn on and control alternate units. If your work requires listing construction tolerances (for example, 3.5 mm +/–0.01), use the Tolerances tab to configure the tolerance format that you want.

The New/Modify Dimension Style dialog box Tolerances tab settings are for adding manufacturing tolerances (for example, **+0.2** or **-0.1**) to the text of ordinary dimensions — the kind of dimensions I cover in this chapter. AutoCAD LT also includes a separate TOLERANCE *command* that draws special symbols called *geometric tolerances.* If you need these symbols, you probably know it; if you've never heard of them, just ignore them. Look up "Geometric Tolerance dialog box" on the Index tab in the AutoCAD LT online help for more information.

Drawing Dimensions

After you copy or create a suitable dimension style, you're ready to dimension. Fortunately, adding dimensions to a drawing using existing dimension styles is usually pretty straightforward.

When you want to dimension something in AutoCAD LT, you can either select the object, such as a line or polyline segment, or select *points* on that object, such as the endpoints of the line or polyline segment. If you select an object, LT finds the most obvious points on it to dimension, such as the endpoints of a line. If you choose to select individual points instead, use object snaps (see Chapter 3). The points that you pick — or that LT finds for you — are called the *origins* of the dimension's extension lines. When you change the size of the object (for example, by stretching it), LT automatically moves the dimension's origin points and updates the dimension text to show the new length.

If you don't use object snaps or another AutoCAD LT precision technique to choose dimension points, the dimension text probably doesn't reflect the precise measurement of the object. This lack of precision can cause serious problems. So when you're dimensioning, always osnap to it!

When you set up a new drawing, make sure that you change the Use Overall Scale Of setting on the Fit tab in the New/Modify Dimension Style dialog box so that it matches the drawing scale factor. Before you draw any dimensions in a drawing that you didn't set up, check this setting to make sure it's correct.

The AutoCAD LT dimension drawing commands prompt you with useful information at the command line. Read the command line prompts during every step of the command, especially when you're trying a dimensioning command for the first time.

Lining up some linear dimensions

Linear dimensions are the most common type of dimensions, and horizontal and vertical are the most common of those. The following example demonstrates all the important techniques for creating horizontal and vertical linear dimensions, as well as aligned dimensions (which are similar to linear dimensions):

1. **Use the Line command to draw a nonorthogonal line — that is, a line segment that's not horizontal or vertical.**

   An angle of about 30 degrees works well for this example.

If you want to apply dimensioning to an object other than a line, use these steps as a general guideline, filling in the appropriate commands and data as applicable to your drawing.

2. **Set a layer that's appropriate for dimensions current.**

   See Chapter 3 for details.

3. **Set a dimension style that's appropriate for your needs current.**

   Choose an existing dimension style from the Dim Style Control drop-down list on the Styles toolbar, or create a new style as in the section, "Creating and managing dimension styles," earlier in this chapter.

4. **Choose Dimension⇨Linear or click the Linear Dimension button on the Dimension toolbar.**

   LT prompts you:

   ```
   Specify first extension line origin or <select object>:
   ```

5. **To specify the origin of the first extension line, snap to the lower-left endpoint of the line by using endpoint object snap.**

   If you don't have endpoint as one of your current running object snaps, specify a single endpoint object snap by clicking the Snap to Endpoint button on the Object Snap toolbar — or holding down the Shift key, right-clicking, and choosing Endpoint from the menu. (See Chapter 3 for more about object snaps.)

   LT prompts you:

   ```
   Specify second extension line origin:
   ```

6. **To specify the origin of the second extension line, snap to the other endpoint of the line by using endpoint object snap again.**

   LT draws a *horizontal* dimension — the length of the displacement in the left-to-right direction — if you move the cursor above or below the line. It draws a *vertical* dimension — the length of the displacement in the up-and-down direction — if you move the cursor to the left or right of the line.

   LT prompts you:

   ```
   Specify dimension line location or
   [Mtext/Text/Angle/Horizontal/Vertical/Rotated]:
   ```

7. **Move the mouse to generate the type of dimension you want (horizontal or vertical), and then click wherever you want to place the dimension line.**

When you're specifying the dimension *line* location, you usually *don't* want to object snap to existing objects — you want the dimension line and text to sit in a relatively empty part of the drawing rather than bump into existing objects. If necessary, temporarily turn off running object snap (click the OSNAP button on the status bar) in order to avoid snapping the dimension line to an existing object.

LT draws the dimension.

If you want to align subsequent dimension lines easily, turn on snap and set a suitable snap spacing — more easily done than said! — before you pick the point that determines the location of the dimension line. See Chapter 3 for more information about snap.

8. **Repeat Steps 4 through 7 to create another linear dimension of the opposite orientation (vertical or horizontal).**
9. **Choose Dimension⇨Aligned or click the Aligned Dimension button on the Dimension toolbar.**

   The prompt includes an option to select an object instead of picking two points (you can use this technique with the DimLInear command, too):

   ```
   Specify first extension line origin or <select object>:
   ```
10. **Press Enter to choose the select object option.**

    LT prompts you:

    ```
    Select object to dimension:
    ```
11. **Select the line or other object that you want to dimension.**

    LT automatically finds the endpoints of the line and uses them as the extension line origin points, as shown in Figure 10-9.

    LT prompts you:

    ```
    Specify dimension line location or
    [Mtext/Text/Angle]:
    ```
12. **Click wherever you want to place the dimension line.**

    LT draws the dimension.

Drawing other kinds of dimensions

After you have the hang of ordinary linear dimensions, you can master other common dimension types quickly. Draw some lines, arcs, and circles (or open a real drawing containing some already-drawn geometry), and try the other dimension commands on the Dimension toolbar or menu.

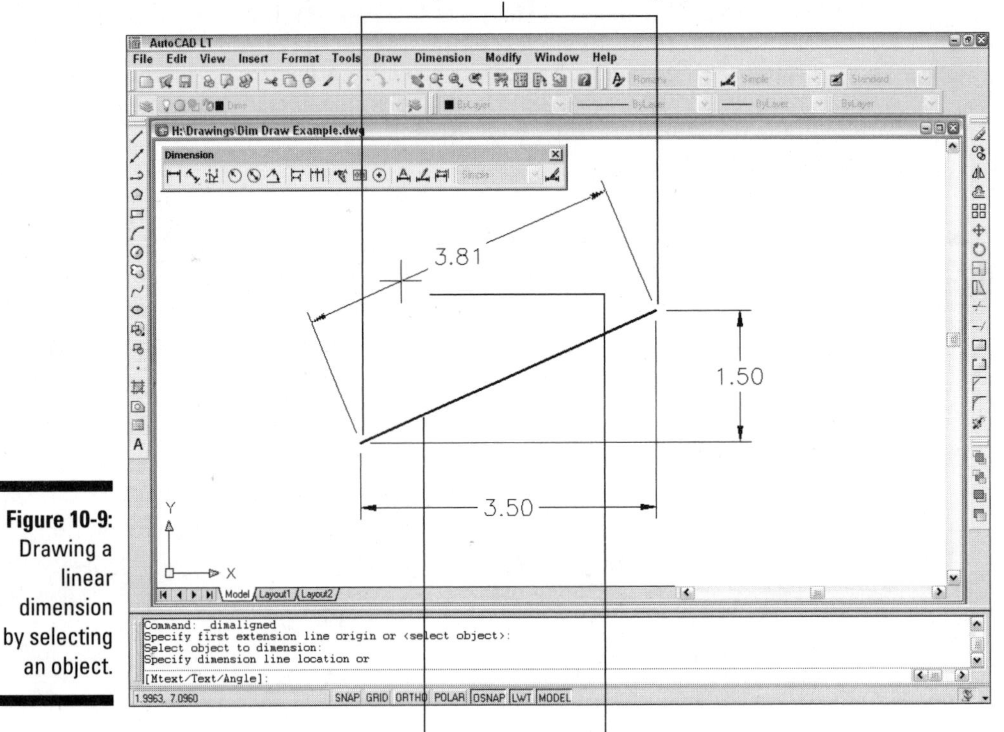

Figure 10-9: Drawing a linear dimension by selecting an object.

Although AutoCAD LT includes special commands for dimensioning the diameter or radius of a circle or arc, you can use the linear dimension techniques described in the previous section to dimension these objects.

To draw a series of side-by-side dimensions whose dimension lines are perfectly aligned, use the DimCOntinue command. To draw an overall dimension above one or more smaller dimensions, use DimBAseline. If you use these commands often in your work, you may find that the QDIM (Quick DIMension) command provides a quick way to draw lots of dimensions in one fell swoop.

Figure 10-10 shows some results of using the more common additional dimensioning commands.

Trans-spatial dimensioning

Trans-spatial dimensioning may sound like the latest New Age fad — after all, most of Autodesk's programmers do work in California — but actually it's just a relatively new (circa AutoCAD and LT 2002) dimensioning feature. There's an age-old argument about whether to draw dimensions in model space, where the geometry that you're dimensioning usually resides, or paper space. (See Chapter 5 for information about model space and paper space.) Most people have settled on dimensioning in model space, but sometimes dimensioning in paper space offers advantages — for example, when you want to dimension different parts of the same geometry in different paper space viewports.

Since AutoCAD LT 2002, the program works much better for dimensioning objects in paper space layouts — when you set the DIMSCALE system variable to 1.0 and then draw dimensions in paper space, LT can associate them with objects in model space.

Get comfortable with dimensioning in model space first. If you later want to try dimensioning in paper space, look up "dimensioning, methods" in the AutoCAD LT online help.

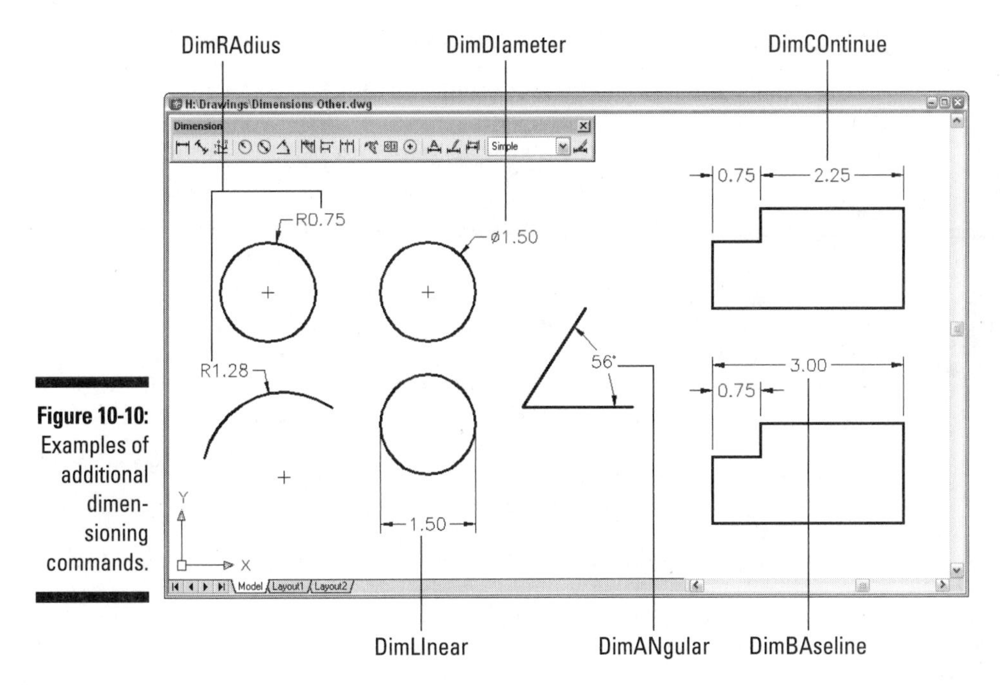

Figure 10-10: Examples of additional dimensioning commands.

Editing Dimensions

After you draw dimensions, you can edit the position of the various parts of each dimension and change the contents of the dimension text. AutoCAD LT groups all the parts of a dimension into a single object.

Editing dimension geometry

The easiest way to change the location of dimension parts is to use grip editing, which I describe in Chapter 7. Just click a dimension, click one of its grips, and maneuver away. You'll discover that certain grips control certain directions of movement. Experiment a few minutes to see how they work.

If you want to change the look of a dimension part (for example, substitute a different arrowhead or suppress an extension line), use the Properties palette. (See Chapter 7 for more on the Properties palette.) All the dimension settings in the New/Modify Dimension Style dialog box (see "Adjusting style settings," earlier in this chapter) are available in the Properties palette when you select one or more dimensions.

If you select one or more dimensions and right-click, the menu displays a number of useful options for overriding dimension settings or assigning a different style.

When you change a setting in the Properties palette, you're *overriding* the default style setting for the currently selected dimension (or dimensions). If you need to make the same change to a bunch of dimensions, creating a new dimension style and assigning that style to them is better. You can use the Properties palette or the right-click menu to change the dimension style that's assigned to one or more dimensions.

You can use the Properties palette to turn on AutoCAD LT 2005's new background mask feature, described in Chapter 9, for the text of individual dimensions: Select the dimensions, display the Text area in the Properties palette, and choose either Background or a specific color from the Fill Color drop-down list. ***Note:*** Turning on background mask in the Multiline Text Editor window, as Chapter 9 tells you to do for regular (nondimension) text, does *not* work for dimension text. You must use the Fill Color setting on either the Text tab of the New/Modify Dimension Style dialog box (as described earlier in this chapter) or the Properties palette.

The AutoCAD LT eXplode command on the Modify toolbar blows a dimension apart, into a bunch of line and multiline text objects. Don't do it! Exploding a dimension doesn't allow you to edit cleanly and eliminates LT's capability of updating the dimension text measurement automatically.

Editing dimension text

In most cases, you don't have to edit dimension text. Assuming that you draw your geometry accurately and pick the dimension points precisely, AutoCAD LT displays the right measurement. If you change the size of the associated object, LT updates the dimension and its measurement. However, you occasionally may need to *override* the dimension text (that is, replace it with a different measurement) or *add* a prefix or a suffix to the true measurement.

AutoCAD LT creates dimension text as a multiline text (mtext) object, so dimension text has the same editing options as ordinary text. Unfortunately, the right-click menu for dimension objects doesn't include a Text Edit option. You can use the Text Override field in the Properties palette, or type **ED** (the keyboard shortcut for the ddEDit command) to edit dimension text in the Multiline Text Editor window.

The default text is <> (that is, the left and right angled bracket characters), which acts as a placeholder for the true length. In other words, AutoCAD LT displays the true dimension length as text in the actual dimension (and keeps the text up to date if you change the distance between the dimension's origin points). You can override the true length by typing a specific length or other text string. You can preserve the true length but add a prefix or suffix by typing it before or after the left- and right-angled bracket characters. In other words, if you enter **<> Max.**, and the actual distance is 12.00, LT displays `12.00 Max.` for the dimension text. If you later stretch the object so that the actual distance changes to 14.50, LT automatically changes the dimension text to read `14.50 Max.` Now you can appreciate the importance of drawing and editing geometry precisely!

Avoid the temptation to override the default dimension text by replacing the angled brackets with a numeric value. Doing so eliminates AutoCAD LT's capability of keeping dimension measurements current, but even worse, you get no visual cue that the default distance has been overridden (unless you edit the dimension text). If you're overriding dimension text a lot, it's probably a sign that the creator of the drawing didn't pay enough attention to using precision techniques when drawing and editing. I'm not going to point any fingers, but you probably know whom to talk to.

Controlling and editing dimension associativity

When you add dimensions by selecting objects or picking points on the objects by using object snap modes, AutoCAD LT normally creates geometry-driven associative dimensions, which are connected to the objects and move with them. This is the case in new drawings originally created in any version of AutoCAD or LT starting with 2002. (Autodesk introduced geometry-driven dimensions in AutoCAD and LT 2002. Before that, AutoCAD and LT normally created dimensions whose parts functioned as a single grouped object but that weren't connected with the dimensioned object.)

In drawings created originally in versions older than AutoCAD or LT 2002, you must set the new DIMASSOC system variable to 2 before AutoCAD LT 2005 creates geometry-driven associative dimensions. An easy way to make this change for the current drawing is to open the Options dialog box (choose Tools⇨Options), click the User Preferences tab, and turn on the Make New Dimensions Associative setting. Be aware that this setting affects only new dimensions that you draw from now on. Thus, you end up with geometry-driven associative new dimensions and less than fully associative existing dimensions in your old drawing. Look up "DIMASSOC system variable" in the AutoCAD LT online help for more information.

You aren't likely to need any of these three commands very often, but if you do, look up the command name in the online help.

- **DIMREASSOCIATE:** If you have dimensions that aren't currently geometry-driven (probably because they were created in older versions of AutoCAD or LT) or are associated with the wrong objects, you can use the DIMREASSOCIATE command (Dimensions⇨Reassociate Dimensions) to associate them with points on the objects of your choice.
- **DIMDISASSOCIATE:** You can use the DIMDISASSOCIATE command to sever the connection between a dimension and its associated object.
- **DIMREGEN:** In a few special circumstances, AutoCAD LT doesn't automatically update geometry-driven associative dimensions (maybe Autodesk should call them "usually geometry-driven but occasionally asleep at the wheel associative dimensions"). In those cases, the DIMREGEN command fixes things.

Pointy-Headed Leaders

No, I'm not talking about your boss (or about you, if you happen to be the boss). I'm talking about arrows that point from your comment to the object or area about which you're commenting. AutoCAD LT treats leaders as a special kind of dimension object (no jokes about dimwitted leaders, now). You can easily draw leaders and text at the same time by using the qLEader (Quick Leader) command, as described in the following steps.

qLEader is an improved version of the old LEADER command, which remains in AutoCAD LT 2005 for compatibility reasons. I recommend that you use qLEader instead of LEADER. Fortunately, the AutoCAD LT 2005 Dimension menu and toolbar choices run the qLEader command.

qLEader is another one of those annoying LT commands that prompts you for some information on the command line and some in a dialog box. Pay close attention to the command line prompts throughout this example:

1. **Set a layer that's appropriate for dimensions current.**

   See Chapter 3 for details.

2. **Set a dimension style that's appropriate for your needs current.**

   Choose an existing dimension style from the drop-down list on the Styles toolbar, or create a new style as in the section, "Creating and managing dimension styles," earlier in this chapter.

3. **Choose Dimension➪Leader or click the Quick Leader button on the Dimension toolbar.**

   The command line prompts you to select the first leader point — that is, the arrowhead point — and gives you the option of changing leader settings first:

   ```
   Specify first leader point, or [Settings] <Settings>:
   ```

   If you want to draw curved rather than straight leader lines or choose a different leader arrowhead style, press Enter now to open the Leader Settings dialog box.

4. **Pick a point that you want to point to.**

   If you use an object snap mode, such as Nearest or Midpoint, to pick a point on an object, LT associates the leader with the object. If you later move the object, LT updates the leader so that it points to the new location.

   The command line prompts you for the next point — LT draws a shaft from the arrowhead to this point:

   ```
   Specify next point:
   ```

5. **Pick a second point.**

   If you pick a second point that's too close to the arrowhead point, LT doesn't have enough room to draw the arrowhead, and thus omits it.

   LT repeats the next point prompt so that you can draw a multisegment shaft if you want to:

   ```
   Specify next point:
   ```

6. **Pick one more point if you want to, or press Enter if you want a leader with a single shaft.**

   Pressing Enter tells the qLEader command that you're finished selecting the points that define the leader shaft. By default, the qLEader command lets you pick up to three points (the arrowhead point and two more points). You can change this behavior in the Leader Settings dialog box (refer to Step 3).

   The command line prompts you to specify the width for word-wrapping the text that you attach to the leader:

   ```
   Specify text width <0.0>:
   ```

The default text width, 0.0, turns off word-wrapping and displays your text on a single line. You can type a width or point and click with the mouse.

Turning off word-wrapping works fine for short notes that fit on one line. If you think your note may be longer, specify a width instead of accepting the default value of 0.0.

7. **Press Enter to suppress word-wrapping, or move the cursor to the right or left to specify a width for word-wrapping; then click.**

   The command line prompts you to type a short note directly at the command line, or press Enter to type your note in the Multiline Text Editor window:

   ```
   Enter first line of annotation text <Mtext>:
   ```

8. **Press Enter to open the Multiline Text Editor window.**
9. **Enter your comment.**
10. **Click OK.**

    The Multiline Text Editor window closes and adds your comment to the drawing, next to the leader.

Figure 10-11 shows several different leaders with notes.

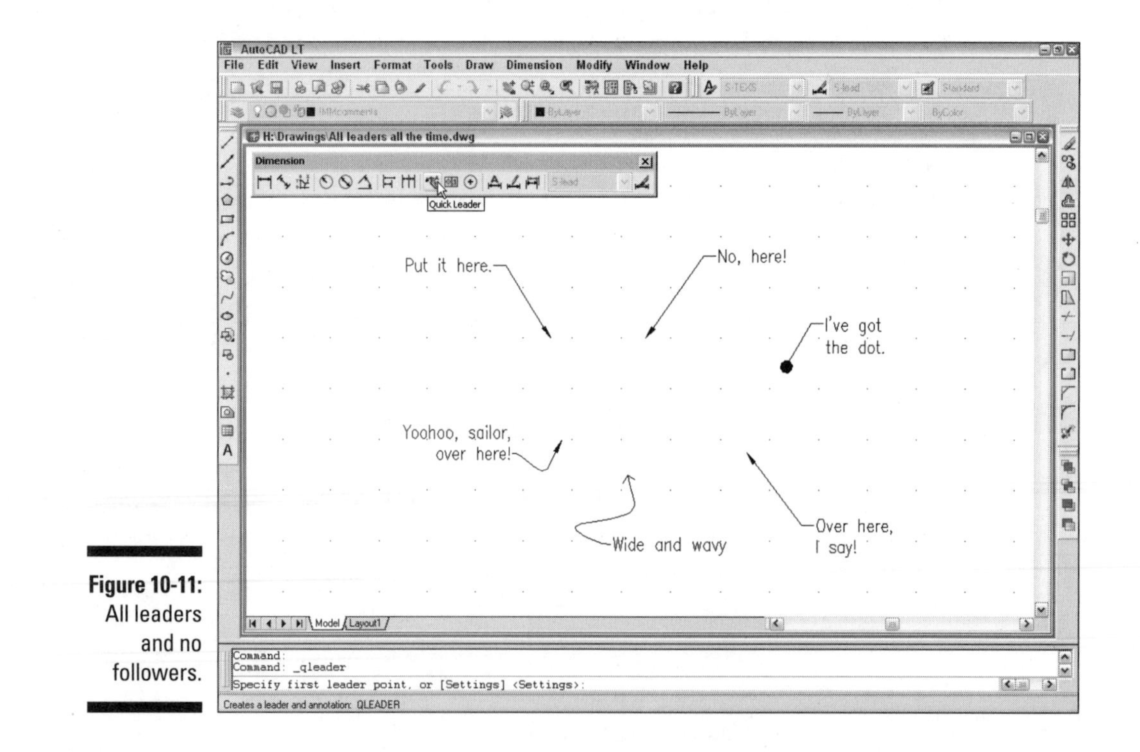

Figure 10-11: All leaders and no followers.

If both the leader arrowhead and the text are the wrong size or appear to be missing entirely, the dimension scale isn't set correctly in the drawing. (As I warn you earlier, AutoCAD LT treats leaders as a special kind of dimension object.) See Chapter 3 for detailed instructions on how to set the dimension scale. After you set the dimension scale properly, erase and re-create the leader and text.

If you add a comment to a drawing and later decide that the comment merits a leader, you can use the qLEader command to draw the leader so that the end of the shaft ends up in the vicinity of the existing text object. Then, when the Multiline Text Editor window appears (Step 8 in the previous steps), click OK without entering any new text.

A leader and the text that you draw with it are partially associated with each other. When you move the text, the leader's shaft follows. Unfortunately, the converse isn't true — moving the leader or one of its vertices doesn't cause the text to follow.

Chapter 11

Hatch Your Fill

In This Chapter

- Adding hatching to your drawings
- Copying existing hatches
- Using predefined and user-defined hatch patterns
- Making solid and gradient fills
- Scaling hatches properly
- Choosing hatching boundaries
- Editing hatches

If you were hoping to hatch a plot (or plot a hatch), see Chapter 12 instead. If you want to hatch an egg, buy my companion book, *Chicken Husbandry For Dummies*. If you need to fill in closed areas of your drawings with special patterns of lines, this chapter is for you.

Drafters often use hatching to represent the type of material that makes up an object, such as insulation, metal, concrete, and so on. In other cases, hatching helps emphasize or clarify the extent of a particular element in the drawing — for example, showing the location of walls in a building plan, or highlighting a swampy area on a map so you know where to avoid building a road. Figure 11-1 shows an example of hatching in a structural detail.

An AutoCAD LT hatch is a separate object that fills a space, which has an appearance dictated by the hatch pattern assigned to it, and that is associated with the objects that bound the space, such as lines, polylines, or arcs. If you move or stretch the boundaries, LT normally updates the hatching to fill the resized area.

Don't go overboard with hatching. The purpose of hatching is to clarify, not overwhelm, the other geometry in the drawing. If your plots look like a patchwork quilt of hatch patterns, it's time to simplify.

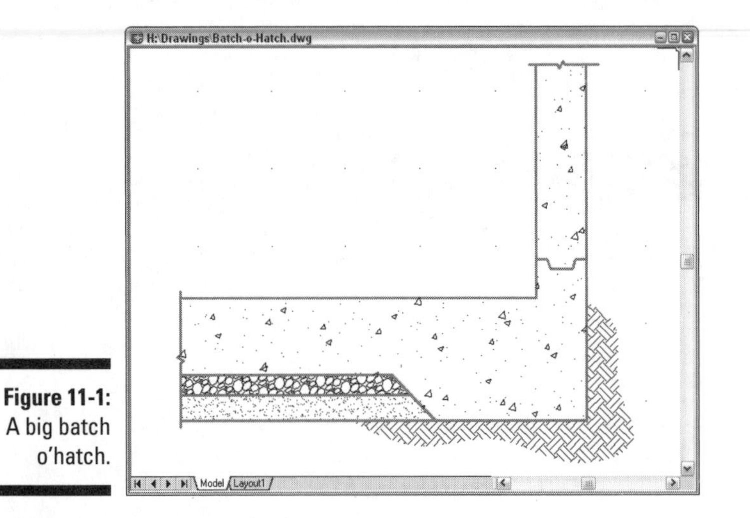

Figure 11-1: A big batch o'hatch.

Hatching is another kind of annotation of your geometry, similar in purpose to text and dimensions. As I describe at the beginning of Chapter 9, you usually are efficient if you save annotation for later in the drafting process. Draw as much geometry as possible first, and *then* hatch the parts that require it. In other words, batch your hatch.

Hatch . . . Hatch . . . Hatchoo

This section outlines the steps you use to add hatching to a drawing with the Boundary Hatch and Fill dialog box, shown in Figure 11-2. You can use this information to get started quickly with hatching. When you need more information about any part of the process, jump to the relevant sections of "Pushing the Boundary (of) Hatch," later in this chapter.

The following steps show you how to hatch an enclosed area by using the "pick points" method of selecting the hatch area (that is, clicking a point inside each of the enclosed areas that you want to hatch):

1. **Open a drawing containing geometry that forms fully closed boundaries, or draw some boundaries with the drawing commands I describe in Chapter 6.**

   The areas you want to hatch must be completely enclosed. The Circle, POLygon, and RECtang commands, and the Line and PLine commands with the Close option, make great hatch boundaries (see Chapter 6 for details).

2. **Set an appropriate layer current, as described in Chapter 3.**

   Putting hatching on its own layer is usually best.

3. **Start the bHatch command by clicking the Hatch button on the Draw toolbar.**

   The Boundary Hatch and Fill dialog box appears (see Figure 11-2).

   For historical reasons, AutoCAD LT 2005 also has a HATCH command, which prompts you at the command line instead of opening a dialog box. Trust me — you want the bHatch command's dialog box.

4. **Choose Predefined, User Defined, or Custom from the Type drop-down list.**

   Predefined or User Defined works best for most purposes. See the next section for details.

5. **If you chose Predefined or Custom in the previous step, select any predefined or custom hatch pattern from the Pattern drop-down list or the Pattern button just to the right of it.**

   If you chose User Defined, you don't need to choose a pattern.

6. **Specify an Angle and Scale for the hatch pattern (or, if you chose User Defined in Step 4, specify Angle and Spacing).**

   See "Getting it right: Hatch angle and scale," later in this chapter, for more information.

Figure 11-2: The Hatch tab of the Boundary Hatch and Fill dialog box.

7. **Click the Pick Points button.**

   The Boundary Hatch and Fill dialog box (temporarily) disappears, and your drawing reappears with the following prompt at the command line:

   ```
   Select internal point:
   ```

8. **Select a point inside the boundary within which you want to hatch by clicking it with the mouse.**

   LT analyzes the drawing and decides which boundaries to use. In a complex drawing, this analysis can take several seconds. LT highlights the boundary that it finds.

   If LT highlights the wrong boundary, right-click, choose Clear All from the menu, and click a different internal point.

9. **Right-click anywhere in the drawing area and choose Enter from the menu to indicate that you're finished selecting points.**

   The Boundary Hatch and Fill dialog box reappears.

10. **Click the Preview button to preview the hatch.**

    The Boundary Hatch and Fill dialog box (temporarily) disappears again, and LT shows you what the hatch will look like.

    ```
    Pick or press Esc to return to dialog or <Right-click to
              accept hatch>:
    ```

11. **Click anywhere in the drawing area to return to the Boundary Hatch and Fill dialog box.**

12. **Adjust any settings and preview again until you're satisfied with the hatch.**

13. **Click OK.**

    LT hatches the area inside the boundary. If you modify the boundary, the hatch automatically resizes to fill the resized area.

Occasionally, AutoCAD LT gets confused and doesn't resize a hatch after you resize the boundary. If that happens, erase and then re-create the hatch in the resized area.

Pushing the Boundary (of) Hatch

The remainder of this chapter shows you how to refine the techniques presented in the preceding section. I describe how to copy existing hatching, take advantage of the various options in the Boundary Hatch and Fill dialog box, and choose more complicated hatching boundaries.

Catch a hatch: Copying hatch properties

One slick way to hatch is by using the Inherit Properties button in the Boundary Hatch and Fill dialog box to copy hatch properties from an existing hatch object. Think of it as point and shoot hatching. If someone — such as you — added some hatching in the past that's just like what you want to use now, click the Inherit Properties button and pick the existing hatching.

Inherit Properties updates the hatch pattern settings in the Boundary Hatch and Fill dialog box to make them the same as the existing hatch pattern object that you picked. You can use the cloned hatch pattern specifications as is or modify them by making changes in the Boundary Hatch and Fill dialog box.

Consistency is a good thing in drafting, especially in computer-aided drafting, in which some or all your drawing may be used for a long time. Thus it's good to use the same hatch patterns, scales, and angles for the same purposes in all your drawings. Find out whether your project, office, company, or profession has hatching standards that apply to your work.

Hatch from scratch

You can use predefined, user-defined, or custom hatch patterns. Most of the time, you choose either predefined or user-defined hatch patterns, unless some generous soul gives you a custom pattern. The next four sections describe the hatch pattern type choices.

Pick a pattern, any pattern: Predefined hatch patterns

To use AutoCAD LT's *predefined* hatch patterns, select Predefined from the Type drop-down list box at the top of the Hatch tab in the Boundary Hatch and Fill dialog box. This selection sets the stage for choosing the hatch pattern.

You specify a predefined hatch pattern in one of two ways:

- If you know the name of the hatch pattern, select it from the Pattern drop-down list. The list is alphabetical, except that SOLID (that is, a solid fill) is at the very beginning.
- If you don't know the pattern's name, or you prefer the visual approach, click the Pattern button (the tiny button with the ellipsis [three dots] to the right of the Pattern prompt and pattern name) to display the Hatch Pattern Palette with pattern previews and names.

AutoCAD LT has about 80 predefined hatch patterns from which to choose. The list includes ANSI (American National Standards Institute) and ISO (International Organization for Standardization) standard hatch patterns. Figure 11-3 shows the Other Predefined hatch patterns, which cover everything from Earth to Escher to Stars. Hatch patterns whose names begin with AR- are intended for architectural and related industries.

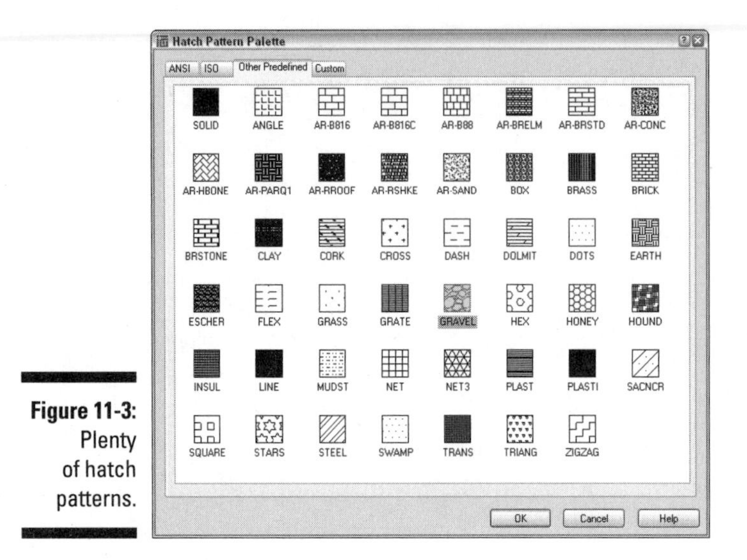

Figure 11-3: Plenty of hatch patterns.

After you select a pattern, specify the angle and scale, as I describe in the section "Getting it right: Hatch angle and scale," in this chapter.

It's up to you: User-defined hatches

A *user-defined* hatch pattern makes a hatch pattern out of parallel lines. Use this option to create a simple pattern and specify the space between the lines in drawing units. For example, you can hatch a wall in a building plan with a user-defined pattern and specify that the hatch lines be three inches apart.

Make it solid, man

Although you may not guess it, AutoCAD LT treats filling an area with a solid color as a type of hatching. Simply choose Solid from the top of the Pattern drop-down list.

Like any other object, a solid hatch takes on the current object color — or the current layer's color if you leave color set to ByLayer. Therefore, check whether the current object layer and color are set appropriately before you use the Solid hatching option (see Chapter 3 for details).

You can create the effect of a solid fill in LT in two other ways:

- If you want a filled-in circle or donut, use the DOnut command and specify an inside diameter of zero.
- If you want one or more line segments with either uniform or tapered widths, use the PLine command's Width option. (Chapter 6 discusses the DOnut and PLine commands.)

Solid fills are a good way to mimic poché — an old hand-drafting technique in which you shade areas with a lighter colored pencil (usually red) to make those areas appear lightly shaded on blueline prints.

After you choose User Defined from the Type drop-down list in the Boundary Hatch and Fill dialog box, you specify the angle and spacing of the lines. You can select the Double check box to achieve a crosshatching effect (two perpendicular sets of hatching lines).

Getting it right: Hatch angle and scale

Predefined and custom hatch patterns require that you enter the angle and scale for AutoCAD LT to generate the hatching. You usually won't have any trouble deciding on an appropriate angle, but a suitable scale can be tricky.

The hatch scale usually is a pattern-specific multiplier times the drawing scale factor. (Drawing scale factor is described in Chapter 5). For example, the EARTH pattern (in the Other Predefined tab of the Hatch Pattern Palette; refer to Figure 11-3) looks pretty good in a full-scale (1 = 1) drawing with a hatch scale of 0.75. If you're adding EARTH pattern hatching to a 1" = 1'–0" detail (drawing scale factor equals 12), try using a hatch scale of 0.75 × 12, or 9.0. This pattern-specific multiplier and drawing-scale-factor approach ensures that hatching looks consistent (that the spaces between the lines are the same) at all scales when you plot.

Assuming that you know your drawing's scale factor, the only complication is figuring out what the pattern-specific multiplier is for a particular hatch pattern. In a more rational world, the pattern-specific multiplier would always be something sensible, like 1.0. Unfortunately, that's not the case for all hatch pattern definitions. Even worse, you can't predict before you use a hatch pattern for the first time what an appropriate pattern-specific multiplier might be. (Autodesk created the hatch patterns whose names begins with AR- — that is, the ones intended for architectural drawings — with a final hatch scale of 1.0 in mind, but in some cases you have to adjust up or down in order to achieve a suitable scale.) You have to use trial and error the first time, and then make a note of the hatch pattern and multiplier for future use.

The first time you use a hatch pattern definition, try 1.0 as the multiplier. Don't forget to multiply by the drawing scale factor. Preview the hatch, and then adjust the hatch scale iteratively; preview after each change. After you settle upon a scale for the current drawing, calculate the corresponding multiplier (for future use); divide the hatch scale by the current drawing's scale factor.

User-defined patterns require that you enter an angle and spacing, not angle and scale. Spacing is expressed in the current drawing units.

Do fence me in: Defining hatch boundaries

After you specify the hatch pattern, angle, and scale you want to use, you define the boundary (or boundaries) into which you want to pour that hatch pattern in one of two ways:

- Picking points within the area(s) you want hatched
- Selecting objects that surround those areas

The actual operation involved in using either of these options is confusing to most people. You probably need a little practice before you get used to it.

The idea behind either definition option is simple when applied to simple areas — that is, closed areas with no additional objects inside them. To define the hatch boundary for a simple area, do one of these two things:

- Click the Pick Points button in the Boundary Hatch and Fill dialog box and then click a point *inside* the boundary.
- Click the Select Objects button and select — that is, pick *on* — one or more objects that form a fully closed boundary.

This simple hatching gets more complicated if you have one closed object inside another, as in Figure 11-4. The AutoCAD LT hatch preview and a bit of experimentation can clarify all these potentially puzzling permutations.

As I warn earlier in this chapter, the default hatch settings require that boundaries be *completely* closed before AutoCAD LT can hatch them. That's one of the reasons to employ the precision techniques from this book whenever you draw or edit objects. If the lines surrounding your boundary don't either meet *exactly* or cross, LT scolds you with a `Valid hatch boundary not found` error message.

The `Valid hatch boundary not found` error message means you need to "repair" lines or other objects so they are a fully closed boundary. Sometimes you can use the Fillet command with a zero fillet radius to force two lines to meet exactly. Another possibility is to use grip editing to align one endpoint precisely with another. Chapter 7 discusses these two editing techniques.

If you don't want to go to the trouble of repairing your drawing in this way, you can use AutoCAD LT 2005's new Gap Tolerance setting, located on the Advanced tab of the Boundary Hatch and Fill dialog box, to tell LT to overlook small gaps when dealing with hatch boundaries.

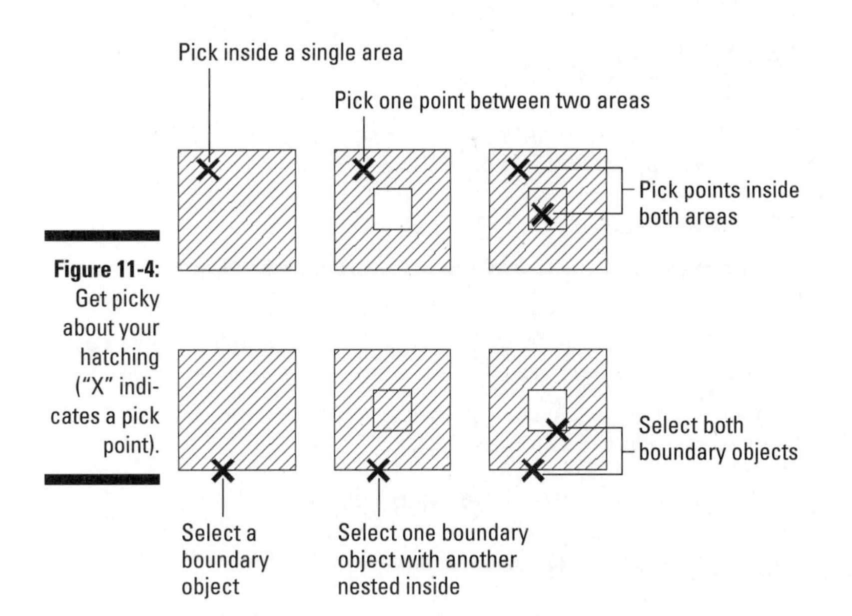

Figure 11-4: Get picky about your hatching ("X" indicates a pick point).

Hatching that knows its place

In AutoCAD LT 2005, the Boundary Hatch and Fill dialog box includes a new Draw Order setting that controls where LT places the hatching with respect to the boundary in terms of object selection. (Refer to Figure 11-2 earlier in this chapter.) The default setting, Send Behind Boundary, puts the hatching "underneath" its boundary for object selection purposes, and that's usually exactly what you want.

Have palette, will hatch

With Tool Palettes, described in Chapter 2, you can create click-and-drag hatch palettes. With a hatch palette, you click a tool (a swatch) and drag into an enclosed boundary to hatch the area. If your hatching needs are simple, you can create a Tool Palette for the patterns and scales you often use. See "hatches, adding to tool palettes" in AutoCAD LT's online help for more information.

Editing Hatch Objects

Editing an existing hatch pattern is simple after you're familiar with the Boundary Hatch and Fill dialog box. Follow these steps:

1. **Select the hatch object.**
2. **Right-click anywhere in the drawing area and choose Hatch Edit from the menu.**

   LT opens the Hatch Edit dialog box and displays the hatch object's current settings.
3. **Make any desired changes, use the Preview button to look them over, and click OK to keep the changes.**

Alternatively, you can use the Properties palette (described in Chapter 7) to make most existing hatch pattern changes. The Properties palette is especially good for changing several hatches at once.

To make one hatch look like another, use the Match Properties button on the Standard toolbar.

The TRim command (described in Chapter 7) is now capable of trimming hatch patterns in most cases — although in some cases it removes associativity of the hatch pattern with the boundary.

Chapter 12

Plotting: Waiting for Your Prints to Come In

In This Chapter

- Configuring printers and plotters
- Plotting model space
- Plotting to scale
- Plotting paper space layouts
- Plotting lineweights and colors
- Controlling plotting with plotstyles
- Using page setups
- Troubleshooting plotting

Despite the increasing number of offices with a computer (or two) on every desk, many people still need to or want to work with printed drawings. Perhaps you thought that using AutoCAD LT means you don't have to rely on hard-copy versions of drawings but can view drawings on-screen instead. Even if that's true, you may need to give hard-copy prints to your less savvy colleagues who don't have AutoCAD or LT. You may want to make some quick prints to pore over during your bus ride home. You may find that checking drawings the old-fashioned way — with a hard-copy print and a red pencil — turns up errors that managed to remain hidden on the computer screen.

Whatever the reason, you'll want to print drawings at some point — probably sooner rather than later. Depending on where you are in a project, plotting is the pop quiz, midterm, or final exam of your drawing-making semester. This chapter helps you ace the test.

You Say Printing, I Say Plotting

Plotting originally meant creating hard-copy output on a device that was capable of printing on larger sheets, such as D size or E size, that measure several feet on a side. (See Chapter 5 for information about drafting paper sizes.) These plotters often used pens to draw, robot-fashion, on large sheets of vellum or Mylar. The sheets could then be run through *diazo blueline machines* — copying machines that create blueline prints — in order to create less-expensive copies. *Printing* meant creating hard-copy output on ordinary printers that used ordinary sized paper, such as A size (letter size, 8½ x 11 inches) or B size (tabloid or ledger size, 11 x 17 inches).

Nowadays, AutoCAD, AutoCAD LT, and most CAD users make no distinction between plotting and printing. AutoCAD veterans usually say "plotting," so if you want to be hip, you can do so, too.

Whatever you call it, plotting an AutoCAD LT drawing is considerably more complicated than printing a word processing document or a spreadsheet. CAD has a larger range of different plotters and printers, drawing types, and output procedures than other computer applications. LT tries to help you tame the vast jungle of plotting permutations, but you'll probably find that you have to take some time to get the lay of the land and clear a path to your desired hard-copy output.

The plotting system in AutoCAD LT 2005 is essentially the same as the one that Autodesk introduced in AutoCAD LT 2000, but with a reorganized, somewhat less imposing Plot dialog box. In addition, Autodesk has improved the page setups feature and added background plotting. I describe all these changes in this chapter.

Get with the system

One of the complications you face in your attempts to create hard copy is that AutoCAD LT has two distinct ways of communicating with your plotters and printers. Operating systems, and the programs that run in them, use a special piece of software called a *printer driver* to format data for printing and then send it to the printer or plotter. When you configure Windows to recognize a new printer connected to your computer or your network, you're actually installing the printer's driver. ("Bring the Rolls around front, James. And bring me a gin and tonic and a D-size plot while you're at it.") AutoCAD LT, like other Windows programs, works with the printers you've configured in Windows. LT calls these *system printers* because they're part of the Windows system.

But AutoCAD LT, unlike other Windows programs, can't leave well enough alone. Some output devices, especially some larger plotters, aren't controlled very efficiently by Windows system printer drivers. For that reason, LT comes with specialized *nonsystem drivers* (that is, drivers that are not installed as part of the Windows system) for plotters from companies such as Hewlett-Packard, Xerox, and Océ. These drivers are kind of like nonunion workers. They ignore the tidy rules for communicating with Windows printers in order to get things done a bit more quickly and flexibly.

Using already-configured Windows system printer drivers usually is easiest, and they work well with many devices — especially devices that print on smaller paper, such as laser and inkjet printers. However, if you have a large plotter, you may be able to get faster plotting, better plot quality, or more plot features by installing a nonsystem driver. To find out more, choose Contents⇨Driver and Peripheral Guide⇨Use Plotters and Printers in the AutoCAD LT online help.

The AutoCAD LT 2005 CD includes a Windows system printer driver for Hewlett-Packard DesignJet large format printers. This driver is optimized for CAD plotting. To install the driver, load your AutoCAD LT 2005 CD, click Install, and then click Hewlett-Packard DesignJet Printer Drivers.

Configure it out

For now, you simply need to make sure that AutoCAD LT recognizes the devices that you want to use for plotting. The following steps show you how:

1. **Launch AutoCAD LT and open an existing drawing or start a new, blank drawing.**
2. **Choose Tools⇨Options to open the Options dialog box, and click the Plot and Publish tab.**
3. **Click the drop-down arrow to view the list just below the Use As Default Output Device option, as shown in Figure 12-1.**

   The list includes two kinds of device configurations, designated by two tiny, difficult-to-distinguish icons to the left of the device names:

   - A little laser printer icon, with a sheet of white paper coming out the top, indicates a Windows system printer configuration.
   - A little plotter icon, with a piece of paper coming out the front, indicates a nonsystem (that is, AutoCAD LT-specific) configuration.

   The nonsystem configuration names always end in *pc3,* because they're stored in special AutoCAD Printer Configuration version 3 files. So, if you can't tell the difference between the icons, look for the *pc3* at the end of the name.

4. **Verify that the list includes the printers and plotters that you want to have available in AutoCAD LT.**

   If not, choose Start⇨Printers and Faxes (in Windows XP) or Start⇨Settings⇨Printers (in Windows 2000), launch the Add Printer Wizard, and follow the instructions. If your printer isn't in the default Windows list, cancel the wizard and hunt down a driver disk that came with your printer, or, better yet, download the current driver from the printer manufacturer's Web site.

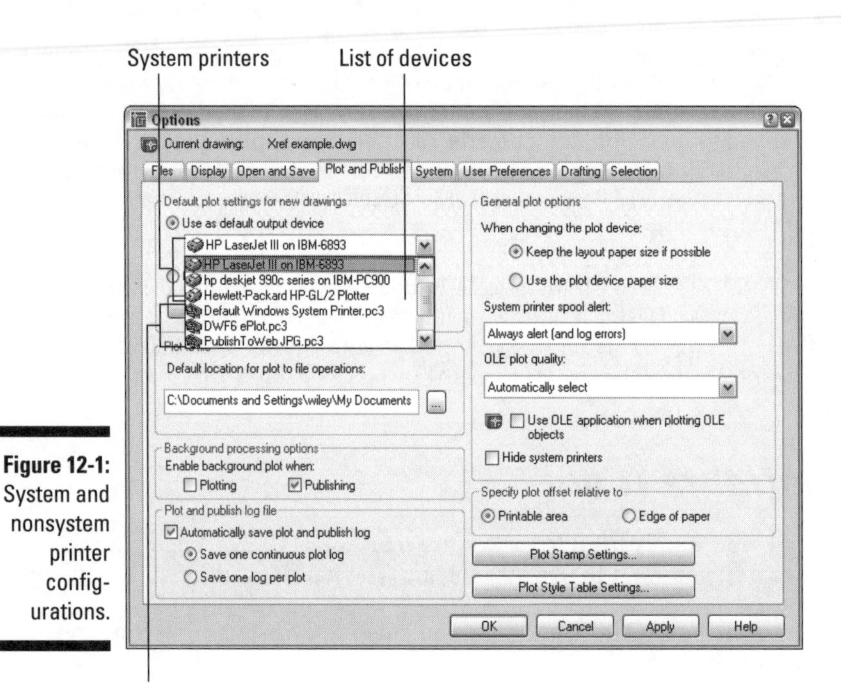

Figure 12-1: System and nonsystem printer configurations.

5. **Choose the output device that you want to make the default for new drawings.**
6. **Click OK to close the dialog box and retain any change that you made in the previous step.**

You use the AutoCAD LT Plotter Manager Add-A-Plotter Wizard to create nonsystem driver configurations. (Choose File➪Plotter Manager to display a window containing a shortcut to the wizard.) This wizard is similar to the Windows Add Printer Wizard; if you can handle adding an ordinary printer in Windows, you probably can handle adding a nonsystem plotter configuration to AutoCAD LT. When you complete the wizard steps, LT saves the information in a PC3 (Plot Configuration version 3) file.

A Simple Plot

Okay, so you believe me. You know that you're not going to master AutoCAD LT plotting in five minutes. That doesn't change the fact that your boss, employee, wife, husband, construction foreman, or 11-year-old son wants a quick check plot of your drawing.

Plotting success in 16 steps

Here's the quick, cut-to-the-chase procedure for plotting a simple drawing — a mere 16 steps! These steps assume that you plot in model space — that is, the Model tab at the bottom of the drawing area shows the drawing in a way that you want to plot. (I cover plotting paper space layout tabs in the section "Plotting the Layout of the Land," later in this chapter.) These steps don't deal with controlling plotted lineweights (see the "Plotting Lineweights and Colors" section later in this chapter for those details). It does, however, result in a piece of paper that bears some resemblance to what AutoCAD LT displays on your computer monitor.

Follow these steps to make a simple, not-to-scale, monochrome plot of a drawing:

1. **Open the drawing in AutoCAD LT.**
2. **Click the Model tab at the bottom of the drawing area to ensure that you're plotting the model space contents.**

   I explain model space and paper space in Chapter 2, and I explain how to plot paper space layouts later in this chapter.
3. **Zoom to the drawing's current extents (choose View➪Zoom➪Extents) so you can verify the area you're going to plot.**

   The extents of a drawing consist of a rectangular area just large enough to include all the objects in the drawing.
4. **To display the Plot dialog box, click the Plot button on the Standard toolbar.**

   The Plot dialog box appears, as shown in Figure 12-2.
5. **In the Printer/Plotter area, select a device from the Name list.**
6. **In the Paper Size area, select a paper size that's loaded in your printer or plotter.**

   Of course, you must make sure that the paper size is large enough to fit the drawing at the scale you want to plot it. For example, if you want to plot a D-size drawing, but you have only a B-size printer, you're out of luck — unless you resort to multiple pieces of paper and lots of tape.
7. **In the Plot Area area (sponsored by the Department of Redundancy Department), choose Extents.**

   If you set limits properly, as I suggest in Chapter 5, then choose Limits instead in order to plot the drawing area that you defined. The Window option — that is, plot a window whose corners you pick — is useful when you want to plot just a portion of your drawing. See the section "Continuing the Plot Dialog" in this chapter for details.

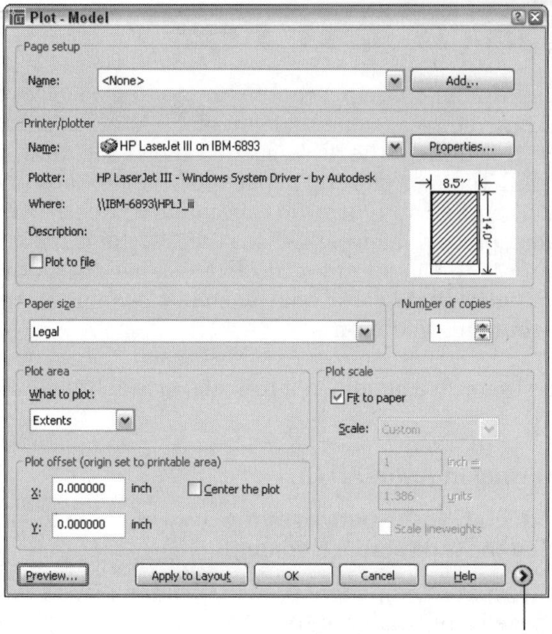

Figure 12-2: The Plot dialog box.

The More Options button

8. **In the Plot Offset area, select the Center the Plot option.**

   Alternatively, you can specify offsets of zero or other amounts in order to position the plot at a specific location on the paper.

9. **In the Plot Scale area, either choose Fit to Paper or uncheck Fit to Paper and specify a scale (by choosing from the drop-down list or typing into the two text boxes).**

   For most real plotting, you plot to a specific scale, but feel free to choose Fit to Paper for now. If you do want to plot to a specific scale, see the "Instead of fit, scale it" section later in this chapter for guidance.

10. **Click the More Options button (at the bottom-right corner of the dialog box, next to the Help button).**

    The Plot dialog box reveals additional settings, as shown in Figure 12-3.

11. **In the Plot Style Table (Pen Assignments) area, choose Monochrome.ctb or Monochrome.stb.**

    LT may ask you whether to "Assign this plotstyle table to all layouts?" Click Yes to make Monochrome.ctb (or Monochrome.stb) the default plotstyle table for the paper space layout tabs as well as the Model tab, or click No to make the change apply only to the current tab.

    The "Plotting with style" section later in this chapter describes plotstyle tables.

Figure 12-3: The expanded Plot dialog box.

12. **In the Plot Options area, make sure that Plot with Plot Styles is on and Save Changes to Layout is off, as shown in Figure 12-3.**

    Leaving Save Changes to Layout turned off tells LT to use any plot settings changes that you make only for this plot — LT reverts to the original plot settings the next time you plot the drawing.

    After you become confident with plotting, you may want to turn on this setting so that LT *does* save your plotting settings changes as the default. Alternatively, click the Apply to Layout button to make the current plot settings the default for future plotting of this tab (that is, the Model tab) in this drawing.

13. **In the Drawing Orientation area, choose Portrait or Landscape.**

    The postage stamp-sized preview in the middle of the Plot dialog box can help you decide on the right orientation. If not, the full preview in the next step tells you for sure.

14. **Click the Preview button and check that the drawing displays on the paper at the correct orientation and size, as shown in Figure 12-4; then right-click and choose Exit to return to the Plot dialog box.**

15. **If you found any problems in the preview, adjust the plot settings (for example, Plot Area, Plot Scale, or Drawing Orientation) and repeat the preview until the plot looks right.**

16. **Click OK to create the plot.**

    When LT finishes generating and sending the plot, it displays a "Plot and Publish Job Complete" balloon notification from the status bar. If you decide that you don't want to see these notifications, right-click the Plot/Publish Details Report Available icon near the right end of the status bar and deselect the Enable Balloon Notification option.

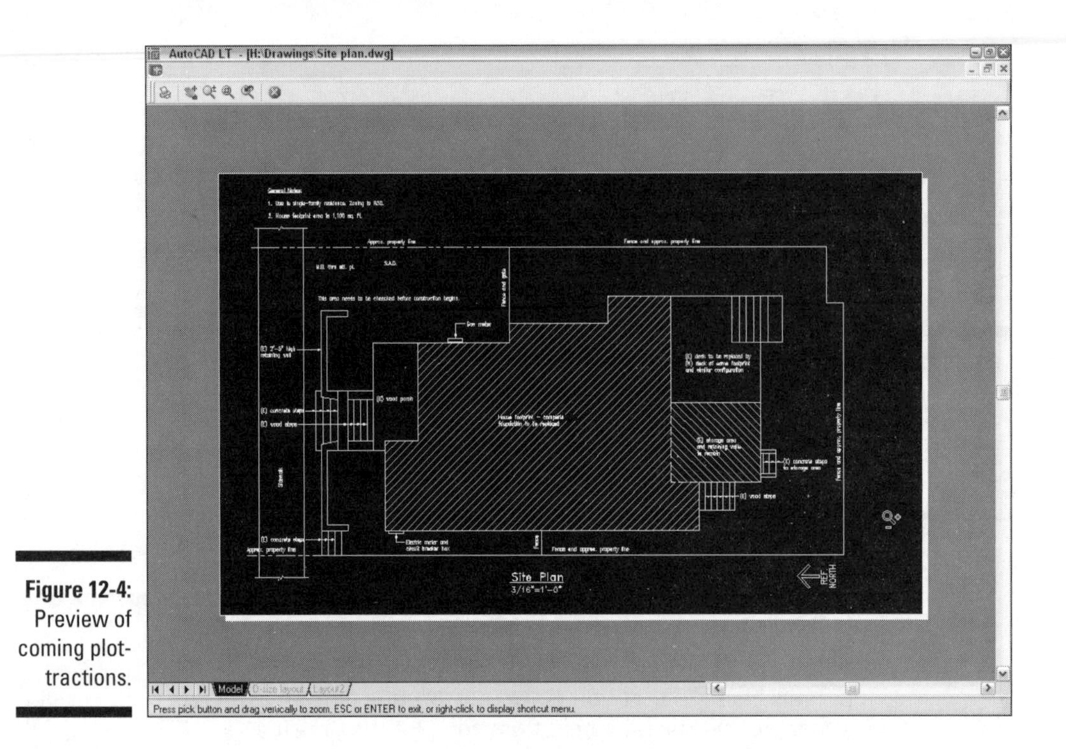

Figure 12-4: Preview of coming plot-tractions.

There — 16 steps, as promised. If for some reason your plot didn't work, well, I warned you that AutoCAD LT plotting was complicated and temperamental! Read the rest of this chapter for all the details about the numerous other plotting options that can cause plotting to go awry. If you're in a big hurry, turn directly to the troubleshooting section, "Troubles with Plotting," at the end of the chapter.

Preview one, two

One key to efficient plotting is liberal use of AutoCAD LT's preview feature. (To maintain political fairness, I recommend conservative use of some other LT options elsewhere in the book.)

The postage stamp-sized partial preview in the middle of the Plot dialog box is a quick reality check to make sure your plot fits on the paper and is turned in the right direction. If the plot area at the current scale is too large for the paper, the partial preview area displays thick red warning lines along the side(s) of the sheet where the drawing will be truncated.

When you point the cursor at the partial preview and pause for a moment, LT displays a ToolTip that informs you of the physical paper size and the printable area (that is, paper size minus margins).

Press the Preview button to see a full preview in a separate window. You see exactly how your drawing lays out on the paper and how the various lineweights, colors, and other object plot properties will appear. You can zoom and pan around the preview by using the right-click menu. (Any zooming or panning that you do does not affect what area of the drawing gets plotted — zooming and panning is just a way to get a better look at different areas of the plot preview.)

Instead of fit, scale it

In most real plotting situations, you want to plot to a specific scale rather than let AutoCAD LT choose an oddball scale that just happens to maximize the drawing on the paper. And if you're going to plot the Model tab of a drawing to scale, you need to know its drawing scale factor. Chapter 5 describes setup concepts, and Chapter 9 provides some tips for determining the scale factor of a drawing that someone else created.

If your drawing was created at a standard scale, such as 1:50 or ¼"=1'–0", then you simply choose the scale from the handy drop-down Scale list in the Plot dialog box. If your scale is not in the list, then type the ratio between plotted distance and AutoCAD LT drawing distance into the two text boxes below the Scale list, as shown in Figure 12-5. The easiest way to express the ratio usually is to type **1** (one) in the upper box and the drawing scale factor in the lower box. (See Chapter 5 for more information.)

Creating half-size plots for some purposes is common in some industries. To plot model space half-size, double the drawing scale factor. For example, a ⅛"=1'–0" drawing has a drawing scale factor of 96, which is equivalent to a plot scale of 1=96. To make a half-size model space plot of it, specify a plot scale of 1=192 (or choose 1⁄16"=1'–0" from the Scale drop-down list). Of course, these kinds of transformations are simpler in the metric system: If you want to make a half-size plot of a 1:50 drawing, just specify a plot scale of 1 mm = 100 or choose 1:100 from the Scale drop-down list.

Even if you work with drawings that are created to be plotted at a specific scale, plotting with a Fit to Paper scale may be the most efficient way to make a reduced-size check plot. For example, drafters in your office might create drawings that get plotted on D size sheets (24 x 36 inch), whereas you have access to a laser printer with a B size (11 x 17 inch) paper tray. By plotting the D size drawings Scaled to Fit on B size paper, you end up with check plots that are slightly smaller than half size (11⁄24th size, to be exact). You can't measure distances on the check plots with a scale, but you probably can check them visually for overall correctness.

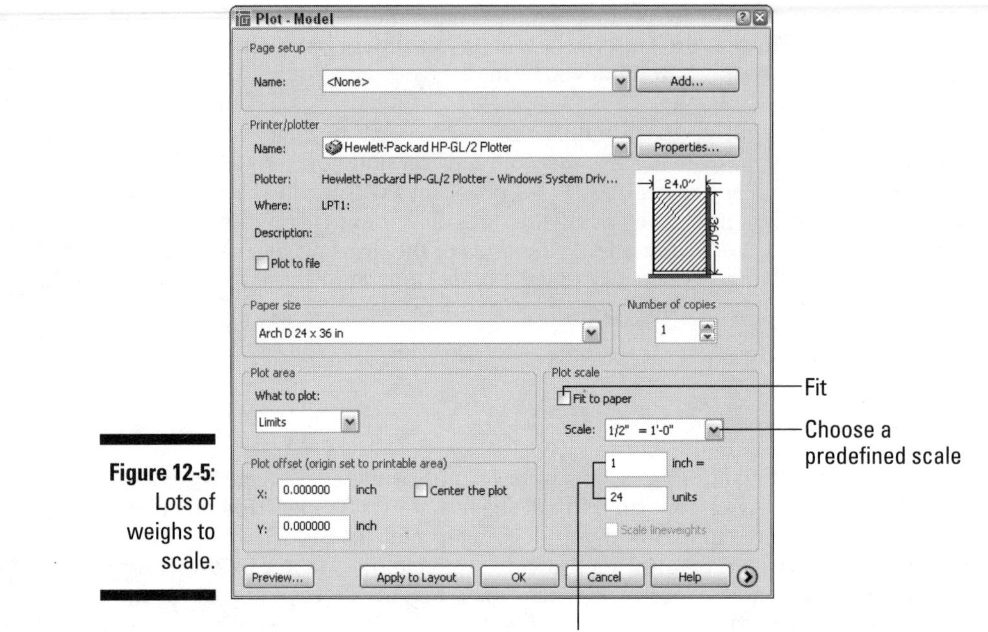

Figure 12-5: Lots of weighs to scale.

Plotting the Layout of the Land

In the previous section, I show you how to plot the model space representation of your drawing by making sure that the Model tab is active when you open the Plot dialog box. However, paper space simplifies plot scaling and gives you additional options for controlling the look of your output. (For example, you can plot the same geometry at different scales or with different sets of layers visible.) So in many drawings, you want to plot a paper space layout instead.

About paper space layouts and plotting

As Chapter 5 describes, you can use AutoCAD's paper space feature to compose one or more *layouts* for plotting your drawing in particular ways. Each layout lives on a separate tab, which you click at the bottom of the drawing area. In addition, AutoCAD LT saves plot settings (plot device, paper size, plot scale) separately for each of the tabs — that is, for each of the layout tabs as well as the Model tab.

Whether to plot model space or a paper space layout in a drawing depends entirely on how the drawing was set up. If you or someone else went through a layout setup similar to the one in Chapter 5, then you probably plot the paper space layout. If not, plot the Model tab.

Don't confuse the Model tab at the bottom of the drawing area with the MODEL/PAPER button on the status bar. The tabs control which view of the drawing (model space or a paper space layout) fills the drawing area. When a paper space layout fills the drawing area, the status bar button controls whether drawing and editing take place in paper space or in model space inside a viewport. When you plot a layout, whether the MODEL/PAPER button says MODEL or PAPER doesn't matter — AutoCAD LT always plots the paper space layout (not just the contents of model space in the viewport).

The presence of a Layout1 tab next to the Model tab at the bottom of the drawing area doesn't necessarily mean that the drawing contains an already set up paper space layout. LT always displays a Layout1 tab when you open a drawing created in AutoCAD LT 97/AutoCAD Release 14 or earlier, and displays a Layout1 and Layout2 tab when you open a drawing created in AutoCAD LT 2000/AutoCAD 2000 or later. Layout1 and Layout2 are simply AutoCAD's default names; the creator of the drawing may have renamed them to something more descriptive.

If you don't have any paper space drawings handy, you can use one of the AutoCAD LT sample drawings, such as the architectural drawing stored in \Program Files\AutoCAD LT 2005\Sample\house plan.dwg.

The path to paper space layout plotting success

Plotting a paper space layout is pretty much like plotting model space, except that you need to find the appropriate layout first and make sure that its tab is selected before you open the Plot dialog box:

1. **Click the layout tabs at the bottom of the drawing area until you find a suitably set up layout.**

   If no one has set up the layout yet, LT creates a default layout. (If the Show Page Setup Manager for New Layouts setting on the Display tab of the Options dialog box is turned on, you see the Page Setup Manager dialog box first — just click the Close button.) The default layout probably isn't useful for real projects, but you can use it to learn about layout plotting. Refer to Chapter 5 for instructions on creating a real layout.

2. **Click the Plot button on the Standard toolbar.**

   The Plot dialog box appears.

3. **Specify a Printer/Plotter Name and a Paper Size.**
4. **In the What to Plot list, choose Layout.**
5. **Specify the Plot Offset (such as zero in both the X and Y directions).**
6. **Specify a Plot Scale of 1:1.**

   One of the big advantages of layouts is that you don't need to know anything about drawing scale in order to plot the drawing — hence the name *paper* space. Figure 12-6 shows the proper settings for plotting a layout.

   To create a half-size plot of a layout, specify a plot scale of 1:2. In addition, turn on the Scale Lineweights setting in order to reduce lineweights proportionally. (I cover plotting lineweights later in this chapter.)

   If you find that the layout is too big for your plotter's largest paper size at a plot scale of 1:1, you can change the What to Plot setting to Extents and then specify Fit to Paper for the Plot Scale. Alternatively, you can exit the Plot dialog box and fix the problem if you want to have a paper space layout that permanently reflects a new paper size. Use the Page Setup dialog box to modify the layout settings, or copy the layout and modify the new layout.

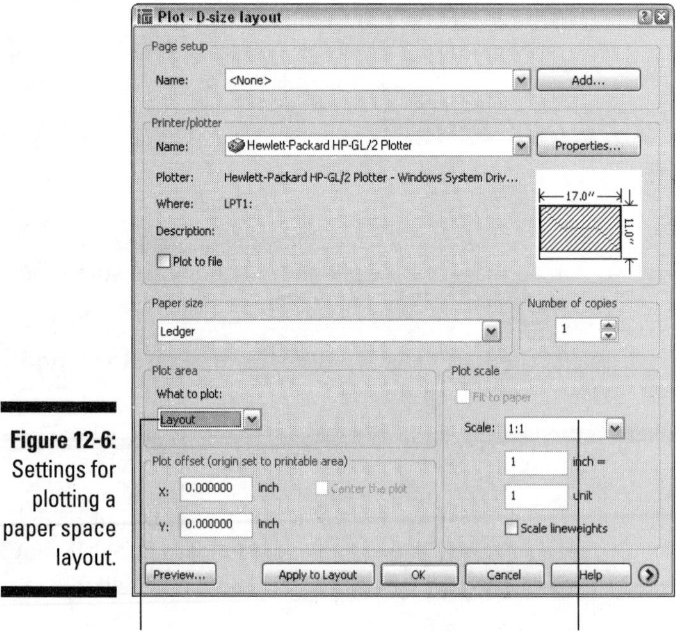

Figure 12-6: Settings for plotting a paper space layout.

7. **Click the More Options button and change any additional plot options that you want to.**

   Refer to Steps 11 through 13 in the section, "Plotting success in 16 steps."

8. **Click the Preview button, check that the drawing displays on the paper at the correct orientation and size, right-click and choose Exit to return to the Plot dialog box.**

   If you found any problems in the preview, change your plot settings and click Preview again until it looks right.

9. **Click OK to create the plot.**

Plotting Lineweights and Colors

In previous sections of this chapter, I help you gain some plotting confidence. Those sections show you how to create scaled, monochrome plots with uniform lineweights in model space or paper space. Those skills may be all you need, but if you care about controlling plotted lineweights and colors, or adding special effects such as screening (plotting shades of gray), read on.

Plotting with style

Plotstyles provide a way to override object properties with alternative plot properties. (See Chapter 3 for information about object properties.) The properties include plotted lineweight, plotted color, and screening (plotting shades of gray). Figure 12-7 shows the full range of options. They come in two exciting flavors:

- Color-dependent plotstyles
- Named plotstyles

Color-dependent plotstyles are based on the standard way of plotting in earlier versions of AutoCAD and LT (before AutoCAD and LT 2000), whereas named plotstyles provide a newer way.

It's remotely possible that you won't need to bother with plotstyles. If the drawings you want to plot have layer and object properties (especially lineweight) that reflect how you want objects to plot, you can dispense with plotstyles. But most people and most drawings use plotstyles, so you have to at least be familiar with them.

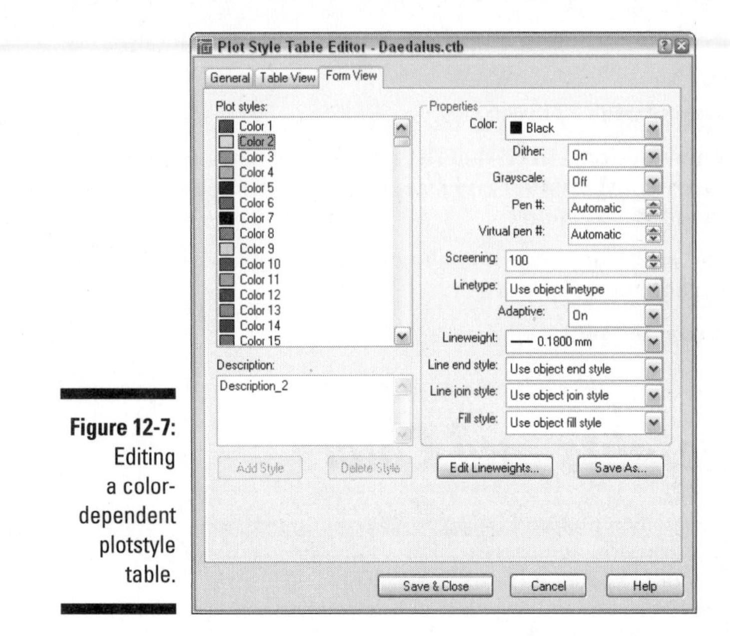

Figure 12-7: Editing a color-dependent plotstyle table.

A couple of common reasons for using plotstyles are to

- **Map screen colors to plotted lineweights.** If this idea seems completely loony to you, try to suspend judgment until you've read the "Plotting through thick and thin" section, a bit later in this chapter.
- **Create *screened* lines on monochrome plots.** Lines that are screened display in various shades of gray, not black. Drafters sometimes use screened lines to deemphasize secondary objects that otherwise overwhelm the main objects in the drawing. Screening is expressed as a percentage, with 100% being completely black and 0% being invisible.

Using plotstyles

If you want objects in your drawing to plot with properties that differ from their display properties, you need plotstyles. For example, you can plot with different lineweights or colors from the ones you're using for display purposes. Or, as I mention in the preceding section, you may need to map display colors to plotted lineweights. AutoCAD LT groups plotstyles into plotstyle tables, each of which is stored in a separate file.

Color-dependent plotstyle tables live in Color TaBle (CTB) files and they map the 255 AutoCAD LT display colors to 255 plotstyles. LT automatically uses the color-dependent plotstyles to figure out how to plot every object, based on — you guessed it — the object's color. Color-dependent plotstyle tables are especially handy for mimicking the old color-mapped-to-lineweight plotting approach of AutoCAD LT 97/AutoCAD R14 and earlier versions; color-dependent plotstyle tables remain the most common method in most companies.

Named plotstyle tables live in Style TaBle (STB) files. After you create a named plotstyle table, you create one or more plotstyles and give them any names you like. Then you can assign the named plotstyles to layers or to individual objects. (See Chapter 3 for more information about object and layer properties.)

"Named" refers to the plotstyles, not to the tables. Both color-dependent plotstyle *tables* and named plotstyle *tables* have names because both are stored in files and files have to have names. But color-dependent plotstyle*s* don't have names and named plotstyle*s* do have names.

To use a plotstyle table, and its included plotstyles (whether they're color dependent or named), you must attach it to model space or a paper space layout. The plotstyle table then affects plotting only for that tab. This approach enables you to plot the same drawing in different ways by attaching different plotstyles to different tabs.

You can attach a plotstyle to model space or a paper space layout by selecting its tab at the bottom of the drawing area, opening the Plot dialog box or Page Setup dialog box, and choosing the plotstyle table name in the Plot Style Table (Pen Assignments) area of the expanded Plot dialog box. See "Controlling plotted lineweights with screen colors," later in this chapter, for an example.

When you start a new drawing in the usual way — that is, by using a template drawing (see Chapter 5), the template drawing's plotstyle behavior determines whether you can choose CTB or STB files. (That's why most of AutoCAD LT's stock template drawings come in Color Dependent Plot Styles and Named Plot Styles versions.) If you want to change from color-dependent plotstyles to named plotstyles (or vice versa) in a particular drawing, use the CONVERTPSTYLES command. If you're converting from color-dependent to named plotstyles, run the CONVERTCTB command first in order to create a suitable STB file.

Creating plotstyles

If you're really lucky, you don't need to use plotstyles. If you're somewhat lucky, you need to use plotstyles, but someone provides the plotstyle table files for you. If that's the case, you must put the CTB or STB files in your Plot Styles folder in order for AutoCAD LT to recognize them. (To find the location of your Plot Styles folder, open the Options dialog box, choose the Files tab, and look for the Printer Support File Path➪Plot Style Table Search Path setting.)

If you're not lucky at all, then you need to be smart — that is, you want to know how to create your own plotstyle table files. Here's how:

1. **Choose File➪Plot Style Manager.**

   The Plot Styles folder opens in a separate window.

2. **Double-click the Add-A-Plot Style Table Wizard program shortcut.**

3. **Read the opening screen and then click Next.**
4. **Choose the Start from Scratch option, or one of the other three options if you want to start with settings from another file. Then click Next.**

   The remaining steps assume that you chose Start from Scratch. If you chose another option, simply follow the wizard's prompts.

   If the creator of a drawing provides you with an AutoCAD R14/AutoCAD LT 97 PC2 (version 2) or AutoCAD R12/AutoCAD LT 95 PCP (version 1) file, choose the Use a PCP or PC2 File option. With this option, the wizard imports color-to-plotted-lineweight settings automatically.
5. **Choose whether you want to create a color-dependent plotstyle table (CTB file) or a named plotstyle table (STB file). Then click Next.**

   Choose Color-Dependent Plot Style Table in order to map screen colors to plotted lineweights. Choose Named Plot Style Table in order to leave screen colors alone (so that the colors plot as you see them on-screen) and to create named plotstyles that you can apply to layers or objects.
6. **Type a name for the new CTB or STB file and then click Next.**
7. **Click the Plot Style Table Editor button.**

   The Plot Style Table Editor dialog box opens (refer to Figure 12-7).
8. **If you created a color-dependent plotstyle table, assign Lineweight, Screening, or other plot properties to each color that's used in the drawing. If you created a named plotstyle table, click the Add Style button and then assign plot properties to each of the named styles that you create.**

   To determine which colors are used in a drawing, switch to the AutoCAD LT window and open the Layer Properties Manager dialog box by clicking the Layers button located on the Layers toolbar.

   To change a setting for all colors or named styles, select all of them first by clicking the first color or named style, holding down the Shift key, scrolling to the end of the list, and then clicking the last color or named style. Any subsequent changes you make apply to all the selected colors or named styles.
9. **Click the Save & Close button to close the Plot Style Table Editor dialog box. Then click Finish to complete the steps for the wizard.**

   The Plot Styles folder now displays your new CTB or STB file.
10. **Close the Plot Styles folder by clicking the X in its title bar.**

Creating your first plotstyle table can be a harrowing experience because you have so many options. Just remember that your most likely reason for creating one is to map screen colors to plotted lineweights (as I describe in greater detail in the next section). Also remember that you may be able to minimize your effort by getting a CTB file from the person who created the drawing that you want to plot.

In Chapter 3, I recommend that you limit yourself to the first nine Standard AutoCAD Colors when defining layers, and not a patchwork of the 255 colors that AutoCAD LT makes available. If you follow my advice, your work to create a color-dependent plotstyle table is much reduced, because you have to assign plot properties for only nine colors, rather than worrying about 255 of them.

Plotting through thick and thin

Long ago, manual drafters developed the practice of drawing lines of different thicknesses, or *lineweights,* in order to distinguish different kinds of objects. Manual drafters did it with different technical ink pen nib diameters or with different hardnesses of pencil lead and varying degrees of pressure on the pencil. Because a computer mouse usually doesn't come with different diameters of mouse balls or a pressure-sensitive button, AutoCAD and its developers had to figure out how to let users indicate lineweights on-screen and on a plot. They came up with two different ways to indicate lineweight:

- Mapping on-screen colors to plotted lineweights. I describe this common approach in Chapter 4.
- Displaying lineweights on-screen to match what the user can expect to see on the plot. This approach was introduced in AutoCAD and LT 2000.

Controlling plotted lineweights with object lineweights

Plotting object lineweights is trivial, assuming that the person who created the drawing took the trouble to assign lineweights to layers or objects (see Chapter 3 for details). Just make sure that the Plot Object Lineweights setting in the expanded Plot dialog box is turned on. Because plotstyles can override the object lineweights with different plotted lineweights, you might also want to turn off the Plot with Plot Styles setting.

As long as you turn on the Plot Object Lineweights setting, you find that (those who hate cheap puns, read no further!) the plot thickens! It also thins, but that's not as funny.

If you *don't* want to plot the lineweights assigned to objects, you must turn off both the Plot Object Lineweights and Plot with Plot Styles settings in the Plot Options area of the Plot dialog box. Turning on Plot with Plot Styles turns on Plot Object Lineweights as well.

Plotting with plodders

Color-as-color and lineweight-as-lineweight seem like great ideas, but Autodesk knew when it added object lineweights back in 1999 that long-time users of AutoCAD weren't going to abandon the old colors-mapped-to-lineweights approach overnight. Thus, you can still control plotted lineweight by display color in AutoCAD LT.

AutoCAD and LT veterans by and large have chosen to stick with their Old Way for now. They've done so for a variety of reasons, including inertia, plotting procedures and drawings built around the Old Way, third-party applications that don't fully support the newer methods, and the need to exchange drawings with clients and subcontractors who haven't upgraded. In summary, the ripple effect of those who need to or want to continue using colors-mapped-to-lineweights is lasting a long time. Don't be surprised if you find yourself going with the flow for a while.

The default setting in AutoCAD LT 2005 is to plot object lineweights, so that's the easiest method if you don't have to consider the historical practices or predilections of other people with whom you exchange drawings. Mapping screen colors to lineweights requires some initial work on your part, but after you've set up the mapping scheme, the additional effort is minimal.

Controlling plotted lineweights with screen colors

To map screen colors to plotted lineweights, you need a color-dependent plotstyle table (CTB file), as I describe in the section "Plotting with style," earlier in this chapter. If you're plotting a drawing created by someone else, that someone else may be able to supply you with the appropriate CTB file, or at least with a PCP or PC2 file from which you can create the CTB file quickly. At the very least, the creator of the drawing can give you a printed chart showing which plotted lineweight to assign to each AutoCAD screen color. Use the instructions in the "Plotting with style" section to copy or create the required CTB file.

Unfortunately, no industry-wide standards exist for mapping screen colors to plotted lineweights. Different offices do it differently. That's why receiving a CTB, PCP, or PC2 file with drawings that someone sends you is useful.

After you have the appropriate CTB file stored in your Plot Styles folder, follow these steps to use it:

1. **Click the tab that you want to plot — the Model tab or the desired paper space layout tab.**
2. **Click the Plot button on the Standard toolbar.**
3. **In the Plot Style Table (Pen Assignments) area on the expanded Plot dialog box, select the CTB file from the Name list, as shown in Figure 12-8.**

   This action attaches the plotstyle table (CTB file) to the tab that you selected in Step 1.

Figure 12-8: Selecting a plotstyle table that maps screen colors to plotted lineweights.

4. **Click the Apply to Layout button.**

   LT records the plot setting change with the current tab's configuration information. Assuming that you save the drawing, LT uses the CTB that you selected as the default plotstyle when you (or other people) plot that tab in the future.

5. **Continue with the plotting as described earlier in this chapter.**

If your drawing uses a named plotstyle table instead of a color-dependent plotstyle table, you follow the same steps, except that you select an STB file instead of a CTB file in Step 3.

You can tell whether the current drawing was set up to use color-dependent plotstyles or named plotstyles by looking at the Properties toolbar. If the last drop-down list (Plot Style Control) is grayed out, the drawing uses color-dependent plotstyles. If this list is not grayed out, the drawing uses named plotstyles.

Plotting in color

Plotting the colors that you see on-screen requires no special tricks. In the absence of a plotstyle table (that is, if you set Plot Style Table (Pen Assignments) to None in the Plot dialog box), AutoCAD LT sends color information as it appears on-screen to the plotter. As long as your output device can plot in color, what you see is what you get.

When in doubt, send it out

Whether you plot to scale or not, with different lineweights or not, in color or not, consider using a service bureau for some of your plotting. In-house plotting on your office's output devices is great for small check plots on faster laser or inkjet printers. Large format plotting, on the other hand, can be slow and time consuming. If you need to plot lots of drawings, you may find yourself spending an afternoon loading paper, replenishing ink cartridges, and trimming sheets.

Good plotting service bureaus have big, fast, expensive plotters that you can only dream about owning. Also, *they're* responsible for babysitting those fancy devices, feeding them, and fixing them. As a bonus, service bureaus can make blueline prints from your plots, if you need to distribute hard-copy sets to other people.

The only downside is that you need to coordinate with a service bureau to make sure it gets what it needs from you and can deliver the kinds of plots you need. Some service bureaus plot directly from your DWG files; others ask you to make PLT (plot) files. Some service bureaus specialize in color plotting, although others are more comfortable with monochrome plotting and making blueline copies.

When you're choosing a service bureau, look for one that traditionally has served drafters, architects, and engineers. These service bureaus tend to be more knowledgeable about AutoCAD, and they have more plotting expertise than the desktop publishing, printing, and copying shops.

Whomever you choose, do some test plots well before the day when that important set of drawings is due. Talk to the plotting people and get a copy of their plotting instructions. Have the service bureau create some plots of a couple of your typical drawings and make sure they look the way you want them to.

If you do lots of plotting with a service bureau, look into whether you can charge it to your clients as an expense (just like bluelines or copying).

If you attach a plotstyle table to the tab that you're plotting (as described in the previous section), you can — if you really want to — map screen colors to different plotted colors. In most cases you don't want that kind of confusion. Instead, leave the Color property in the plotstyle table set to Use Object Color.

If your goal is *not* to plot color, make sure that you set the Color property for all plotstyles to Black. If you try to plot colors on a monochrome device, you may find that objects appear in various shades of gray, like in a black-and-white newspaper photograph, with lighter colors mapped to lighter shades of gray and darker colors to darker shades of gray. This process of mapping colors to shades of gray is called *monochrome dithering,* and it usually is *not* what you want in a CAD drawing. To override it, use the Plot Style Table Editor, as described in the section "Creating plotstyles," earlier in this chapter, to set the Color option for all colors to Black (the default setting is Use

Object Color). If you don't already have a plotstyle table that you want to use, choose Monochrome.CTB (for color-based plotstyles) or Monochrome.STB (for named plotstyles), both of which come with AutoCAD LT.

It's a (Page) Setup!

Page setups specify the plotter, paper size, and other plot settings that you use to plot a particular tab of a particular drawing. AutoCAD LT maintains separate page setups for model space and for each paper space layout (that is, for each tab you see in the drawing area). When you click the Apply to Layout button in the Plot dialog box (or turn on the Save Changes to Layout setting and then click OK to plot), LT stores the current plot settings as the page setup for the current tab.

You also can give page setups names and save them. The advantage of doing so is that you can switch quickly between different plot settings and copy plot settings from one drawing tab to another. Named page setups are stored with each drawing, but you can copy them from another drawing into the current one with the Page Setup Manager dialog box (which I describe later in this section).

If your plotting needs are simple, you don't need to do anything special with page setups. In the Plot dialog box, just click the Apply to Layout button or turn on the Save Changes to Layout setting to save any plotting changes with the tab you're plotting.

If you want to get fancier, you can create named page setups in order to plot the same layout (or the model tab) in different ways, or to copy plot settings from one tab to another or one drawing to another. Click the Add button in the Plot dialog box to create a named page setup from the current plot settings. After you create a named page setup, you can restore its plot settings by choosing it from the Page Setup Name list.

For even greater control, choose File⇨Page Setup Manager to create, change, and copy page setups. In the Page Setup Manager dialog box, shown in Figure 12-9, you can create new page setups and modify existing ones. Click the Modify button to open the Page Setup dialog box, which is almost identical to the Plot dialog box. The primary difference is that you're changing plot settings rather than actually plotting. The Set Current button copies the page setup that you select n the Page Setups list to the current layout tab. With the Import button, you can copy a layout from another drawing (DWG) or drawing template (DWT) file.

Figure 12-9: The Page Setup Manager dialog box.

Continuing the Plot Dialog

In previous sections of this chapter, I cover most of the important options in the Plot dialog box. This section reveals a few more fine points that can make your plotting life easier. I don't cover every minute, obscure, useful-only-at-cocktail-party-discussions detail. But I do point out some occasionally useful options that increase your vocabulary when you're communicating with the Plot dialog box:

- **Printer/Plotter:** As I describe in the section "Configure it out," earlier in this chapter, you use the Name list to select the Windows system printer or nonsystem driver configuration that you want to use for plotting.

  The Properties button opens the Plotter Configuration Editor dialog box, with which you can change media (type of paper) and other properties that are unique to the currently selected plotter or printer. In particular, you can define custom paper sizes.

  As if AutoCAD LT's Plot dialog box settings weren't overwhelming enough, some plotter drivers hide important settings in the Plotter Configuration Editor dialog box, typically behind the Custom Properties button near the bottom of the dialog box. (For example, if you're using the HP enhanced Windows system driver mentioned earlier in this chapter, you can click the Custom Properties button and then the More Sizes button to specify which paper sizes are available to you on the Plot Settings tab of the main Plot dialog box.)

To make matters even more confusing, if you make any changes in the Plotter Configuration Editor dialog box, LT prompts you to save the changes to a separate PC3 file. Choose `Save Changes to the Following File` (that is, create a new AutoCAD LT-specific configuration that includes the revised settings) and type a configuration name that you can recognize later. When you want to plot with custom settings, remember to choose the AutoCAD LT-specific PC3 configuration near the end of the Plotter Configuration Name list, and not the Windows system printer configuration near the beginning of the list.

- **Plot to File:** If you need to plot to a file rather than directly to your plotter or network printer queue, select this option. When you click OK to plot, LT asks you for a plot filename and location.

This option is especially useful when you want to use the ePlot feature to publish a DWF file. (See Chapter 15 for details about using DWF files.) You also may need to create files to send to a plotting service bureau.

- **Plot Stamp On:** Use this option to turn on and off and configure the contents of a text string that AutoCAD LT adds automatically to the corner of each plot. The plot stamp can include useful information such as the drawing filename and plot date and time.
- **Plot Area:** Specify the area of the drawing to plot. Your choices include Display, Extents, and Window, regardless of whether you're plotting a paper space layout or the model space tab. If you defined named views in the drawing, LT adds a View option. The additional choice is Layout for a paper space layout tab or Limits for the model space tab.
  - *Display* means the drawing as it's currently displayed in the drawing window (including any white space — or black space — around the drawing objects).
  - *Extents* means the rectangular area containing all the objects in the drawing.
  - *Limits* means the model space area that you specified (or should have specified) when you set up the drawing. See Chapter 5 for details.
  - *Window* means a rectangular area that you specify.
  - *View* means a named view, which you select from the drop-down list (Chapter 8 describes named views and how to create them).

Usually, you choose to plot Layout in paper space. For model space, the choice depends on whether the drawing was set up properly and what you want to plot. If you set limits properly, as I suggest in Chapter 5, then plot Limits in order to get the whole drawing area. If you're trying to plot a drawing in which the limits weren't set properly, try Extents instead. Use Window or View if you want to plot just a portion of model space.

- **Plot Offset:** A plot offset of X=0 and Y=0 positions the plot at the lower-left corner of the plottable area. If you want to move the plot from this default position on the paper, enter nonzero numbers or select the Center the Plot option. (The Center the Plot option is available only when you haven't selected Layout from the What to Plot list.)
- **Shaded Viewport Options:** If your drawing includes viewports showing shaded objects that you created or rendered 3D models that an AutoCAD user created (Chapter 1 describes LT's 3D limitations), use this area to control the plotted appearance.
- **Plot Options:** The Plot Object Lineweights option and the Plot with Plot Styles option control whether LT uses the features described in the "Plotting with style" and "Plotting through thick and thin" sections earlier in this chapter.

  The Hide Paperspace Objects option controls whether AutoCAD LT hides objects that are behind other objects when a 3D model displays in a viewport. You can ignore this option unless you create extruded, 2½D objects or plot 3D models from AutoCAD users.
- **Plot Upside-Down:** Turn on this setting if you want to rotate the plot 180 degrees on the paper (a handy option for plotting in the southern hemisphere, or for avoiding having to cock your head at an uncomfortable angle as you watch plots come out of the plotter).

Use the Plot dialog box's quick help to find out more about any part of the dialog box:

1. **Click the question mark next to the close button in the dialog box's title bar.**
2. **Point the cursor at the part of the dialog box that confuses you and click.**
3. **Click the Help button at the bottom of the dialog box if the pop-up help isn't enough.**

   The AutoCAD LT 2005 Help window opens and displays the Plot Dialog Box help page.

AutoCAD LT normally generates plots in the foreground — that is, the plotting process takes over the program for the entire time that the program is creating the plot. AutoCAD LT 2005 includes a new background plotting feature that returns control of the program to you more quickly. If you have a reasonably fast computer with adequate memory, turn on this feature in the Options dialog box: Choose Tools➪Options, click the Plot and Publish tab, and turn on Plotting in the Background Processing Options area.

If you want to automate plotting for a batch of drawings, check out Chapter 15.

Troubles with Plotting

No matter how many times you read this chapter or how carefully you study the AutoCAD LT documentation, you occasionally run into plotting problems. You're especially likely to encounter problems when trying to plot other people's drawings because you don't always know what plotting conventions they had in mind. (Plotting conventions aren't where spies meet; they're a standardized approach to plotting issues — see Chapter 14 for suggestions.) Table 12-1 describes some of the more common plotting problems and solutions.

Table 12-1 Plotting Problems and Solutions

Problem	*Possible Solution*
Nothing comes out of the plotter (system printer driver).	Check whether you can print to the device from other Windows applications. If not, it's not an AutoCAD LT problem. Try the Windows Print Troubleshooter (Start⇨Help and Support⇨Printing and faxing [in Windows XP] or Start⇨Help⇨Contents⇨Troubleshooting and Maintenance [in Windows 2000]).
Nothing comes out of the plotter (nonsystem printer driver).	Choose File⇨Plotter Manager, double-click the plotter configuration, and check the settings.
Objects don't plot the way they appear on-screen.	Check for a plotstyle table with weird settings, or try plotting without a plotstyle table.
Objects appear "ghosted" or with washed-out colors.	In the plotstyle table, set Color to Black for all colors or named plotstyles.
Scaled to Fit doesn't work right in paper space.	Change the plot area from Layout to Extents.
The HP enhanced Windows system driver that came on the AutoCAD LT 2005 CD, and the available paper sizes aren't right (for example, no architectural paper sizes).	On the Plot dialog box's Plot Device tab, click the Properties button, and then the Custom Properties button (near the bottom), and then the More Sizes button to specify the standard and custom paper sizes. See the "Continuing the Plot Dialog" section earlier in this chapter for more information.
Something else is wrong.	Check the plot log: Click the Plot/Publish Details Report Available icon near the right end of the status bar and look for error messages.

Part IV

Collaboration Makes the Drawings Go 'Round

"Ironically, he went out there looking for a 'hot spot.'"

In this part . . .

After you get the lines and text right, you may be justified in thinking that your work in AutoCAD LT is done. But LT enables you to do so much more! Blocks and external references help you manage data within drawings, between drawings, and across a network. If you plan to share drawings (whether among your own projects, with people in your office, or with folks in other companies), you need to think about consistency in presentation and drawing organization — in other words, CAD standards. The Internet is the biggest ongoing swap meet in human history, and AutoCAD LT offers some unique trading possibilities — and potential pitfalls — via e-mail and the Web. With the information in this part, you can teach LT how to give and receive in no time.

Chapter 13

Be a Block-Head (And an Xref-Man)

In This Chapter

- Introducing blocks and external references (xrefs)
- Creating block definitions
- Inserting blocks
- Using attributes in blocks
- Attaching and managing xrefs
- Controlling xref paths

Chapter 7 shows you how to copy objects within a drawing or even to another drawing. That's one way to use CAD to improve drafting efficiency. You can copy a DWG file and then modify it to create a similar drawing — an even better productivity booster, as long as you're in the habit of making similar drawings. But all those are baby steps compared to the techniques that I cover in this chapter: treating drawings and parts of drawings as reusable and updateable modules. If you want to make drafting production more efficient with CAD, then you want to know how to use blocks and xrefs.

- A *block* is a collection of objects grouped together to form a single object. You can *insert* this collection more than once in the same drawing, and when you do, all instances of the block remain identical, even after you change the *block definition*. Although a block lives within a specific drawing, you can transfer copies of it into other drawings. You can add fill-in-the-blank text fields called *attributes* to blocks.
- An *external reference, or xref,* is like an industrial-strength block. An external reference is a pointer to a separate drawing outside the drawing you're working on. The referenced drawing appears on-screen and on plots as part of your drawing, but it continues to live as a separate document on your hard drive. If you edit the externally referenced drawing, the appearance of the drawing changes in all drawings that reference it.

Blocks and external references enable you to reuse your work and the work of others, giving you the potential to save tremendous amounts of time — or to cause tremendous problems if you change a file on which other peoples' drawings depend. Use these features when you can to save time, but do so in an organized and careful way so as to avoid problems.

The way you use blocks and especially xrefs depends a lot on the profession and office in which you work. Some disciplines and companies use these drawing organization features heavily and in a highly organized way, although others don't. Ask your colleagues what the local customs are and follow them.

Rocking with Blocks

First, a little more block theory and then you can rock right into those blocks.

To use a block in a drawing, you need two things: a block *definition* and one or more block *inserts*. AutoCAD LT doesn't always make the distinction between these two things very clear, but you need to understand the difference to avoid terminal confusion about blocks. (Maybe this syndrome should be called *block-headedness?*)

A block definition lives in an invisible area of your drawing file called the *block table*. (It's one of those *symbol tables* that I describe in Chapter 3.) The block table is like a book of graphical recipes for making different kinds of blocks. Each block definition is like a recipe for making one kind of block. When you insert a block, as I describe later in this chapter, AutoCAD LT creates a special object called a *block insert*. The insert points to the recipe and tells LT, "Hey, draw me according to the instructions in this recipe!"

Although a block may look like a collection of objects stored together and given a name, it's really a graphical recipe (the block definition) plus one or more pointers to that recipe (one or more block inserts). Each time you insert a particular block, you create another pointer to the same recipe.

The advantages of blocks include

- **Grouping objects together when they belong together logically:** You can draw a screw by using lines and arcs, and then make a block definition out of all these objects. When you insert the screw block, AutoCAD LT treats it as a single object for purposes of copying, moving, and so on.
- **Saving time and reducing errors:** Inserting a block is, of course, much quicker than redrawing the same geometry again. And the less geometry you draw from scratch, the less opportunity you have to make a mistake.

- **Efficiency of storage when you reuse the same block repeatedly:** If you insert the same screw block 15 times in a drawing, AutoCAD LT stores the detailed block definition only once. The 15 block inserts that point to the block definition take up much less hard drive space than 15 copies of all the lines, polylines, and arcs do.
- **The ability to edit all instances of a symbol in a drawing simply by modifying a single block definition:** This one is the biggie. If you decide that your design requires a different kind of screw, you simply redefine the screw's block definition. With this new recipe, AutoCAD LT then replaces all 15 screws automatically. That's a heck of a lot faster than erasing and recopying 15 screws!

WARNING!

Blocks *aren't* as great for drawing elements used in multiple drawings, however, especially in a situation where several people are working on and sharing parts of drawings with one another. That's because blocks, after they get into multiple drawings, stay in each drawing; a later modification to a block definition in one drawing does not automatically modify all the other drawings that use that block. If you use a block with your company's logo in a number of drawings and then you decide to change the logo, you must make the change within each drawing that uses the block.

TIP

External references enable you to modify multiple drawings from the original referenced drawing. You can find out more about external references in the section "Going External," later in this chapter.

TIP

If all you need to do is make some objects into a group so that you can more easily select them for copying, moving, and so on, use the AutoCAD LT *group* feature. Type **Group** and press Enter to open the Group Manager dialog box. Then select some objects, click the Create Group button, and type a name for the group. When you're editing drawings containing groups, press Ctrl+H to toggle "group-ness" on or off. If you toggle "group-ness" on, picking any object in a group selects all objects in the group. If you toggle it off, picking an object selects only that object, even if it happens to be a member of a group.

Creating block definitions

To create a block definition from objects in the current drawing, use the Block Definition dialog box. (The other way to create a block definition is by inserting another drawing file into your current drawing as a block, which I explain in the next section.) The following steps show you how to create a block definition with the Block Definition dialog box:

1. **Click the Make Block button on the Draw toolbar.**

   The Block Definition dialog box appears (see Figure 13-1).

Figure 13-1: The Block Definition dialog box.

Layers matter when you create the objects that make up a block. Block geometry created on most layers retains the characteristics, such as color and linetype, of those layers. But if you create a block by using geometry on Layer 0, that geometry has no characteristics, such as color and linetype of its own; chameleonlike, it takes on the features of the layer into which it's inserted.

2. **Type the block definition's name in the Name text entry box.**

   If you type the name of an existing block definition, LT will replace that block definition with the new group of objects you select (see Step 9 for details.). This process is called *block redefinition*.

   To see a list of the names of all the current blocks in your drawing, pull down the Name list.

3. **Specify the base point, also known as the insertion point, of the block, using either of the following methods:**

   - Enter the coordinates of the insertion point in the X, Y, and Z text boxes.
   - Click the Pick Point button and then select a point on the screen. (In this case, use an object snap or other precision technique, as described in Chapter 3, to grab a specific point on one of the block's objects.)

   The *base point* is the point on the block by which you insert it later, as I describe in the next section.

Use an obvious and consistent point on the group of objects for the base point, such as the lower-left corner, so that you know what to expect when you insert the block.

4. **Click the Select Objects button and then select the objects that you want as part of the block.**

   LT uses the selected objects to create a block definition. Figure 13-2 shows the base point and group of selected objects during the process of creating a new block definition.

5. **Select a radio button to tell LT what to do with the objects used to define the block: Retain them in place, Convert them into a block instance, or Delete them.**

   The default choice, Convert to Block, is usually the best. See Step 9 for a description of what happens with each choice.

6. **Choose Create Icon from Block Geometry in the Preview Icon area.**

   Go ahead and create the icon; it helps you and others find the right block to use later.

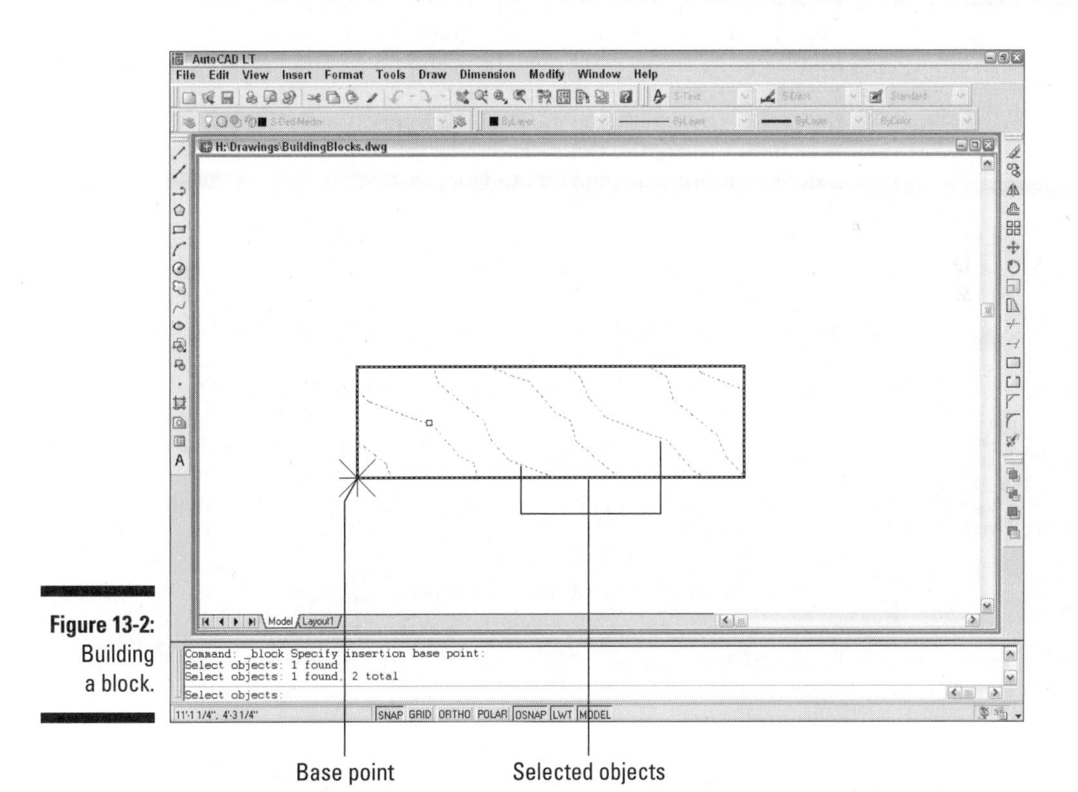

Figure 13-2: Building a block.

7. **Specify the Insert units to which the block will be scaled in the Drag-and-Drop Units drop-down menu.**

   When you or someone else drags the block from one drawing into another via the DesignCenter (see Chapter 3) or Tool Palette (described later in this chapter), the units you specify here and the units of the drawing you're dragging into control the default insertion scale factor.

8. **Enter the block Description.**

   Now is the time to think like a database manager and enter a useful description that identifies the block to yourself and others.

9. **Click OK to complete the block definition process.**

   If you typed the name of an existing block definition in Step 2, LT warns you that you redefine that block definition. Click Yes to redefine, which updates all instances of the block in the current drawing to match the changed block definition.

   LT stores the block definition in the current drawing's block table. If you chose the Convert to Block radio button (the default) in Step 5, LT also creates a block insert pointing to the new block definition — the objects look the same on-screen, but now they're an instance of the block rather than existing as separate objects. If you chose the Retain radio button, the objects remain in place but aren't converted into a block insert — they stay individual objects with no connection to the new block definition. If you chose the Delete radio button, the objects disappear (but the block definition still gets created).

You can include in a block definition a special kind of variable text object called an *attribute definition*. When you insert a block that contains one or more attribute definitions, LT prompts you to fill in values for the text fields. Attributes are useful for variable title block information (sheet number, sheet title, and so on) and symbols that contain different codes or callouts. I describe how to create and use attribute definitions later in this chapter.

Keep your common symbol drawings in one or more specific folders that you set aside just for that purpose. You may want to use one of the following techniques to develop a *block library* of symbols that you use frequently:

- Create a separate DWG file for each symbol (using WBLOCK, or simply by drawing each one in a new drawing).
- Store a bunch of symbols as block definitions in one drawing and use DesignCenter to import block definitions from this drawing when you need them.

Block and WBLOCK

The Block command, which opens the Block Definition dialog box, is great for use within a drawing, but what if you want to use the block definition in multiple drawings? The easiest method is to use DesignCenter to copy a block definition from one drawing to another, as described in Chapter 3.

Another method involves the WBLOCK and Insert commands. I don't cover this method here because it's less intuitive than using DesignCenter. But you may hear AutoCAD drafters talk about "wblocking" part of a drawing. So that you can keep these block-y names straight:

- The Block command creates a block definition from objects in the current drawing.
- The WBLOCK command creates a new DWG file from objects in the current drawing, or from a block definition in the current drawing.

Inserting blocks

AutoCAD LT provides a number of ways to insert a block, but the most commonly used and most flexible is the Insert dialog box. Here are the steps for inserting a block:

1. **Set an appropriate layer current, as described in Chapter 3.**

   Inserting each block on a layer that has something to do with its geometry or purpose is a good idea:

   - If all the objects in the block definition reside on one layer, then insert the block on that layer.
   - If the block geometry spans several layers, choose one of them to insert the block on.

   If any of the block definition's geometry was created on layer 0, then that geometry inherits the color, linetype, and other object properties of the layer that you insert the block on. It's like the chameleon changing color to match its surroundings or a politician changing his position to match the day's opinion polls.

2. **Click the Insert Block button on the Draw toolbar.**

   The Insert dialog box appears, as shown in Figure 13-3.

3. **Enter the block definition name or external filename by using one of the following methods:**

   - Use the Name drop-down list to select from a list of block definitions in the current drawing.
   - Click the Browse button to select a DWG file and have LT create a block definition from it.

Figure 13-3: The Insert dialog box.

You can use an external drawing to replace a block definition in your current drawing. If you click Browse and choose a file whose name matches the name of a block definition that's already in your drawing, LT warns you and then updates the block definition in your drawing with the current contents of the external file. This process is called *block redefinition*, and as described in Steps 2 and 9 in the preceding section, LT automatically updates all the block inserts that point to the block definition.

4. **Enter the insertion point, scale, and rotation angle of the block.**

   You can either click the Specify On-Screen check box in each area, to specify the parameters on-screen at the command prompt, or type the values you want in the Insertion Point, Scale, and Rotation text boxes.

   Check the Uniform Scale check box to constrain the X, Y, and Z scaling parameters to the same value (which in almost all cases you do).

5. **If you want AutoCAD LT to create a copy of the individual objects in the block instead of a block insert that points to the block definition, click the Explode check box.**
6. **Click OK.**
7. **If you checked Specify On-Screen for the insertion point, scale, or rotation angle, answer the prompts on the command line to specify these parameters.**

After you insert a block, all the objects displayed in the block insert behave as a single object. When you select any object in the block insert, LT highlights all the objects in it.

Another way to insert a block is to drag a DWG file's name from Windows Explorer and drop it anywhere in the current drawing window. AutoCAD LT then prompts you to choose an insertion point and optionally change the default scale factor and rotation angle. Similarly, you can drag a block definition's name from the Blocks section of DesignCenter and drop it into the current drawing window. (Chapter 3 describes DesignCenter.)

If you drag a DWG file's name from Windows Explorer and drop it in the gray area of the AutoCAD LT program window — that is, an area that's not occupied by any currently open drawing — LT opens the drawing for editing instead of inserting it into another drawing.

AutoCAD LT provides one additional way of inserting blocks: the Tool Palettes, which are described in Chapter 2. As is true of using the Tool Palettes for hatching (Chapter 11), you first must create and configure appropriate tools — that is, swatches. The easiest method is right-clicking a drawing in DesignCenter and choosing Create Tool Palette. A new page is added to the Tool Palettes area containing all the block definitions from the drawing that you right-clicked. Simply click and drag a tool to insert its corresponding block into a drawing. As with hatching, you don't get the chance to specify a different insertion scale. You also can't use all of AutoCAD LT's precision tools to specify the insertion point precisely, so you may need to move the block into place after inserting it. I recommend that you first master the other block insertion methods that I describe in this chapter — especially the Insert dialog box and DesignCenter. Then, if you find yourself inserting the same blocks frequently, consider creating a Tool Palette containing them. See "tool palettes, adding drawings from" in the AutoCAD LT online help for more information.

Be careful when inserting one drawing into another. If the host (or parent) drawing and the inserted (or child) drawing have different definitions for layers that share the same name, the objects in the child drawing takes on the layer characteristics of the parent drawing. For example, if you insert a drawing with lines on a layer called Walls that's blue and dashed into a drawing with a layer called Walls that's red and continuous, the inserted lines on the wall layer turn red and continuous after they're inserted. The same rules apply to linetypes, text styles, dimension styles, and block definitions nested inside the drawing you're inserting.

Attributes: Fill-in-the-blank blocks

You may think of attributes as the good (or bad) qualities of your significant other, but in AutoCAD LT, attributes are fill-in-the-blank text fields that you can add to your blocks. When you create a block definition and then insert it several times in a drawing, all the ordinary geometry (lines, circles, regular text strings, and so on) in all the instances are exactly identical. Attributes provide a little more flexibility in the form of text strings that can be different in each block insert.

For example, suppose that you frequently designate parts in your drawings by labeling them with a distinct number or letter in a circle for each part. If you want to create a block for this symbol, you can't simply draw the number or letter as regular text with the mText or TeXt command. If you create a block definition with a regular text object (for example, the letter A), the text string is the same in every instance of the block (always the letter A). That's not much help in distinguishing the parts!

Instead, you create an *attribute definition,* which acts as a placeholder for a text string that can vary each time you insert the block. You include the attribute definition when you create the block definition (as I demonstrate in the "Creating block definitions" section earlier in this chapter). Then, each time you insert the block, AutoCAD LT prompts you to fill in an *attribute value* for each attribute definition.

The AutoCAD LT documentation and dialog boxes often use the term *attribute* to refer indiscriminately to an *attribute definition* or an *attribute value*. I attribute a lot of the confusion about attributes to this sloppiness. Just remember that an attribute definition is the text field or placeholder in the block definition, and an attribute value is the specific text string that you type when you insert the block.

If you've worked with databases, the correspondences in Table 13-1 between AutoCAD LT objects (blocks and attributes) and database terminology may help you understand the concept.

Table 13-1 Attribute and Database Comparison

AutoCAD LT	*Database*
block definition	database table structure
block insert	one record in the table
attribute definition	field name
attribute value	value of the field in one record

Attribute definitions

You use the Attribute Definition dialog box to create attribute definitions (clever, huh?). The steps are similar to creating a text string, except that you must supply a little more information. Create attribute definitions with the following steps:

1. **Change to the layer on which you want to create the attribute definition.**
2. **Choose Draw⇨Block⇨Define Attributes to run the ATTDEF command.**

   The Attribute Definition dialog box appears, as shown in Figure 13-4.

   You rarely need to use any of the Mode settings (Invisible, Constant, Verify, or Preset). Just leave them unchecked. If you're curious about what the modes do, use the dialog box help to find out more.

Figure 13-4: The Attribute Definition dialog box.

3. **In the Attribute area, type the Tag (database field name), Prompt (user prompt), and Value (default value).**

   The Tag can't contain any spaces. The Prompt and Value fields may contain spaces.

4. **Make sure that the Specify On-Screen box in the Insertion Point area is checked.**

   You specify the attribute definition's insertion point in Step 7.

5. **In the Text Options area, specify the Justification, Text Style, Height, and Rotation.**

   The text properties for attribute definitions are the same as those for single-line text objects — see Chapter 9.

6. **Click OK.**

   LT closes the Attribute Definition dialog box and prompts you for an insertion point:

   ```
   Specify start point:
   ```

7. **Specify an insertion point for the attribute definition.**

   An attribute definition's insertion point is like a text string's base point (which I describe in Chapter 9). Remember to use snap, object snap, or another precision tool if you want the attribute value to be located at a precise point.

   LT creates the attribute definition, using the Tag that you typed in Step 3 as its label.

8. **Repeat Steps 1 through 7 for any additional attribute definitions.**

If you need to create a series of similar attribute definitions, create the first one by using Steps 1 through 7. Then copy the first attribute definition and edit the copy with the Properties palette. Alternatively, if you need to create more attribute definitions directly below the first one, select the Align Below Previous Attribute Definition check box in the Attribute Definition dialog box. When you check this box, LT automatically places the new attribute definition below the previously created one.

Block definition containing attribute definitions

After you create one or more attribute definitions — and any other geometry that you want to include in the block — you're ready to create a block definition that contains them. Follow the steps in the section, "Creating block definitions," earlier in this chapter.

At Step 4 in the section, "Creating block definitions," select any attribute definitions first before you select the other geometry. Select each attribute definition one by one (clicking each attribute definition rather than selecting multiple attributes with a selection window), in the order that you want the attribute value prompts to appear in the Enter/Edit Attributes dialog box (see Figure 13-5). If you don't select the attributes one by one, your block and attributes still work, but the order of the attribute prompts in the Enter/Edit Attributes dialog box may not be what you want.

Attributes are particularly useful for creating a title block. Use regular AutoCAD LT commands, including mText or TeXt, to draw the parts of the title block that remain the same in all drawings. Then use the ATTDEF command to create an attribute for each text string in the drawing that might change on different sheets.

Insert a block containing attribute definitions

After you create a block definition that contains attribute definitions, you insert it just like any other block. Follow the steps in the section, "Inserting blocks," earlier in this chapter. At the end of the steps, AutoCAD LT displays the Enter Attributes dialog box, shown in Figure 13-5. The dialog box contains one row for each of the attribute definitions and has any default values filled in. You simply edit the values and then click OK.

The ATTDIA (ATTribute DIAlog box) system variable controls whether AutoCAD LT prompts for attribute values in a dialog box (ATTDIA=1) or at the command line (ATTDIA=0). If you insert a block and see command line prompts for each attribute value, type a value and press Enter for each attribute value. When you return to the command prompt, type **ATTDIA**, press Enter, type **1**, and press Enter again. When you insert blocks with attributes in this drawing in the future, LT displays the Enter Attributes dialog box instead of prompting you at the command line.

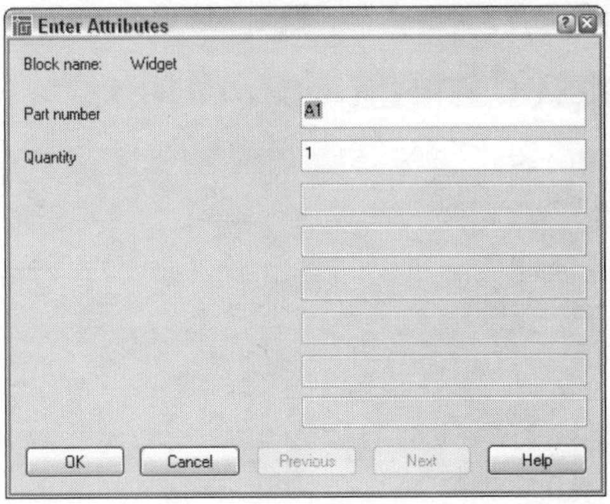

Figure 13-5: The Enter Attributes dialog box.

Edit attribute values

After you insert a block that contains attributes, you can edit the individual attributes in that block insert with the ATTEDIT command (ATTtribute EDIT — nothing to do with changing your long distance company). Choose Modify⇨Object⇨Attribute⇨Single and click any object in the block insert. AutoCAD LT displays the Edit Attributes dialog box with the current attribute values available for editing, as shown in Figure 13-6. This dialog box looks just look the Enter Attributes dialog box described in the preceding paragraph.

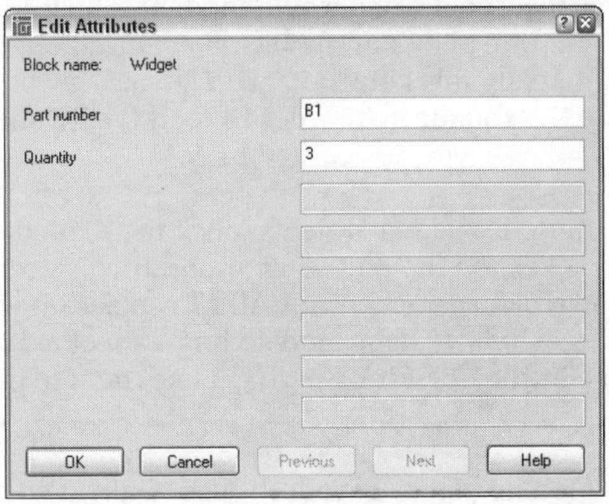

Figure 13-6: The Edit Attributes dialog box — déjà vu all over again!

Many people use attributes in the way I've described so far — as fill-in-the-blank text fields in blocks. But attributes also can serve as data extraction tools. For example, you can export attribute values, such as part numbers and quantities, to a text, spreadsheet, or database file for analysis or reporting. You use the Attribute Extraction dialog box (Tools⇨Attribute Extraction) to perform this feat. To find out more, look up "ATTEXT (ATTribute EXTtract) command" in the AutoCAD LT online help.

Purging unused block definitions

Each block definition slightly increases the size of your DWG file, as do other named objects, such as layers, text styles, and dimension styles. If you delete (or explode) all the block inserts that point to a particular block definition, then that block definition no longer serves any purpose.

Run the PUrge command periodically in each drawing and purge unused block definitions and other named objects. Choose File➪Drawing Utilities➪Purge to display the Purge dialog box (shown in the figure). Click the Purge All button in order to purge all unused named objects in the current drawing.

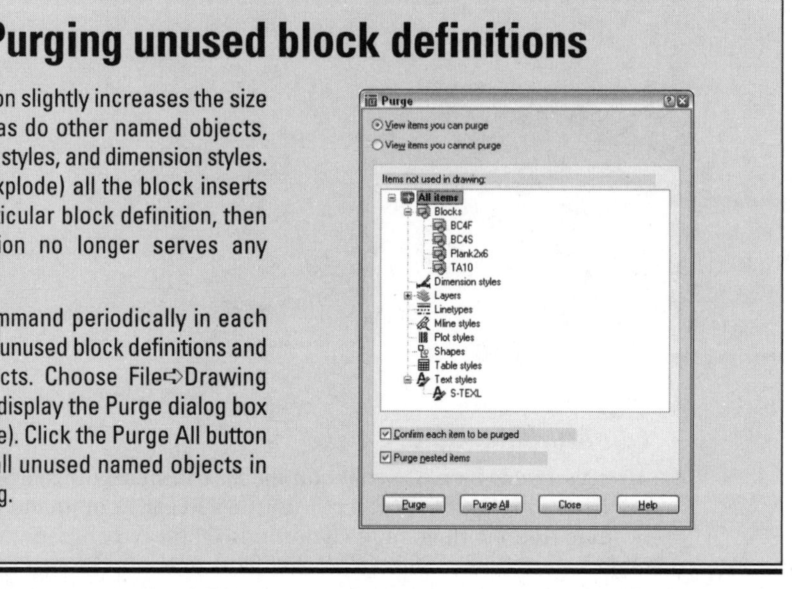

Exploding blocks

The objects in each block insert act like a well-honed marching squadron: If you move or otherwise edit one object in the block insert, all objects move or change in the same way. Usually this cohesion is an advantage, but occasionally you need to break up the squadron in order to modify one object without affecting the others.

To *explode* a block insert into individual objects, click the Explode button (which looks like a firecracker) on the Edit toolbar and then select the block insert. When you explode a block insert, AutoCAD LT replaces it with all the individual objects — lines, polylines, arcs, and so on — specified in the block definition. You then can edit the objects or perhaps use them to make more block definitions.

Don't make a habit of exploding blocks cavalierly, especially if you're working in someone else's drawing and aren't sure why the objects are organized as blocks. Most people use blocks for a reason, and if you go around exploding them left and right, you're likely to be treated the same way that anyone who blows up a lot of things gets treated.

If you explode a block that contains attributes, the attribute *values* change back to attribute *definitions*. This change usually isn't the sort that you want. If you really need to explode the block insert, you probably want to erase the attribute definitions and draw regular text strings in their place.

Going External

In AutoCAD LT, an *xref,* or external reference, is a reference to another, *external* file — one outside the current drawing — that you can make act as though it's part of your drawing. Technically, a reference is simply a pointer from one file to another. The xref is the actual pointer, but many people call the combination of the pointer and the external file the xref.

Drawings that you include as xrefs in other drawings often are called *child* drawings. Drawings that contain pointers to the child drawings are called *parent* drawings. This family terminology gets a little weird when you realize that a child drawing can have lots of parent drawings that refer to it — apparently it's the commune version of family relations. If you find such relationships odd, you can, like the AutoCAD LT online help, refer to the parent drawing as the *host* drawing. I prefer the terms *parent* and *child,* in part because they're easily extendable to describing more complex hierarchies, such as a parent drawing, which xrefs a child drawing, which in turn xrefs a grandchild drawing.

Xrefs have a big advantage over blocks: If you change a child drawing, AutoCAD LT automatically loads the change into all the parent drawings that reference the child drawing.

LT loads all xrefs into the parent drawing each time the parent drawing is opened. If the child drawing has been changed, LT automatically incorporates those changes into the parent drawing.

When you open a drawing containing xrefs, AutoCAD LT displays a little symbol (which looks like papers with a binder clip) on the right end of the status bar. This symbol alerts you to the fact that some of the things you see in the drawing are actually parts of other, xrefed drawings. If an xref changes while you have the parent drawing open (because you or someone else opens and saves the child drawing), the status bar xref symbol displays an `External Reference Files Have Changed` balloon notification. You can use the Reload option in the Xref Manager dialog box to show the updated xrefs. See the "Managing xrefs" section later in this chapter for details.

Another advantage of xrefs over blocks is that their contents aren't stored in your drawing even once. The hard drive storage space taken up by the original drawing (that is, the xref) isn't duplicated, no matter how many parent drawings reference it. This characteristic makes xrefs much more efficient than blocks for larger drawings that are reused several times.

But you can always buy more hard drive space, so the storage issue isn't crucial. The key benefit of xrefs is that they enable you to organize your drawings in a modular way so that changes you make to a single drawing file automatically "ripple through" all the parent drawings to which it's xrefed. This benefit is even greater on larger projects involving multiple drafters, each of whose work may be incorporated in part or in whole in the work of others.

The automatic update feature of xrefs is a big advantage only if you're organized about how you use xrefs. Suppose that an architect creates a plan drawing showing a building's walls and other major features that are common to the architectural, structural, plumbing, and electrical plan drawings. The architect then tells the structural, plumbing, and electrical drafters to xref this background plan into their drawings, so that everyone is working from a consistent and reusable set of common plan elements. If the architect decides to revise the wall locations and updates the xrefed drawing, everyone sees the current wall configuration and can change their drawings. But if the architect absent-mindedly adds architecture-specific objects, such as toilets and furniture, to the xrefed drawing, or shifts all the objects with respect to 0,0, everyone else has problems. If different people in your office share xrefs, create a protocol for who is allowed to modify which file when, and what communication needs to take place after someone modifies a shared xref.

Becoming attached to your xrefs

Attaching an external reference is similar to inserting a block, and almost as easy. Just use the following steps:

1. **Set an appropriate layer current, as described in Chapter 3.**

   I recommend that you insert xrefs on a separate layer from all other objects. ***Note:*** If you freeze the layer an xref is inserted on, the entire xref disappears. (This behavior can be either a handy trick or a nasty surprise.)

2. **Choose Insert⇨Xref Manager from the menu bar to start the XRef command.**

   The Xref Manager dialog box appears (see Figure 13-7).

   Don't choose Insert⇨External Reference. This menu choice jumps ahead to Step 4, which is confusing at this point.

Figure 13-7: The Xref Manager dialog box.

3. **Click Attach.**

   The Select Reference File dialog box appears.

4. **Browse to find the file you want to attach, select it, and then click Open.**

   The External Reference dialog box appears.

5. **Specify the parameters for the xref in the dialog box.**

   Parameters include the insertion point, scaling factors, and rotation angle. You can set these parameters in the dialog box or specify them on-screen, just as you can do when inserting a block, as described earlier in this chapter.

   You can choose the Attachment or Overlay radio button to tell AutoCAD LT how to handle the xref. The choice matters only if you create a drawing that uses xrefs, and then your drawing is in turn used as an xref. Attachment is the default choice, and it means to always include the xrefed file with your drawing when someone else uses your drawing as an xref. Overlay, the other choice, means that you see the xrefed drawing, but someone who xrefs your drawing doesn't see the overlaid file. By choosing Overlay, you can xref in a map, for example, to your drawing of a house, but not have the map show up when someone else xrefs your house drawing. (That person can xref the map, if need be.) I recommend that you use the default Attachment reference type unless you have a specific reason to do otherwise.

   The Path Type drop-down list provides more flexibility in how the xref's path gets stored. See the "Forging an xref path" section later in this chapter for more information. For now, I recommend that you choose Relative Path instead of the default Full Path.

6. **Click OK.**

   The externally referenced file appears in your drawing.

Layer-palooza

When you attach or overlay an xref, AutoCAD LT adds new layers to your current drawing that correspond to the layers in the xrefed DWG file. The new layers are assigned names that combine the drawing name and layer name; for example, if you xref the drawing MYSCREW.DWG, which has the layer names GEOMETRY, TEXT, and so on, the xrefed layers are named MYSCREW|GEOMETRY, MYSCREW|TEXT, and so on. By creating separate layers corresponding to each layer in the xrefed file, AutoCAD LT eliminates the potential problem I warned you about with blocks when layers have the same name but different color or linetype in the two drawings.

LT also creates new linetypes, text styles, dimension styles, and block definitions for each of these items in the xrefed file — for example, MYSCREW|DASHED, MYSCREW|NOTES, MYSCREW|A-DIMS, and MYSCREW|LOGO.

Creating and editing an external reference file

To create a file that you can use as an external reference, just create a drawing and save it (or use the WBLOCK command to create a new DWG from geometry in the current drawing). That's it. You then can create or open another drawing and create an external reference to the previous one. The xrefed drawing appears in your parent drawing as a single object, like a block insert. In other words, if you click any object in the xref, AutoCAD LT selects the entire xref. You can measure or object snap to the xrefed geometry, but you can't modify or delete individual objects in the xref — you open the xref drawing in order to edit its geometry.

Forging an xref path

When you attach an xref, AutoCAD LT by default stores the xref's full path — that is, the drive letter and sequence of folders and subfolders in which the DWG file resides, along with the filename. This default behavior corresponds to the Full Path setting in the Path Type drop-down list. (Figure 13-8 shows the three xref path options.) Full Path works fine as long as you never move files on your hard drive or network and never send your DWG files to anyone else — which is to say, it almost never works fine!

Figure 13-8: Chart your path when you attach an xref.

At the other end of the path spectrum, the No Path option causes LT not to store any path with the xref attachment — only the filename is stored. This option is the easiest and best if the parent and child drawings reside in the same folder.

If you prefer to organize the DWG files for a particular project in more then one folder, then you'll appreciate AutoCAD LT's Relative Path option, shown in Figure 13-8. This option permits xrefing across more complex, hierarchical folder structures, but avoids many of the problems that Full Path can cause. For example, you may have a parent drawing H:\Project-X\Plans\First floor.dwg that xrefs H:\Project-X\Common\Column grid.dwg. If you choose Relative Path, AutoCAD LT stores the xref path as ..\ Common\Column grid.dwg instead of H:\Project-X\Common\Column grid.dwg. Now if you decide to move the \Project-X folder and its subfolders to a different drive (or send them to someone else who doesn't have an H: drive), LT can still find the xrefs.

When you use Relative Path, you see xref paths that include the special codes . and .. (single and double period). The single period means "this parent drawing's folder" and the double period means "the folder above this parent drawing's folder" (in other words, the folder of which the parent drawing's folder is a subfolder).

If all these path options and periods have got you feeling punchy, you can keep your life simple by always keeping parent and child drawings in the same folder and using the No Path option when you attach xrefs.

Managing xrefs

The Xref Manager dialog box includes many more options for managing xrefs after you attach them. Important dialog box options include

- **List of external references:** You can change between a List and a Tree view of your drawing's external references just by clicking the appropriate button at the top of the dialog box. You also can resize the columns by dragging the column dividers or re-sort the list by clicking the column header names, just as in other Windows dialog boxes.
- **Detach:** Completely removes the selected reference to the external file from your drawing.

  Note: Using the Detach button is the *right way* to remove an xref from the current drawing. If you use the ERASE command instead, the xref disappears from the current drawing but LT retains the xref information in the Xref Manager dialog box.
- **Reload:** Causes AutoCAD LT to reread the selected xrefed DWG file from the disk and update your drawing with its latest contents. This feature is handy when you share xrefs on a network and someone has just made changes to a drawing that you've xrefed.

- **Unload:** Makes the selected xref disappear from the on-screen display of your drawing and from any plots you do of it, but retains the pointer and attachment information. Use the Reload button to redisplay an unloaded xref.
- **Bind:** Brings the selected xref into your drawing and makes it a block. You might use this function, for example, to "roll up" a complex set of xrefs into a single archive drawing.

  In many offices, binding xrefs without an acceptable reason for doing so is a crime as heinous as exploding blocks indiscriminately. In both cases, you're eliminating an important data management link. Find out what the policies are in your company. When in doubt, keep yourself out of a bind. And even when you do have a good reason to bind, you generally do it on a copy of the parent drawing.

None of these options affects the xrefed drawing itself; it continues to exist as a separate DWG file. If you need to delete or move the DWG file that the xref refers to, do it in Windows Explorer.

The fact that the xrefed drawing is a separate file is a potential source of problems when you send your drawing to someone else; that someone else needs *all* the files that your drawing depends on, or it is useless to the receiving party. Make sure to include xrefed files in the package with your drawing. See Chapter 15 for the steps.

AutoCAD (but not AutoCAD LT) includes an additional xref feature called *xref clipping*. AutoCAD users can use the XCLIP command to clip an externally referenced file so only part of it appears in the parent drawing. AutoCAD LT doesn't include the XCLIP command, but if you open a drawing containing an xref that was clipped in AutoCAD, the clipped view is preserved.

Blocks, Xrefs, and Drawing Organization

Blocks and xrefs are useful for organizing sets of drawings to use and update repeated elements . It's not always clear, though, when to use blocks and when to use xrefs. Applications for xrefs include

- The parts of a title block that are the same on all sheets in a project
- Reference elements that need to appear in multiple drawings (for example, wall outlines, site topography, column grids)
- Assemblies that are repeated in one or more drawings, especially if the assemblies are likely to change together (for example, repeated framing assemblies, bathroom layouts, modular furniture layouts)

- Pasting up several drawings (for example, details or a couple of plans) onto one plot sheet
- Temporarily attaching a background drawing for reference or tracing

On the other hand, blocks remain useful in simpler circumstances. Situations in which you might stick with a block are

- Components that aren't likely to change.
- Small components.
- A simple assembly that's used repeatedly, but in only one drawing.
- When you want to include *attributes* (variable text fields) that you can fill in each time you insert a block. Blocks let you include attribute definitions; xrefs don't.

Everyone in a company or workgroup needs to aim for consistency in when and how they use blocks and xrefs. Check whether guidelines exist for using blocks and xrefs in your office. If so, follow them; if not, developing some guidelines is a good idea. Chapter 14 discusses how to start such guidelines.

LT Is No Raster Master

A *raster* file (also called a *bitmap* file) stores a graphical image as a series of dots. Raster files are good for storing photographs, logos, and other images, whereas CAD *vector* files are good for storing geometrical objects, such as lines and arcs, along with text and other annotations for describing the geometry.

Sometimes combining raster images with CAD vector files is handy. AutoCAD (but not AutoCAD LT) includes another xref-like feature: the ability to attach raster images to drawings. This feature is useful for adding a raster logo to a drawing title block or placing a photographed map or scene behind a drawing.

When AutoCAD users attach a raster file, they do so in a way that's much like attaching an external reference. The raster image isn't stored with the drawing file; instead, AutoCAD establishes a reference to the raster image file from within the drawing. Popular raster image file formats include TIF, JPG, GIF, and BMP.

AutoCAD LT can open, view, and plot drawings containing attached raster images, but LT can't do the attaching. Raster masters require full AutoCAD. However, you can view a list of attached raster images and unload and reload them by using the AutoCAD LT IMage command, which opens the LT Image Manager dialog box.

Chapter 14

CAD Standards Rule

In This Chapter

- Making the case for CAD standards
- Choosing from existing standards
- Rolling your own standards
- Taking advantage of standards tools

If you've ever worked with other people to create a multichapter, visually complex, frequently updated text document, then you probably understand the importance of coordinating how everyone works on the parts of the document. Even if you're someone who churns out documents from your one-person office or lonely cubicle, you probably try to ensure a reasonably consistent look and feel in similar documents. You employ consistent fonts, the same company logo, and the same paper size in most documents — or if you don't, you probably at least think that you should!

CAD exacts similar demands for reasonable consistency, only more so:

- You take pride in the clarity and consistency of your drawings. Sloppy drawings with randomly varying text heights and lineweights don't reflect well on you, and they also make your drawings harder to read.
- CAD drawings that don't conform with some logically consistent scheme usually are harder for you to edit and to reuse on other projects, and present the same problems for others with whom you work.

This stuff is important enough in CAD that it has a special name: *CAD standards.* Those people compulsive enough to fret about it all the time and sadistic enough to impose their fretting on others also have a special name: *CAD managers.* This chapter doesn't turn you into a CAD manager — a reassurance you're probably grateful for — but it does introduce the most important CAD standards issues. This chapter also suggests some ways to come up with your own simple CAD standards, in case you're going it alone and don't have the benefit of a ready-made company or project CAD standards document to guide you. The chapter ends with an overview of AutoCAD LT tools that can help you comply with and check conformity to CAD standards.

Why CAD Standards?

Throughout this book, I emphasize things like setting up your drawings properly, drawing objects on appropriate and consistent layers, and specifying suitable text fonts and heights. These practices amount to conforming to a CAD standard.

You need to do these things if you work with or exchange drawings with others. If you don't, several bad things can happen. You're pegged as a clueless newbie by experienced drafters who understand the importance of CAD consistency. Even if your ego can handle the contempt, you make everyone's work slower and more difficult. And if the project has electronic drawing submittal requirements, you may find that your client rejects your DWG files and demands that you make them conform to the CAD standards in the contract.

Even if you work solo and don't have any particular requirements imposed from outside, your own work can go more smoothly and look better if you adhere to a reasonably consistent way of doing things in AutoCAD LT. You certainly find plotting easier and more predictable.

CAD standards originally grew out of a desire to achieve a graphical consistency on the plotted drawings that mirrored the graphical consistency on hand-drafted drawings. Before the days of CAD, most companies had manual drafting standards that specified standard lettering (text) sizes, dimension appearance, symbol shapes, and so on. Sometimes these standards were based on standard industry reference books, such as the *Architectural Graphic Standards*.

As CAD users became more sophisticated, they realized that CAD standards needed to incorporate more than just the look of the resulting plot. CAD drawings contain a lot more organizational depth than printed drawings — layers, screen colors, blocks, xrefs, text and dimension styles, and the like. If these things aren't subject to a modicum of standardization, people who work on the same drawings or projects are likely to end up stumbling over — or throwing things at — one another. And if you work alone, standardization keeps you from stumbling over *yourself* — consistency enables you to know what to predict when you open, edit, and plot your drawings.

In short, the first job of CAD standards is to impose some graphical consistency on plotted output. CAD standards also encourage consistency in the way that people create, assign properties to, organize, and display objects in the CAD file.

The aesthetics of CAD

Manual drafting veterans frequently complain that CAD drawings don't look as good as the drawings that they used to create by hand. "Too 'flat,' too cartoonish, and inconsistent" are some of the refrains that you hear. These complaints are not just the whining of old-timers. Good manual drafters were justifiably proud of the appearance of their drawings. They focused on making the finished blueline prints look sharp and read well.

When computers and CAD software got into the act, focusing on the screen image and paying less attention to the plotted output became easy for CAD drafters. In the early days, CAD users struggled with a new way of making drawings and didn't have as much time to make them look good. By the time that CAD became commonplace, a new crop of CAD users had grown up without the benefit of learning how to make good-looking drawings on paper.

There's no reason that CAD drawings can't look as good as manual drawings. It's a matter of understanding the look that you're after and caring enough to want to achieve it. If you see some especially clear and elegant printed drawings, find out who drew them and take that person out to lunch. You'll probably find some techniques that you can translate into making better CAD drawings. You may also gain new respect for the skills of those who made handsome and functional drawings with the simplest of tools.

Which CAD Standards?

If CAD standards are as important as I claim, you may expect that industries would've settled on a standardized way of doing things. No such luck. Although the manual drafting conventions in many professions have carried over to some degree into CAD, a lot of the things that need standardization have been left to the imagination of individual companies, departments, or people. For example, you find that different companies usually name layers differently and employ different schemes for mapping object screen color to plotted lineweight (see Chapter 12). In particularly disorganized companies, you find that different drafters use different layers and color-to-lineweight. And in the worst cases, the same drafter does these things differently in different drawings — or even in the same drawing!

As you can imagine, this proliferation of nonstandard standards makes sharing and reusing parts of CAD drawings a lot more difficult. You can at least minimize the pain within your own office by conforming to any existing CAD standards or, if there aren't any, by developing some. (Later in this chapter, I give some suggestions for how to get started.)

Even if you're lucky or perseverant enough to get a well-rounded set of CAD standards in your office, that may not be the end of it. CAD-savvy people from different companies who collaborate on projects often want to minimize the pain of inconsistency during drawing exchange. Although each company may have its own CAD standards house in order, there's no way that all those standards are the same. Thus, one or more companies (often the lead consultant) may impose a set of *project-specific* CAD standards. Project-specific standards don't necessarily need to be as detailed as a full-blown company CAD standards document, but depending on the project and the person who created the project-specific CAD standards, they might be.

The result of this confusing muddle of industry practices, company CAD standards, and project-specific CAD standards is that you find yourself switching among different standards as you work on different projects. Before you start making drawings, find out whether any particular CAD standards apply. To start off conforming to those standards is a lot easier than to fix nonconforming drawings later.

Industry standards

Professional, trade, and governmental groups in some industries have made an attempt to promulgate CAD standards for the benefit of everyone in the industry. For example, the American Institute of Architects (AIA), together with several professional engineering associations, published a *CAD Layer Guidelines* document, which has become part of a so-called National CAD Standard that's now promulgated by the U.S. government's National Institute of Building Sciences, or NIBS (see `www.nationalcadstandard.org`). The International Organization for Standardization, or ISO (the acronym reflects the French ordering of the words), publishes ISO standards document 13567 (see `www.iso.org`). This document, which comes in no fewer than three parts, attempts to provide a framework for CAD layer standards in the building design industries throughout the world.

These documents may be useful to you in your search for standards, but they aren't a panacea. The majority of CAD-using companies has ignored officially promulgated CAD standards because these companies developed their own standards and practices years ago and are loath to change. That doesn't mean you can't use the officially promulgated standards, but they don't suddenly make you a part of some mythical CAD standards mainstream. Also, practical implementation of most official CAD standards in a specific company requires a generous amount of clarification, modification, and additional documentation. In other words, you don't just buy the document and then get to work; you need to tailor it to your company and projects. And finally, some of these officially promulgated CAD standards documents are shockingly expensive. Apparently these organizations haven't found that the way to make something popular is to post it on the Web for free!

What Needs to Be Standardized?

If you are in a company or on a project without any CAD standards, put together at least a minimal set of guidelines. First, impose some consistency on *plotted appearance* and *use of layers*. If you make a few rules for yourself before you start, you end up with drawings that are more professional looking and easier to edit — and more likely to be useful on future projects.

A spreadsheet or word processing program is great for documenting your CAD standards decisions as they firm up. Many CAD standards components work best as tabular lists of layers, colors, and so forth. (See Tables 14-1 and 14-2 in this chapter for examples.) Use the cells in a spreadsheet or the tables feature in a word processor to organize your CAD standards documentation.

Before you start, make sure that you're familiar with managing properties (Chapter 3) and plotstyles (Chapter 12). You need a good understanding to make intelligent decisions about your plotting and layer standards. (If you want to make *unintelligent* decisions, don't worry about those chapters!)

Plotting

If you plan to use color-dependent plotstyles (most people do), develop a color-to-lineweight plotting chart like Table 14-1. If you choose the more logical but lonelier named plotstyles approach, make a similar chart, with plotstyle names instead of color in the first column. (See Chapter 12 for information about color-dependent and named plotstyles.) After you complete a plotting chart, create a plotstyle table (CBT file for color-dependent plotstyles or STB file for named plotstyles), as described in Chapter 12.

Your life is easier — and your plotting chart much shorter — if you limit yourself to a small portion of the 255 colors in the AutoCAD Color Index (ACI). The first nine colors work well for many people.

If your work requires *screened* (shaded or faded-out) lines, extend the plotting chart to include a couple of additional AutoCAD colors. For each color, list the plotted lineweight and screen percentage ranging from 0% for invisible to 100% for solid black.

Table 14-1 Sample Color-to-Lineweight Plotting Chart

AutoCAD Color	*Plotted Lineweight*
1 (red)	0.15 mm
2 (yellow)	0.20 mm
3 (green)	0.25 mm
4 (cyan)	0.30 mm
5 (blue)	0.35 mm
6 (magenta)	0.40 mm
7 (white/black)	0.50 mm
8 (dark gray)	0.10 mm
9 (light gray)	0.70 mm

Layers

After you work out your plotting conventions, you're ready to develop a chart of layers. A chart of layers takes more thought and work, and you probably revise it more frequently than the plotting chart. Find a typical drawing from your office or industry and identify the things you'll draw — such as walls, text, dimensions, and hatching. Then decide how you want to parse those objects onto different layers (see Chapter 3). Here are some guidelines:

- **Objects that you want to plot with different lineweights go on different layers.** Assign each layer an appropriate color, based on how you want the objects to appear on-screen and on plots. If you're using object lineweights (Chapter 3) or named plotstyles (Chapter 12), include a column for these settings in your chart. In all cases, let the objects inherit these properties from the layer.
- **Objects whose visibility you want to control separately go on different layers.** Turn off or freeze a layer in order to make the objects on that layer, and only the objects on that layer, disappear temporarily.
- **Objects that represent significantly different kinds of things in the real world go on different layers.** For example, doors go on different layers from walls in an architectural floor plan.

As you make your layer decisions, you develop a layer chart that resembles Table 14-2. If you use named plotstyles instead of color-dependent plotstyles, add a Plot Style column to the chart.

Table 14-2 Sample Layer Chart

Layer Name	*Color*	*Linetype*	*Use*
Wall	5	Continuous	Walls
Wall-Belo	3	Dashed	Walls below (shown dashed)
Cols	6	Continuous	Columns
Door	4	Continuous	Doors
Text	3	Continuous	Regular note text
Text-Bold	7	Continuous	Large/bold text
Dims	2	Continuous	Dimensions
Patt	1	Continuous	Hatch patterns
Cntr	1	Center	Centerlines
Symb	2	Continuous	Annotational symbols
Nplt	8	Continuous	Nonplotting information

The layer chart in Table 14-2 is simpler than the layer systems used by experienced drafters in most companies. The layer names in the table are based on names in the *AIA CAD Layer Guidelines* document mentioned in the "Industry standards" sidebar. That document recommends adding a discipline-specific prefix to each layer name: A-Walls for walls drawn by the architectural team, S-Walls for walls drawn by the structural team, and so on.

Other stuff

The following settings and procedures deserve some consistency, too:

- **Text styles:** Decide on text fonts and heights and use them consistently. (See Chapter 9 for more information.)

Manual CAD drafting standards often specify a minimum text height of ⅛ inch or 3 mm, because hand-lettered text smaller than that becomes difficult to read, especially on half-size prints. Plotted 3⁄32 inch or 2.5 mm CAD text is quite legible, but half-size plots with these smaller text heights can result in text that's on the margin of legibility. Text legibility on half-size — or smaller — plots depends on the plotter resolution, the lineweight assigned to the text, and the condition of your eyes. Test before you commit to using smaller text heights, or use ⅛ inch or 3 mm as a minimum.

- **Dimension styles:** Create a dimension style that reflects your preferred look and feel. (See Chapter 10.)
- **Hatch patterns:** Choose the hatch patterns that you need and decide on an appropriate scale and angle for each. (See Chapter 11.)
- **Drawing setup and organization:** Set up all the drawings on a project in the same way, and use sheet sets, blocks, and xrefs in a consistent fashion.

After you make standards, create a simple test drawing and make sure that the plotted results are what you want. You'll undoubtedly revise and extend your standards as you go, especially on your first few projects. In time, you find a set of standards that work for you.

Tools to Make Standards Easier

Most of the hard CAD standards work happens outside of AutoCAD LT — thinking, deciding, documenting, revising, and so on. But ultimately you need to translate that work into your CAD practice, and LT includes a couple of tools to make the job easier.

Template drawings, or DWT files, provide a straightforward way to create new drawings that start with a standard set of layers, text styles, dimension styles, and other named objects. (Chapter 3 describes named objects.) After you make your main CAD standards decisions, create one or more template drawings that contain the layers and other objects that you're likely to need in most drawings. Chapter 5 describes template files in detail and shows you how to create and use them.

DesignCenter, described in Chapter 3, is a great tool for copying layers, text styles, dimension styles, block definitions, and other named objects from one drawing to another. If you or someone else has created one drawing with a reasonably standardized set of layers, text styles, or whatever, open DesignCenter and copy its named objects into other drawings.

As Chapter 3 warns, DesignCenter does not change named objects (layers, text styles, and so on) whose names match those of the objects you're copying. So if you copy layers from a drawing called Good_standards.dwg to a drawing called No_standards.dwg, and No_standards.dwg already contains some of the layers that you're trying to copy (but with different color or other settings), DesignCenter doesn't change the settings for the settings in No_standards.dwg. In other words, DesignCenter can't help you correct non-standard settings; it only helps you create new named objects whose settings match those of the named objects in another drawing.

AutoCAD LT's Tool Palettes, described in Chapter 2, also can help with CAD standards. You can add your standard hatch patterns and blocks (for example, drafting symbols) to palette tabs in order to make dragging them into any drawing easy. Look up "Tool Palettes" in the AutoCAD LT online help for more information and instructions on how to create custom tool palettes.

If your company does have CAD standards in place, someone may have created custom tools to help you comply with those standards. For example, the CAD manager may have put together template drawings with customized settings or block libraries of standard symbols. CAD managers sometimes create custom menu choices, scripts, or utility programs for the company's CAD standards.

Chapter 15

AutoCAD LT Meets the Internet

In This Chapter

- Understanding AutoCAD LT Internet features
- Exchanging drawing files via e-mail and FTP
- Using the Reference Manager to view and fix file dependencies
- Using the Drawing Web Format and ePlot
- Making multiple Web and paper plots with PUBLISH
- Viewing and plotting drawings without AutoCAD or LT
- Opening password-protected drawings

Unless you've been living under a rock for the past five years, you know that the Internet is causing major changes in the way that people work. (And even if you have been living under a rock, someone probably is offering broadband service to it by now!) Because of the Net, most of us communicate differently, exchange files more rapidly, and fill out express delivery forms less frequently.

AutoCAD users were among the online pioneers, well before the Internet burst onto the public scene. Despite this early adoption, the CAD world has been relatively slow to take the full-immersion Internet plunge. Exchanging drawings via e-mail and using the World Wide Web for CAD software research and support are pretty common nowadays. But finding drawings incorporated into Web pages or Web-centric CAD applications is still uncommon. That's partly because CAD drafters have traditionally been somewhat insulated from the general computing community — they spend most of their time cranking out drawings and leave all that new-fangled Web design stuff to people who don't have real work to get done, thank you very much! Even the more forward-thinking CAD users tend to display a healthy, and often reasonable, skepticism about whether any particular innovation can help with the pressing job of getting drawings finished on deadline.

This chapter shows you how — and when — to use AutoCAD LT's Internet features. I also cover how the Internet features can connect with traditional CAD tasks, such as plotting. The emphasis of this chapter is on useful, no-nonsense ways of taking advantage of the Internet in your CAD work.

Your ticket to most of the features described in this chapter is an account with an Internet service provider (ISP). You probably already have Internet access through work or a private ISP account — or both; but if not, now is the time to get connected. Other CAD users expect to be able to send drawings to you and receive them from you via e-mail. Software companies, including Autodesk, expect you to have Web access in order to download software updates and support information. Dialup modem access to the Internet is acceptable, but if you're doing much drawing exchange or want to download software updates without waiting all day, consider springing for broadband access, such as DSL (Digital Subscriber Line) or cable modem.

The Internet and LT: An Overview

As with all things Internet-y, AutoCAD LT 2005's Internet features are a hodgepodge of the genuinely useful, the interesting but still somewhat immature or difficult to use, and the downright foolish. I steer you toward features and techniques that are reliable and widely used today. I warn you about "stupid pet trick" features that might impress a 12-year-old computer geek but leave your project leader wondering what planet you come from. On the other hand, a few of today's questionable features are likely to become the reliable, commonplace ones of tomorrow. I give you enough context to see how everything works and where it may lead. Table 15-1 summarizes the AutoCAD LT 2005 Internet features and tells you where in this book to find more information.

Table 15-1 AutoCAD LT 2005 Internet Features

Feature	*Description*	*Comments*	*Where You Can Find More Info*
ETRANSMIT command	Package DWG files for sending via e-mail mail or FTP or posting on the Web	Useful to most people	"Send it with ETRANSMIT" in this chapter
File navigation dialog box	Can save to and open from Web and FTP sites	Potentially useful for people who routinely work with files on Web or FTP sites	Chapter 2

Feature	*Description*	*Comments*	*Where You Can Find More Info*
DWF files	A lightweight drawing file format for posting drawings on the Web or sharing them with people who don't have AutoCAD or LT	The recipient must have Autodesk DWF Viewer installed; potentially useful for sharing drawings with people who don't have AutoCAD or LT	"Drawing Web Format — Not Just for the Web" in this chapter
PUBLISH command	Create DWF files, plot (PLT) files, or paper plots in batches	Can help automate the traditional plotting procedure; if DWF files ever catch on, can streamline their creation	"Making DWFs (or Plots) with PUBLISH" in this chapter
Publish to Web	A wizard that builds and publishes a Web page containing drawings	Like most wizards, fairly easy to use, but limited; possibly useful as a quick-and-dirty Web publishing approach	"PUBLISHTOWEB command" in the AutoCAD LT online help
Insert hyperlink	Add hyperlinks to objects in drawings	Of questionable use, except in specialized applications	"Hand-y objects" in this chapter
Password protection	Requires a password in order to open a drawing	Useful for limiting access to sensitive DWG or DWF files; LT can't password protect drawings but does allow you to open drawings that an AutoCAD user password protected (if you know the password, of course)	"The Drawing Protection Racket" in this chapter
Digital signatures	Provide electronic confirmation that someone has approved a particular version of a particular drawing	Requires an account with a digital certificate provider; new technology, so look before you leap — and talk to your attorney first	"Digital signatures, learning more about" in the AutoCAD LT online help

Sending Strategies

E-mail and FTP (File Transfer Protocol) have largely replaced blueline prints, overnight delivery, floppies, and higher capacity disks as the standard means of exchanging drawings. Some companies even use specially designed Web-based services, such as Autodesk's Buzzsaw, as a repository for project drawings from all the companies working on a particular project. Whether you're exchanging drawings in order to reuse CAD objects or simply to make hard-copy plots of someone else's drawings, you need to be comfortable sending and receiving drawings electronically.

Sending and receiving DWG files doesn't differ much from sending and receiving other kinds of files, except for the following:

- **DWG files tend to be bigger than word processing documents and spreadsheets.** Consequently, you may need to invest in a faster Internet connection, such as cable or DSL.
- **You can easily forget to include all the dependent files.** I tell you in the next section how to make sure that you send all the necessary files — and how to pester the people who don't send you all their necessary files.
- **It's often not completely obvious how to plot what you receive.** Read Chapter 12 and the section, "Bad reception?" in this chapter to solve plotting puzzles.

Whenever you send DWG files together, follow the Golden Exchange Rule: "Send files unto others as you would have them sent unto you." That means sending all the dependent files along with the main DWG files, sending plotting support files (CTB or STB files — see Chapter 12), and including a description of what you're sending. And ask the recipient to try opening the drawings you send them right away, so you both have more time to respond if there's any problem.

Send it with ETRANSMIT

Many people naively assume that an AutoCAD drawing is always contained in a single DWG file, but that's often not the case. Each drawing file created in AutoCAD or LT can contain references to other kinds of files, the most important of which I describe in Table 15-2. Thus, before you start exchanging drawings via e-mail or FTP, you need to assemble the drawings with all their dependent files.

Table 15-2 Other Kinds of Files that DWG Files Commonly Reference

Description	*File Types*	*Consequences if Missing*	*Where the Use of These File Types Is Explained*
Custom font files	SHX, TTF	AutoCAD or LT substitutes another font	Chapter 9
Other drawings	DWG (xrefs)	Stuff in the main drawing disappears	Chapter 13
Raster graphics files	JPG, PCX, TIF, and so on	Stuff in the drawing disappears	Chapter 13
Plotstyle tables	CTB, STB	Lineweights and other plotted effects don't look right	Chapter 12

As you can see from the table, the consequences of not including a custom font aren't that dire: The recipient still sees your text, but the font is different. Of course, the new font may look odd or cause text spacing problems within the drawing. If, on the other hand, you forget to send xrefs or raster graphics that are attached to your main drawing, the objects contained on those attached files simply are gone when the recipient opens your drawing. Not good!

Table 15-2 doesn't exhaust the types of files that your DWG files might refer to. Custom plotter settings (such as custom paper sizes) may reside in PC3 or PMP files. An FMP file controls some aspects of font mapping. (Like so much else in AutoCAD LT, the tools and rules for mapping missing fonts are flexible but somewhat complicated. Look up the "FONTALT" and "FONTMAP" system variables in the AutoCAD LT online help for detailed information.)

Rapid eTransmit

Fortunately, the AutoCAD LT ETRANSMIT command pulls together all the files that your main DWG file depends on. Follow these steps to assemble a drawing with all its dependent files with ETRANSMIT.

1. **Open the drawing that you want to run ETRANSMIT on.**

   If the drawing is already open, save it. ETRANSMIT requires that you save any changes to the drawing before proceeding.

2. **Choose File⇨eTransmit.**

   The Create Transmittal dialog box appears, as shown in Figure 15-1.

Figure 15-1: Rapid eTransmit.

3. **On the Files Tree or Files Table tab, remove the check mark next to any file that you want ETRANMSIT *not* to copy with the main drawing.**

   Unless you have assigned custom font mapping, you can omit the Aclt.fmp file.

4. **Select a transmittal setup from the list.**

   Transmittal setups are new in AutoCAD LT 2005. They contain settings that control how ETRANSMIT processes the drawings and creates the transmittal package. Click the Transmittal Setups button to create new or modify existing setups. The default Standard transmittal setup works fine for many purposes, except that you probably want to turn on the Include Fonts setting, as described in the next paragraph. In any case, you view the settings (click the Modify button) just to see what options you can change if you need to later.

   If you want ETRANSMIT to include SHX and TTF font files, including any custom fonts that you're using, you must select the Include Fonts setting in the transmittal setup. (Click Transmittal Setups, click Modify, and check the Include Fonts box.) Note, however, that many SHX and TTF files are custom fonts, which work like licensed software. Sending them to others is just like sharing your AutoCAD LT program CD with others. No, I don't mean that it's easy and fun; I mean that it's illegal and unethical. Before you send a custom font file to someone else, find out what the licensing restrictions are on the font and be prepared to work within them.

5. **Click the View Report button.**

   You see a report listing the files that ETRANSMIT will copy, along with warnings about any files that it can't locate.

6. **Review the report and make sure that ETRANSMIT finds all the files.**

7. **Click OK.**

   ETRANMSIT displays a file dialog box so that you can specify the name and location of the transmittal package (which is a ZIP file by default).

8. **Click Save.**

   ETRANSMIT creates the transmittal package (which is a ZIP file by default).

Although AutoCAD LT 2005 automatically compresses its DWG files, zipping files manages to compress them even further (about 20 percent more, in my experience). More important, zipping creates a single, tidy package of all your DWG, raster image, plotstyle table, and font files. No one likes to receive an e-mail message carrying an endless cargo of attached files. Do everyone a favor: be hip and zip.

The only downside to zipping is that creating a zipped file and extracting files from it require a separate zip/unzip program. Several good shareware utilities are available, including WinZip (`www.winzip.com`).

Transmitting multiple drawings

In many cases, you want to send more than one drawing to a recipient. In this situation, you can open each drawing and run ETRANSMIT on each in turn. (In the transmittal setup, set Transmittal Package Type to Folder (Set of Files), specify the Transmittal File Folder to copy the files to, and use Transmittal Options to control whether the files copy to one or more than one folder.) When you process all the drawings, use a program like WinZip to package the files into a single zipped file before sending it.

FTP for you and me

FTP, or *File Transfer Protocol,* is a simple but robust protocol for copying files over the Internet. A computer that's connected to the Internet can act as an FTP *server,* which means that part of its hard drive is accessible over the Internet. The person who configures the FTP server can place restrictions so that only people who enter a particular logon name and password can see and download files. FTP overcomes the file size limitations that often occur with e-mail.

Because of all these FTP benefits, it's increasingly common for people at larger companies to place drawing files on their company's FTP site and tell you to go get them. This approach relieves them of having to e-mail you the files, and relieves you of waiting for that 10MB e-mail download when you least expect it.

In most cases, the person making the files available to you via FTP sends you a Uniform Resource Locator (URL) that looks like a Web page address, except that it starts with `FTP://` instead of `HTTP://`. If you open your Web browser and enter the FTP URL into the address field, the browser connects to the FTP site, asks you for a location and name to use for the file when it copies to your system, and begins downloading the file. If the FTP site uses password protection, you have to enter a logon name and password first.

If you want fancier FTP download options, you can use an FTP utility program such as WS_FTP (`www.ipswitch.com`).

Even if you work for a small company, you may be able to post files on your ISP's FTP server in order to make them available to others. Check with your ISP to find out whether you can do it and, if so, what the procedures are.

FTP transfers are more prone to user confusion problems than are e-mail files, especially if the recipient hasn't used FTP before. For example, it's common for the person posting the files to forget to tell the recipient the logon name and password, or for the recipient not to have an FTP program — or to not know how to use it. Check with your recipient the first couple of times you use FTP to transfer files to make sure they got the files successfully — and don't be surprised if they ask you to use e-mail or overnight delivery instead.

Bad reception?

Other sections in this chapter focus on sending files to others. What happens when you're on the receiving end? Not everyone is as conscientious as you are about following the Golden Exchange Rule. You'll receive drawings with missing dependent files and no information or support files for plotting.

When you receive an e-mail message or FTP download containing drawings (zipped, I hope!), copy the file to a new folder on your hard drive or a network disk and unzip the files.

Check at least a few of the drawings in the package to make sure that the sender included all the xrefs, fonts, and raster image files. You can perform this check by opening each main drawing in that folder. After you open each file, press the F2 key to view the command line window, and look for missing font and xref error messages of the following sort:

```
Substituting [simplex.shx] for [helv.shx].
Resolve Xref "GRID": C:\Here\There\Nowhere\grid.dwg
Can't find C:\Here\There\Nowhere\grid.dwg
```

A `Substituting...` message indicates that AutoCAD LT couldn't find a font and is substituting a different font for it. A `Can't find...` message indicates that LT couldn't locate an xref. Any missing raster files appear as rectangular boxes with the names of the image files inside the rectangles. Alternatively, you can open the Xref Manager or Image Manager dialog box, which reveals any missing xref or raster image files. (See Chapter 13 for details.)

Write down each missing file and then tell the sender to get on the ball and send you the missing pieces. While you're at it, tell that person to buy this book and read this chapter!

Press the F2 key after opening *any* drawing that you didn't create so that you know right away if any fonts and xrefs are missing.

If you receive drawings with custom TrueType font files (files whose extensions are TTF), you must install those files before Windows and AutoCAD LT recognizes them. Choose Start⇨Settings⇨Control Panel. (In Windows XP, choose Start⇨Control Panel and then click the Switch to Classic View link in order to see the Fonts applet.) Double-click the Fonts icon to open the Fonts window, and then choose File⇨Install New Font.

Drawing Web Format — Not Just for the Web

In a previous section of this chapter, I explain how you can exchange drawings via e-mail and FTP. That's all the Internet connectivity that many AutoCAD and LT users need, but if you're curious about connecting drawings to the Web or sharing drawings with people who don't have AutoCAD or LT, this section is for you.

The AutoCAD and AutoCAD LT Web features are built on two pieces of technology:

- A special lightweight drawing format called DWF that Autodesk originally developed especially for putting drawings on the Web.
- A free program from Autodesk called Autodesk DWF Viewer that enables anyone to view and print DWF files without having AutoCAD.

All about DWF

The AutoCAD DWG format works well for storing drawing information on local and network disks, but the high precision and large number of object properties that AutoCAD and LT use make for comparatively large files.

To overcome this size problem and encourage people to publish drawings on the Web, Autodesk developed an alternative lightweight vector format for representing AutoCAD drawings: DWF (Design Web Format). A DWF file is a more compact representation of a DWG file. DWF uses less space — and less transfer time over the Web and e-mail — because it's less precise and doesn't have all the information that's in the DWG file.

DWF hasn't exactly taken the Web by storm; Autodesk has gradually recast it as a format for electronic plotting, or *ePlotting*, including for sharing drawings with people who don't have AutoCAD or LT. In other words, Autodesk is pushing DWF as a CAD analogue to Adobe's PDF (Portable Document Format). Thus you can create DWF files from your drawings and send the DWFs to people who don't have AutoCAD or LT. Your recipients can view and plot the DWF files after they download the free Autodesk DWF Viewer program, which is available on the Autodesk Web site, `www.autodesk.com`.

ePlot, not replot

A DWF file captures a single, plotted view of your drawing, so, unlike a DWG file, it can provide a relatively unambiguous snapshot of what you want to see on paper. With a DWG file, on the other hand, you have to provide lots of information to other people — drawing view, scale, plotstyle settings, and so on — in order for them to get the same plotting results that you did.

Potential ePlotting scenarios include

- Architects and other consultants on a building project periodically upload DWF files to the project Web site. Architects and engineers with some minimal CAD knowledge can review the drawings on-screen and create their own hard-copy plots, if necessary. Principals and clients who don't want anything to do with CAD, or even with computers, can have their secretaries or other employees create hard-copy plots for them to examine.
- When Internet-savvy people need hard-copy prints of your drawings, you e-mail a zipped file containing DWF files, along with the URL for Autodesk DWF Viewer and simple instructions for creating plots from the DWF files. (Be ready to walk them through the process by phone the first time or two to reduce anxiety on everyone's part.)
- A CAD plotting service bureau encourages its customers to send DWF files instead of DWG files for plotting. The DWF files are much smaller and require less intervention on the part of the service bureau's employees.

The ePlot concept debuted in AutoCAD and LT 2000 and hasn't yet caught on in a big way. Autodesk hopes to establish ePlot and the DWF format as a standard for CAD documents similar to what Adobe's PDF has become for word processing documents. It remains to be seen whether ePlotting will become a popular way to generate hard-copy output. In particular, many people outside of CAD-using companies don't have access to large-format plotters. They're limited to 8½-x-11-inch — or, at best, 11-x-17-inch — reduced-size check plots. Consequently, many people can't plot your DWF files to scale, and may not plot them large enough to read everything.

Don't be afraid to try ePlotting with colleagues inside or outside your company, but don't become too dependent on it until you see whether the rest of the CAD world shares your enthusiasm. Otherwise, you risk becoming the only one who's willing to use your DWF files for plotting — in which case the next version of the feature will be called mePlot.

AutoCAD LT 2005 uses version 6 of the DWF format, which Autodesk introduced with AutoCAD and LT 2004. (The DWF format changes at least as often as the DWG format, as Autodesk adds new features to AutoCAD and new Design Web Format capabilities.) The most important new feature in DWF 6 is multiple sheets in a single DWF file, as shown in Figure 15-2. It's like stapling together a set of drawings, except that you never have to worry about your stapler being empty.

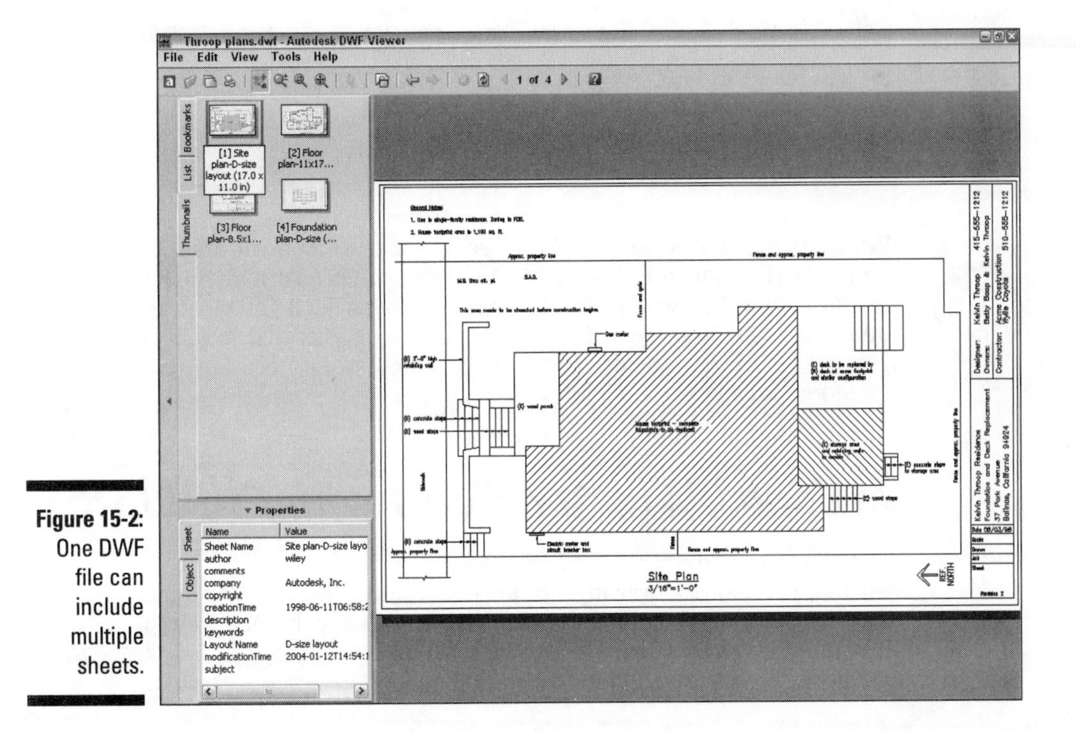

Figure 15-2: One DWF file can include multiple sheets.

Making DWFs with ePlot

As I describe in the previous section, AutoCAD LT treats DWF files like electronic plots, or ePlots. You create a DWF file from the current drawing just as if you're plotting it to a piece of paper, as I describe in Chapter 12. The only difference is that, in the Plot dialog box's Printer/Plotter area, you choose the plotter configuration named `DWF6 ePlot.pc3`, as shown in Figure 15-3. When you do so, AutoCAD LT automatically turns on the Plot to File setting. Then when you click OK to generate the ePlot, LT displays a file dialog box in which you specify a filename and location for the DWF file that gets created. The location can be a folder on a hard drive or a Web server.

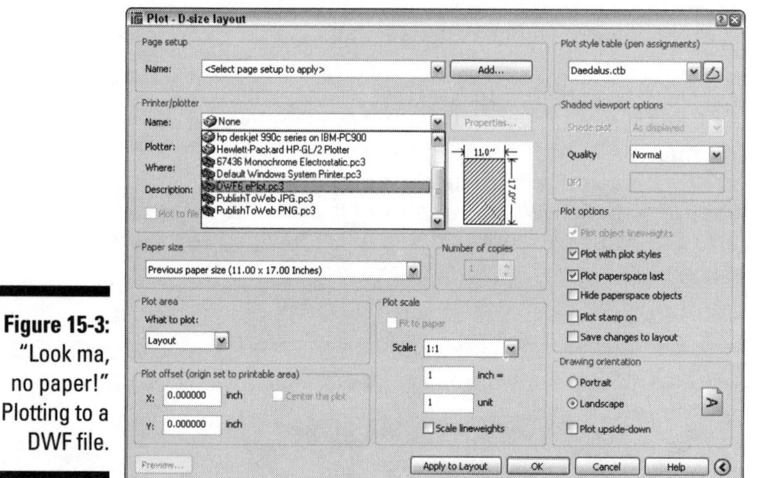

Figure 15-3: "Look ma, no paper!" Plotting to a DWF file.

Pay particular attention to the Scale setting in the Plot Scale area. If you're creating a DWF simply for viewing in a browser, you can turn on the Fit to Paper setting rather than worry about a specific plot scale. If you want to enable others to ePlot your DWF file to scale, as described earlier in this chapter, you need to choose the desired plot scale factor. Chapter 12 describes how to choose an appropriate plot scale factor.

Making DWFs (or Plots) with PUBLISH

The ePlot method of creating DWF files described in the previous section works fine for single drawings. But if you want to create DWF files for a lot of drawings or plot a bunch of drawings the good ol' fashioned way (on paper, that is), you can use the Publish dialog box, shown in Figure 15-4, to speed the process.

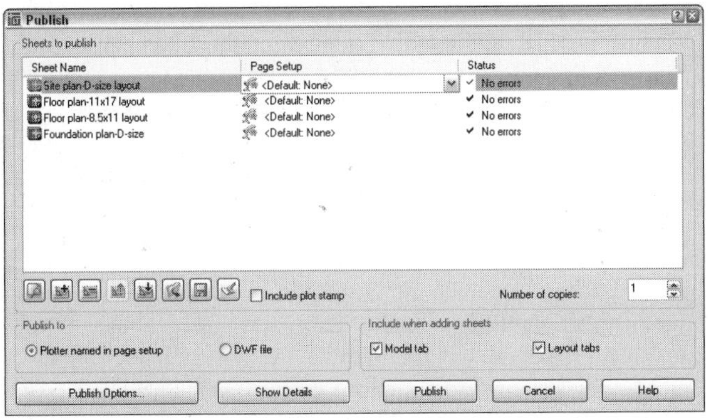

Figure 15-4: Hot off the presses: AutoCAD LT Publish dialog box.

Although the Publish dialog box is wired to support DWF as well as regular (paper) plotting, for now, more people are likely to use it for paper plotting. (An alternative use is creating plot files to send to a plotting service bureau.) But if you do decide to go into large-scale DWF publishing, including multi-sheet DWF files, use the Publish Drawing Sheets dialog box, as in the following steps.

1. **Choose File⇨Publish.**

   The Publish dialog box appears (refer to Figure 15-4). The dialog box lists all tabs (Model and paper space layouts) of the current drawing for plotting. The Publish dialog box refers to each tab as a *sheet.*

2. **Use the buttons below the sheet list to preview any sheet, add sheets from other drawings, remove sheets from the to-be-plotted list, or rearrange the plotting order.**

   With the additional buttons, you can save and recall lists of sheets. See Step 4 for more information.

3. **After you specify the sheets that you want to plot, specify whether you want to plot them to an actual plotter, plot (PLT) file, or a DWF file.**

   You can select a specific plotter configuration for each sheet by choosing a Page Setup in the sheet list. See Chapter 12 for more information about page setups.

4. **Click the Publish Options button to display a dialog box containing additional settings.**

   Most of these options are of concern only if you're creating DWF files. The one exception is Default Output Directory, which also applies to creating plot (PLT) files.

5. **Click the Save Sheet List button to save the current drawings and settings list, if you anticipate having to publish the same group of drawings again.**

6. **Click the Publish button to start the process.**

Don't confuse the PUBLISH command (File⇨Publish) with the PUBLISHTOWEB command (File⇨Publish to Web). The PUBLISH command creates sets of DWF files, plot files, or actual plots. The PUBLISHTOWEB Wizard creates a Web page containing images of your drawings. The results of this wizard won't put any Web designers or programmers out of work, but you can use it to create primitive Web page paste-ups of your drawings. See "PUBLISHTOWEB command" in the AutoCAD LT online help if you want to give it a whirl.

Hand-y objects

No Web file format is complete without hyperlinks, and DWF has those, too. You can attach a hyperlink to any drawing object in AutoCAD LT, not just to a text string. As you pass the cursor over an object with a hyperlink, the cursor changes from the ordinary pointer to a globe and two links of a chain (as in "World Wide Web" and "link," not "world-wide chain gang"). Right-click the object and select the Hyperlink option from the menu, which opens your browser and navigates to the URL that's attached to the object. If you create a DWF file that includes objects with hyperlinks, Autodesk DWF Viewer embeds the links in the DWF file so that you can Ctrl+click to navigate to them.

Hyperlinks on objects are a clever trick, but they're of limited practical value in most DWG and DWF files:

- The drawing images are so small that distinguishing the hyperlink on one object from the hyperlink on another object is difficult.
- Most people aren't used to associating hyperlinks with individual lines and other objects. The interface is likely to leave them perplexed.

If you want to experiment with hyperlinks in objects, look up "HYPERLINK command, about" in the online help.

Autodesk DWF Viewer

After you create DWF files, whether with ePlot or PUBLISH, you or the recipient of your DWF files can use Autodesk DWF Viewer to view and print them. Autodesk DWF Viewer (refer to Figure 15-2) is a free viewer from Autodesk. You can download the current version from the Autodesk Web page, `www.autodesk.com` (click Products and then Autodesk DWF Viewer).

When you install AutoCAD LT 2005, the setup program by default installs Autodesk DWF Viewer as well. Choose Start⇨Programs⇨Autodesk⇨Autodesk DWF Viewer, or simply double-click a DWF file in Windows Explorer, to launch it.

The Drawing Protection Racket

Many people who send DWG (or DWF) files are concerned about the misuse (that is, by the wrong people or for the wrong purposes), abuse (for example, modification without your consent), or reuse (on other projects or by other people without due compensation to you) of those files.

AutoCAD, but not AutoCAD LT, includes a password-protection feature. AutoCAD users can lock a DWG or DWF file so that only those who type the password that they specify can open, insert, or xref it. If you try to open, a DWG file that an AutoCAD user has password protected, you see a dialog box similar to the one shown in Figure 15-5.

Figure 15-5: Password, please.

AutoCAD LT, as well as AutoCAD, can password protect DWF files. Use the PUBLISH command and click the Publish Options button in the Publish dialog box.

Both AutoCAD and LT also include a *digital signature* feature — a high-tech way to add an electronic marker to a DWG file that verifies that someone approved the drawing. Autodesk's digital signature feature relies on fairly new technology by Microsoft. You must first get an account with a digital certificate provider, who serves to authenticate you and your computer. Of course, for this feature to be useful, you need to send drawings to someone who wants to receive digitally authenticated drawings from you (or vice versa) and who has the technological savvy to deal with digital certificates. For more information, see "digital signatures, learning more about" in the AutoCAD LT online help.

Although electronic security features such as the ones described in this section are useful as part of a strategy to protect your work from misuse, they're not a substitute for communicating clearly, preferably in the form of written contracts, what constitutes appropriate use of drawings that you send to or receive from others. `http://markcad.com/autocad/elecdwgexchange.htm` outlines the issues and suggests how to play well with your drawing exchange buddies.

Part V
The Part of Tens

In this part . . .

Tens sounds a lot like *tense,* and tense is how AutoCAD LT may make you feel sometimes. But never fear — help is on the way! Checklists are always a big help in getting things right and fixing things that are wrong. And a Top Ten list is a good way to quickly spot the best — or the worst — of almost anything, AutoCAD LT included. This Part of Tens features lists that help you keep your drawings healthy and trade drawings with other people and programs.

Chapter 16

Ten Ways to Do No Harm

Hippocrates of Greece is famous for many things, not least of which is the Hippocratic oath sworn by doctors. It begins "First, do no harm." This oath is not a bad approach to take when editing existing drawings with AutoCAD LT, whether the drawings were created originally by you or by someone else. Although you usually take several days to accomplish several days of productive work, you can accidentally undo days or weeks of work by yourself and others in minutes. (Of course, you also can *purposefully* undo days or weeks of work by yourself and others in minutes, but I can't give much advice to stop you if you want to do that!)

Follow these guidelines to avoid doing harm to the hard work of others and the productive potential of yourself.

Be Precise

Throughout this book, I remind you that using precision techniques such as snap, object snaps, and typed coordinates is a fundamental part of good CAD practice. Don't try to use AutoCAD LT like an illustration program, in which you eyeball locations and distances. Use one of the many LT precision techniques *every* time you specify a point or distance.

Control Properties by Layer

As I describe in Chapter 3, AutoCAD LT gives you two different ways of controlling object properties such as color, linetype, and lineweight: by layer and by object. Unless you have a *really* good reason to assign properties by object — such as instructions from your company's CAD manager or the client for whom you're creating the drawing — use the by-layer method: Assign colors, linetypes, and lineweights to layers, and let objects inherit their properties from the layer on which they reside. Don't assign explicit color, linetype, or lineweight to objects.

Know Your Drawing Scale Factor

Chapter 5 describes the importance of choosing an appropriate drawing scale factor when you set up a drawing. Knowing the drawing scale factor of any drawing you're working on is equally important whether you set it up or not. You need this number in order to calculate lots of scale-dependent objects, such as text, dimensions, and hatching. Chapter 9 includes tips for figuring out the drawing scale factor of an existing drawing.

Know Your Space

Understand the difference between model space and paper space (described in Chapter 2) and know which space the different parts of the drawing you're looking at on-screen reside in. Above all, make sure that you draw objects in the appropriate space. When you're viewing a paper space layout, keep an eye on the status bar's MODEL/PAPER button so that you know which space the cursor currently is in. (Chapter 5 describes how to keep your model and paper space bearings.) When you plot, ensure that you select the right tab — either Model or one of the paper space layout tabs.

Explode with Care

The eXplode command makes exploding polylines (Chapter 6), dimensions (Chapter 10), hatches (Chapter 11), and block inserts (Chapter 13) into their constituent objects easy. The only problem is that someone probably grouped those objects together for a reason. So until you understand that reason and know why it no longer applies, leave the dynamite alone.

Don't Cram Your Geometry

Cramming for a geometry test is okay, but don't cram geometry, dimensions, text, or anything (and everything) else into your drawings. A real temptation exists to put a lot of stuff into every square inch of your drawing, using AutoCAD LT's flexible panning and zooming capabilities to really work over all the available space. If you succumb to this temptation, you discover that editing is more difficult and adding more information may be impossible! In addition, reading the resulting drawing probably is harder.

Instead of cramming stuff onto the sheet, use white (empty) space to surround areas of dense geometry. Put details on separate sheets. Attach a page of notes instead of putting a ton of text onto your drawing. Managing a reasonable number of drawings with less on each one is easier than having two or three densely packed sheets crammed with every bit of geometry and annotation needed for the project.

Freeze Instead of Erase

Starting with an existing drawing from another discipline is common when you want to add, say, an electrical system to a floor plan. But if you remove the landscaping around a building because you don't need it for the wiring, you may cause a great deal of rework when the landscaping information is needed again. And what if the person who did the landscaping work has, in the meantime, decided to leaf? (Sorry . . .) Unless you know that objects are no longer needed, use the AutoCAD LT Freeze or Off layer setting to make objects on those layers invisible without obliterating them. These settings are in the Layer Properties Manager dialog box, as described in Chapter 3.

Use CAD Standards

Become knowledgeable about CAD standards in your industry and company, and take advantage of any standardized resources and approaches available to you. (See Chapter 14 for suggestions.) By following standards consistently, you can apply your creativity, expertise, and energy to the interesting parts of the job at hand, not to arguing about which hatching patterns to use. And if you find that things are a mess in your company because no one else pays much attention to industry standards, well, knowing those standards makes you very employable as well.

Save Drawings Regularly

As with all computer documents that you work on, get in the habit of saving your current AutoCAD LT drawing regularly. I recommend every ten minutes or so. Each time you save, LT writes the current state of the drawing to the *drawingname*.dwg file, after renaming the previously saved version *drawingname*.bak. Thus, you can always recover the next-to-last saved version of your drawing by renaming *drawingname*.bak to *somethingelse*.dwg and opening it in AutoCAD.

AutoCAD LT also includes an automatic drawing save feature. It's useful as a secondary backup save, but don't rely on it exclusively. LT creates automatic save files with inscrutable names like `Drawing1_1_1_1478.SV$` and puts them in the folder specified by the Automatic Save File Location setting on the File tab of the Options dialog box. Save your drawing and save yourself the pain of lost work and the hassle of trying to locate the right automatic save file.

If you find yourself in the unfortunate position of needing an automatic save file, move the SV$ files file from the automatic save folder to another folder. Rename the files from SV$ to DWG, open them in AutoCAD LT, and look for the one that corresponds to the drawing you're trying to recover. ***Note:*** LT deletes the SV$ file after you close the drawing, so it's usually useful only after a software or computer crash.

Back Up Drawings Regularly

Backing up your data is prudent advice for any important work that you do on a computer, but it's doubly prudent for CAD drawings. A set of CAD drawings is a lot harder and more time consuming to re-create than most other computer documents. Unless you're willing to lose more than a day's worth of work, develop a plan of daily backups onto tape, CD-RW (CD ReWritable) discs, or another high-capacity medium.

Don't be lulled into complacency by the increasing reliability of hard drives. Although hard drive failure is increasingly rare, it still happens, and if it happens to you *sans backup,* you quickly understand the full force of the phrase "catastrophic failure." Also, backups aren't just protection against drive failure. Most of the time, backups help you recover from "pilot error" — accidentally erasing a file, messing up a drawing with ill-advised editing, and so on. Even if you're conscientious and never make mistakes, there's a good chance someone else in your office with access to your DWG files hasn't quite achieved your exalted level of perfection. Protect your work and minimize recriminations with regular backups.

Chapter 17

Ten Ways to Swap Drawing Data with Other People and Programs

At various times, you probably need to transfer information from one kind of document to another. You even may have taken the CAD plunge because you want to import AutoCAD drawing data into your word processing or other documents. If so, this chapter is for you. It covers exchanging AutoCAD and LT drawing data with other programs — what works, what doesn't, and how to do it. I also tell you when to give up and reach for the scissors and glue.

This chapter frequently mentions *vector* and *raster* graphics file formats:

- A vector format stores graphics as collections of geometrical objects (such as lines, polygons, and text). Vector graphics are good for high geometrical precision and for stretching or squeezing images to different sizes. These two characteristics make vector formats good for CAD.
- A raster format stores graphics as a series of dots, or *pixels*. Raster graphics are good for depicting photographic detail and lots of colors.

Exchanging AutoCAD LT drawing data with other programs sometimes works great the first time you try it. Sometimes, you have to try a bunch of techniques or exchange formats to get all the data to transfer in an acceptable way. Occasionally, no practical exchange method exists for preserving formatting or other properties that are important to you. Where your exchange efforts fall in this spectrum depends on the kind of drawings you make, the other programs you work with, and the output devices or formats that you use. I provide recommendations in this chapter, but be prepared to experiment.

Table 17-1 lists exchange formats between common programs and AutoCAD LT.

Table 17-1 Swapping Between AutoCAD LT 2005 and Other Programs

Swap	*Recommended Formats*
AutoCAD LT to AutoCAD (same version)	DWG
AutoCAD or LT 2005 to AutoCAD R14	R12/LT2 DXF
AutoCAD LT to another CAD program	DXF or DWG
AutoCAD LT to AutoCAD	DWG
AutoCAD or LT 2005 to AutoCAD R14	R12 DXF
AutoCAD LT to another CAD program	DXF or DWG
AutoCAD LT to humans who don't have AutoCAD or LT	PDF or DWF
AutoCAD LT to Word	WMF
Word to AutoCAD LT	RTF or TXT
AutoCAD LT to paint program	BMP
Paint program to AutoCAD LT	No straightforward way — need AutoCAD in order to attach raster images with the IMage command
AutoCAD LT to draw program	WMF
Draw program to AutoCAD LT	WMF
AutoCAD LT to the Web	JPG, PNG, or DWF
Excel to AutoCAD LT	Windows clipboard, using Paste Special (see Chapter 9)
AutoCAD LT to Excel	CSV using AutoCAD LT's TABLE-EXPORT command (see "TABLE-EXPORT command" in LT's online help)

The remainder of this chapter gives you specific steps for making most of the exchanges recommended in this table, as well as others.

DWG

DWG, AutoCAD and LT's native file format, is the best format for exchanging drawings with other AutoCAD or LT users. Use the SAVE and SAVEAS commands to create DWG files and the OPEN command to open them.

AutoCAD LT can't *create* every kind of object that AutoCAD can — raster attachments and most 3D objects, for example — but it can successfully *read* and *save* DWG files that contain these objects.

AutoCAD LT 2005 can't save to the AutoCAD Release 14/AutoCAD LT 97 DWG format. If you need to send drawings to AutoCAD R14 users, save them in R12 DXF format instead of a DWG format. (See the "DXF" section for instructions.)

Autodesk does not document the native AutoCAD DWG file format, and recommends that all file exchanges between AutoCAD and other CAD programs take place via DXF files (see the next section). But several companies have reverse-engineered the DWG format, and it's now common for other CAD programs to read and sometimes write DWG files directly, with greater or lesser accuracy. Because the DWG format is complicated, isn't documented, and gets changed every couple of years, no one ever figures it out perfectly. Thus, exchanging DWG files with non-Autodesk programs always involves some compatibility risks.

When you send DWG files to other people — whether they use AutoCAD, AutoCAD LT, or a different CAD program — you need to make sure that their software can read the DWG file version that you're sending. See Chapter 1 for information about AutoCAD and LT DWG file versions.

Round-trip DWG fare

The most demanding — and elusive — kind of data exchange is called *round-trip transfer. Round trip* means that you create and save a file in one program, edit and save it in another program, and then edit and save it in the first program again. A perfect round trip is one in which all the data survives and the users of both programs can happily edit whatever they want to. Unfortunately, the perfect round trip, like the perfect visit to your cousins, rarely happens.

In CAD, round-trip transfer becomes an issue when two people want to work on the same drawings with different CAD programs. AutoCAD and AutoCAD LT have excellent round-trip compatibility, as Chapter 1 explains. Expect a bumpier road if you're exchanging drawings with users of other CAD programs. Perform some test transfers before you assume that your drawings can get from here to there and back again unscathed.

When you send DWG files to other people, remember to use the ETRANSMIT command to ensure that you send all the dependent files (fonts, xrefs, and raster images). See Chapter 15 for details.

DXF

DXF (Drawing eXchange Format) is the Autodesk-approved format for exchanging between different CAD programs. (Some other vector graphics applications, such as drawing and illustration programs, read and write DXF files, too.) DXF is a documented version of the DWG format. Because DXF more-or-less exactly mimics the DWG file's contents, it's (usually) a faithful representation of AutoCAD and LT drawings.

How well DXF works for exchanging data depends largely on the other program that you're exchanging with. Some CAD and vector graphics programs do a good job of reading and writing DXF files, while others don't. In practice, geometry usually comes through well, but properties, formatting, and other nongeometrical information can be tricky. Test before you commit to a large-scale exchange, and always check the results.

To create DXF files, use the SAVEAS command (File⇨Save As) and choose one of the three DXF versions in the Files of Type drop-down list. To open a DXF file, use the OPEN command (File⇨Open) and choose DXF from the Files of Type drop-down list.

DWF

As Chapter 15 describes, DWF is Autodesk's special "lightweight" drawing format for posting drawings on the Web or sharing them with people who don't have AutoCAD or LT. Those people can use the free Autodesk DWF Viewer program to view and print DWF files. Chapter 15 describes how to create and use DWF files.

PDF

Adobe's PDF (Portable Document Format) is the most popular format for exchanging formatted text documents among users of different computers and operating systems. PDF also does graphics, as you probably know from having viewed PDF brochures on Web sites.

Autodesk has worked hard to make DWF the PDF for CAD drawing exchange, but DWF hasn't yet caught on in a big way. When AutoCAD and LT users need to send drawings to people who don't have either program, many prefer to convert the drawings to PDF files. Most potential recipients are familiar with PDF and already have the free Adobe Reader installed on their computers, neither of which can be said of DWF.

The free Adobe Reader views and prints PDF files, but won't create them. In order to convert an AutoCAD LT drawing (or any other Windows document) into a PDF file, you need additional software. Adobe sells Acrobat Standard and Professional for this purpose — see `www.adobe.com/acrobat/` for details and a trial version. Many other companies offer commercial and shareware PDF-creation programs. One such utility is Pdf995 (`www.pdf995.com`), which, despite its under-$10 price, does a good job of creating PDF files from AutoCAD LT drawings.

WMF

There are lots of different vector and raster graphics file formats, but Microsoft has been pretty successful at making its WMF and BMP formats the *lingua franca* — or should that be *lingua bill-a*? — for exchanging graphical information in Windows.

WMF (Windows MetaFile) is a vector format, so it does a decent job of representing AutoCAD objects such as lines, arcs, and text.

To create a WMF file showing some or all the objects in a drawing, use the EXPORT command (File⇨Export) and choose `Metafile (*.wmf)` in the Files of Type drop-down list. After you create a WMF file in AutoCAD LT, use the other program's file insertion command to place the image in a document.

AutoCAD LT puts objects in the WMF file with the colors and display lineweights that you see on the LT screen. To create a WMF file that looks like a *monochrome plot* — that is, with varying lineweights and all objects black — you need to set layer and object properties in LT so that the objects look that way on-screen before you create the WMF file.

You can go the other direction, from a WMF file into AutoCAD LT, by using the WMFIN command (Insert⇨Windows Metafile).

BMP, JPEG, TIFF, and Other Raster Formats

BMP (BitMaP) is the standard Windows raster format. AutoCAD LT can create BMP files from drawing objects (via the BMPOUT command). When you export AutoCAD LT drawing objects to a BMP file, all the objects get converted to dots. Turning a line into a bunch of dots isn't a swell idea if you want to change the line again. But it is useful if you need to copy a drawing into a company brochure.

One problem with BMP files is their big file size. Unlike some other raster formats, BMP doesn't offer compression. Because CAD drawings usually are fairly large in area, they can turn into monstrously large BMP files.

Creating a BMP file showing some or all the objects in a drawing is similar to creating a WMF file: Type the BMPOUT command at the command line, press Enter, specify a BMP filename, and select the objects to include in the BMP image. After you create a BMP file in AutoCAD LT, you use the other program's File⇨Open to open it or the graphics file insertion command to place it in an existing document.

Although BMP is a standard Windows format for exchanging raster data, it's certainly not the preferred format of many programs. Other common raster formats include PCX, JPEG, and TIFF (the latter two appear as JPG and TIF in Windows). Among their other advantages, these formats offer image compression, which can reduce the size of raster files dramatically.

If the program that you're trying to work with works best with other formats, or you want to avoid huge BMP files, you have a couple of options:

- Create an AutoCAD LT-friendly format (such as WMF or BMP) and translate it to another graphics format with a translation program such as HiJaak (`www.imsisoft.com`) or VuePrint (`www.hamrick.com`).

  AutoCAD LT includes JPGOUT, PNGOUT, and TIFOUT commands for creating JPG, PNG, and TIF files in the same way that you export WMF and BMP files. Type the command name, press Enter, specify a raster filename, and select the objects to include in the image file. These commands use the current drawing area background color as the background color for the image. If you want your image background to be white, make sure that the AutoCAD LT drawing area color is white when you run the command. (Choose Tools⇨Options⇨Display⇨Colors to change display colors.)

- If you need to convert drawings to a raster format other than BMP or TIF, the second option is to use the AutoCAD LT Raster File Format driver. This driver enables you to "plot" to a file by using one of nine raster formats, including PCX, JPEG, and TIFF. Before you can use the Raster File Format driver, you must create a new plotter configuration: Choose File⇨Plotter Manager and then run the Add-A-Plotter wizard. After you create the Raster File Format driver configuration, you use the Plot dialog box as described in Chapter 12 to generate "plots" to raster files.

If you want to go the other direction — a raster file into a drawing — you need full AutoCAD's IMage command, as described in Chapter 13. AutoCAD LT cannot attach raster files to drawings, but it does display any raster images that an AutoCAD user has attached.

Windows Clipboard

If you need to transfer lots of WMF or BMP figures, you can do it a bit more quickly with the Windows Clipboard, which bypasses the creation of WMF and BMP files on disk. Instead, Windows uses your computer's memory to transfer the data. Choose Edit⇨Copy in the program from which you want to copy the data and Edit⇨Paste Special in the program to which you want to copy it. In the Paste Special dialog box, choose Picture to paste the image in WMF format or Bitmap to paste it in BMP format.

OLE

Microsoft Windows includes a data transfer feature, Object Linking and Embedding, or OLE. (In case you're wondering, that's "OLE" pronounced like the Spanish cheer, not like the Cockney way of saying *hole.*) Microsoft touts OLE as an all-purpose solution to the challenge of exchanging formatted data between any two Windows programs.

If you want to share data between two OLE-aware programs (and most Windows applications are OLE-aware), creating an embedded or linked document isn't much more complicated than cut and paste. That's the theory.

Here's how it works. In OLE lingo, the program that you're taking the data from is the *source*. The program that receives the data is called the *container*. For example, if you want to place some word processing text from Microsoft Word into an AutoCAD LT drawing, Word is the source, and LT is the container.

In Word, you select the text that you want to put in the AutoCAD LT drawing and choose Edit⇨Copy to copy them to the Windows Clipboard. Then, you switch to LT and choose Edit⇨Paste Special. The Paste Special choice displays a dialog box containing the choices Paste and Paste Link. The Paste option creates a copy of the object from the source document and *embeds* the copied object into the container document. The Paste Link option *links* the new object in the container document to its source document so any changes to the source document automatically reflect in the container document. In other words, if you link word processing text to an AutoCAD LT drawing, changes that you make later in the Word document get propagated to the LT drawing automatically. If you embed the same spreadsheet object in an LT drawing, changes that you later make to the text in Word don't reflect in the drawing.

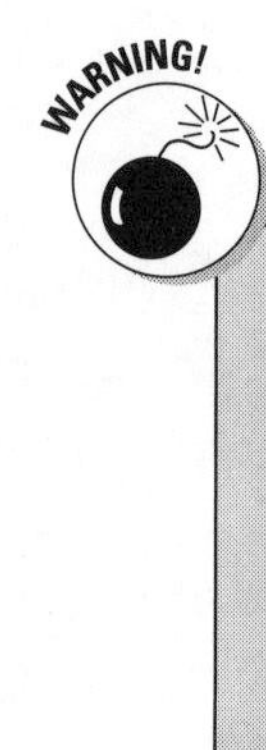

That's how it's *supposed* to work. In practice, the container application sometimes doesn't display or print all the linked or embedded data correctly. See the "Should you shout, 'OLE!'?" sidebar for details.

Should you shout, "OLE!"?

Unfortunately, OLE is afflicted with several practical problems.

- Compound OLE documents can slow performance — a lot. If you plan to use OLE, you need a fast computer with lots of memory — or lots of time on your hands.
- Supporting OLE well is a difficult programming job, and many applications, including AutoCAD LT, suffer from OLE design limitations and bugs. (For example, when you link or embed a word processing document, only the first page appears in AutoCAD LT.)
- Previous versions of LT exhibited more OLE problems than AutoCAD LT 2005. In particular, plotted OLE output often underwent creative but undesirable transformations. If you exchange drawings with users of earlier versions, what they see on-screen and plot may not match what you created.

AutoCAD LT 2005 includes a bevy of OLE improvements, which address some of the limitations:

- You can control text size more easily, via the MSOLESCALE system variable and OLESCALE command.
- Editing of OLE objects with commands such as Move and CoPy is more consistent with editing of native AutoCAD LT objects.
- You can control the quality of plotted OLE objects with a setting on the Plot and Publish tab of the Options dialog box.

Even with the OLE improvements in AutoCAD LT 2005, consider carefully and test extensively before embedding or linking documents into drawings. If you want to play it safe, use the alternative methods described in this chapter, and save OLÉ for your next trip to Spain.

Screen Capture

If your goal is to show the entire AutoCAD LT program window, not just the drawing contained in it, create a *screen capture*. Most of the figures in this book are screen captures. You might use similar figures to put together a training manual or to show your mom all the cool software you use.

Windows includes a no-frills screen capture capability that is okay for an occasional screen capture. It works like this:

1. **Capture the whole screen or active window with one of these steps:**
   - Press the Print Screen key to capture the entire Windows screen, including the desktop and taskbar.
   - Hold down the Alt key and press the Print Screen key to capture just the active program window (for example, AutoCAD LT).

   Windows copies a bitmap image to the Windows Clipboard.
2. **Paste the bitmap image into another program. You have two options:**
   - Paste into a paint program (such as the Paint program in Windows). Use that program to save a raster image as a BMP file format.
   - Paste the bitmap image directly into a document (such as a Word document or an AutoCAD LT drawing) without creating another file.

If you do lots of captures, a screen capture utility program makes the job faster and gives you more options. You can control the area of the screen that gets captured, save to different raster file formats with different monochrome, grayscale, and color options, and print screen captures. One good screen capture utility program is FullShot by Inbit, Inc. (`www.inbit.com`).

When you create screen captures, pay attention to resolution and colors:

- High screen resolutions (for example, above 1280 x 1024) can make your captures unreadable when they get compressed onto an 8½-x-11-inch sheet of paper and printed on a low-resolution printer.
- Some colors don't print in monochrome, and a black AutoCAD drawing area is overwhelmingly dark. For most of the screen captures in this book, I used 1024 x 768 resolution, a white AutoCAD LT drawing area, and dark colors — mostly black — for all the objects in the drawing.

TXT and RTF

TXT (Text, also called ASCII for American Standard Code for Information Interchange) is the simplest format for storing letters and numbers. TXT files store only basic text, without such formatting as boldface or special paragraph characteristics. RTF (Rich Text Format) is a format developed by Microsoft for exchanging word processing documents (text plus formatting).

To import a TXT or RTF file, choose Import Text from the Multiline Text Editor window's right-click menu. AutoCAD LT imports plain text from TXT and RTF files. When you import an RTF file, LT even brings along most of the text formatting and alignment. Chapter 9 covers the Multiline Text Editor window.

Because no sane person uses AutoCAD LT as a word processor, LT doesn't provide any special tools for exporting text. You can select AutoCAD LT text, copy it to the Windows Clipboard, and then paste it into another program.

Chapter 18

Ten Ways to Work in an AutoCAD World

As Chapter 1 makes clear, AutoCAD LT plays well in the AutoCAD world, but there are several important differences and a slew of lesser ones. This chapter highlights the things that match up well, describes the differences, and tells you what you can do about those differences.

DWG Is Your Friend

As I explain in Chapter 1, one of AutoCAD LT's biggest advantages is that it uses AutoCAD's DWG as its own native file format. Thus, you usually don't need to worry about file translation problems when you work on drawings with AutoCAD users or exchange drawings with them — just open and save in the usual way. AutoCAD and the DWG format being as complicated as they are, AutoCAD and LT occasionally display the same drawing slightly differently. (The technical term for such differences is *bug*.) Fortunately, however, such glitches are very rare.

AutoCAD Users Are Your Friends

Your friendly, neighborhood AutoCAD user can be an unparalleled resource as you're mastering AutoCAD LT or when you run into obscure problems later down the road. Many AutoCAD users have been churning out drawings every hour of the day and every day of the week for years now, and some of them know the innards of AutoCAD better than some of the programmers at Autodesk! Most of what these AutoCAD veterans know applies to AutoCAD LT as well, so get to know the ones around you, treat them well, and ask whether you can tap into their considerable experience and insight.

A Pox on Proxies

AutoCAD and AutoCAD LT aren't the only CAD programs in Autodesk's large and growing herd. You may well find yourself opening drawings created by users of discipline-specific Autodesk programs such as Architectural Desktop or Mechanical Desktop. These programs make use of special application-defined objects, such as doors and walls that know how to interact with each other. The problem with application-defined objects is that only the application that created them (for example, Architectural Desktop) knows all about them; regular AutoCAD and AutoCAD LT can view and print these objects, but depending on the application and the objects, you may have limited editing control over the objects.

When you open drawings that contain application-defined objects, AutoCAD LT displays a dialog box saying that it's converting them to *proxies*. A proxy is a simplified version of the application-defined object composed of ordinary lines, circles, and so on. The proxy version looks the same on the LT (or AutoCAD) screen as the full-fledged application-defined object looks in the application that created it, but its abilities may be more limited. The dialog box warns of you of this possibility.

Forget Sheet Sets

Perhaps the biggest news in AutoCAD 2005 is *sheet sets*, a new set of features for creating, organizing, and managing a set of drawing sheets for a project. Autodesk decided not to include the sheet sets features in AutoCAD LT, so you continue to organize drawings by means of suitable filenames and folder structure. AutoCAD 2005 users who decide to take advantage of sheet sets can share drawings with you, but you don't see the organizational information — you just deal with the drawings as separate DWG files.

Raster Disaster

As I mention in Chapter 13, AutoCAD includes a raster file attachment feature that's missing from AutoCAD LT. If you exchange drawings with AutoCAD users frequently, sooner or later you come across DWG files with attached logos, background photographs, or maps in the form of bitmap files (JPG, TIF, GIF, BMP, and so on). Fortunately, AutoCAD LT has no problem viewing and printing these attached raster images. But you can't add or change attached raster files. If you find that you need to do so, this is the time to call on the good graces of your AutoCAD-using friends or colleagues.

Xclip Exemption

AutoCAD LT includes AutoCAD's all-important xref feature, as described in Chapter 13, but LT cannot *clip* (that is, show only a portion of) xrefs. Once again, LT has no difficulty showing xrefs that have been clipped in AutoCAD, but you can't modify the clipping area or clip an xref yourself.

From Flatland to 3D

Most people who know anything at all about the differences between AutoCAD and AutoCAD LT cite the latter's lack of 3D capabilities as the main difference. The limitation described in the next section is more significant for most people, but that AutoCAD LT doesn't do true 3D is nonetheless true. If you open 3D models created in AutoCAD (or another 3D-savvy Autodesk program, such as Mechanical Desktop or Architectural Desktop), you see the objects in their full 3D glory, but you aren't able to do much editing of them or create new 3D objects. Your ability to move around the drawing in 3D space also is more limited because LT lacks AutoCAD's slick 3Dorbit command. (You can use the VPOINT and DDVPOINT commands to move around a 3D model, but neither command is particularly intuitive.)

The Customization Limitation

As Chapter 1 explains, AutoCAD add-on programs of all levels of sophistication and scope play a central role in AutoCAD's popularity. You can find everything from simple AutoLISP or Visual Basic programs written by ordinary drafters to full-blown, discipline-specific applications developed by professional programmers. If AutoCAD itself doesn't do something that some people find useful, there's a good chance that someone has written an add-on program to do it.

Unfortunately, almost none of these add-ons work with AutoCAD LT. So when you hear your AutoCAD-using buddy going on about the cool, new freeware program that he came across for AutoCAD, you may have to suppress some envy.

The add-on tools that *you* can use with AutoCAD LT are scripts (SCR files), menu macros, custom drawing templates (DWT files) files, and block libraries (DWG files containing useful symbols).

Other Differences

The preceding sections cover the main differences between AutoCAD LT and AutoCAD. Other differences include the following:

- AutoCAD includes a lame MLine command for drawing series of two or more parallel straight lines; LT includes a slightly less lame DLine command for drawing series of two straight lines or arcs.
- AutoCAD has a *profiles* feature, with which users can create different AutoCAD "personalities" (for example, for different users of the same computer or different AutoCAD applications).
- AutoCAD includes standalone Reference Manager and CAD standards tools that can make managing drawings and standards easier.

Trading Up (or Trading Down!)

If you bump up against one or more of these limitations one too many times, then you may need to consider trading up to full AutoCAD. Get out your wallet, though. Besides AutoCAD's much steeper cost, Autodesk doesn't typically offer any break to AutoCAD LT users who want to "upgrade" to full AutoCAD.

You may find some solace knowing that, in recent years, some AutoCAD users have *downgraded* to LT! AutoCAD LT has most of what a lot of AutoCAD users need, and the fee to upgrade AutoCAD over several versions can easily add up to more than the cost of a new copy of AutoCAD LT.

Index

• Symbols & Numbers •

• A •

• B •

• C •

• E •

• F •

• G •

• H •

• I •

• J •

• K •

• L •

• M •

• N •

• O •

• P •

• T •

• U •

• V •

• W •